Second Edition

ATTACK PROOF

The Ultimate Guide to Personal Protection

Grand Master John Perkins

10th degree black belt Guided Chaos

Lt. Col. Al Ridenhour, USMC

Master, Guided Chaos

Matt Kovsky

5th degree black belt Guided Chaos

Human Kinetics

Library of Congress Cataloging-in-Publication Data

Perkins, John, 1951 Mar. 31-
  Attack proof : the ultimate guide to personal protection / John Perkins, Al Ridenhour,
Matt Kovsky. -- 2nd ed.
    p. cm.
  Includes bibliographical references and index.
  ISBN-13: 978-0-7360-7876-4 (soft cover : alk. paper)
  ISBN-10: 0-7360-7876-2 (soft cover : alk. paper) 1. Crime prevention. 2. Violent crimes--Prevention.
3. Self-defense. I. Ridenhour, Al, 1964- II. Kovsky, Matt, 1957- III. Title.
  HV7431.P453 2009
  613.6'6--dc22
                    2009001456

ISBN-10: 0-7360-7876-2
ISBN-13: 978-0-7360-7876-4

This publication is written and published to provide accurate and authoritative information relevant to the subject matter presented. It is published and sold with the understanding that the author and publisher are not engaged in rendering legal, medical, or other professional services by reason of their authorship or publication of this work. If medical or other expert assistance is required, the services of a competent professional person should be sought.

The Web addresses cited in this text were current as of March 2009, unless otherwise noted.

Acquisitions Editor: Justin Klug; **Developmental Editor:** Kevin Matz; **Assistant Editor:** Elizabeth Watson; **Copyeditor:** Ann Prisland; **Proofreader:** John Wentworth; **Permission Manager:** Martha Gullo; **Graphic Designer:** Joe Buck; **Graphic Artist:** Kim McFarland; **Cover Designers:** Joe Troy and Keith Blomberg; **Photographer (cover):** Joe Troy; **Photographer (interior):** Timothy J. Carron of TLC Photo (www.tlcphotostudio.com), Cold Spring, NY; **Photo Production Manager:** Jason Allen; **Art Manager:** Kelly Hendren; **Associate Art Manager:** Alan L. Wilborn; **Printer:** McNaughton & Gunn

Human Kinetics books are available at special discounts for bulk purchase. Special editions or book excerpts can also be created to specification. For details, contact the Special Sales Manager at Human Kinetics.

Printed in the United States of America   10 9 8 7 6 5 4 3 2

The paper in this book is certified under a sustainable forestry program.

Human Kinetics
Web site: www.HumanKinetics.com

United States: Human Kinetics
P.O. Box 5076
Champaign, IL 61825-5076
800-747-4457
e-mail: humank@hkusa.com

Canada: Human Kinetics
475 Devonshire Road Unit 100
Windsor, ON N8Y 2L5
800-465-7301 (in Canada only)
e-mail: info@hkcanada.com

Europe: Human Kinetics
107 Bradford Road
Stanningley
Leeds LS28 6AT, United Kingdom
+44 (0) 113 255 5665
e-mail: hk@hkeurope.com

Australia: Human Kinetics
57A Price Avenue
Lower Mitcham, South Australia 5062
08 8372 0999
e-mail: info@hkaustralia.com

New Zealand: Human Kinetics
P.O. Box 80
Torrens Park, South Australia 5062
0800 222 062
e-mail: info@hknewzealand.com

Dedicated to Coy Perkins Sr., who started it all.

—John Perkins

CONTENTS

Drill Finder   vi

Acknowledgments   x

Introduction: Life on the Streets   xi

Part I	Body and Mind Principles of Close Combat	1

CHAPTER 1   Awareness 2

CHAPTER 2   Basic Strikes and Strategies 13

Part II	Body and Mind Principles of Guided Chaos	48

CHAPTER 3   Looseness 51

CHAPTER 4   Body Unity 73

CHAPTER 5   Balance, Rooting, and Footwork 82

CHAPTER 6   Sensitivity 103

Part III	Guided Chaos for Superior Self-Defense	151

CHAPTER 7   Applying the Principles to Motion 153

CHAPTER 8   Economy of Movement 169

CHAPTER 9   Grabs and Locks 182

CHAPTER 10   Ground Fighting 194

CHAPTER 11   Stair Fighting 219

CHAPTER 12   Weapons Fighting 226

Afterword: The Survival Manifesto   247

Creating a Training Regimen   262

Glossary   264

References and Resources   268

Index   269

About the Authors   275

DRILL FINDER

DRILL NAME	CLOSE COMBAT	LOOSENESS	BALANCE	BODY UNITY	SENSITIVITY	GRIP	TENDON STRENGTHENERS	GUN AND KNIFE DEFENSES	PARTNER	PAGE NUMBER	PART NUMBER
Advanced Ninja and Vacuum Walks			•							89	II
Anywhere Strikes I	•	•		•						37	I
Anywhere Strikes II	•	•		•			•			38	I
Anywhere Strikes III	•	•	•	•						39	I
Anywhere Striking Full-Power Footwork: The Rocket Step	•		•	•						38	I
Back Walk			•		•				•	121	II
Ball Compression				•						124	II
Basic Knife-Fighting Drill		•	•					•	•	234	III
Battle-Ax Box Step			•	•			•			94	III
Body Writing				•						76	II
Box Step			•	•						92	III
Box-Step Over the Line			•	•						97	II
Chair			•					•	•	234	III
Circle Box Step		•		•						98	I
Circle Clap		•		•						70	I
Close-Range Takedown Pre-emption Within Contact Flow		•	•	•	•				•	203	III
Coin Chase					•				•	121	II

DRILL NAME	CLOSE COMBAT	LOOSENESS	BALANCE	BODY UNITY	SENSITIVITY	GRIP	TENDON STRENGTHENERS	GUN AND KNIFE DEFENSES	PARTNER	PAGE NUMBER	PART NUMBER
Coin Dance					•				•	120	II
Combat-Draw Movement								•		243	III
Contact Flow	•	•	•	•	•				•	135	II
Contact Flow on Stairs	•	•	•	•	•				•	224	III
Contact Flow Variations	•	•	•	•	•			•	•	138	II
Crazy Walk			•							90	II
Crazy Walk on Stairs			•							223	III
Dead-Fish Arms		•							•	62	II
Drop-Striking the Grappler		•	•	•					•	203	III
Falling in Your Favor	•					•				204	III
Finger Creep						•				190	III
Focus Your Fear	•									25	I
Fold Like a Napkin		•							•	61	II
Free-Form Body Unity			•							79	II
Free-Stepping and Kicking on Stairs		•	•	•					•	223	III
Free-Striking Box Step			•						•	93	II
Fright Reaction I	•								•	27	I
Fright Reaction II	•		•						•	28	I
Fright Reaction III	•		•						•	28	I
Fright Reaction IV	•		•						•	218	III
Gang Attack I	•								•	36	I
Gang Attack II	•								•	41	I
Gang Attack III	•								•	215	III
Gorilla Walk		•								70	II
Grab to Destroy						•				190	III
Ground Fighting on Stairs		•	•	•	•					224	III
Ground Fighting Warm-Ups		•								210	III
Ground Versus Ground		•			•				•	215	III
Ground Versus Standing		•			•				•	214	III
Guided Chaos Form	•		•	•						90	II
Gun Defense I								•	•	239	III

(continued)

DRILL NAME	CLOSE COMBAT	LOOSENESS	BALANCE	BODY UNITY	SENSITIVITY	GRIP	TENDON STRENGTHENERS	GUN AND KNIFE DEFENSES	PARTNER	PAGE NUMBER	PART NUMBER
Gun Defense II								•	•	240	III
Hackey-Sack		•	•							98	II
Hula		•								63	II
Interview	•									29	I
Iso-Strike							•			191	III
Knife Skip								•	•	233	III
Knife Spin					•			•	•	233	III
Leg Mania		•						•		212	III
Meet Jason	•								•	34	I
Mexican Hat Dance	•	•								41	I
Middle-Linebacker Hitting	•			•						29 & 124	I & II
Modified Anywhere Strikes	•	•	•	•						180	III
Ninja Walk			•							87	II
Ninja Walk and Vacuum Walk on Stairs			•							221	III
Opening the Door				•						78	II
Polishing the Sphere I		•	•	•						131	II
Polishing the Sphere II		•	•	•						132	II
Polishing the Sphere III		•	•	•						132	II
Psycho-chimp		•								69	II
Psycho Tango			•							147	II
Puppeteering			•	•						80	II
Relaxed Breathing		•								61	II
Relationship of Human Energy to Movement (RHEM)		•	•	•						134	II
Rolling the Energy Ball/Striking Sequence	•	•	•	•						129	II
Rooted Multidirectional Step			•							96	II
Row the Boat		•		•						180	III
Sand Bucket						•				191	III
Seven-Step Dropping Drill				•						123	II
Small Circle Dance		•	•							69	II

DRILL NAME	CLOSE COMBAT	LOOSENESS	BALANCE	BODY UNITY	SENSITIVITY	GRIP	TENDON STRENGTHENERS	GUN AND KNIFE DEFENSES	PARTNER	PAGE NUMBER	PART NUMBER
Solo Circle Flow		•		•						67	II
Speed Flow		•					•			192	III
Split-Brain Air Writing		•								71	II
Stair Steps				•						122	II
Starting the Mower				•						77	II
Stepping Over the Line			•							97	II
Stepping Off-Line Drill			•							98	II
Sticks of Death		•							•	68	II
Sticky Fingers		•							•	68	II
Stop the Charge			•	•					•	203	III
Stumble Steps				•					•	122	II
Swimming		•		•						64	II
Swimming Backstroke		•		•						66	II
Swimming Sidestroke		•		•						66	II
Switch Feet			•							97	II
Turning		•		•						64	II
TV Cut					•					124	II
Two-Minute Push-Up							•			191	III
Unitized Long-Stepping			•	•						80	II
Vacuum Walk			•							88	II
Washing the Body		•	•	•	•					132	II
Weaving Python		•							•	62	II
Whirling Dervish Box Step		•	•	•						95	II
Wood Surfing			•							91	II

Acknowledgments

Special thanks to guided chaos third-degree Ari Kandel, who was instrumental in the creation of this expanded second edition of *Attack Proof*. His lucid, detailed, and compelling prose makes up large portions of the new material, which is pulled from his dedicated training and teaching experiences in John Perkins' classes and seminars.

Also thanks to the following people:

- Tim Carron of TLC Photo (www.tlcphotostudio.com) in Cold Spring, New York, for his flawless photography
- Graphic artist Joe Troy for the cover concept
- Killeen Good, Breanna Good, David Randel Jr, Joseph Martarano, Kevin Harrell, Michael Watson, Tony Dey, and Samantha Fox for modeling their techniques and expertise in the photographs
- Bryan Hopkins, aka Dr. Macintosh, for his computer expertise
- David Pirell for his peerless artistry
- Mary Ann Celente for her organizational precision
- Phyllis O. Burnett (you know why)

Grand Master John Perkins would like to thank Professor Bradley J. Steiner for his inspiration, Grandmaster Ik Jo Kang for his patient teaching, Master Waysun Liao for his philosophy, and Dr. Drew Miller for his insights. Special thanks to Dr. Peter Pizzola and Dr. Peter DeForrest for their guidance on the world of forensic science. John also wants to acknowledge George and Stathis Kaperonis for contributing to his knowledge of Elephtheri Pali (an ancient Greek fighting art) and Tony Dey for his MMA expertise. Most of all, John would like to thank Cheryl Adler for her wisdom and support.

Lieutenant Colonel Al Ridenhour would like to acknowledge his wife, Lani, and his son, Spencer, for all their love and support over the years and without whom none of this would be possible.

Matt Kovsky would like to thank his wife, Kerri, for her love and endurance through the lengthy birth (and rebirth) of this book.

Introduction

LIFE ON THE STREETS

Anyone who's been overseas in a real war, ambushed by subhuman deviants on city streets, or attacked in his or her own bed at night by an invisible assailant can tell you that true fighting is not a game, sport, movie, or choreographed dance. It is complete and total anarchy. Chaos. Adrenaline furiously pumping, muscles fiercely straining, fists and teeth whipping and snapping, bones cracking; confusion, blood, and, heart-bursting fear. In short, it's a hell storm, a tornado, a hurricane. And guess who's in the eye.

The Harsh Reality of Naked Violence

There are hundreds of martial arts in existence, and many times that number of books about them. Nevertheless, most are pretty much the same, both in content and approach. What you are about to read, however, is unlike any other self-defense book you've ever come across.

We're not going to sugarcoat it for you: Self-defense is warfare. In war, there is a distinct difference between what works and what doesn't, between what is real and what we would like to be real. War is a filter for figments of the imagination. Through a deadly process of attrition, whether you like it or not, useless knowledge is disposed of. What you're left with are survival skills.

In the modern era, the focus of hand-to-hand combat training has become lost, especially for civilians. The reasons for this are varied but include economic, cultural, and egotistical influences; political and personal rivalries overseas between individuals and governments have spawned secretiveness, repression, and financial hardship among many Old World masters and financial greed in many New World disciples. In fact, an entire volume could be written on just this subject, but that is beyond the scope of this work. What we need to recognize is, whether by plan or accident, self-defense training on almost all levels has become inadequate, overstylized, unnatural, and in many cases, too sportive. To teach large numbers of people in a short time, instructors boil down defensive moves into simple, regimented, robotlike techniques that bear no resemblance to actual fighting. Similarly, some originally authentic systems of fighting have developed into highly artistic and dancelike art forms that are appropriate for demonstration purposes only.

Although marketed as self-defense, they are now too elaborate and cumbersome for the violent mayhem of real-life situations.

In addition, the current craze for mixed martial art (MMA) tournament fighting in the form of the Ultimate Fighting Championship (UFC) and the like has created a powerful, false association in the mind of the public between sportive competitions and life-and-death combat. Although UFC contests provide the ultimate arena for superb athletes to use maximum skill and power, the object of these events—to secure submission through tapout or knockout—is far different from the goals and training implicit in life-and-death warfare. When you train to compete within rules meant to protect the competitors, you begin the dangerous process of ingraining in your nervous system and reflexes self-limiting habits fraught with peril. Although this perspective causes tremendous antagonism in the MMA community, a simple examination of the UFC's own rules prohibiting specific "dangerous" attacks within matches underscores the point over and over that the way you train is the way you fight. These attacks are prohibited by the UFC:

1. Butting with the head
2. Gouging at the eyes
3. Biting
4. Hair pulling
5. Fish hooking
6. Attacking the groin
7. Putting a finger into any orifice, cut, or laceration on an opponent
8. Manipulating an opponent's small joints
9. Striking the spine or back of the head
10. Striking downward using the point of the elbow
11. Making throat strikes of any kind, including grabbing the trachea
12. Clawing, pinching, or twisting the flesh
13. Grabbing the clavicle
14. Kicking the head of a grounded opponent
15. Kneeing the head of a grounded opponent
16. Stomping a grounded opponent
17. Kicking to the kidney with your heel
18. Spiking an opponent to the canvas on the head or neck
19. Throwing an opponent out of the ring or fenced area
20. Holding the shorts or gloves of an opponent
21. Spitting at an opponent
22. Engaging in unsportsmanlike conduct that causes injury to an opponent
23. Holding the ropes or fence

Rather than being avoided, all of the above can and should be trained (both their delivery and defense) as part of a realistic self-defense curriculum. If dealt with properly, there are ways of practicing these attacks with little risk to the participants. Certain maneuvers, such as holding ropes or fences, have real-world analogs that are vital to survival in varied and chaotic environments, something we cover in depth within the art of guided chaos.

Teaching Soldiers to Die

If self-defense for civilians has become confused and inadequate, the situation for soldiers in our military has become even worse.

In World War II, our military's entire hand-to-hand combat training was revamped with the prospect of confronting Japanese soldiers skilled in judo and karate. This revamping resulted in a highly simplified system of strikes and strategies designed to do one thing: kill the enemy. Through a political process too convoluted and distressing to elaborate on here, over the years, this hand-to-hand training has become convoluted, misdirected, and ineffective except under so-called sportive or competitive (i.e., unrealistic) conditions.

In the meantime, the Russians instituted a hand-to-hand combat methodology in 1989 that far surpassed ours in terms of simplicity and effectiveness. Ironically, it was nearly identical to the system our military used in World War II. In addition, several years ago in Manchester, England, an alleged Al Qaeda training manual was recovered that was used in several terrorist trials. It taught exactly the kinds of killing techniques that our military used to teach. What's wrong with this picture?

Without overelaborating, sport fighting proponents within the services have come to believe that sportive techniques are suitable for the battlefield when, in fact, they are nothing more than a recipe for disaster. Sport fighting proponents are teaching locking, grappling, and restraining maneuvers that our soldiers are supposed to use against an enemy trying to kill them. All you have to do is watch a few episodes of *COPS* on TV to see how well that works against street thugs. The videotape doesn't lie: It often takes five officers piled on top of a crazed criminal to cuff him. What does any of this have to do with man-to-man, hand-to-hand, life-or-death combat?

Granted, some missions require soldiers to roll people up and detain them with basic arm-control techniques, but such skills should be taught only after soldiers learn how to kill the enemy (it should also be noted that sportive throwing and grappling techniques require tremendous physical ability in order to make them work—highly impractical for the battlefield when you're wrapped in 71 pounds [31.75 kg] of battle rattle).

If the simple, deadly tactics employed in World War II were resurrected, some fear that soldiers would be apt to use them against civilians—or on each other. But when you consider that soldiers are taught to fire rifles and pistols all the time, and there is nothing to stop them from going to a local pawn shop, buying guns, and sniping at people from the bell tower, you realize these fears about using fighting tactics are absurd. There are several possible reasons why people might think this way:

1. They've never seen real down and dirty street fights and don't know what people are capable of: The speed and ferocity are just on a different level.
2. Their impression of real fighting (like that of most people in our culture) has been shaped by sportive fighting, movies, and TV, so they have no frame of reference based on truth.
3. They may have a fear of stepping into the dark world of real, up-close and personal, life-and death combat. Many people pontificate on it, but to actually acknowledge the chaotic savagery of real violence is to acknowledge the fact that some of our preconceptions about life-and-death combat are just plain wrong.

Think about it: Soldiers, who are wearing an average of 71 pounds of gear, are being expected to go to the ground and grapple with people who are probably trying to kill them, and then to do what? Control the attackers with a lock? This is insane, yet it's what passes for military combatives today.

And as bad as our soldiers have it, our police have it far worse because they have to be politically correct and follow the letter of the law while encountering far more hand-to-hand mayhem than any marine is ever likely to face. Hamstrung as they are, law enforcement officers are being taught techniques that put them at great risk.

The methodologies in this book address all of these misconceptions and are the result of extensive real-world testing. These methodologies have nothing to do with belts, tournaments, rankings, egos, or the preservation of traditions that no longer reflect the effectiveness of their original forms. Their creator, John Perkins, is a retired New York police detective and an expert on the dynamics of violence at homicide scenes. His research experiments for Dr. Peter Deforrest (head of Forensic Science at John Jay College of Criminal Justice) and Dr. Peter Pizzola (current director of the New York Police

Department crime lab), involving thousands of experiments in blood-spatter pattern interpretation, were crucial to Perkins' understanding of various aspects of very violent events. For Perkins, these experiments revealed that fights to the death don't go down the way most people think.

But there is far more to Perkins' unique perspective on violence than his police work. In an era drowning in martial art hyperbole and sportive myth-making nonsense, the following may seem like more of the same, but it is nevertheless true: John Perkins was raised from the age of five to be a warrior. Some would call it child abuse and others reality training, but the fact remains that John's part Cherokee, part Welsh West Virginian father and uncles were determined (they had their reasons) that he master both World War II close-quarters combat and Native American catch-as-catch-can wrestling. His preparation included brutal training with knife, tomahawk, and spear, and all begun before he entered kindergarten. His father and uncles were large, powerful men, and they taught John both evasion and destruction for his own good. Planted in the back of John's mind was a restless thirst to overcome everything he was taught with something even better.

Thus began a martial arts odyssey that included bone-breaking fights on the streets of Yonkers, New York, illegal pit fighting on the docks of Hoboken and New Orleans, tai chi, kempo, the ancient Greek art of Elephtheri Pali (ruthless combat), as well as hundreds of bloody melees as a cop that resulted in trips to the hospital or morgue for the losers. An entire book could be written about his adventures and misadventures, but the greatest imperative imparted by all these experiences was survival.

John Perkins applied the reality principles he was evolving to the development of a unique and dynamic fighting system. This system is currently used by some highly trained Marines, SWAT teams, and FBI personnel, as well as state and local law enforcement officers. This self-defense methodology is probably different from anything else you've ever come across. It had to be to address the paradox that has plagued the field of self-defense for some time: If all life-and-death struggles are hell-storms of unchoreographed chaos and confusion, then why do self-defense systems train you with repetitive, patterned techniques? In everything from formalized kata to standardized punching, the nervous systems and reflexes of students and professionals are being trained from the beginning for a reality that doesn't exist: preplanned fighting.

This book prepares the highly skilled martial artist and the non–martial artist to face the two most dangerous adversaries: the psychopathic, violent criminal and ignorance. Self-defense, although it may be raised to the level of an art form, is neither a game nor a sport. The psychopathic, violent criminal is not a movie character but a living beast who enjoys senseless acts of brutality—the maiming or killing of innocent people—to release seething rage. This criminal may be lucid or acting under the influence of mind-altering substances. He or she may be a prison-trained monster or may have been taught on the street. He or she may be anyone, from a next-door neighbor or an ex-husband to a rogue police officer or fellow passenger on a jetliner secretly bent on a terrorist act. This criminal attacks instantly and decisively, relying on surprise or subterfuge, either armed or bare-handed. He or she gives no quarter and may care little about being killed. This is what you may come up against.

The bottom line for you is to prepare for potential confrontations, both physically and mentally. To do so, you're going to have to learn to do things a little differently. Learning some magical technique is not going to help you deal with real-life mayhem. Neither is retreating into Eastern or New Age mysticism. You need to take a swan dive into reality with both eyes and all your senses wide open. With the help of this book—and hard work—you're going to become a practitioner of guided chaos. You're going to learn how to deal with violence the way it really happens: unplanned, unformatted, unstylized, unchoreographed, furious, and wild. In short, chaotic. But rather than force limited, rigid, florid, or sportive choreography onto chaos, we're going to show you something totally unique, yet so simple in concept that we're almost embarrassed to teach it. You are going to learn how to adapt and flow with the chaos.

This book provides martial artists with unique principles that enhance what they already know; it gives novices the bare bones of survival strategy as well as a training methodology that will enhance their overall coordination, timing, balance, and inner and outer harmony. But, which is not the case with purely meditative training, that inner peace will become more profound because it will be based on physical and mental abilities and on a true representation of fighting dynamics.

YONKERS BLOODBATH

John Perkins

In one documented example, a police officer responded to a radio call for help from an injured colleague at an infamous Yonkers, New York, lounge. The responding officer was highly trained in various styles of karate and kung fu, and he plunged through the open door of the bar, ready for action. As he ran across the threshold, his first step into the dimly lit room was straight into a pool of blood. As if on ice, he slipped and slammed down hard on his back. Immediately, a huge brute dove on him and began alternately pummeling his face and strangling him. In a frenzy, the officer grabbed his nightstick and swung it wildly at the attacking man's head. Instead, the heavy nightstick crashed against a bar stool and blew apart. It was now useless as a bludgeoning weapon.

What saved the officer was that as a child, he had been trained by his father in Native American fighting principles that embodied looseness, spontaneity, and unbridled, free-form viciousness. These now emerged. He began to use the broken nightstick as a stabbing weapon, hammering it against the thug's temple. This, working in concert with his raging adrenaline, enabled him to evade strikes, adapt to the broken nightstick, and avoid serious injury to himself.

This fighting methodology is different from other organized styles of martial arts in many ways, yet it can complement most of them. How different is it? To begin with, the methods presented here have no forms. That is, there are no set and sanctified techniques, no prearranged responses to specific types of attacks, and no learn-by-the-numbers choreography to clog the mind and reflexes with unnecessary strategic calculations. How is this possible? We invert the entire learning process. With guided chaos, we start your training where most systems should end—with improvisation and adaptability—and work backward from there.

We do this because during a real fight for your life, it is virtually impossible to deliver a stylized technique effectively; the speed, chaos, viciousness, confusion, and utter terror associated with a real fight preclude this. Your nervous system simply becomes overloaded with the flood of sensory stimuli. You can't treat your brain like an electronic dictionary full of self-defense responses and expect it to select the right technique to counter a matching attack under extreme duress. It simply doesn't work that way.

If you've been programmed by practicing a specific response to a specific attack, your defense will fail if the attack changes by even one inch from the way you've trained. This is true whether you know one technique or a thousand. How will your body know when to deliver the strike if the sensory data it is being bombarded with have no correlation to your practice? All serious (nonsparring) fights are literally hell-storms of chaos; therefore, you cannot rely confidently on choreographed training. This is not conjecture. It has been proven through exhaustive experience, countless police and morgue reports, and testimonials from police officers with high-ranking belts from various martial arts styles whose classical training failed them when the spit hit the fan.

This book contains documented examples of real people under horrific circumstances. It helps to be reminded over and over that violence rarely unfolds the way it does in the ring, in martial arts school, or on TV or in the movies.

PSYCHOTIC REACTION

John Perkins

A fact of life is that no matter how strong, large, or fast you are, there's always someone stronger, larger, or faster. Typically, these are the people who attack you. Also, no matter what the attacker looks like, you never know who you're dealing with. An otherwise diminutive individual can become so enraged by drugs, psychosis, or sheer terror that he or she literally has the strength of a lion.

In one instance, police officers found a small, homeless woman lying motionless in the street, muttering to herself. When they asked her to move, all hell broke loose. Between the street where she was discovered and the mental hospital where she was finally locked down, one cop had his uniform torn to shreds, another had flesh ripped from his body, and two large hospital orderlies who tried to restrain her in the cell were seriously injured. Their cries for help could be heard through the heavy door meant to contain her. Caught by surprise, a 220-pound (100 kg) cop with a black belt hit the woman with a reverse punch square in the solar plexus and sent her crashing against a wall. This only enraged her. She let out a deep, guttural growl that would have made an exorcist cower in fear, and then she exploded. In the end, the first effective thing available with which to subdue her without serious injury was a 200-pound iron hospital bed. Despite her size, the woman was a human tornado.

This book offers a proven alternative form of thinking, training, and fighting that takes the following issues head-on:

- Training in a hard style of martial art that emphasizes brute strength may not adequately prepare you for real, life-and-death confrontations.
- Training in a soft style with technically complex forms can clog the mind when every millisecond of a real fight is totally unpredictable.
- Training in a rules-based, sportive, and competitive manner, even with full speed and power, is dangerously detrimental to the development of true self-defense and instinctive reflexes.

Now don't get us wrong. With time, dedication, talent, and first-class teaching, classical training has turned out (and continues to turn out) superb fighters. Sport fighting trains those with already superior genetics and makes them even better competitors. Nevertheless, we submit a different approach to learning realistic self-defense, one that's more focused on the end result of taking average people and adapting them to the inherent unpredictability of random violence. Weigh the arguments carefully and draw your own conclusions. Our methodology focuses on training in a noncooperative manner from the very start, stressing the unexpected.

Contrast this with the training routine of many popular soft styles. On cue, one person attacks another in a pre-set manner, with both parties knowing the precise technique that will be used. For example, one person faces another, pretending to attack with a knife held about waist high. The attacker slowly moves forward, while the defender steps confidently to one side, brushing the knife away. The defender then grabs the attacker's knife arm, twisting the wrist. The attacker then jumps into the air, flips over, and lands on one side, whereupon the defender puts the knife hand into a wrist lock, supposedly vanquishing the attacker. This is as close to pure choreography as you can get, yet it's a scene duplicated in many martial arts schools and police academies. Students are led to believe that these techniques will work in the real world, when in fact, this idea is a dangerous fallacy. Police reports show that an enraged, untrained, 100-pound (45 kg) woman with a large knife can slice a trained martial artist to ribbons in seconds.

Take a reality test: Face off against a training partner armed with a felt-tip marker representing a knife. Both of you slather your arms with oil (the oil represents the shockingly slippery blood that would almost certainly be covering your arms in any real knife attack). Now, with the attacker slicing and stabbing wildly at maximum adrenaline speed like a crazed sewing machine, try to effect a knife disarm. You will find, in addition to being covered with hundreds of ink marks (representing your body being carved into hamburger), that it's impossible to get a grip on your slippery attacker. Congratulations: You have survived a simulation; in real life, your corpse would've been shredded almost beyond recognition. Train unrealistically and unnaturally, and you cannot fight for real. As obvious as this concept seems, it is one of the most overlooked aspects of martial arts training.

Don't misunderstand—it is always helpful to be fit to have the best chance in an attack. That is, achieving and maintaining cardiovascular fitness and muscular strength means you will be better able to move quickly and protect yourself. However, since the reality is that most real fights last less than four seconds, adrenaline and trained reflexes are the true keys to survival. Even if you win the fight, however, you could still lose: If you're not in shape, your body can suffer cardiovascular and structural trauma simply recovering from the stresses your adrenaline-fired responses placed on it. We will help you develop only those physical attributes necessary for self-defense at the expense of those that would help you win a body-building contest, an arm wrestling match, or a triathlon.

We will say this again and again: Classical training is very often beautiful, cooperative, and predictable, but combat is ugly, nasty, and chaotic. Board breaking, high kicks, and flashy Russian splits are all great and praiseworthy athletic accomplishments. But they have absolutely nothing to do with self-defense. It's very simple: The way you practice is the way you fight. So if you can't depend on fixed techniques, and you can't rely on muscling your assailant, what are you left with?

> In the real world, attacks are not choreographed. They happen when least expected and under the worst circumstances. They are anarchic and spontaneous by nature, and they require a different mindset and method of training.

Another Way

To free the mind and allow it to function at the gross, animalistic level best suited for survival, you need to train in paradoxical ways by learning principles of movement that are simultaneously random, spontaneous, and free, yet singularly effective. What we mean by principles of movement are the laws of balance, ballistics, body unity, inertia, momentum, speed, weight, looseness, sensitivity, and coordination best suited for the human body in mortal combat.

This is what we call an education in guided chaos. During a fight, the only constant is change—change in direction, attack angles, weapons, balance, environment, lighting, number of assailants, friction, speed, force, tactics, footing, emotions, pain, and any number of other variables. Therefore, in this methodology, what you will be learning and practicing are principles and exercises to help you to become a master of motion, randomness, improvisation, and change rather than a master of techniques.

> *Now an army may be likened to water, for just as flowing water avoids the heights and hastens to the lowlands, so an army avoids strength and strikes weakness. And as water shapes its flow in accordance with the ground, so an army manages its victory in accordance with the situation of the enemy. And as water has no constant form, there are in war no constant conditions. Thus, one able to gain the victory by modifying his tactics in accordance with the enemy situation may be said to be divine.*
>
> —Sun Tzu, The Art of War

This is as true today as it was over 2,000 years ago.

Because our approach to self-defense is unusual, the material in *Attack Proof* is laid out differently from what you might expect. There are virtually no common conditioning exercises or repetitive drills. Although we detail many physical exercises that may double as effective, low-impact aerobics, the mission of *Attack Proof* is to teach you principles of motion that can help you save your life.

THE BEFUDDLED MASTER

John Perkins

A great master of the soft style mentioned on page xi (who was second only to the style's creator), lost in a mock fight with an untrained cameraman who was filming him. On a whim, the master decided to use this cameraman in an impromptu demonstration. Unfortunately, this cameraman, as you can see in the film, did not know how to "cooperate" with the master, who had a difficult time trying to put him on the ground. In fact, it took quite a long time and much effort for the master to win. The fight was a clumsy mess and was probably very embarrassing for the master. Surprisingly, this did not serve as a lesson: The style is still taught today as if cooperation is always going to be present. This is because many people who say they want to learn self-defense really want a sport—or a religion. This is why so many martial arts schools concentrate on the superfluous instead of the essential.

For those of you who have the first edition of *Attack Proof*, you will be happy to see that we have expanded virtually every chapter, adding in things that were originally deleted because of space limitations. There are also new chapters applying the principles to even wilder scenarios.

In part I we detail and dispose of certain faulty preconceptions about handling violence. Chapter 1 prepares you mentally for what is to follow. If this sounds frightening, don't worry; once you begin to understand what you are dealing with and how you are going to deal with it, you will build a new perspective on self-defense—and perhaps life—that is both calming and fortifying. You will also learn the single most important tool of self-defense, which, ironically, has nothing to do with fighting. Chapter 2 briefly describes basic strikes, some obvious and some unusual, that make up the elementary tools you'll use to defend yourself. This includes treating misconceptions about kicks and explaining how and when they are appropriate. We have culled all this from a system created to rapidly train U.S. soldiers during World War II to deal with Japanese troops allegedly proficient in judo and karate. A simplified system called close combat has been devised from these methods. It is lethal and, with little training, provides effective self-defense for the average person. (We'd like to point out that Perkins' close combat differs from all the currently popular World War II combatives in that it incorporates some of the far more advanced guided chaos principles.) We round out the chapter with some very unusual drills to unify the mental principles described in chapter 1 with the physical principles explained in chapter 2. It is important, however, that you do not attempt fanatical perfection of the strikes explained in chapter 2; if you do, you will fall into the most common trap in martial arts: fixating your mind and body on a technique. What you'll learn is that the strike itself is not as important as acquiring the opportunity to deliver it. Learning this close combat material first will ensure that you develop the right attitude for self-preservation before launching into the heart of this book—the study and training of guided chaos and its related principles in parts II and III.

What, then, is the relationship between the close combat described in part I and the guided chaos described in parts II and III? We believe that learning to punch and kick is the easy part. All you need is the knowledge to discriminate between useless and effective striking; that's what close combat does. Then, once you understand what basic strikes are and what they're supposed to do, you can focus your attention on the real business of learning self-defense: how to make the strikes work. That's where guided chaos comes in. Guided chaos is the language of fighting. We cannot emphasize enough that great physical strength, hand-toughening routines, and high-flying wheel kicks aren't required. All you need are gravity, perseverance, and an open mind.

Part II explains in detail the primary principles of guided chaos. Their chief purpose is to make your movements free and creative. Each chapter has its own exercises for integrating the principles into unified, mind–body responses. We say "unified" because, as you'll see, your own mind can be your biggest enemy.

OVERQUALIFIED?
John Perkins

In one of our seminars, an arrogant teacher of a particular style that emphasizes knife work (who also happened to be a police trainer) thought he was overqualified for a particular drill using rubber knives. He was matched with an untrained, 5-foot-2-inch (1.6 m) woman. Before the exercise began, she was pulled to the side and told to imagine that she was a Native American warrior, and that settlers had captured her family. The only thing standing between her and her children was the self-assured man standing in front of her. She was given permission to do whatever she wanted. With a yell, the woman ran straight at the man. At the last second, she slid on her knees and stabbed the police trainer five times in the groin with the rubber knife. Stunned, he managed one feeble swipe at her head, which she blocked, before falling backward on the ground. The woman jumped on top of the police trainer and finished him with a stab to the throat. Not surprisingly, the police trainer was crestfallen. He was obviously highly skilled, but he suffered from a reactive handicap: pattern recognition. Because what the woman had done resembled no pattern he had ever practiced, he could not respond to her movement effectively.

Part III shows you how to apply the principles of part II to combat, including those involving weapons and multiple attackers. By explaining additional modifying principles and exercises in chapter 7 (Applying the Principles to Motion) and chapter 8 (Economy of Movement), you begin to apply the "guided" in guided chaos. Chapter 9 (Grabs and Locks) uses the preceding principles to protect you from one of the most dangerous traps in fighting: falling in love with controlling tactics. Finally, in chapter 10, we explain in great detail the guided chaos approach to ground fighting. There is a world of difference between these methods and those currently popular in MMA.

Chapter 11 is an exploration of stair fighting and how the principles can be adapted to a demanding environment (many of Perkins' patrols took him into crime-infested housing projects). Chapter 12 covers attack and defense using kicking, sticks, knives, guns, and canes.

Afterword: The Survival Manifesto was written primarily by guided chaos master Lt. Col. Al Ridenhour, who gives his unique perspective as an Iraq War combat veteran on self-defense mind-setting. This brings us full circle by reiterating and amplifying the critical survival principle of part I: self-defense as warfare. We have included in the afterword some real-life horror stories that are definitely not for the faint of heart. If you are not mentally prepared to train for the realities recounted in these stories, your chances of survival are slim.

Throughout *Attack Proof* we present various self-defense awareness strategies that make up a body of street smarts, covering everything from home, work, and school to defense while traveling by car or airliner, including in hotels and during hijackings.

If you are already an advanced black belt or want to put teeth in your tai chi, you needn't dispose of everything you know. What you'll find is that guided chaos makes everything you know work better.

Special Note: DVDs augmenting parts I, III, and III are available from www.attackproof.com.

BODY AND MIND PRINCIPLES OF CLOSE COMBAT

Before we launch into the more advanced guided chaos methodology that makes our approach so different from that of other martial arts, part I provides you with critical close combat fighting basics that should be part of every serious self-defense student's knowledge. These consist of awareness and general self-defense decision making (chapter 1) and basic close combat strikes and strategies (chapter 2). As noted in the introduction, these close combat methods alone are lethal and, with little training, provide effective self-defense for the average person. They also provide the necessary foundation on which you can build your knowledge and practice of guided chaos, which is presented in parts II and III.

CHAPTER ONE

AWARENESS

The concept of awareness is so simple that we're almost embarrassed to teach it. Ironically, though, it's one of the most ignored yet effective forms of self-defense available. There are also many misconceptions about what to do with this concept. Consider this scenario: You're walking to some destination on a city street. You need to make a left at the next corner. As you make the turn, you notice two men loitering against a car. They don't necessarily look dangerous, but there's just something, a feeling, that disturbs you slightly about them. Do you

- walk down the opposite side of the street and avoid eye contact so you won't seem confrontational;
- walk straight toward them, confident, head held high, the way you may have learned in an assertiveness training class; or
- reach into your pocket (handbag, holster) and rest your fingers lightly on your knife, mace, or pistol?

The correct answer? None of the above. Rather, you use your awareness and walk down another street. It's logical: If you're not there, they can't attack you. No one is going to pin a medal on you for bravery if you're already dead. Let the next person be the hero.

Learn to respect your intuition and use your awareness in any situation. Everyone has awareness, yet many people silence their inner voice and ignore their better judgment. A gross example of this is people who walk around with their heads down, contemplating some inner scenario, or grooving with their iPods completely oblivious to their surroundings. This behavior is an accident waiting to happen. Even though most of us look where we're going, we don't really see anything.

Even if you are licensed to carry a handgun and have sought the necessary professional training to be able to use your gun safely and effectively, it's important that you remain aware so that you can reach for it in time. Without adequate hand-to-hand fighting knowledge, you won't be able to get your gun out before you're overpowered. And your assailant may get to it first, which could really escalate the seriousness of the situation. We've done workshops in which gun owners had their worlds rocked by a simple test: They found that when they were charged at by a knife-wielding attacker from across a large room, they were cut down long before they could pull their weapons.

By reminding you to be aware of your surroundings, we are not talking about descending into some New Age, Zen-like state of mind, but about the importance of training yourself to casually notice your surroundings all the time. This is vital because in nearly 100 percent of assaults, the victim had a feeling that something was wrong before anything actually happened. Our primitive instincts are still fully functional, screaming at us; we're just not listening to them.

It's important to take notice of your surroundings all the time.

Try this simple exercise every time you're on the street: Decide to look for something during the course of your walk. For example, look for people with red shirts or men with mustaches. This gets you to open your awareness to your surroundings on a regular basis.

You don't have to go around in a continuously paranoid state, however. Simply keep your attention outward, and if something looks amiss, you'll notice it. Best of all, if you are aware, any predator out there will notice that you're cognizant of your surroundings and so won't be an easy target.

Learn to trust your feelings. For example, if a complete stranger insists on helping you fix a flat tire or carry packages, or offers to do any other unsolicited favor, you may feel a tightness in your stomach and ignore it because you want to be polite. Predators count on this. They approach you this way to earn your trust and then get you to a private location. Don't back down. Seek out a third person, such as a store employee or a neighbor, if the stranger's insistent. Or start screaming; there are more dead polite people than you'd like to know about. Be aware and be vocal. The best self-defense is never having to use it in the first place.

Learn Awareness Strategies

The following tips provide some specific ways to be aware and prevent robbery, assault, and murder (some ways to combat rape are discussed in chapter 2). Whether you're at home, at the office, in a parking lot, at an ATM, in a car, or on a train, the best self-defense is awareness. You don't have to be on red alert all the time. Fear can actually stifle your sensitivity. Simply take notice of your environment—and daydream only when you know you're safe.

Note: All the awareness material culminates in the special section titled Self-Defense Aboard Airliners at the end of chapter 2. This section distills awareness, mind-set, close combat striking, and environmental weapons into a particular reaction scenario that almost anyone can learn from.

Being Aware at Automated Teller Machines (ATMs)

ATMs are potentially dangerous anytime but especially at night and when you're alone. Avoid using an ATM at night or in an isolated area. Robberies at ATMs are bad enough, but assault, rape, and murder are sometimes part of the equation. If possible, try to avoid using them if you're the only customer. Carefully stick to these guidelines to help protect yourself:

- Scan the area before leaving your car to approach an ATM.
- At drive-up ATMs, keep the car in drive or in gear with the clutch depressed. Keep your foot securely on the brake. If something goes wrong, hit the gas.
- If a vehicle pulls out ahead of you and suddenly stops, the driver may be counting his money—and maybe not. Don't enter any area where your car can be immobilized. Wait until there's no potential for blockage.
- Use ATMs only while in the public eye. Naturally, criminals prefer darkness and isolation.
- Some criminals study the habits of regular ATM users. Don't visit ATMs on a schedule. Vary the days, times, and ATMs you visit.
- If your ATM card is lost or stolen, you may be contacted by telephone. The caller may sound official and ask for your personal identification number (PIN). Don't give it

out. Instead, offer a reward if he or she turns your lost property over to the police. Or offer to meet him or her in a public place—and bring a friend.

Staying Safe When Traveling

Be especially vigilant when traveling. Hotels and motels are prime crime areas. Follow these tips to help you stay safe when traveling:

- Call the front desk if someone suspicious is lurking about or tries to gain entry to your hotel room, using some excuse such as "I have to check your TV."
- Watch out for ruses. Many travelers fall victim to criminals posing as employees. Always verify by calling the front desk. Some criminals manipulate legitimate employees to gain access to your room.
- If you're going on a trip or are a constant traveler, purchase one or two portable door alarms that attach to the doorknob. You can find these alarms in electronics supply stores. If someone tries to enter your front door or the door between your room and an adjacent one, he or she will activate a high-pitched siren. You can also purchase a portable alarm with a built-in delay feature to place on the inside of the door while you're out. Be aware, however, that the delay feature is not good for personal protection when you're in.
- If you have valuables, put them in the hotel safe.
- If you suspect that something is wrong before you enter your room, have a staff member check it first.
- Have your room cleaned while you're present.
- Keep a "Do not disturb" sign on your door and a radio or TV playing while you're out.
- Always find out who's calling you in your room. Don't give your name until you're satisfied you've got a legitimate caller. If the caller says he or she is from room service, ask the name and verify by calling room service. If the caller says he or she is calling from the front desk, call the front desk back and verify.
- If you're out partying, whether away from home or not, be aware that there are many kinds of drugs that can be slipped into your drink by a person who has gained your confidence. Do not leave your drink unattended. Get to know whom you're dealing with. Allowing another person to return to your room with you is dangerous.
- Keep conversations with cab drivers or hotel personnel courteous, but don't give out personal information. It may be used for criminal purposes.
- If you're traveling in an urban area, stay away from the edge of train and subway platforms. Every year some psycho somewhere pushes an oblivious victim in front of an oncoming train.
- Remain sober while traveling. The need may arise for you to be lucid and take physical steps to survive.

Distinguishing Phony Police

A person posing as a police officer is a disturbingly popular scam used by the most heinous predators. Here are some tips to help you distinguish imposters from real police:

- If you're going about your business and are accosted by a person or persons in plain clothes flashing badges and IDs, be extremely wary, especially if you know you've done nothing wrong. If they ask you for nonpersonal information and their IDs look legitimate, you could answer their questions.
- If they want to place you in a vehicle or move you to another location, or if you have doubts, be courteous and ask them to communicate with headquarters and call for a uniform patrol car to respond. Don't jump into an unmarked car with potential masqueraders.

- If you're in an unmarked car and something the people say or do clearly tells you they're not real police, crash the car.
- If you receive a phone call from someone claiming to be a police officer, find out which precinct he or she is calling from and call back to verify.
- If you're approached on foot by someone flashing a badge, don't just follow blindly if asked—demand a uniform patrol car be sent.
- If you're driving lawfully and carefully in an isolated area and a suspicious, unmarked car pulls up with a plainclothes driver asking you to pull over, take no chances. Even if you see a flashing dashboard and single roof light, be careful. Anyone can buy a badge or light for a car. Authentic-looking uniforms can be purchased by anybody. Signal to the suspect officer to follow you to a safer, crowded area. If you're stopped, request that a uniform patrol car be sent. Keep your car locked with the windows up and engine running. Ask for the phone number of the precinct. Call 911 if you feel you're in danger, and let the others see you doing it. This points to the necessity of always carrying a charged cell phone—don't leave home without it.

Avoiding Purse Snatchers, Pickpockets, and Muggers

To thwart these kinds of robbers, carry your valuables, such as license, keys, and credit cards, separate from your wallet or purse, especially when traveling. Purchase a money belt or pouch that can be easily concealed. Follow these tips as well:

- If a purse snatcher grabs your bag, don't fight back. Let it go. Many have been injured or killed because they valued their possessions more than their personal safety.
- Be aware that most street robberies are perpetrated by one or more criminals who use a diversion. It could be as simple as asking the time or some other question. You're being assessed as a potential target.
- Don't stop on the street. Keep walking and politely decline requests for information, directions, the time, or money. Say you're in a hurry, you have no money, whatever. If the person attempts to stop you physically, be ready to escape. If you can't escape, be ready to fight.
- Keep in mind that you don't know if the person accosting you is working with an accomplice and setting you up for rape, robbery, assault, or murder. In the case of panhandlers in public places, you could have some loose change to give them, but don't ever go into your purse or wallet to get change. If you're actually being robbed, and the robber asks for your money, don't fish around for bills. Give the robber your whole purse or wallet.
- If you're walking, somehow become cornered by one or more people, and your inner alarm goes off, attack immediately and ruthlessly (study chapter 2 and the section on multiple attackers in chapter 10). As soon as you can, escape. Hit hard and fast, disable the one closest to you, push that attacker aside, and run through the gap. If escape is impossible, you'll need everything you will learn in this book. You can survive.

Defending Yourself at Home

More than half of all rapes and a great percentage of robberies, assaults, and murders happen in the home. Defend your home or apartment like a castle:

- Get a dog. Most criminals avoid homes with dogs. Some breeds provide better defense than others, so do some research.
- Keep your windows clear of shrubbery, which can hide a burglar or rapist while he is jimmying your window.
- Get outdoor motion sensor lights.
- Consider installing an alarm system made by a reputable security company.

- Join your Neighborhood Watch program, or form one if it doesn't already exist.
- Keep your valuables out of easy sight and away from ground-floor windows.
- Make sure that your garage door is secure. Many thieves and violent criminals gain access this way.
- Have a peep sight and/or an intercom system installed in your front and rear door. Don't open your door for anyone. If someone at your door is in an emergency, call 911 for them. Rapists, robbers, and murderers often use this ruse. They may pose as plumbers, letter carriers, or telephone or power company employees. They may be women or children with adult male backup. Fake injuries are also used to get past your front door.
- If you reach the door to your house or apartment and the key won't go into the lock or your entry is damaged, get away immediately and call the police. Don't enter your home without the police checking it out first.
- If you're on your way home and suspect you're being followed, verify this by making four left or right turns around a block. If the vehicle is still behind you, don't go home. Criminals will simply follow and jump you in your own driveway. Drive to the local police or fire department or some other highly public area. Use your cell phone and call 911.
- Reinforce your bedroom door with a secure lock to slow down an intruder. Keep a cell phone and gun (that you've been trained to use) by the bed. A shotgun has the highest deterrent value, and anyone with an ounce of brains will run when they hear it cocked. This may seem extreme but think of the simple logic: If the intruder is not discouraged by motion lights, alarms, and a dog and is still determined to get in, you've got a serious problem. All the previously listed obstacles and the reinforced door are meant to slow down an intruder; having a cell phone gets around a cut phone line. You know what the gun's for. If it's come to this, don't hesitate to empty your gun into the intruder.
- Create an escape plan. The advice so far is good if you've got no children, or there's no other exit. If you do have children or another way out, remember that the first line of defense is awareness, and the second is escape. Create and practice an evacuation plan for your entire family. Everybody needs to try to get out through the nearest window or door and get a neighbor's attention.

Jogging Safely

Pepper spray has limited effectiveness against an enraged and determined attacker. In John Perkins' personal experience, it has worked only about half the time, even when it's shot straight in the eyes at close range. Use pepper spray in conjunction with a defensive strategy: spray and run, or spray, hit, and run. Here are more commonsense tips for jogging safely:

- Never jog with headphones on—you jeopardize your awareness, making yourself a sitting duck.
- Stay away from unlit, thick shrubbery adjacent to trails and paths. Remain at least 10 feet (3 m) away from the sides of buildings and parked cars as you round blind corners. This can provide the critical space you need to defend yourself against an ambush.
- Do not jog alone.
- Vary your jogging times and routes. Predictability aids a predator's planning.
- Wear a personal alarm that you can set off with one hand.
- If you believe at any time you're being followed by a vehicle as you're out jogging, turn around immediately and run in the opposite direction—preferably toward home or another secure area. Don't be assertive. Don't be coy. Just get out of there!

Awareness can prevent you from getting into other potentially hazardous situations, from entering a strange bar at 4:00 a.m. on New Year's Eve to leaving your drink unattended (and susceptible to a date-rape drug cocktail). In addition to the awareness guidelines provided throughout this chapter, two excellent books that promote self-defense awareness are *Strong on Defense* by Sanford Strong and *The Gift of Fear* by Gavin de Becker.

Establish Your Personal Comfort Zone

It's an unfortunate fact of life, but there are people in this world who simply can't live in peace with their fellow human beings. You try to cultivate a love your neighbor philosophy, and then some mutant wrecks it by killing you. Regrettably, one violent encounter can cut short a lifetime of altruism. So you must make a personal decision either to be wholly trusting (and vulnerable) or ever vigilant. Vigilance doesn't mean you have to walk around angry. Indeed, if you take the emotion out of it, vigilance merely becomes a relaxed, practical exercise for fully participating in life.

For example, establish a personal comfort zone that no stranger is allowed to enter. This is not paranoia, just good practical sense. You need a trigger that allows you to stay relaxed most of the time. At a minimum, the zone is about as far as you can extend your arm or leg. This is also known as your sphere of influence, which we cover later. Maintaining this zone may require that you walk around people so they don't get too close. Refusing to give space needlessly is a senseless provocation and another liability of so-called assertiveness training. Don't create or let yourself be pulled into senseless confrontations. You never know who you're dealing with. Maintaining your personal comfort zone is difficult in a crowded subway or elevator, but in these situations, your awareness is already heightened. Also, potential attackers are discouraged from attacking in such crowded conditions: There are witnesses, and the attacker's escape route is usually obstructed.

Practice Hostile Awareness

What you think and do before a fight is often more important than the fight itself. We'll call this next section your prefight orientation because you're going to have to make some hard, philosophical decisions about your attitude as a victim. But first, try this: From time to time, strictly as an exercise, when you walk down a busy sidewalk with people going by at different angles, directions, and speeds, visualize how you would respond to a random attack from a stranger. Calmly imagine counterattacks that are appropriate to someone else's position in space in relation to yours. How would you strike? When could you run? Do you have sturdy shoes with which to kick? If you're really aware, you may need to make a practical decision about your footwear. Shoes can be stylish and still pack a punch. If you're truly serious about self-defense, it is now possible to purchase almost any type of casual shoe with a steel toe. This effectively turns your feet into sledgehammers that are always at the ready and easier to bring into action than almost any pocket weapon.

Look around and check your surroundings. Are there natural weapons (bricks, sticks, bottles, and the like) nearby? Perhaps you have a ballpoint pen handy to use as a stabbing weapon to the head or soft body parts. Don't get nervous—this is your life we're talking about protecting. This is only a drill, but drills are best practiced initially while you are calm; hostile awareness will become easier as you learn and practice the methodologies in this book. After a while, it will become second nature, and your subconscious won't be so startled if the real thing should happen. The point is, practicing hostile awareness isn't an exercise in creating social or emotional dysfunction. Instead, you're looking for potential hostility in your environment, not building your own. This prepares your nervous system to respond in an attack.

Remember, reckless anger can be detrimental to self-defense because it robs you of your ability to stay loose and be physically sensitive. You're merely engaging in neural programming, what's called visualization in advanced sports training.

Note: Continue to practice hostile awareness (strike and evasion visualization) and environmental awareness (availability of natural weapons) even after you've mastered everything in this book.

The Decision-Making Process

Does this attitude of passive vigilance seem extreme? Perhaps some sobering statistics are in order. But first another quiz: If you're involved in a mugging or some other form of assault in which the assailant attempts to take you to another place (in other words, a kidnapping, carjacking, or a robbery moved to a remote location), do you

- try to reason with your captor,
- go along quietly so you can escape or be rescued later, or
- tell your captor you're expected someplace and that people will come looking for you?

Once again, the correct answer is none of the above. Police statistics show that if you go along with the attacker to a second crime scene, the odds of being killed or being so severely injured that you might wish you had been killed are extremely high. By the same token, if you make your stand right there and either run (if you can) or fight for your life, the odds are reversed. So, you see, your decision-making process is greatly simplified. But let's be absolutely clear about what we mean by this: If you're asked for money by a mugger, be very polite and respectful, and then give it to him. All of it. Don't fish around for bills; give him your whole handbag or wallet and quickly. In some situations where you have a good deal of distance (at least 15 feet, or 4.6 m) between you, you can simultaneously throw your wallet and run the other way (although we discourage this because some psychos could get ticked off and blow you away anyway).

Regardless, if the mugger wants you to come with him, it's because he has a lot more in mind. This is the moment of truth. We detail what you actually do in your counterattack in chapter 2, but it's important to know the reality of the situation. Despite what you may have been told or seen in movies, there's no magic solution that will get you out of this situation completely unscathed. You'll probably sustain some sort of injury even if you get away successfully. The key thing, however, is that you survive. If you don't run or fight back, you probably won't.

With a knife right against your throat or a gun in your face, this changes, but only to the extent that your attacker needs to be taken slightly off guard before you resist. We detail specific maneuvers to increase your chances in these situations in chapter 12 (Weapons Fighting), but the point is, don't wait until the attacker has taken you to a secure location. Keep in mind that most assaults take place without a weapon being introduced, at least initially.

Hostile Awareness During a Carjacking

Hostile awareness can be extended to other dangerous circumstances that demand immediate action to prevent later tragedy. What if you're in your car, boxed in by traffic, and one or more carjackers jump in suddenly through carelessly unlocked doors and windows and demand to take you someplace? Prevent the assault from moving to a second crime scene by doing whatever it takes to crash the car quickly. Bite, scratch, and rip the intruder's eyes out; then grab the wheel and smash into something big. Carjackers lose interest in you fast when this happens, and the injuries you might sustain will probably be less than any the attacker might give you. A crash also attracts a lot of attention. In short, don't go with the attackers if you want to live. Be careful: There are actually many cars that automatically open the door locks when you turn off the ignition and/or remove the key. We know of one woman who was ambushed in the driver's seat and had a knife put to her throat precisely because of one automaker's stupidity.

Here are some other tips to help you survive a carjacking:

- Always park in well-lit areas. Scan parking areas before parking your car. Scan again before leaving your car. When returning to your car, scan the area before approaching. This applies especially to parking lots in malls. If something looks suspicious, go back to the mall, tell a security guard, or use your cell phone to call the police—

don't second-guess yourself. Many horrific tragedies in the news could have been prevented if people had followed this ridiculously easy and simple advice. Have your keys ready. Once inside, lock the windows and doors.

- Avoid driving through bad areas of town. If you must, and you get a flat tire, drive on the rim as far as you need to in order to leave the area. The cost of a new wheel is a small price to pay for your life. When you're driving, if someone outside the car points to your wheel and says you've got a flat, respond with thanks and keep driving to the nearest safe area. The person may even have put a slow leak in your tire and followed you. This phony Good Samaritan scenario is the oldest trick in the book.

- Always carry a car charger for your cell phone and an extra battery.

- When in traffic, always maintain some space in front and behind your car so you can escape or at least ram another car and then escape.

- Beware of fender-bender scams. If you're hit, never pull over in a deserted area. Signal to the other driver that you want to drive to a populated area or some business establishment where you can trade insurance information. If the other driver doesn't like it, too bad. You can tell the judge you were afraid for your safety. Better to be judged by 12 than carried by 6.

- If you're stopped on a deserted highway with severe car trouble, your cell phone won't connect, and someone stops to "help" you, tell that person you just called the highway police for assistance, but you'd also like to call AAA and your battery just died. Ask the person if he or she could go to a phone and call for you. If the person insists on helping you and then gets out of the car, leave the ignition key in place, get out immediately, and put distance between you and the other person. Don't get trapped in your car. Remember, a law-abiding person would never put you through this.

- Prepare your family for carjacking incidents. Practice escaping through the nearest window or door and scattering in different directions at the first indication of danger or at a prearranged signal from you (e.g., "Run!").

- If you're alone and a predator suddenly enters through a window or door before you can hit the gas, leave the keys and get out the other door. Give the intruder the car.

- Don't go with an abductor. Crash the car. Hard. If the abductor is driving, wait until you're doing at least 25 miles per hour (40 km per hour) and then scratch his eyes out, bite his ear off, go berserk, and make him lose control. That's what you want. Grab the wheel. Don't reach for the keys; it's a dangerous waste of time.

THE BATTERED KICKBOXER

Mercy can be a liability, even for the well trained. Mary (not her real name), a competitive kickboxer, was assaulted out of nowhere by a homeless man who spat corn chips in her face and then attacked her. To her credit, Mary reacted instantly, punching and kicking him with tremendous force. The man fell to the ground, apparently hurt badly.

Unfortunately, what she did next almost got her killed. Mary leaned over him to make sure the man wasn't seriously injured. Suddenly, he leaped up, struck her in the face, and began pummeling her. She recovered and again fought back, only to be pulled off him by the authorities. At first, they thought he was the victim because he was covered with blood. In actuality, his first strike to her face had been with a concealed punch knife that had pierced her nasal cavity between the eye and nose. The blood had literally poured out of her onto the homeless man. After much reconstructive surgery, Mary eventually healed, but she was lucky to have survived.

The moral of the story? Do what's necessary, then run. Often, weapons aren't pulled until later in the fight. If you can't get away, then be sure to incapacitate the attacker. After all, he or she attacked you, and your family or loved ones won't be consoled if an act of pity on your part deprives them of you forever.

THANKSGIVING DAY MELEE

John Perkins

A huge fight took place one Thanksgiving Day at a football game in Yonkers, New York. Knives were involved, and many people were hurt. A police officer (who also happened to be an instructor of controlling tactics) applied a wrist lock to one of three extremely large, belligerent individuals and was actually raised off the ground by his lock and tossed like a toy against a 4-inch (10 cm) iron pipe protruding from a fence. Another officer (Perkins) was then forced to subdue all three of these extremely powerful men by himself.

This story teaches us the following:

1. Training for life-and-death situations by practicing controlling tactics is like taking major league batting practice with a flyswatter. In both cases, you'll strike out big time.

2. As a private citizen, you're under no obligation to respect the rights of someone who is trying to maim or kill you. You have the right to fight back and to be left alone.

3. By training to use deadly force instead of training to contain, control, or even worse, "submit" to the attacker (as if you were in some televised UFC bout!), you have the ability to decide the level of punishment. You can always back off from maximum force. Once you start with submission tactics, you may never get back in the fight. In the preceding story, it was fortunate for the first cop (the controlling tactics instructor) that Perkins got there in time to provide the right kind of backup.

The three linchpins of self-defense are

- scan,
- avoid, and
- carry a cell phone.

- If it's gotten to the point that abductors are going to place you in the trunk, you're in big trouble. What we said earlier about not going to the second crime scene applies here. Fight like a rabid dog. Don't think that by complying you'll have a better chance of surviving later. If, however, you wind up in the car's trunk, rip out as many wires as you can once the car starts moving. Inoperative tail lights may attract a cop's attention. In many cars, you can punch out the tail lights from inside the trunk and actually stick your hand out and wave to attract attention.

- Fill your tank in the daytime. Scan the gas station and the store before pulling up.

- The instant you see a gun, run (provided the gun's not right on your body and you're not being restrained). Don't even wait for the attacker to say anything. This is best illustrated by an incident that happened to one of the authors' wives. A thug jumped out from between two parked cars and waved a handgun. The woman took off the instant she saw gunmetal, leaving the attacker speechless. He never even had a chance to say, "Give me your money!" The odds of him shooting at this point were small because it would have attracted attention; the odds of that attacker hitting the intended victim at all (much less with a lethal shot) were even smaller. You'd be surprised how fast and far an adrenaline-fueled person can run, even with several poorly placed bullets in them.

Understand Your Perspective as a Victim

Law enforcement personnel are in an unenviable position. With their lives on the line, they must subdue and arrest extremely dangerous individuals who are often quite willing to rip their heads off. The question each cop in such a situation asks is "Does this suspect actually harbor this intent or is he just bluffing? Can I take the risk?" Then, once a fight begins, only reasonable force may be used. In the heat of battle, every cop is expected to have a legal computer implanted in his or her skull to weigh the results of any actions and avoid excessive tactics that may save the officer's life and the lives of innocent victims, yet provoke a lawsuit by the perpetrator.

The legal implications of every action have created a market for tactics that don't use lethal force (locks and holds rather than strikes and chokes), which protect the criminal more than the cop or other victim. Even so, the effectiveness of these nonlethal tactics is also controversial. This book is not the place to discuss this issue in depth without getting into an argument over department policy, local politics, and civil rights; however, we will say that geared-down "lethal" force training often winds up being safer for both perpetrator and policeman than locks and holds. Understand this well: A cop who can't fight will be far more likely to use a gun. The point is that as a civilian, you are under no such constraints.

Challenge No One

We are teaching the pacifism of a warrior. Unless you or a loved one is in imminent physical danger, no fight is worth it because you never know who you are dealing with.

Even when you win, you can be seriously injured. Remember that self-defense isn't about honor; it's about survival, and macho posturing is a form of insecurity. What are we talking about? Suppose you are in a bar and someone bumps you, then makes some remark intended to insult your sexual orientation or claim to have intimate knowledge of your sister. You say confidently, "Excuse me," admit you're a eunuch, and wish him well with your sister. If necessary, claim you're a coward and leave, but don't sound like a coward. This puts just a hint of doubt in the bully while providing an excuse not to escalate. Walking away from confrontation has three advantages:

1. It lets you avoid petty squabbles and later entanglement with the legal system.
2. It restricts fights to those you absolutely must undertake to save your life.
3. It relieves you of the moral indecision and guilt when you have no other choice but to do what must be done. This mindset alone triples your fighting power.

The principle of challenging no one, although philosophical, will also prepare you for its vital physical counterpart when we launch into the guided chaos principles in part II.

DON'T FIGHT

Many years ago before he began training in guided chaos, author Kovsky was entering a building for his high school reunion when a small, wiry man pushed past him, knocking him into the door. Kovsky said, "Hey, watch it!" to the man, who wheeled around and screamed, "F--k you, asshole!" Kovsky, sensing he could crush the punk because of his small size, stepped forward just as a third person intervened and de-escalated the situation (he knew the punk's brother). Later, Kovsky asked the third person, "Why did you stop me? I could've kicked his ass!" The other replied, "Because everybody in the neighborhood knows he just got himself a new gun, and he's been itching to try it out."

Respond According to Your Environment

Your environment can play a huge part in your response. If you're in an area with other people, such as on a crowded train, it's effective to be loud, assertive, and vocal to attract attention to your position, especially if you're experiencing stealthy harassment by a pickpocket or a subway groper. Simply screaming at the offender will turn heads and discourage the person. However, if the person is not discouraged, or if you're in an area where no one is likely to help you (or care), the material in chapter 2 comes into play.

Preventing Common Mistakes

➤ Don't try to be polite to a stranger who gives you a bad feeling. This is potential suicide. Run.

➤ Release your fear. Self-defense skills are useless if you can't channel and focus your fear. Memorized self-defense techniques are too slow for the nervous system to process in a rapidly changing crisis.

➤ Avoid trouble. Being inappropriately or unnecessarily assertive with a criminal is an invitation for disaster. Standing up to verbal bullying in a bar is not self-defense; it's ego.

➤ Don't be manipulated.

➤ Don't resist a simple robbery. Do resist an abduction with everything you've got. Don't look on a conflict as a personal challenge. Avoid confrontations at all costs: Run away first. Fight only when you have no choice.

➤ Be a pacifist warrior. Obscurity is the best security.

CHAPTER TWO

BASIC STRIKES AND STRATEGIES

You develop your awareness, you avoid dangerous situations, and you confidently claim cowardice and walk away from confrontations. Nevertheless, some mutant has picked you as his target du jour. If you're jumped without notice or your attacker wants to move you to another location and you can't run, you now know, at least mentally, that it is time to make your stand and let loose the dogs of war. (If you still think playing nicey-nice with neat little McDojo techniques or the latest MMA ground and pound moves you learned will allow you to walk away without wrinkling your shirt, you need a serious reality check. Skip to the end of this book and read "The Survival Manifesto" with special focus on the section called mind-setting. Go ahead, we'll wait.)

Got your mind right? Good. But what do you actually do, and how do you train for it?

The Interview and Preemptive Strike

Unless you're the victim of an assassination-style attack in which you're simply ambushed and executed, most confrontations begin with an interview. The interview situation refers to an impending mugging or attack that begins with a verbal distraction, such as "You got the time?" or "You got some change?" or the ever-popular "Do you know how to get to . . . ?" It also can refer to that all-important point in the beginning stages of a confrontation in which someone attempts to provoke you with the what-you-gonna-do-about-it rap. If the person gives you the slightest bad feeling (a feeling based on your awareness, which you need to trust), your verbal response is to say "Nothing," "No," or "I don't know" and back away, keeping your eyes on the person. Quickly scan around for accomplices but instantly bring your eyes back to the speaker. This should only take a millisecond. Never just turn your back on someone with disdain, or it may be your last memory. By the way, no one says you can't immediately run away screaming. If your gut instinct is that strong, listen to it. Regardless, since you aren't challenging (see chapter 1, p. 11), you give this individual every opportunity to disprove your suspicions when you back away. A law-abiding person won't pursue you. You react to the interview this way so you can take full responsibility for what happens next.

Despite your withdrawal, if a stranger (or a hostile acquaintance) physically enters your personal comfort zone (see chapter 1, p. 7) with a gesture, strike, or attempt to touch you for the purpose of causing you harm, and you can't escape or run, you need to resort to preemptive striking—an action that Bradley Steiner, president of the International Combat Martial Arts Federation, calls "attacking the attacker"—quickly and decisively (*Tactical Skills of Hand to Hand Combat* by Bradley J. Steiner, copyright 1977, Paladin reprint edition 2008). You don't want to spar with the enemy. If the fight lasts longer than four seconds, you're in deep trouble. You want to disable him or her as quickly as possible and run. If you feel as if your life is in danger, your actions may involve using immediate, deadly strikes to the eyes and throat. In close combat, there are basic defensive postures that enable you to use preemptive striking effectively.

The Jack Benny Stance

If you're old enough to know who the great comedian Jack Benny was, you'll picture this immediately (but it's no joke!). Jack used to stroke his chin while he pondered his next punchline. This is the same stance you want to take during the interview at your first inkling of danger (which you will feel instantly—even with scam artists—if you start learning to pay serious attention to your gut instincts). The animal in you recognizes danger instantaneously, while your brain says *be civilized*.

To assume the Jack Benny stance, stand sideways to your aggressor (far enough away so that he or she must step forward to reach you) and bring your lead hand near your face with the elbow down in a seemingly nonaggressive position (see figure 2.1*a*). Or, this could be a nervous gesture of indecision such as scratching your head, rubbing your mouth, or, if cornered in an elevator, raising both hands up in a kind of meek, why me? posture (see figure 2.1*b*).

Figure 2.1

Don't attempt to look threatening with an en garde posture as if you know karate. The last thing you need to do is get your aggressor's adrenaline flowing faster than it already is. Instead, like Jack Benny, look small, passive, and harmless. Depending on the situation, it may help you to look terrified (this may be closer to how you actually feel than you'd like, but we're going to teach you how to use terror as an energy source). This immediately lets the other person think he won't have to work too hard to get what he wants. You're basically setting a trap. But wouldn't being assertive just make him back off? Unless you're a great actor and have pressure-tested your frothing-at-the-mouth-pyscho routine, no. Remember, he's already picked you out. He expects you to be scared. If you're normal, you *are* scared. If you look as if you are, your aggressor will be lulled slightly before you explode in his face like a hand grenade. Tell him, "You're the man, you got me, what do you want?"

But let's be absolutely clear: If it's money he wants, give it to him promptly. Be super polite, and hopefully he'll take your dough and go. Don't fish around for bills in your purse or wallet; give him the whole wallet. Don't fight simply because he wants your money.

If the aggressor wants more than you can give and attempts to harm you, or especially if he or she wants you to go somewhere, you must act immediately. Because you've looked like easy pickin's until now, the aggressor's defenses will be down slightly. This is good, because you'll be attacking him or her preemptively, by striking in the middle of a sentence, while you're cowering (attacking the attacker). If you're getting the idea that playing possum has its advantages, you're on the right track. In a nutshell, you're assuming a physical posture that does three things:

- It makes you less threatening to the attacker, and relaxes him or her slightly.
- It automatically provides cover for your head and throat and protects you from an accomplice's rear choke.
- It aligns your arm for a straight shot to the thug's chin, eyes, or throat, while deflecting any strike.

With your arms in the Jack Benny stance, and while acting meek, shoot your lead (upraised) hand straight out as you step forward onto your lead leg with all your weight, moving in a falling motion. This adds power to the blow. The lead hand smashes your attacker under the chin with your palm while your fingers drive deep into the eye sockets (see figure 2.2a on p. 16). This type of combination strike is called a chin jab. A relatively weak person, powered by adrenaline, can wrench a larger person's neck with this strike because the vertebral support is weak.

You can also chop to the front or side of the throat with the edge of your hand on the pinkie side (see figure 2.2b on p. 16). Or you can just stab the attacker straight in the eyes with your fingers. Which first strike you pick will be determined by your training. Some people prefer chopping, and some prefer chin jabbing. A smaller person with skinny arms might prefer gouging straight to the eyes (this is advantageous because skinny arms are harder to block). Regardless of your first strike, follow up instantaneously with the other arm by blasting your palm up under his chin, into the side of his jaw, or into his temple (depending on what's available). Step forward with each strike, as if launching a shot put. This is only the first in a series of rapid, straight, and screaming blows you should unleash like a wild, enraged jungle cat (you'll learn others, starting on p. 18). While doing this, hunch your shoulders and sink your head down so that you protect your face and neck. Your arms will occupy the line your attacker might take to attack you. This accomplishes your deflection automatically. How is this possible?

When you're standing sideways in the Jack Benny stance, because both hands shoot out (one behind the other), you'll automatically deflect a strike from either of the attacker's hands if he or she should move first. This forms a kind of instantaneous defensive arc around your head. To understand how this works, imagine the hull of a boat, or better yet, an icebreaker. The V-shaped hull cracks the ice at the prow, the point of maximum force combined with the narrowest surface area. The ice then slides around the sides. Similarly, without blocking, your hands go straight for the chin, eyes, and throat, while your arms (the prow) shield against his attack.

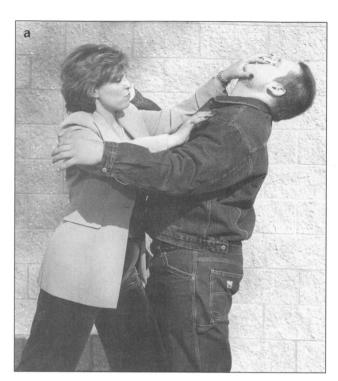 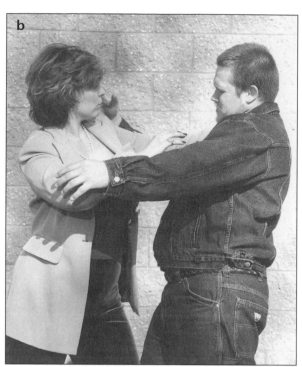

Figure 2.2

Don't block. If your energy is directed toward blocking his hand, you'll be committed to this direction and will waste perhaps your only opportunity to strike unimpeded. Also, he'll probably overpower your block, anyway. Because you want to disable the attacker, focus on driving his head back, spearing his eyes, or chopping the side of his neck. Because of the shape of your response (the position of your arms coming out of the Jack Benny stance), you will block the initial attack anyway. If he reaches for or strikes at you from the outside left (see figure 2.3a) he'll be deflected and struck at the same time. If he reaches or strikes from the outside right, the outcome will be the same. If he reaches straight forward (figure 2.3b), either his attack will be deflected, or both your first strike and his will neutralize each other—except that your other hand, which has been simultaneously traveling to the same target, will hit its mark.

If he reaches for you with both hands (typically attackers don't hit with both hands simultaneously), the shape of your attack will split his two hands like a wedge. Remember, your chin jab, eye gouge, or chop is not happening in isolation. You are not posing to strike like a kung fu movie star. Your move is merely the first in a continuous barrage of screaming, ripping, wildcatlike, buzz-saw strikes. In short, forget about looking good or admiring your handiwork; just go berserk. Attacking the attacker is efficient because you don't block. Your strikes are your blocks. We detail these and other strikes as well as drills to practice them later in this chapter. You will also learn the remarkably simple close combat universal entry (CCUE), which ties all these principles together.

No strike occurs in isolation.

Blind Attacks and the Fright Reaction

More dangerous than the interview is the blind attack. In the blind attack, you're ambushed with no prior warning (as described in The Williams Brothers' Attack, chapter 5, p. 101). Provided you aren't killed instantly—with a knife or gun—your defense depends on your body's natural fright reaction and not on rigid, stylized techniques. There's virtually no defense against a planned assassination anyway, even if you're Mike Tyson armed with an M16. However, since most assaults have a different objective in mind (robbery, rape, or intimidation), you usually have some options.

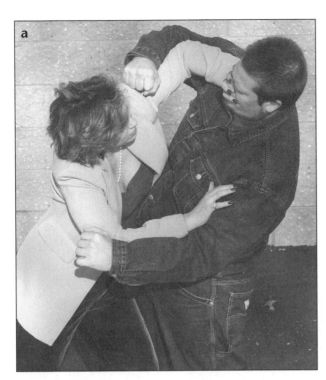
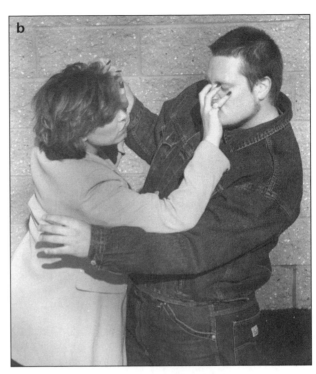

Figure 2.3

The fright reaction uses your body's natural, adrenaline-fueled response to sudden shock and fear. Ever been attacked by a swarm of bees? Ever had a firecracker thrown in your face or heard a gunshot? What did you do? Your whole body instinctively dropped its center of gravity, your back curved out protectively, your head sank low between your upraised shoulders, and your arms and elbows came up around your face and neck (figure 2.4a). Dropping your center of gravity in this way strengthens your stability and

Figure 2.4

It is a waste of time to block because this may be the only opening you ever get. If the attacker reaches for you first, resist the temptation to stop his or her hand. Go straight for the eyes and throat. Done correctly, your strike will deflect your attacker's strikes.

adds to your power and balance. This fundamental, instinctive reaction involves a vital motion principle called dropping (described later in this chapter); we will fully exploit this principle in parts II and III. For now, though, understand that simply lowering your head, hunching your shoulders, and raising your arms protects vital areas (especially your throat) from strikes and rear-approach strangling attacks (figure 2.4b). And you tend to do all this naturally without any training (provided your instincts haven't been smothered by some bogus martial art). The fright reaction is an ideal defensive position and should not be substituted with some stylized kung fu stance.

What you do immediately after the fright reaction is critical, and it must be simple and focused. Turn toward the attacker and hit like a banshee. Jab his chin, chop his neck, and spear your fingers straight into his eye sockets. We will give you drills that will help you discover which strikes work for you, but train them all so they can be delivered like a buzz saw when you need them. Eye strikes are especially nasty and hard for the enemy to block. If you've ever been accidentally poked in the eye, such as in a basketball game, imagine how devastating a purposeful strike could be. We describe these and other follow-up strikes in the next sections.

Basic Close Combat Strikes

Many of the strikes detailed in this section can be lethal if practiced properly. They do not involve complicated movements. Most of them are culled from methods taught to U.S. soldiers during World War II to defeat the Japanese, who were all presumed to be skilled in judo, jujitsu, and karate. These strikes are also the elementary weaponry used in guided chaos principles, described beginning in chapter 3.

Speaking of guided chaos, we will briefly illustrate one of its key principles here because it can amplify all your close combat strikes. Simply put, we want you to deliver every strike as if you were sneezing. "Sneezing?" you say. That's right. Not straining, not winding up, but convulsing spasmodically, as if your strike had been shot out of your body like your breath during a sneeze. We call this principle dropping; it involves an instantaneous tightening and relaxing of the whole body like a whip. This principle will make more sense when we discuss it in relation to the energy principles described in chapter 6, but for now, apply this sensation to every strike you practice.

Figure 2.5

Chin Jab

As described earlier, you direct this strike at the face while moving forward. The idea is to cause massive trauma to the head and spine by striking with the heel of the palm, especially underneath the chin. You actually walk through the strike, driving your attacker back. By striking under the chin, the head snaps back, creating pressure on the spinal cord and either knocking the assailant unconscious or breaking the attacker's neck. At the end of each chin jab, use your fingers to gouge out the eyes or drive through them with power, pushing them back into their sockets. Yes, it's gory, but your goal is to survive, not to be a guest at your own funeral.

Deliver these palm strikes exactly as if you were throwing a shot put. A common mistake beginners make when delivering palm strikes (and punches) is to get too close and overbend the elbows so that they wind up pitty-patting the target using nothing but their triceps (figure 2.5).

Keep your arms relatively straight at impact and drive through the head, not with muscular strength but with your root—your connection with the ground. This is something you should do on all strikes. Your root is an esoteric principle from martial arts; it means your ability to drive all your strikes from your feet. You will train yourself to root automatically when you learn more about the principles in part II, but for now, recognize that your legs are far stronger than your upper body. Also, using your arm muscles exclusively makes you tight and slow. Drive from the ground through your legs at high speed, extending the energy through your hips and back to your hand and out your fingertips as if you were pushing a stalled car. Use this visualization, however, only to get the right alignment. The way you actually hit the target will be more like a jackhammer. Slam it but don't overcommit to it, or you will end up losing your balance.

You might ask, "Why not use a fist?" There are many disadvantages to using a closed fist (see p. 21). One of them is that a closed fist is easier to block. A chin jab can slip under an opponent's deflection because the hand is shaped more like a spear when it comes out, offering less surface area.

Chops, Spears, Ridgehands, and Claws

You direct these strikes at the side of the neck, Adam's apple, eyes, or back of the neck at the base of the skull. A relatively unfamiliar but extremely effective target for the spear is the center of the armpit. Executed correctly, these blows are deadly. When employing a chop, hold your hand flat with your wrist straight and your fingers together but relaxed. Keep the thumb extended out at a 90-degree angle from the hand (figure 2.6).

This is different from many styles where you are told to keep all your fingers tightly together; we have found this tightness slows the speed, power, and reaction time of your strikes significantly (see chapter 3). Aim for the soft tissue of the neck and strike with the pinkie side of your hand, using either the bony prominence of the wrist or the fleshy area one inch above it. Create a loose, dropping motion when striking the side or back of the neck, using the weight of your body without tightening your muscles. Drop your entire body weight into the shot. There is a far more sophisticated way of dropping that we will get into later, but for now, you want to almost fall into the chop, so that the power is not a by-product of muscular exertion but of body mass in motion. You do this by lunging forward and relaxing the front leg so that for a split second your knee collapses about two inches (5 cm). This dropping action adds power to the strike because you're turning and dropping your body weight down onto the opponent's neck like an ax. If you look at old films of world champion boxer Jack Dempsey, you'll see that he would often step and suddenly drop his weight onto his lead leg as he jabbed. This is a rather crude form of dropping, but it worked. Dempsey hit like a wrecking ball.

When hitting straight into the throat, blast through it, using the same dropping motion. Again, this adds power to your attack, even if the chop is upward. The body propels the chop outward. The chopping shoulder moves to the inside, while the other shoulder moves away; this is because the whole body is turning like a windmill, as you can see in figure 2.7. You can deliver chops at an almost infinite

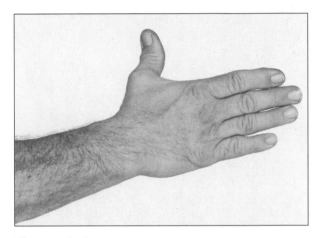

Figure 2.6

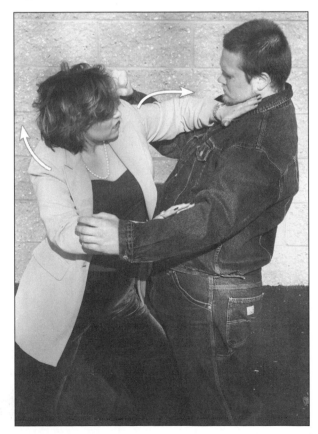

Figure 2.7

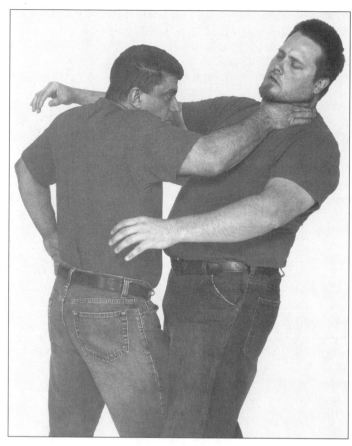

Figure 2.8

number of angles. When you become familiar with the principles of guided chaos in parts II and III, you'll see how they're used in the context of a real fight. Ridgehands are similar to chops, except that you deliver them with the thumb side of the flat hand.

When using a spear hand strike, keep your fingers together and almost straight, aiming for the eyes and throat. These are your primary targets. No matter how big or strong a person is, no matter how much he or she lifts weights, there is nothing he or she can do to make the eyelids or throat stronger. Your eyelids will not stop a person's fingers from going through them. If your hand is in a clawing position, like a bear or a cat, you don't need to press your fingers together. At least one of your fingers will find an eye socket without precise aiming. Also, as a bonus, the momentum of a clawing strike sends your palm into the attacker's nose or chin. If you imagine you're throwing a shot put or a banana pie into someone's face, your hand will be in the right position.

A yoking, or V-shaped, spear hand strike to the Adam's apple is also potentially lethal. With your hand in a chopping position, move your thumb out about 3 inches (7.6 centimeters) to create a V, the vertex of which you thrust out and drive into the throat (figure 2.8). This is useful at close range.

Rips and Tears

Contrary to what you may have been taught in classical methods of self-defense, rips and tears can comprise some of your most effective weaponry. Rips and tears have the effect of opening the attacker to other strikes. Rip by using your hands to squeeze and tear at any soft tissue areas of the body. Any time someone pulls away from you, it presents an opportunity to rip and tear. Pull at the eyes, neck, throat, ears, groin, lips, hair, fingers, or any lose fold of skin, such as around the underarms, waist, or corners of the mouth. Ripping, tearing, and pinching (discussed next) are the only tactics for which we recommend a regimen of pure strength training for the hands because the stronger your grip, the more you will hurt your attacker. You can substitute rips and tears when you attack the attacker if that works for you. If you've ever seen how cats fight, you'll get the idea. This is distinguished from wrenching where you'd be using your hands to break and snap bones, tendons and cartilage.

> With chops, on impact snap your hand open further, stretching your fingers, and then instantly relax. This solidifies the weapon from liquid looseness to rock-hard ice, then back to liquid.

Pinches

If, despite everything you've done, you wind up with your arms pinned to your opponent's body, dig your fingers in or grab some flesh between the bent second joints of your index and middle finger and pinch and twist with every ounce of strength in one, fast, convulsive movement. If your attacker is experiencing an adrenaline rush, a pinch will not cause him or her to collapse in pain (unless you pinch in a vital area, such as the throat, face, or groin). Pinches are dramatically more effective on some body types than others (ectomorphs and some mesomorphs yes; endomorphs no), but this is not a calculation you need to make. Pinches often provide an opening for you to hit through when your attacker reacts. If it allows you to follow with a stab in the eye, perfect. One other particularly effective target for a pinch (or rip) is the edge of the pectoral muscle where it overhangs the armpit. This can be very nasty—which leads us to the subject of biting.

Bites

You're being held tightly by his arms; you can't move. Chances are, however, that your mouth is free. If so, you can use it to rip and tear into his flesh like a wild dog. Don't be shy: This is your life we're talking about, and you could die if you don't act. Worry about diseases later. The second your attacker flinches, start gouging with your fingers, hitting with your elbows, and ramming with your head.

Head Butts

You've probably seen these in movies, but it's important to know what part of the head to hit with, or you'll suffer more damage than you'll dish out. Use the thickest part, which is the top of the forehead, right at the hairline. The straight butt is particularly effective in an upward strike against a tall opponent (figure 2.9). Your target can be any part of the face, temple, or jaw. Just don't hit your attacker's forehead. You can also slash with this part of the head sideways like a hook punch. Be sure to practice head butts at all possible angles on a heavy bag, but remember to warm up, stretch your neck muscles first, and start slowly.

Figure 2.9

Elbow Strikes

You can use elbow strikes anywhere: to the head, neck, throat, base of the skull, chin, upper and lower arm, hand, shoulder, chest, rib cage, and so on. When done correctly, an elbow strike is equivalent to hitting someone with a baseball bat because the elbow's striking power penetrates deep into the body. Moreover, you can use the elbow strike in a spearing motion. This tool is virtually limitless in its applications and the variety of angles at which you can deliver it. It is vastly underused in most martial arts. Practice elbow strikes using a variety of angles. (Part II teaches other uses for the elbow beyond striking.) The only limitation of this weapon is that you can only use it at short range.

Some of the less familiar angles that we recommend you practice include the up elbow (figure 2.10a on p. 22) and the downward-spearing elbow (figure 2.10b), delivered as a thrust with the upper body rather than as a swing. The downward-spearing elbow is similar to the horizontal-spearing elbow (figure 2.10c). You deliver the inverted up elbow (figure 2.10d) like a shoulder shrug, and you can use it as part of an upward-turning body rotation that ends in a chop to the throat. You should practice every angle you can think of. Be creative. You never know what position you may find yourself in.

Closed-Fist Strikes

You may be wondering why we placed these strikes at the end of this list of offensive hand weapons. Although these strikes are the most popular, they're the least effective for self-defense, especially when striking to the head. Ironically, using the fist is practically a conditioned response in most people.

Believe it or not, a fist has too much give in it to be an effective weapon unless it is highly trained; the wrist is likely to bend on impact. The hand itself is constructed of many small bones and tendons, each with the cushioning potential of a small shock absorber. When making contact, the hand must first compress until there is no more flex remaining before it can deliver any power. Along the way, there is great potential for injury to the puncher. This is why boxers tape their wrists before a fight.

When you use an open-handed strike such as the palm heel, it's already in the position it needs to be when it makes contact. There's little skeletal movement because the

Learning how to make a proper fist takes a lot of practice and is actually difficult to execute in a panic, compared to a palm strike.

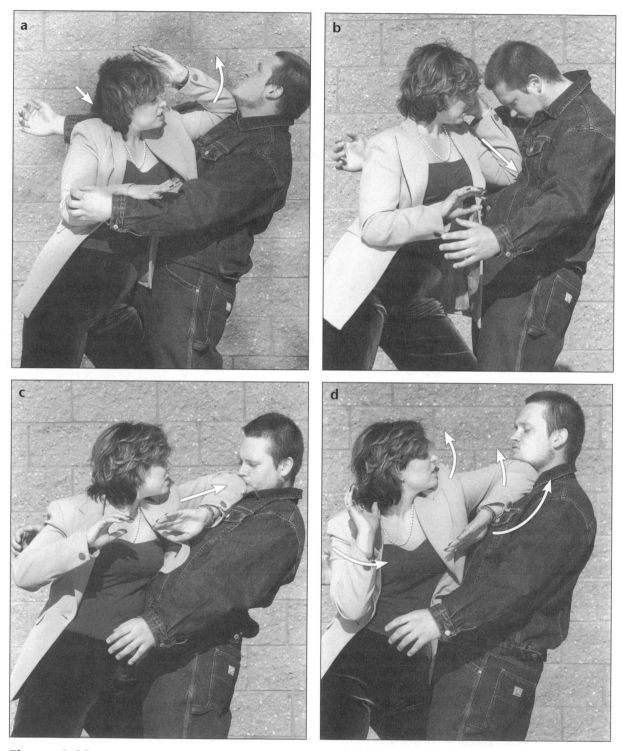

Figure 2.10

bones in the lower part of the hand and arm are already in line with each other. There's little flex or give because the hand sits right on the end of the forearm bone. This allows maximum power transfer to the target.

This is not to say that closed-fist punches have no use. When you do use them, target the soft areas of the body: the nose, ribs, kidneys, and the like. When delivering them, keep the hand loose and relaxed. When you strike, tighten the hand on contact as if grabbing a bar and then instantly relax it. This creates a vicious snapping or slashing effect on the opponent's body. But you need to understand that the punch has limitations. If you're still not convinced, slam your palm into a brick wall. Sure, it hurts. But would you want to repeat that with your fist? A punch to the skull would have a similar effect. Unlike in the movies, when you punch someone in the head, it's your hand that breaks. Save shots to the skull for open-handed strikes, which can snap the neck back like a twig, when your life is on the line.

A more practical use of the punch is as a hammer fist. Here, the striking surface is similar to the chop, except that the impact is more bludgeoning (figure 2.11). Hammer fists have a wide variety of targets that can overwhelm an attacker when blended with the rest of your arsenal. They can be made even more powerful with slambag training (coming later in this book), which helps harden the pinkie muscle. Eventually, this muscle can become so strong that the striking surface of the hammer fist feels like a steel hammer

There is another use for fists that involves destroying incoming limbs like a lumberjack cutting down trees. In guided chaos, we call this combat boxing, but it requires extensive slambag training and is beyond the scope of this book. See the resources and www.attackproof.com for class and seminar info.

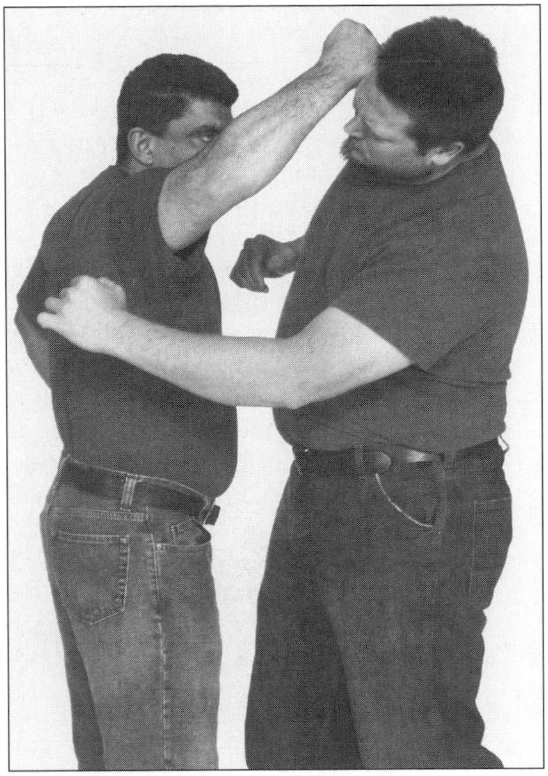

Figure 2.11

Knee Strikes

Keep your knee strikes low, using them on your attacker's thighs (inside and out), hips, sides of the knee joints, tailbone, abdomen, or groin. Don't jump up to knee-strike someone in the head, the way you see in the movies, unless you want to get slammed to the ground. Use a convulsive action to drive your knee forward as if you are coughing. This contracts the diaphragm explosively, pulling in the stomach muscles and adding speed to your knee strike.

Kicks and Stomps

It is essential to practice low kicking without chambering, or setting up. Chambering is a martial arts term for the practice of first raising the knee high before driving the kick out. We consider this motion a big time waster that merely serves to announce your intention to kick. It also raises your center of gravity so you can get knocked on your butt.

You should be able to deliver a kick without telegraphing your intention to your opponent. If you think you need to chamber to get power, remember this: The kick is useless if you can't get it off the floor in time to take advantage of an opening. It's better to deliver short, snappy, crushing, stomping, or stabbing kicks with the points of your shoes or the edge of your heel than to thrust out a big, high, looping side kick like you see in the movies. Such big kicks are easy to block and may only push the attacker back, giving him or her a chance to regroup. Your most practical kick could well turn out to be a crushing stomp on the toes (with practice, this can be done without looking down). Deliver your kicks quickly, economically, and loosely as if kicking a soccer ball. Kick low and step fast, repeatedly, like a flamenco dancer. Later, we will show you a drill for developing this.

Unless you're attacked in the shower or on the beach, you'll never need to kick barefoot. Wearing sturdy shoes changes the dynamics of your kicks and effectively puts hammers at the ends of your feet. Steel-toed shoes are now available in almost every style, from sneaker to boot to dress shoe (sorry ladies, no pumps!). They are a wise addition to your everyday wardrobe. You should always practice with them on.

When do you kick? If you're only being harassed, and your opponent wants to spar, just walk away, keeping an eye on him. If he approaches you, you can turn toward him and employ the stomping, drop-step kick. If you're just beyond arm's length, stomp with

Is the Groin an Ideal Target?

One myth that needs to be dispelled is the effectiveness of a single strike to the groin. We've been conditioned through TV and movies to think that one shot to this area will instantly incapacitate an assailant. This is usually emphasized as an option for women in street self-defense classes. Unfortunately, it is a dangerous fallacy.

First, most men have almost a sixth sense when it comes to getting hit in the groin and will instinctively block it if given half a chance. In a bloody melee this strike may have little effect if not aided by the element of surprise and accompanied by other strikes.

Over and over, in police reports and testimony from average civilians, we have found that all a groin strike does to an enraged thug or a meth or crack-addict is piss him off. So much so, in fact, that what might have been a quick hit-and-run mugging can turn into a psychotic bloodbath. Granted, if you're simply being harassed by a nonserious, sober pest, a kick, chop, or hammerfist to the groin will leave him gasping and doubled over after about a two-second delay. If an opponent is adrenaline fueled, however, hitting this target has little stopping power unless it is accompanied by a barrage of other strikes. This is why we emphasize going straight for the throat and especially the eyes in a preemptive strike. Or you can strike these areas immediately after a strike to the groin with the hand or knee if that's what's available. Throat and eye strikes have tremendous stopping power, sometimes greater than a gun would have. If you poke a 300-pound (136-kilogram) sumo wrestler in the eye with your thumb or finger, the fight is essentially over before it starts. You can now run away or attack at will, if necessary. However, you should still learn to use multiple strikes because you should never rely on only one "magic" blow.

your lead leg right where it is or move it forward a few inches, and instantly bring your rear leg forward to kick, like a soccer player. If the attacker is farther away (because you tried to back away first, and he moved toward you), make up the distance by first stepping forward with your rear leg and stomping with it as it lands. Immediately follow that stomp with a low kick with the other leg. In either case, deliver the whole stomp-step-kick sequence at high speed to your attacker's shins or ankles; there should be only a split second between the stomp-step and the kick. It should look like you're kicking a field goal (figure 2.12, *a–b*). However, keep the kick short and snappy. Do *not* follow through or you may wind up on your butt if you miss. We call this *containing the over-travel* and cover it in more depth in chapter 5.

The stomp part of the kick is important because it gains power from the ground and also stabilizes you on slippery surfaces, such as water, ice, blood, or oil. Police officers and bouncers using this strategy have proven its effectiveness. However, don't stomp at an angle, or you may slip. Your lower leg and especially the foot must hit the ground perpendicularly.

Do the stomp as if your lead leg had been kicked out from beneath you, and your weight collapsed downward as you recovered your footing. This intentional stumbling forces you to involve your complete body mass whether you want to or not. The momentum the stomp generates then drives the kick. Thus, if you weigh 110 pounds (49.9 kilograms), your kick has more than that amount of force behind it—because momentum is mass times velocity. When you're within arm's length of your attacker, use a lead-leg stomp to close the distance and add power to a chop, spear, or chin jab. This adds significantly more force than you could generate with just arm strength. Not using muscle power exclusively also helps you remain loose and less likely to be seriously injured in a fight.

When you learn the CCUE (Close Combat Universal Entry, p. 31), you'll learn more ways of incorporating low kicks. We also get into the far more advanced guided chaos kicking in part III.

Figure 2.12

Close Combat Drills

Now that you have a basic understanding of predator methodology and a vocabulary of basic strikes, we can begin to speak the language of close combat and combine these strikes into drills. Many of them are completely different from what you may be used to doing in classical martial arts. (Note: We've provided a method for structuring all the drills into a training regimen beginning on p. 262.)

Visualize your attacker as clearly as you can. This mental component of training is often neglected, but it is vital for programming your nervous system and fright reaction for danger. Although it's important to perform these drills seriously and realistically, maintain an attitude of play and improvisation at all times. As we get further into the guided chaos methods discussed in part II, it's important to keep your movements and your mind free.

It is critical that you do the first two drills regularly. Although simple, they fill the biggest gap in your self-defense, which is learning to overcome the paralysis of fear (see Lightning Strikes Twice p. 36).

Focus Your Fear

After awareness, your first line of defense is to run, run, run. Get used to the idea. Your second line of defense is to fight as if you and your family are going to die. We know we're being blunt—and repetitive—but there really is no other way to approach self-defense. The prospect of this may be terrifying, but when you consider what the alternative (dying) would mean to your family, you can mix in another emotion: anger. When you combine these two emotions with regular training and develop a sense of competence, the result is self-defense dynamite. You will become calmer, less prone to being sucked into asinine confrontations, and better at controlling the force level of your response if you must fight.

The Ugly Reality of Eye-Gouging

MMA enthusiasts often state that eye gouges just piss people off, or that they've seen fighters in the UFC routinely shake off illegal eye gouges and go on fighting.

This is going to be crude, but the reason those half-hearted attempts failed is because

- in a sportive contest, you're not thinking, "I'm going to die if I don't do something," or
- you lack the proper mindset for life and death combat. The definition of *gouge* is to remove or scoop out material, usually with a pointed object, in this case a finger or thumb to remove part of the eye.

Gouging should only be done in immediate life-or-death situations. To properly gouge the eyes, drive a finger or thumb deeply into the eye socket, causing the eyeball to hemorrhage or crush. Simply poking or scraping your fingers over the eyes of an enraged attacker will not stop him. A scratch to the eye will not suffice against a person who is under the influence of a narcotic or other pain-numbing drug. A true crushing push into the eye socket has worked and will work.

If the situation is dire and must be ended instantly, then a deep thrust of the finger deep into the eye socket and down past the occipital bone can be applied, which will cause convulsions or death. True life-or-death gouging is simplified by the funnel shape of the skull around the eyes, which guides the determined attack to its target. This is accomplished with the kind of extreme close combat sensitivity and dexterity developed by the principles in parts II and III—and not with the kind of Three Stooges eye pokes taught in many styles—because most people will flinch if an object is seen approaching the eye from some distance.

You can practice an eye poke or gouge by using a toy hockey mask and taping it to a striking mit. Practice striking the facial area and sliding your finger or fingers into the holes in the mask. A training partner is needed for this. Your partner holds the target still while you practice striking to the eyes; your partner then moves the mask around, which allows you to practice under more realistic conditions. The training partner could mimic high-speed head turning similar to what some grapplers try to keep the opponent's fingers from finding their mark. In real life, it is virtually impossible to elude eye strikes at grappling range without the kind of highly trained sensitivity that's developed with contact flow (chapter 6).

It is anathema to most human beings to thrust their fingers into the eyes of another. This is why we caution not to get into fights for any reason except where there is the threat of death and no escape is available. John Perkins has used eye gouges and even pushed his little finger through the corner of an attacker's eye. This action caused the attacker's nervous system to shut down instantly during a multiple-attacker altercation.

Caution: Never push into a person's eye because that person wants to show you how he or she can withstand the push. Those people are idiots. Some macho men can't deal with the fact that they have any vulnerability, so they will try to wish it away or fool themselves or others. A person cannot build up the eyelid or facial muscles to ward off a serious poke or gouge. We have heard the story many times about how a poke to the eye only enraged an attacker. A serious poke is no joke. Don't be fooled by fools.

This drill teaches you to channel and focus your fear, allowing you to run or successfully mount a counterattack.

1. Go into a room, close all the windows and doors, and turn off all the lights.
2. Close your eyes.
3. Stand completely relaxed and slowly breathe through your nose deep into your belly.
4. Visualize tension leaving through your exhalation and the power of the sun entering

through your inhalation, flooding every cell of your body with energy. Do this for a full five minutes.

5. Now imagine that the most depraved criminal you can think of is about to enjoy attacking and psychotically torturing the person who depends on you most, the person you're closest to in the world. But first, he's going to torture and kill you to get you out of the way. Not if you can help it.

6. Visualize the dark, tragic future this criminal could create: the tears, the regret, the shame. Now take all your fears, frustration, and helplessness and crush them deep into the bottom of your stomach. Take all the wrongs and humiliations that have been dealt you in life, all the anger and blind rage, and set them to burning. Ignite them with a sense of justice unfulfilled. Unfulfilled . . . until now.

7. From the pit of your gut, drive the fire into your feet, and then let it roar back up through your legs, hips, back, chest, shoulders, and then out your hands and mouth in the loudest, deepest animal scream your diaphragm can handle. We call this the warrior cry. You may have to yell into a pillow or wait until you're alone in the house, out in the woods, or in a self-defense class. But you need to release the potential paralysis that can occur in a moment of crisis—and become familiar with it. You need to know that you can explode and act when you're terrified and your family depends on it.

8. Do this once a week even after you've become proficient at everything else in this book.

In our society, we are conditioned to be polite, listen, obey, and behave. The psychopathic criminal knows this. He relies on your tendency to be socially correct. You need to relearn what an animal knows to do at the first sign of danger: It fights or runs for its life!

Not in every instance, but often enough, there is a moment of suspicion before violence or an actual abduction takes place. If you question the victims of violent crime, you will find that nearly all of them had an inkling beforehand that something was just not right. This first inkling of danger is when you run, not after. Forget about being polite to a suspicious stranger; your personal safety is your first responsibility.

Fright Reaction I

In some segments of society today, individuals (especially teenage girls) have separated themselves from their basic instincts. Because of the inundation of senseless violence in film, television, and especially music in our materialistic culture, some young people act as if they've been anaesthetized when first presented with simulated assault drills. In short, many have become desensitized to violence. Unless they've been actual victims, kids are hip, cool, blasé, and detached—just as teen culture has taught them. It's almost as if their instinct for self-preservation has been drained out of them. Nothing could be more dangerous. On the flip side, however, some teens are so wound up by popular culture, sugar, and so-called energy drinks that they have become nervous wrecks. (There are political and sociological implications to this also, but we won't go into that.) This drill deals with both conditions and helps you channel fear-generated adrenaline into effective defensive reaction instead of frozen terror.

1. Find a partner to help you perform this drill.

2. Stand quietly with your eyes closed and your arms at your sides. Breathe slowly into your stomach, saying *in* to yourself with each inhalation and *out* with each exhalation. Feel the tension escape with each exhalation and your body relax and sink deeper with gravity into your feet. Relax and quiet your mind. Tune into the sensation of air moving over your skin.

3. Now, have your partner touch you, as gently as a fly, somewhere around your head (this may remind you of annoying mosquitoes on a hot summer night).

4. The instant you feel anything, open your eyes and drop explosively into the fright reaction—lower your center of gravity, widen your stance, bring your hands up around your face, and sink your head low between your shoulders.

5. Have your partner make the touch lighter and lighter (thus making you more sensitive) as he or she touches annoying areas: your eyelids, ears, hair, and the like.

6. React as early and as quickly as you can, each time returning to the starting position with your eyes closed and arms relaxed at your sides.

7. Do this drill 20 or 30 times per session, and you'll begin to feel very alert and alive. Do not confuse this state of mind with anxiety, which can actually lessen your sensitivity. When you're in a dark alley or other remote location, this feeling is exactly what you want.

Your partner should try to get his or her touching hand out of the way as fast as possible, while you try to keep it off you. However, you're not trying to grab or hit your partner directly; you're simply reacting reflexively without thought or plan, both of which would slow you down. The key is to develop your reflexive sensitivity and dropping so that, in a blind attack, your whole body will begin to move as early as possible so it's ready for what comes next.

Fright Reaction II

This fright-reaction drill and those that follow are vital for understanding that fear is good when used to your advantage. This drill helps you channel your fear-generated adrenaline into effective defensive reaction instead of frozen terror.

1. Find a partner to help you perform this drill.

2. Stand quietly with your eyes closed and your arms at your sides. Breathe slowly into your stomach, saying *in* to yourself with each inhalation and *out* with each exhalation. Relax and quiet your mind. Tune into the sensation of air moving over your skin.

3. Spin around several times and then walk forward, keeping your eyes closed.

4. Keep walking. Within a few steps, your partner will shove you forcefully with a padded kicking shield (available at martial arts stores). The shove should come from an indiscriminate angle.

5. Open your eyes and go into the fright reaction at the instant of contact (or as early as you can).

6. Consider your reaction. Your balance, of course, will be totally blown. The point of this drill is to get you to drop your weight and spread your stance so quickly that eventually you can eliminate all stumbling. Repeat the drill again and again, regaining your balance each time by bending your knees and widening your stance, thus lowering your center of gravity. With practice, you will land as balanced as a jungle cat, no matter how hard you're pushed and from any angle.

Fright Reaction III

Now that you're getting comfortable with the fright reaction, let's add in attacking the attacker.

1. Find a partner to help you perform this drill.

2. Stand quietly with your eyes closed and your arms at your sides. Breathe slowly into your stomach, saying *in* to yourself with each inhalation and *out* with each exhalation. Relax and quiet your mind. Tune into the sensation of air moving over your skin.

3. Spin around several times and then walk forward, keeping your eyes closed.

4. Keep walking. Within a few steps, your partner will shove you forcefully with a padded kicking shield (available at martial arts stores). The shove should come from an indiscriminate angle.

5. From whatever position you end up in, open your eyes, go into the fright reaction, and then immediately launch yourself into the shield with fast, furious, full-power, alternating palm strikes.

6. Step forward with each strike. Nothing fancy here—simply drive forward as fast and straight as you can. Don't push the shield; hit it hard and fast as if smashing cockroaches on a red-hot frying pan to kill them without being in contact with the pan long enough to be burned. Hit as hard as you can and bounce off the surface into the next strike. Do not overcommit your balance to the shield, or you will fall over if it moves (contain the over-travel). Rely on your own balance, not the target's. This is an important concept that we will develop throughout this book. As a variation, try ripping and shredding as you hit. In other words, immediately after striking and as you retract your hands as fast as lightning, try to rip the leather off the face of the shield. Ideally, this should have no effect on your striking speed.

7. Scream like a banshee with each strike.

8. Keep advancing on the target, but don't get so close that you cramp the full extension of your arms on impact. (This is a common fault of beginners—they wind up pitty-patting the shield because their elbows remain bent at less than 90 degrees.)

9. Turn your back and shoulders into each strike so that your trunk and hips (rather than just the unbending action of your elbows) are driving your arms out. Ideally, you should also step in with each strike. Hit as fast and hard as you can. After four or five shots, run away.

Middle-Linebacker Hitting

If you've played football you probably remember this one:

1. With your hands in front of you, pick your feet up and step in place as fast as you can.

2. Here's where we modify it: With each step, shoot out a palm-heel strike with the alternate hand. In other words, as your right foot lands, hit with the left palm heel and vice versa.

3. Make your steps smaller and smaller and faster and faster until your feet are barely leaving the ground. You could call this the supersonic shuffle. At the same time, try to keep your palm striking in sync with your steps.

4. Try this drill against a heavy bag; then, try coordinating palm strikes with the step on the same side (left hand step, left palm strike, etc).

The point of this drill is to get you to put your entire body weight behind every strike. By stepping, you force this to happen. By taking smaller and faster steps, you increase your coordination and the ability to marshal all your power instantaneously and loosely without muscling up. This is actually a high-speed dropping drill (a full explanation of dropping is coming up in chapter 6).

Interview

This drill incorporates the personal comfort zone and the Jack Benny stance. It is so simple you might think it's unnecessary, but it's vital to practice because, when in danger, most people react to the wrong stimuli at the wrong time.

Remember that the interview, as opposed to an assassination, involves a short period of time where the assailant is sizing you up. Selecting you was the first step. You can minimize being selected somewhat if you appear to be aware of your surroundings, but don't count on it. For whatever reason, there's now someone almost in your face, and you're his chosen prey.

In chapter 1, you learned how to establish your personal comfort zone (see p. 7). If the aggressor makes a move to cross this boundary, or the content of the conversation sets off alarm bells in your stomach (that's your good friend Mr. Adrenaline at your service), you must strike like lightning, stopping only when you can run. Or just run immediately.

Now since your first contact with this person is verbal, and you probably will be surprised, you might feel a slight fright reaction coming on. However, the interview stimulus is still not so dangerous that you'll just go off, as you would in a blind attack; instead, you raise your arm by assuming the Jack Benny stance (p. 14) or a similar nonthreatening posture that raises your hands. This is not so unnatural, because touching your face nervously and moving away sideways is a sign of fear and discomfort. If you think standing tall with your chest out is going to discourage a predator, remember this: He's already picked you out. Now he wants to see how hard he's going to have to work to get what he wants. Unless you've perfected your frothing-at-the-mouth routine he's going to go through with whatever he's got in mind. It's better now to appear weaker, so that he lets down his guard slightly.

This drill helps you practice delineating and maintaining your comfort zone, checking for accomplices, moving off-line, and deciding to avoid petty squabbles. By doing these four things, you give the enemy every opportunity to change his mind. If he enters your zone (your sphere of influence), he will have to deal with a wild animal. He has made your choice for you.

1. Find a partner to help you perform this drill. Have your partner put on a focus glove (available at martial arts stores) with two eyes drawn on it.

2. Spin around in circles with your eyes closed, then stop and walk forward.

3. Open your eyes when your partner, holding the focus glove, addresses you verbally.

   - If your partner says, "Come with me" or "Get in the car," run away immediately. If you see a gun or knife and he's not holding you, run away immediately (use rubber knives and guns for the drill).

   - If your partner starts with some seemingly innocuous chatter such as "You got change?" "You got the time?" or "How do you get to . . . ?" say no and keep on walking; be alert for a rear or side attack from the assailant or an accomplice.

   - If, however, after opening your eyes you see that your escape is blocked by a wall, furniture, or other objects, then immediately adopt the Jack Benny stance and back away slowly as far as you can. Backing away is important to justify what is to follow. (By the way, a scam artist, kidnapper, or rapist will often address you with reassuring conversation. Don't be taken in; it's meant to lower your guard before the attacker gets physical.)

4. Somewhere in the conversation, your partner should reach for you or, to make it more belligerent, should strike at you. If someone physically enters your personal comfort zone under these circumstances, attack the attacker right then with everything you've got. For the purposes of this drill, you will be responding the same way as in Fright Reaction III" with a barrage of strikes. Try both of the following as your first strike:

   - Stomp-step and strike with your lead hand, using a chin jab.

   - Spear straight for the eyes on the focus glove or chop to the front or side of the throat (the side of the focus-glove hand—not your partner's!) Make sure both your hands come out almost simultaneously, with the closer one hitting first.

5. Without pausing, continue ripping at the focus glove's eyes or slam the glove with your palm heels, driving your partner back, screaming from the gut the whole time. Keep your arms pumping like jackhammers, driving with your legs and powering your arms with your back and waist. If you're clawing at the eyes like an insane alley cat, try to rip the leather from the skin of the glove. You want to imagine yourself tearing the attacker's face off his skull.

6. Hit 5 to 10 times and then run away. Keep in mind that when your partner reaches or

strikes at you, his or her hand will be deflected incidentally by the curve of your arm as you go straight toward your target, just as water is deflected by the hull of a boat. This holds true for your other arm, too, in case your partner strikes with his other hand, which will happen half the time. Remember, it's a waste of time to block the attacker's hand; practice to eliminate this dangerous habit.

When you are practicing this drill, remember that you should not perform the stomping first strike in isolation. It's merely the first in a series of snarling, slashing, crushing blows. In general, as initial strikes, chin jabs, and eye gouges work better for smaller individuals than throat chops. However, if you do practice eye strikes, train yourself mentally to spear right through the eye sockets. Ghastly as this may sound, we have experience with students who trained physically but not psychologically to perform these strikes. In an actual fight, with their lives in peril, they had their fingers right on their attacker's eyeballs but couldn't bring themselves to drive through them. Luckily, the students were advanced enough to use other strikes and get away with their lives.

The above drill is one way of responding to the enemy. Following is another method that is slightly more advanced but has the advantage of being virtually universal in its application. As you improve, you should practice it within the interview scenario described earlier.

Close Combat Universal Entry (CCUE)

There are two problems with multiple technique–based responses to a straight-on attack: (1) you don't know if the attacker is coming with the right hand or left, and (2) your brain isn't fast enough to know the difference or to select a perfectly corresponding defense. Most martial arts styles say you should respond one way to a left-handed attack and a different way to a right-handed attack, multiplied by the type of strike and the incoming angle. This is movie-inspired lunacy. All you need to realize is that in an initial attack, the attacker is coming directly toward you from wherever he or she is. If the attacker moves in an erratic fashion with plenty of feints and jives, this is sparring, not fighting. Leave the area, watching the person the whole time. If the attacker steps back, you step back. Afterwards, you'll need to examine how you ever got involved in this stupidity in the first place.

In a real assault (where the attacker crosses your personal comfort zone), the most important thing to do first is to step off-line. Just like the matador in the bullfight, you step in but at a 45-degree angle. If you just step off and away to the side, you will give the attacker time and space to recover from what we are about to describe.

From the Jack Benny or similar dissuasive position, you are going to do three things simultaneously (for the sake of clarity, the pictures that follow show each step in isolation):

1. Step off-line in your favorite direction. If you're a righty in a left lead, this will probably be to the right with your right foot (shown in photo); experiment to see which way you're faster and stronger (figure 2.13*a* on p. 32).
2. Intercept and clear the incoming attack (figure 2.13*b* shown clearing with the right hand).
3. Attack the attacker with a chop (figure 2.13*c* shown chopping with left hand).
4. Follow instantly with a palm to the face (figure 2.13*d* shown with right palm to jaw hinge).

The above four steps are performed as follows: with a motion like the swimming sidestroke, your right hand comes sweeping down and in from upper right to lower left, smashing the incoming strike out of the way with a splashing (not pushing) motion. Simultaneously, your left hand shoots in with a circular motion from wherever it is to where your right hand was an instant earlier (up and outside to the right and above the

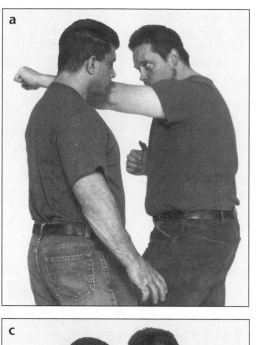
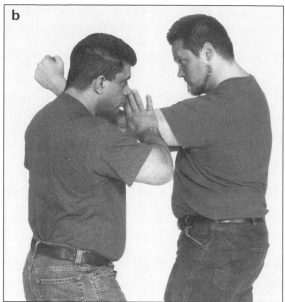
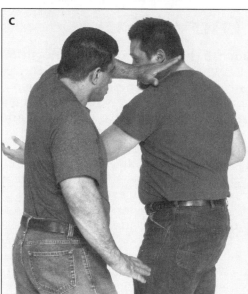
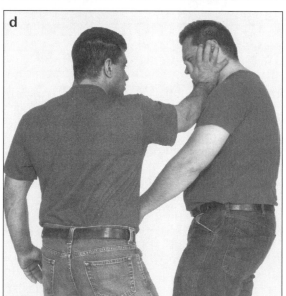

Figure 2.13

path of the right arm); it then slashes down and inside to the left like an ax, with a chop to the attacker's neck or spine. This is immediately followed by a palm heel to the temple with the other hand (the one that did the clearing motion). As an alternative, you can substitute clawing strikes (like a cat or bear) for the clearing, chopping, and palming movements. As you read this, you may have thought the motion is complicated and time consuming, when in actuality, it is lightning fast because it happens all at once and economically combines stepping, clearing, and striking (figure 2.14 shows all movements combined in reality). This all happens explosively and will be greatly enhanced when you learn about dropping energy in part II and apply that to both the clearing and chopping motions.

But there is one thing even better about this entry, and that is its universality (as you will see when you practice it): If the attacker throws a straight left, your right hand easily smashes it out of the way, clearing a path for the chop to the neck (figure 2.15a). However, if the attacker throws a straight right, the devastation will be even worse because there will be nothing to clear in the first place (figure 2.15b). Let's say, however, that the attacker throws a left hook. What you will find is that by virtue of the body's innate fear or flinch reaction and the very nature of the CCUE's motion, your right hand will automatically check the hook by moving to the outside right (but inside the strike). In the meantime, your guillotining left chop will come crashing in on its mark with nothing to stop it (figure 2.15c).

It doesn't matter what the assailant attacks you with because your response is a complete no-brainer. And this is all because in a real assault, the attacker comes right at you, so stepping off-line in your favorite direction is still effective. What if he jumps you so fast that you can't get the full CCUE off? It doesn't matter because a CCUE cut short by space is simply an ordinary fright reaction. It just comes out that way. The attacker winds up eating an elbow straight to his face—all because you got scared and reacted naturally and instinctively.

But this is not the end of the CCUE. The chop is immediately followed by a knee strike (left or right is determined simply by the natural steps you take with the chop/palm) so that a high-low attack is delivered in an instant (figure 2.16 on p. 34). This will be addressed later in the Ground Fighting chapter as another no-brainer response to a takedown attempt, but for now, picture this: The attacker dives at you; you don't know if he's throwing a right, a left, or a big roundhouse hook, but in a microsecond, he's gone from sight because it turns out he actually dove for your legs. No matter—he just ate your knee with his face because it was part of your CCUE anyway.

Figure 2.14

A more advanced way of stepping off-line that Master Perkins prefers is much more subtle and thus easier to screw up as a beginner. In the previous scenario, in a left lead, instead of stepping in obliquely to the right with the right foot, drop-step forward (see chapter 6, dropping energy) very slightly to the right with the left foot (figure 2.17 on p. 34). This is even faster (and more powerful because the impact is shocking), but the margin for error is greater because you are essentially crashing inside with the most economical degree of off-lining. The sequence of your arms remains the same although your right knee now follows naturally instead of your left.

Be aware that if you're a lefty or if you just prefer moving left, all the above is reversed. It also doesn't hurt to practice both directions. Just remember that the way you train is

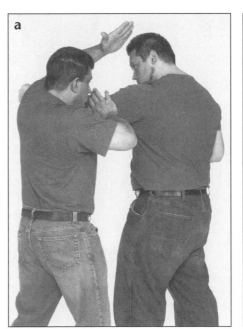

Figure 2.15

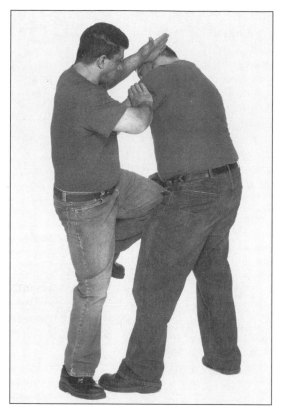

Figure 2.16

Figure 2.17

the way you fight, and you don't want to have a computer meltdown picking one or the other when violence strikes. Pick the direction you like best and use it for everything.

A slight variation of the clear/chop may be used against very big and strong attackers where you simply don't have enough force to intercept the incoming strike. If the attacker throws a left to your face, you simply smash it in and down with your left elbow (like a fright reaction) and instantaneously follow with a left chop to the neck.

The following concept is advanced and may not make sense until you read the rest of the book. The CCUE is a *patterned* close combat technique, even though the rest of this book talks about eliminating all patterned techniques and responses. That is because close combat defines what you do in the opening instant of an attack when you are not yet in tactile sensitivity range. Close combat may be all you ever need, but *do not,* we repeat, do not count on it, or you will fall into the same trap as those who follow every other system. That is because you never know exactly how a fight will go, and you must learn how to flow and adapt with the chaos—something you can't really do until you are in actual physical contact with your attacker. Although it's very effective, if the close combat CCUE hasn't destroyed the enemy in the first second of the fight, you're in big trouble. This is why Perkins invented guided chaos. Parts II and III will explain all this in great detail.

Meet Jason

Besides being used for the horror movie *Halloween,* a goalie's mask taped to a focus glove is an excellent training aid for practicing eye gouging.

1. Have your partner wear a focus glove with a goalie's mask taped to it.
2. Practice eye gouging through the holes of the goalie mask. Learn to deliver the gouges one immediately after the other as if you were an enraged alley cat.

Surviving Rape

Rape is horrible enough. However, many women can live through a rape and recover psychologically. The problem is that there's no guarantee the monster will stop with just rape. This is a choice only you can make. Often, the rape is followed by torture and murder. What you need to know is that most rapes are committed without a weapon. So chances are you won't have to deal with that factor. With most rapes, there are slim windows of opportunity where the rapist is vulnerable. You need to seize those opportunities the way a cornered wildcat would; your life may depend on it.

The most important thing is not to let this scenario happen in the first place. All the awareness material in chapter 1 plays a big part in staying safe and is underscored by a story that appeared in New York City a few years ago. A young woman was approached by a man from behind in broad daylight on a crowded street. The man hissed menacingly, "Don't turn around. I've got a gun pointed at you! Walk with me and look normal!" He then began to search for the ideal secluded location to rape her. The woman was terrified. She never saw the gun, but she looked beseechingly into the eyes of passersby as she and her captor moved from one place to another. No spot was ever good enough for the hapless rapist. He eventually gave up and just walked away. The woman was unbelievably lucky. Contrast this with another New York City incident where a man jumped out from between two parked cars with a gun and approached a woman walking on the sidewalk. In this case she didn't even wait for the attacker to say anything. As soon as she saw gunmetal, she was out of there. As author Ridenhour likes to say "they'll be cleaning the skid marks for a week!" The attacker was left speechless with the gun hanging at his side. This goes back to what we said earlier: Unless you're being restrained, and the gun is shoved right in your face or into your back, run! Even if the gun is in your face or back, if you're being taken to another location, fight right now, or you may never get another chance.

If the attack is going down, you're alone, and you haven't been able to escape, you could appear to submit slightly to get to those moments of vulnerability we spoke of earlier. If the rapist is armed with a gun or a knife and you are in a standing position, you can use the strategies outlined in this chapter and chapter 12. If, however, you are in a prone position, you could wait for the attacker to put down the weapon for a second while he undoes his pants or makes any other preparation for the rape. You could be just a little difficult to handle so he is taken off guard, giving you the opportunity to attack him in the eyes. When his pants are down, submit momentarily and bite or crush his testicles. Get up immediately, launch into eye and throat strikes, and then run. There are other opportunities during a rape when the rapist may become vulnerable, but we will leave those to your imagination. Yes it is ugly, but if you are serious about self-defense, failing to plan is planning to fail.

Another strategy that could cause your assailant to reconsider is to pick up the knife or weapon your attacker puts down and plunge it into his neck. If the rapist is bare-handed and pulls you from behind, respond as in Fright Reaction II (p. 28). If you go to the ground, the strategies for ground fighting in chapter 10 will be useful.

Mace may only enrage a determined rapist and immediately turn a sex crime into a brutal attack or homicide. Women need to seriously consider carrying a real weapon that can be employed instantly, like a knife; however, be forewarned that you will then enter into a legal gray area where a court may actually find you more at fault in a crime than your attacker, and you may wind up serving prison time instead of the monster who assaulted you. There are certain knives (for example, push-daggers and punch knives) that require very little skill or strength to use effectively; they have the added advantage of being very hard to dislodge even when wet with blood. These kinds of knives are illegal virtually everywhere. Don't be overconfident if you have a permit to carry a handgun, either. Believe it or not, unless there is a lot of distance between you and the attacker, it is very difficult to draw your weapon during an actual assault. More on this in chapter 12. There is also a comprehensive gun defense DVD available from www.attackproof.com that covers far more scenarios than can be addressed in this book.

3. Have your partner keep the target moving.

4. Try the drill with your back to the glove, so that when you turn, you have to find it and hit without pausing.

5. Alternate eye gouges with palm strikes, driving in with full extension and body weight. What you will find is that palm strikes and eye gouges actually blend together because the fingers of a palm strike tend to drift into the eyes anyway, while the heel of your hand collapses into a palm strike during an eye gouge.

Gang Attack I

Ideally, you will have five training partners for this drill. This drill trains your peripheral awareness and your ability to react and move powerfully in random directions.

1. Have four individuals arrange themselves in a circle facing you, the "victim." Each should be holding kicking shields (available at martial arts supplies stores). Have the fifth individual stand outside the circle and act as an instigator.

2. Face the instigator with your eyes closed.

3. Wait while the instigator preselects an attacker from the circle by pointing to him.

4. Now, open your eyes. The instigator will engage you in conversation. The content need not be hostile. In fact, the instigator should pick a subject that you become involved in and have to think about, for example, how to fix a car or bake a cake. The goal is for the instigator to create an innocuous mental distraction (something scam artists do well).

5. Continue until, somewhere in this exchange, the preselected attacker simultaneously yells and charges at you.

6. Whip around to face the attacker, scream, stomp-step, chop, and palm-strike the shield. If the attacker is very close, go into your fright reaction and then hit.

LIGHTNING STRIKES TWICE
John Perkins

During one of my classes, a group of female students told me a story. They related that they knew of a woman who had been raped and beaten by an unknown assailant. As part of her recovery, she was advised to take up a martial art. And so she did. She attended one of the major karate mills and trained for four years, receiving a first- and then a second-degree black belt. She was good at both forms and sparring, and she was in great physical shape.

One evening, she and a female co-worker were the last to leave their office when a man holding a short stick in his hand suddenly appeared out of a utility closet. He was about 5 feet, 10 inches (1.78 m) tall and weighed approximately 180 pounds (81.7 kg). He stated to the women that he did not want to hurt them and was only interested in robbing the office. He then instructed both women to take off their clothes and go inside the utility closet until he left. They complied.

While both women were waiting naked inside the closet, the monster jumped in, beat, and then raped them. Despite all her training, the woman with a second-degree black belt could not fight back because she had never been taught how to use awareness strategies, how to deal with paralyzing fear, or how to fight at close range. She is still under psychiatric care today.

I know that this is an extreme example of not receiving the right psychological as well as physical training. And truthfully, it may have been the first trauma that made the woman a victim twice. But when you are face-to-face with a psychotic criminal bent on a mission, you have to be charged with the survival energy and mind-set of a cornered sewer rat.

This drill brings up an interesting point. In a multiple-attacker situation, if you're standing still and focusing on one stranger's conversation, you're a sitting duck. So, when engaged in conversation with someone who makes you uncomfortable, even if you think it's rude, look around (without turning your head); keep your hands and feet moving as if you're a nervous commuter waiting for a train. The slightest shift in body position can be enough to keep a lunging attacker from getting a perfect fix on you. This has been especially useful for cops when questioning a suspect on the street. Often, the suspect has unseen friends nearby. By staying in motion, you throw a monkey wrench into their attack. Don't become hypnotized by a stranger's chatter.

Anywhere Strikes I

If you surveyed 100 martial arts books, chances are not one of them would train you the way this drill does. This extremely vital exercise will build your ability to hit randomly, freely, and powerfully from any angle without plan. This exercise will come into focus with the information on guided chaos in part II, but for now, you can start training your nervous system to simply react and recognize bizarre openings without interference from your brain dictating the angle or type of strike.

1. Choose a target such as a hanging, heavy bag (available at most sporting goods stores), B.O.B. (Body Opponent Bag), or Fighting Man Dummy (both available on the web). Alternatively you can use a tree or basement support pole.

2. Take any strike, let's say a chop, and begin hitting the target slowly, using only one hand. Practice turning your entire body behind every strike. Drive from your feet, through your legs, and turn your hips. Unwind your back and align your shoulder so that you have one continuous, uninterrupted chain of power coming up from the floor and into your hand on every chop. Your arms are almost straight at impact. Be sure not to stand too close and crimp your arms; this is a common fault of beginners.

3. Now, begin to change the angle of delivery so that the pattern of strikes moves around the bag like the hands of a clock. You will see that the mechanics of the strikes change as you go beyond the range of a specific joint. For example, with your right arm at about one o'clock (figure 2.18*a*), you begin to look like a very nasty waiter delivering a bowl of soup. At about four o'clock, the chop becomes a ridgehand to the thigh or groin (figure 2.18*b*). At seven o'clock, it becomes a chop again (figure 2.18*c*).

4. Work around the clock three times with about 40 strikes, moving slowly and concentrating on delivering each chop with your full body weight. Then go counterclockwise.

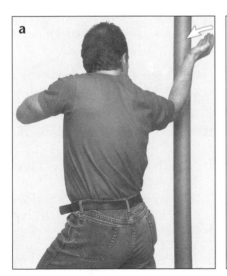 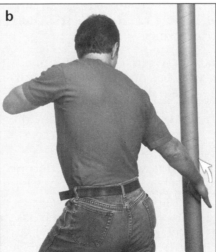 

Figure 2.18

5. Switch hands and go around the other way. Be aware that, like any good tennis player, you should reposition your feet for every shot so that maximum power and balance are available to you. This is paramount.

6. Perform this drill with elbows, palm strikes, clawing motions, and hammer fists. Notice that elbow blows can be delivered with horizontal or vertical spearing motions straight ahead as well as circular. Add those to the mix.

Anywhere Strikes II

You have to practice spontaneity to be spontaneous. Get loose and let fly.

1. Perform the previous drill again, but this time, add speed and rhythm, using fast-paced music as your guide.

2. Despite the increase in speed, be sure your feet move and readjust for maximum power delivery with each strike.

3. Practice the drill with different weapons.

When you hit, retract the strike faster than it goes out so that you're bouncing your shots off the target.

Anywhere Striking Full-Power Footwork: The Rocket Step

There is a quality to your footwork that must be addressed here even though it involves principles of dropping energy that aren't fully explained until chapter 6. If you like, you can skip ahead, but it's not entirely necessary.

Since these drills call for hitting a heavy bag with speed and power, we want to eliminate right now all the major footwork flaws so common to striking.

Whenever you hit, whether it's a bag or a person, never

- rise up on your toes,
- swivel your feet together in a misguided attempt to hit with the whole body,
- lean forward or backward,
- crowd the target, or
- fall into the strike expecting the target to support your balance. This principle is so important that we've given it a name: *containing the over-travel*. Dropping completely eliminates this tendency.

To deliver the most power in a way that immediately prepares you for the next strike while maintaining your balance, treat your legs like independent, compressed springs. We will take the anywhere strikes drill example of a combination chop and palm series:

1. Stand facing the heavy bag at just less than arm's length but a little to the right of the bag.

2. Load all your weight onto your right foot, keeping the knee bent. Your left toe is just touching the ground to your left with zero weight on it, similar to the ninja walk concept (covered in chapter 5). Your left toe is probing the ground for your next step.

3. As if you're a coiled lion exploding toward its prey, drive laterally off the right leg (without rising) onto your left foot, which has stepped about 6 inches (15.2 cm) further to the left. As you do this, deliver a chop to the bag with your left hand followed instantaneously by a right palm heel as you land on the left foot with 99 percent of your weight.

4. The chop and palm should both hit the bag dead center so that the bag is dented and does not spin. Do not push the bag and do not maintain contact with it after impact. The quality of your strike should be a piercing splash: Imagine that you're trying to annihilate a cockroach on a red-hot frying pan. You must hit the cockroach so fast and so hard that you obliterate it without burning your hand. The frying pan would essentially bounce into the air from the impact. Maintain the same distance from the heavy bag the entire time you perform this drill. Do not fall into it. Pass the bag; don't crowd it.

5. The instant after you spring off your right foot and land on your left, your right foot steps to the left also, but because 99 percent of your weight is now transferred to the left, your right foot lands by merely tapping the ground sharply with the toe (figure 2.19). The toe-tap landing is about 2 to 2 1/2 feet (.6 to .7 m) to the right of your left foot. What your right toe immediately does then is probe the ground for the next root it will spring to when you deliver the same strikes springing back to your right. We say "probing" because where you step depends entirely on where the target is. In the case of a moving enemy (or heavy bag), this quality of a mobile root is critical for delivering maximum balanced power into your next strike. If you were fighting an immobile enemy, you could just drop (see dropping, chapter 6) into both feet right where you stand, but typically the enemy is not hanging around waiting to be pounded a second time (except in the movies.)

Figure 2.19

6. After impact, both your arms have swung through the target and are now poised to your left for a right chop and a left palm moving to the right. This has a loose swinging feel, like the arms of an ape. As before, drive off your bent, coiled left leg and deliver the chop and palm combination like a machine gun as you land with 99 percent of your weight on your right foot (which has stepped about 6 inches [15.2 cm] further to the right); your left foot comes up sharply nearby, with the toe popping into the ground—again probing for its next root because you will chop and palm to the left again.

7. Spring back and forth, crushing the bag with the chop and palm combo. Each time you hit, take two steps: left-right, right-left, left-right, and so on. It should sound like Bam-Bam, Bam-Bam, Bam-Bam, etc.

8. Do not rise when you step. Do not lunge and do not leave the back foot "in the bucket." What you will notice is that you will hit harder, faster, and sharper than you ever have before; you'll always be balanced and spring-loaded for the next strike. This is because the rocket step forces you to use full body unity (chapter 4) as well as dropping energy (you'll see why in chapter 6) when you step.

Do not fall in love with the stepping in this drill. This is because how you step is always dependent upon how the enemy moves and can always change. Instead, understand the principle behind the quality of this movement and apply it when necessary.

Anywhere Strikes III

We cannot emphasize enough that it's best to have no preconceived plan of what you're going to strike with. The crazier you get, the better. This drill takes anywhere strikes I and II one step further to sharpen your ability to deliver spontaneous, random strikes.

1. Perform anywhere strikes II, but now use both hands and strike with no pattern whatsoever. Let your mind go blank and hit with totally random chops and ridgehands. Don't plan; just let them come out however your imagination creates them the moment they're delivered.

2. Double and triple up occasionally on the same strike to the same spot. For many people accustomed to rigid, classical self-defense training, hitting this randomly presents a problem: They want to work like boxers, in fixed combinations. You must, however, forget about looking cool and just let the strikes flow. With time, you'll have no idea what you're doing, nor should you. And if you don't know what you're doing, heaven knows your opponent won't have a clue.

3. Apply this method of practice to any weapon. With the elbow, you will find that you can deliver certain angles with a spearing action, rather than a bludgeon. Try head butting from every conceivable angle, just don't knock yourself out—butt against a heavy bag! Remember to use your forehead just below the hairline.

4. After trying each different strike solo, mix them up. Creativity is the key. Add your shoulders. How many different ways can you hit with them? It's up to you to find out. Add your knees and feet. Hit with your butt (this is useful to create space). Remember to use the principles described earlier in this chapter regarding close combat strikes. Once you have fully understood dropping energy (described in part II), come back to this drill and try to drop on every strike. The idea is not to hit hard, although you should go for maximum power when you get used to the drill. The idea is to develop familiarity with the motion of random hitting, so that no matter what position you find yourself in, you can deliver with power, alignment, and balance. You'll be able to hit *from* anywhere *to* anywhere.

After a while, you'll notice something interesting. You'll see that certain strikes flow right into others, within the same movement. For example, a right backhanded elbow strike to the head flows nonstop into a right backhanded chop to the head (figure 2.20*a*), which in the same full-body turn a millisecond later flows into a left inside palm strike, followed by a left inside elbow (figure 2.20*b*). This has all occurred within one whole-body, step-and-turn movement to the right. Your arms are merely acting like the teeth of a rotary blade, and your waist has become like the drive shaft. This multihitting principle, discussed in chapter 8, is extremely effective when combined with the other guided chaos principles you will learn in parts II and III.

To continue with this example, after your body has completed the ape-like or pendulum-like swing of blows to the right, it can immediately unleash a similar barrage of blows as

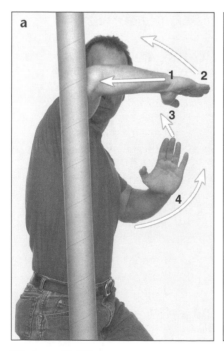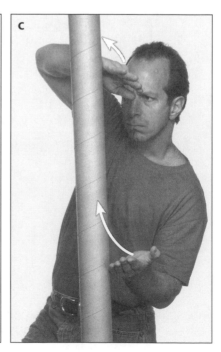

Figure 2.20

it swings back to the left. Using the anywhere principle, you can also direct this swinging vertically or diagonally. For example, merely change the angle of your waist and back and the position of your feet, and the blows serve to knock the assailant's head skyward in one direction (figure 2.20c) and into the ground in the other. As you can see, practicing this drill adds a vital attribute to your self-defense skills. Once you fully understand looseness (also in part II), come back to this drill and add pocketing and yielding to your interaction with the bag as it swings.

Mexican Hat Dance

Or the Spanish Flamenco, Irish Jig, or whatever; the name's not important. What is important is that this drill teaches how kicks are used combatively at close range while moving around your attacker. The silly names describe a maneuver that's no laughing matter if you're the dance partner. If you have one or more opponents, an effective tactic is to go into a wild, rapid, foot-stomping dance as if you were trying to crush 50 beer cans in five seconds and then kick them into hockey goals. You won't believe how fast people back up to avoid getting their toes smashed, only to get their shins kicked. Since they can't find a place to put their feet down, their balance is upset, and this creates openings for you to run or attack further. Your foot is effectively bouncing or ricocheting from stomp to stomp and stomp to kick, gaining speed and energy from each impact like a ping-pong ball. In short, learn to instantaneously switch feet as you stomp so you look like you're doing a Mexican hat dance. This is not simply a technique but a way of moving. If you want your kicks to look like a kung fu movie star's or a ballet dancer's, this isn't for you. If you want to cause great havoc and survive an attack, it is.

1. Find a target, such as a low, heavy bag or large tree.
2. Bounce or ping-pong your foot between the ground and the target as if you were trying to stomp 50 cockroaches or kick 50 soccer balls in five seconds. The ground itself is a target because you are simulating crushing toes and insteps with your heel. Drop your body weight like a loose sack of potatoes every time your foot hits the ground; pick up speed as your foot ricochets back up to a low, short shin kick, front kick, or roundhouse kick. Relaxation is the key, not muscular exertion.
3. Start delivering knee strikes with a convulsive action, as if on every strike you were coughing or sneezing violently. This causes your back and stomach muscles to pull your legs up at reflex speed (as fast as your nervous system can operate).
4. Be sure you bounce between strikes from, for example, a knee to the thigh or a heel stomp to the toes, scraping the shins along the way. Once you begin to perform the contact flow drill (part II), you should be adding in these multiple toe and shin crushing attacks. As your sensitivity increases, you will be able to "feel" exactly where your partner's feet are without looking at them. If in the midst of a fight you were to crush the attacker's feet while simultaneously delivering hand strikes, you could potentially end the assault right there. One additional important point when practicing the Mexican Hat Dance is that no matter how hard you kick or stomp, you should never overcommit your balance. You don't want to be falling on your butt if you miss. This is a vital balance principle that will be fully explained in part II, along with drills to practice it.

Gang Attack II

This drill simulates actual upright fighting conditions very closely. Be warned, however, that this particular drill is exhausting; do it at maximum speed and intensity for no longer than 10 to 15 seconds at a time. Make sure you're in good physical condition first. This drill also requires a long, heavy bag (also called Muay Thai bags).

1. Get four or more partners, three of them with their own large kicking shields. Have the fourth person stand by the room light switch and rapidly flick the lights on and off (mostly off).

2. Close your eyes and spin.

3. Have two of your partners slam you with their shields while the third throws several loose shields at your feet, trying to trip you. Not surprisingly, this is very disorienting.

4. At first contact, open your eyes, regain your balance with a fright reaction, find the heavy bag, and attack it.

5. Simultaneously avoid and attack the partners holding shields; focus on the heavy, hanging bag as your primary target.

6. Continue stomping, both to get your balance and to crush the loose kicking shields on the floor as if they were attackers' feet. Because of the flashing lights, you will need to keep reorienting yourself; at the same time, try to keep the heavy bag between you and the nearest shield-carrying attacker. Just go nuts. Have no plan. Simply be fast, loose, balanced, and relaxed. Scream on every blow.

7. As with the anywhere striking drills, insert as many strikes as randomly as possible within your flow of movement. As you move in, elbows follow palm strikes, head butts follow elbows, knees follow both, and biting follows clawing. However, this is not a rule. In a real fight, there are no rules. Spontaneity is king. Move with your whole body.

8. Be sure not to crimp your shots by getting too close to the bag. When you learn dropping energy, you'll be able to hit harder in less space.

If you're practicing solo and have the space and funds, you can perform this drill inside a circle of three Muay Thai heavy bags.

If you do this drill several times a week, the results will be incredible. What you will find is that, just as in a real fight, all techniques and planned counters go right out the window. The way to get better is by becoming looser, quicker, and better balanced, not by fighting your body's natural motion. Classical purists will be uncomfortable with this training and will make all kinds of excuses about why they can't get their stuff off or make it look pretty. As you learn the guided chaos principles in parts II and III, however, you'll become more creative, efficient, and lethal with gang attack II.

Although knives and guns can enter into close combat, most assaults take place without a weapon; even if you have a weapon, you still need hand-to-hand combat skills to create enough room to get it out. For this reason, we present these basic hand-to-hand close combat principles and skills in isolation from weapons. We specifically address how to deal effectively with knife and gun attacks in chapter 12. We've chosen not to include those topics in this chapter because they introduce higher levels of sensitivity and awareness that you will gain with the principles and exercises presented in parts II and III of this book. Obviously, guns and knives also introduce a whole new set of tactical problems.

Close Combat Battlefields: School, Work, and Travel

Personal safety in the schools has become a growing concern in America. Today's high school student needs not only to be book smart but to be street smart as well. Students need to be prepared for all types of predators, including bullies, criminals, gangs, and even suicidal gunmen. Odds are students will encounter at least one of these dangerous aggressors at some point in their high school experience. Close combat can equip students with the tools they need to prevail when faced with the serious challenges presented by these threats.

The bully is the most common school predator that your son or daughter will most likely have to deal with at some point. A bully is someone who is habitually cruel to those who are weaker; bullies use violence or the threat of violence to intimidate others. This

COURTHOUSE FRENZY
John Perkins

With only a few classes of close combat under her belt, a petite woman entered an elevator in a New York courthouse. Just before the doors closed, a huge, 300-pound (136 kg) man rushed in and immediately hit the button for the basement. He was a paroled rapist, wandering the halls of the courthouse looking for a victim.

As he turned to face the diminutive woman, she cowered (she was terrified) and put her hands up to her mouth in horror (a modified Jack Benny stance). This put the giant more at ease. Smelling her fear, he lowered his hands, brought his face closer, and opened his eyes wide, practically salivating at the prospect of easy prey. The woman's hands suddenly exploded straight out, her fingers stabbing deep into his eye sockets. The man screamed in pain, but she continued to hit and kick him while simultaneously pushing every button she could reach with her elbow. The doors opened, and the elevator stopped six inches below the floor. The man fell out and tripped as she continued to kick and palm-heel his head. When security arrived on the scene, they pulled her off him, thinking it was a domestic disturbance. The man suffered a torn retina among his many injuries.

is done for personal edification or to increase social status. Sometimes bullies are out for profit, but stealing someone's property through the use of physical force or threat of violence is a crime. We consider those people criminals and will speak about dealing with them later. As for the bully, he or she wants the attention of other people and is trying to prove toughness in front of an audience. The key to protecting yourself from a bully is not to play into their game.

The bully usually follows a three-step attack process.

1. The in ya face   2. The bump or push   3. The attack

The in ya face step is when the bully gets in close, right in front of your face. Usually this is accompanied with a barrage of insults designed to make you angry and get you off balance both physically and mentally. Eventually, one of the people involved has had enough, and the encounter moves to the next step: the bump or push. Then the bully uses the attack step, with a right hook or overhand punch to the face. A flail of hooks and punches follows. This is the bully's game, and it works—but if you don't play the game, you can't lose.

All the awareness material previously described comes into play here. Avoid confrontation at all costs. Do not engage in tough talk back. If you're continually being hounded, notify school security. This is important because if it comes to blows later, you properly gave authorities advance warning. Never stand toe-to-toe with a bully. That is playing into the bully's hands and into his or her game. When you first become aware of the bully, face him or her but keep moving; keep the bully outside your personal comfort zone or sphere of influence. It's very difficult to push someone who is moving around you. Keep your hands up by your face in the Jack Benny or similar "I don't want to fight" posture so that you are also ready for a rear attack from an accomplice. Do not assume a fighting stance; to do so would be to play the bully's game. Try to de-escalate the situation. Loudly say, "Leave me alone. I am outta here. I am not getting in trouble 'cause of you; this is not worth it." These are statements that let people around you know that you are not the aggressor. This will help you later on because if despite all your attempts to gain space, the bully moves into your personal comfort zone or inside your sphere of influence, all the material in chapters 1 and 2 comes into play. Because you are now at immediate risk of physical injury, attack the attacker. There should be no shortage of witnesses to the bully's initial threat posture since it was preceded by close-in, verbal abuse loudly broadcasting to an audience the bully's intent to mess you up.

If you have to fight, then fight like a victim—don't ball up your hands into fists. Hitting someone with a closed fist can be considered assault. It appears aggressive and combative to any bystanders. Fists are also less effective than open-hand strikes.

Step in but off-line using the CCUE. If the bully hasn't swung first, he'll be caught completely off guard. If he has, the CCUE will let you bypass his strike and insert your own chops and palm strikes. If he dives for your legs, the step off-line and CCUE knee strike will crush his face as your elbow slams his neck or your fingers tear at his eye sockets (this is only if you perceive the bully has deadly intent).

When striking, shout, "Help! Get Back! Leave me alone! Get this psycho off of me! I am not fighting you!" These words let first responders know that you are the victim.

Remember, escape the instant you are able. After a good, open-palm strike, the bully will probably have second thoughts about messing with you. Do not beat the bully to a pulp if he or she becomes unable to fight. Use only the force necessary to get away from your opponent. Get to a dean, teacher, or school security personnel and let that person know what happened. Explain the steps you took to de-escalate the situation. Odds are you are not the first person this bully has bothered. If you are afraid of being seen reporting a bully, a superb resource is www.schooltipline.com (not available in all states). Here, bullies can be reported anonymously. Parents need to ask all states and all schools to use this Web site. Remember, do not become the aggressor. Self-defense is about defending your body from injury; it is not about your pride.

The second threat in schools is criminals. They come in all ages, shapes, and sizes, and all ethnic and social groups. Some students steal because they can't or don't want to pay for something. Some steal just for the rush of doing something bad. Whatever the reason, your best defense is tactical awareness. Be conscious of your environment and always try to know where you are: know the building, floor, and address. Do not leave your valuables unattended. Don't give out you locker combination and don't bring anything to school that you are scared of losing. Fancy jewelry, electronics, cameras, and cell phones are all better left at home. Granted, in an extreme situation like terrorism or kidnapping a cell phone can be a lifesaver, but the odds of your accessing the phone during an actual assault are nil. You will have to balance the risks of theft versus utility. One option is not to bring the latest awesome cell phone/MP3/web ready model to school, period. No criminal is going to be interested in taking a plain, lame, 3-year-old phone away from you.

If someone comes up to a student and threatens violence in order to take something, that's not bullying, that's robbery. If the aggressor displays a weapon while threatening, that's robbery. If the aggressor uses something not usually thought of as a weapon to amplify the threat, this is robbery, too. For example, if a criminal displays a chain or bike lock and tells the student, "If you don't give up your cell phone, I'll bust you in the head," that's a robbery. This aggressor is not a bully; he or she is a criminal. Even if no weapon or improvised weapon is displayed or used, but the threat of force is communicated or implied, it is a strong-arm robbery. Remember, a bully is someone who intimidates or harasses you. The moment that person tries to take your property or your life, he or she is a criminal.

Another group of criminals in the schools is a gang. There are many different gangs covering lots of varied ethnic and social groups. Some wear colored bandannas tucked into pockets; some wear colored beads to identify them as members of a particular gang. This is referred to as flagging. If you or your child is ever approached by a group wearing (or taking out and displaying) these so-called flags, this should raise your suspicion and concern. If you see these groups approaching you, get away immediately but use your street smarts and tactics. Go to any public phone and call 911. Even if you have a cell phone, use a public phone if possible because the police can know immediately where you are. Even if it isn't practical to talk to the operator because of an immediate threat, just call 911 and let the phone hang. Police will then be dispatched to investigate the 911 call. When you see a police car, wave it down. Tell the officers a large group was acting menacingly, and you felt you needed help.

If an attack is unavoidable or if you are taken by surprise, this is usually called getting jumped. This is a group assault in which the victim is kicked and punched by multiple attackers, who then flee the scene after their attack. Your best bet is to follow the principles of guided chaos involving multiple attackers found later in this book. If you fail, use the techniques of modified Native American ground fighting: Fight to evade. Strike to escape. Do not get surrounded.

The final predator students may come into contact with is the suicidal gunman; this is the most rare but the most dangerous of the predators. An example was the Columbine High School shooting. On April 20, 1999, Columbine High School was the scene of a terrible school shooting where 23 people were injured, and 12 students and a teacher were killed by two of their classmates. In the event of an emergency situation involving armed gunmen, your first and best option is to escape through the nearest exit and get as far away from the scene as possible. If the attackers order you to stop, do not listen. Run for your life. Stay low, hunch your body forward, and keep your head down. A common myth is that it is best to run in a zig-zag pattern to avoid getting hit by bullets; that is not necessary. Just stay low and run for your life. If you are able to escape, get to a phone and dial 911. Be prepared to give as much information as possible to help the police.

If you cannot escape, try to find cover or concealment. Cover is something that protects you from a projectile or explosion. This could be a wall or column of a building, the engine block of a car, a fire hydrant, or a large, thick tree. The next and least favorable tactic is concealment. This is something, including a bush, a hedge, curtains, or cardboard boxes, which blocks you from your assailant's view but offers no ballistic protection. Use concealment to buy time to escape or find cover. Don't wait out a situation behind concealment; you need to get to real cover.

If you are put into a situation where you believe combat is your only chance for survival, then fight with the savagery of a cornered sewer rat. Grab anything handy as a weapon: A pen, pencil, ruler, or even the corner of a hard-cover book can become an improvised stabbing weapon. Yell, scream, stab, claw, bite, scratch, and rip. Do not stop until the threat is neutralized. Remember that you only use improvised weapons in this extreme case. The minute you use something as a weapon, you will be held accountable for your actions.

All of these tactics, legalities, awareness methods, and fight strategies apply equally to bullying, robbery, and attack situations in the workplace.

Self-Defense Aboard Airliners

The monstrous events of September 11, 2001, instantly raised awareness of the dangers that can unfold aboard a commercial airliner. An airliner's passenger cabin can become a terrorist war zone that threatens not only your safety as a passenger, but also the safety of entire metropolitan areas.

Although countermeasures put in place by the airlines and the federal government make it unlikely that a full repeat of the September 11 attacks will occur, other dangers still exist aboard airliners. Locked, reinforced cockpit doors make it unlikely that a terrorist could take control of the airplane. However, terrorists as well as disruptive or emotionally disturbed passengers can certainly threaten the safety of the passengers and crew, and possibly bring down the plane. Therefore, if you travel on commercial airplanes, it makes sense to study how to protect yourself and others in flight.

As usual, awareness is key. Surreptitiously scan the passengers in the waiting area before boarding the plane, noting anyone who looks or acts suspicious, nervous, or unstable. Don't be obvious about this. You do not want to be mistaken for a federal air marshal or other law enforcement officer because that could make you a primary target in the event of an incident. Terrorists are trained to surprise and take out military and police officers and other capable-looking individuals in the first moments of any assault. As you board the airplane, note where anyone suspicious is seated.

Once on board, balancing awareness against comfort is a choice you have to make. Obviously, you will not be aware of what is going on in the cabin if you are drunk or asleep. Your awareness will likewise be limited to a degree by using headphones and personal electronic devices, or by getting engrossed in a book or magazine. However, it is difficult for most people to get through a long flight without some form of distraction. If you choose to read, watch television, or use a computer, be sure to look up every few minutes to avoid getting completely absorbed in what you're doing.

Be familiar with the safety features and emergency procedures of the airplane. Read the card! Note where the closest emergency exits are. If you are sitting in an exit row, be sure you know how to operate the exit and mentally rehearse opening it. In the event of an emergency and if everyone is trying to get to the emergency exits in a panic, the quickest way to get there, if you are physically able, may be to climb over the seats rather than attempt to move through a jammed aisle.

Although purpose-built weapons are obviously not allowed on airliners, take note of the myriad of improvised weapons that are available to you:

- A cane can be used as a weapon. If you seem to need a cane in order to walk, you will be able to take one onboard. See the section in chapter 12 about cane fighting. The narrow confines of an airliner's aisle magnifies the effectiveness of the thrusting motions guided chaos emphasizes. Be sure you have a cane up to the task. Attack-proof.com has sturdy chromalloy steel canes.

- A sturdy pen can be a very effective stabbing weapon. Thick, metal pens with rubberized plastic grips and flat buttons on top for driving with the thumb are best.

- Steel-toed boots or any other sturdy footwear can enhance your kicking ability, effectively putting a pair of sledgehammers on the ends of your legs. Composite-toe footwear is available that is just as strong as steel but lighter. This type is now available in almost any kind of shoe or sneaker.

- Big, heavy, solid objects are but a latch lift away in the overhead bins. Feel free to use someone else's luggage as a bludgeon, shield, or projectile against a blade-wielding maniac or terrorist. Seat cushions can be used not only as floatation devices, but also as shields or projectiles.

- The corner of a laptop computer can be used to smash into a hijacker's face with short, explosive, two-handed, hatchet-like or spearing motions. There are also metal handles that screw on to many laptops available online; these handles allow you to swing a laptop with surprising power (as well as carry your computer more conveniently). In addition, your laptop or cell phone's AC power supply can be placed in a sock and swung with tremendously damaging force.

- An ordinary glossy magazine (preferably one with book-style binding) can be turned into a rigid stabbing weapon. Fold the magazine diagonally so that one corner containing the binding becomes the apex of a triangle. Fold it over a second time, and the apex becomes a sturdy spike that can be thrust with two hands like a jackhammer into the hijacker's face.

- Anything that can cause a person to blink or look away can be an effective distraction device, allowing you to follow up against a temporarily blind, off-balance, or unprepared attacker. A pocket full of change or a drink (either thrown or spit) can work nicely.

Be aware of how the aircraft environment can limit but also enhance your fighting capabilities. The narrow aisle obviously decreases the space you have to move off-line or swing or kick from outside angles. Straight, direct strikes and kicks are the rule in this environment. When we train federal air marshals for unarmed combat aboard an airplane, we emphasize the development of extreme, short-range dropping power in straight strikes, which allows the marshals to stop, crush, and run over people moving in the aisles.

The seats on either side of the aisle offer a unique opportunity to enhance your balance and double your kicking power. Use your hands to hold on to and push off from the seats beside you as you launch straight front kicks. If you are physically able, you can use the added balance and leverage offered by the seats to launch your entire body forward, hitting with one or both feet into the torso or throat of the enemy. Because of the narrow aisle, the attacker will be unable to get out of the way, and the speed and power you can gain in your kicks from holding onto the seats or even the overhead bins (if you're tall enough) can be devastating. In a workshop we conducted for flight attendants shortly after 9/11, a 100-pound (45.4-kg) female flight attendant was able to knock a 300-pound (136.1-kg) instructor who was holding the kicking shield ass-over-teakettle using this method. Practice this method by holding the backs of two sturdy chairs while you kick at a kicking shield.

If a terrorist is coming down the aisle past your seat, and you have a pen, you can ambush him as follows: Just as he passes your seat, rise, get behind him, reach around to his front with both hands, and pull your pen down hard into his jugular notch (which will act like a funnel) with both hands. As you do this, fall backward, pulling him down on top of you as cover against other terrorists, and continue to work the pen into his throat until you hit spine. If the throat stab somehow fails, gouge deeply into the eye sockets with your pen or your fingers, attempting to penetrate the brain.

If you need to subdue an emotionally disturbed person, and you can enlist others to help, a blanket can be an effective device to gain initial control. Once several people can secure the blanket over the person's head so that he or she is disoriented and slightly restrained, it should be easier to upset the person's balance and pin him or her on the floor without causing undue injury, where additional blankets can be used as restraints. Remember, however, that your safety and that of the other passengers must come first. Emotionally disturbed persons (EDPs in cop-speak) can be insanely strong (no pun intended) and destructive, and it may require harsher measures to get them to stop.

If a terrorist attempts to set off a bomb (e.g., the infamous Shoe Bomber), the terrorist must be stopped as quickly as possible by any means necessary. Leaving the would-be terrorist conscious may allow him or her to set off the bomb, even if restrained.

Contrary to popular belief, bullets and even hand grenades will in most cases not bring down a plane (although they can be very damaging to the passengers). Relatively small penetrations of an airliner's skin will not result in a huge suction effect or catastrophic depressurization. Bullets and small explosions can damage electronics, hydraulics, and other aircraft systems, but modern commercial airliners have sufficient redundancy and safety mechanisms built in to survive such damage.

If you never do anything but study and practice the skills and strategies presented in this chapter, you will become quite formidable to an attacker. However, what if you become the victim of someone possessing the same or similarly devastating skills? This was the problem confronting John Perkins when he was a child. His father and uncles who were training him to be a warrior were all highly proficient in fighting arts similar to close combat. In addition to having these warrior skills, John's father could punch a hole in a refrigerator, and his uncle could lift the front end of a car. This is why the guided chaos principles were devised—to give you a fighting chance against the physical monsters of the world and the most advanced practitioners of other martial arts. The material in parts II and III is radically different from anything else you may have ever encountered and was designed to let you confront these scenarios head-on.

Preventing Common Mistakes

➤ Trust your instincts early on and run from danger.

➤ Stand sideways in the Jack Benny stance when you sense a threat. Beginners usually stand square to their opponents, creating a much larger target area.

➤ Protect your personal comfort zone when necessary but don't block or reach for the attacker's hand. Go straight for his eyes and throat. Deflect and strike in one motion with the arc of your arm and shoulder, your head tucked low.

➤ Practice multiple palm strikes without crimping or overextending your elbow. Drive with your legs, hips, back, and shoulders.

➤ Step in but off-line when using the CCUE (and indeed with any defense where you attack the attacker). This effectively throws a monkey wrench into the assault.

➤ Remember to breathe, scream, and run.

BODY AND MIND PRINCIPLES OF GUIDED CHAOS

The main concept underlying guided chaos is this: Why train patterned movements when every real fight is made up of unpatterned movements? Throughout a lifetime of fighting, and as a forensic scientist reconstructing homicides for the police, John Perkins has meticulously analyzed the movement dynamics of horrific life-and-death bloodbaths. Unlike fight scenes in movies, these are far from choreographed. Through research and plenty of terrifying hands-on experience, he's concluded that the main thing all melees have in common is utter chaos and mayhem. Any system of self-defense training that doesn't appreciate this fully is dangerously delusional. By following our methodology, you endeavor to understand and exploit chaos and then channel its energy. We want you to thrive in chaos. How do you do this?

In most classical martial arts schools, you're taught from the outside in. They tell you, "This is what you're supposed to do against this certain kind of attack." They give you choreographed or sportive moves to deal with every kind of assault. They impose form upon function, as if you were preparing to learn the tango. Eventually, after decades of external practice, what you're supposed to achieve is an internal state of balance, relaxation, and sensitivity—what some people would call chi. What they don't tell you is that brawls aren't ballets. Your attacker is not going to dance the same steps as you.

In addition, to their credit, many of the more innovative styles try to borrow techniques from other disciplines. As if they're adding spokes to a wheel, they try to make their styles well rounded, complete, and natural. However, there is a potential trap: If the techniques are never integrated subconsciously and dissolved, or the techniques can only function in a rules-based environment, all you'll have are a million defensive moves waiting for a million matching attacks. When the spit hits the fan, will you pick the right one? And should this even be a job for the brain to handle at that instant? The last thing you want to do is lock up your brain with calculations and defense formulas during a fight.

Guided chaos bypasses this neural traffic jam entirely by teaching principles of effective combat through play and experimentation so that you can quickly absorb information subconsciously. When you were a child, you learned to walk and talk not from a textbook but by natural trial and error. Similarly, guided chaos will teach you to defend yourself using your own instincts by maximizing your human physical attributes.

It has been said that there are many paths up the mountain, but from the top, everything looks the same. Similarly, after 30 years of tai chi (if your patience holds out) or taekwondo (if your body holds out), what you might finally begin to develop after endless, arduous hours of memorization, imitation, sweat, and "perfect" execution, are the four pillars of combat that everything else rests on: looseness, body unity, balance, and sensitivity, culminating in the elusive fifth principle: complete freedom of action and an anything-goes adaptability. Well, here's a wild idea: Why not train these principles first?

Don't misunderstand us. It's possible for high-quality classical training to turn out superb fighters, but there are potential traps along the way that preclude the development of spontaneity in the unwary. In parts II and III, we present a realistic approach to self-defense, an approach that stresses principles, not techniques. The reason we harp so much on principles is that they're easier to apply to a lot of different situations in a pinch. In this methodology, you still train hard, just differently. With guided chaos principles, you train like a jazz musician improvising on a theme, letting it flow and evolve with the rhythm and energy of the music. A martial artist who learns only forms and techniques is akin to a jazz musician practicing only scales—that musician will never be able to jam with confidence. You learn to jam by jamming, and you learn to improvise and adapt by adopting a training model that emphasizes combat-effective improvisation over everything else.

> Guided chaos does not train technique. It trains response-ability.

The Language of Combat

Combat, as opposed to a sparring match with rules, is not like a song you know, with a beginning, middle, and end. Extending the improvisational jazz analogy, no one, not even the musician, knows exactly where the song will go, or how it will get there. Yet, there's a method to the madness. The musician who is more relaxed, adaptable, and loose with his or her talent, balanced with the instrument, sensitive to the flow of notes, and able to put his or her whole body and soul into the groove will make the better music.

In terms of self-defense, training in guided chaos will hypertune your balance, allowing you to hit with power from any position. It also allows you to get your entire body mass behind every blow—what we call body unity. This is impossible unless you also train supreme looseness into all your muscles and joints so you can achieve angles of attack and defense most people would think impossible. Developing this kind of looseness makes you as hard to hit as water, but as nasty as a bullwhip on offense. When you combine these attributes with highly trained sensitivity, you will be able to detect the slightest change in your opponent's attack—often before your attacker changes anything. This allows you to reflect and amplify that attacker's own energy back at him or her with devastating consequences. None of these principles will work unless you employ them simultaneously. Though guided chaos training does not involve learning specific techniques, concentrating on these principles will make you the better fighter.

To get this formless art down on paper, we have had to compromise somewhat by reducing movements that characterize guided chaos to general principles that follow natural laws and human anatomy instead of forcing the body into a classical box. The principles provide guidelines, but the actual execution and shape of the movements are determined by you and your experiences. We have given these principles—and the typical movements that arise out of employing them—names as a matter of convenience. You should know, however that John Perkins' best student, who's lethal beyond comprehension, employs all these principles masterfully yet has no names for most of them. He believes some things are better left unspoken, undefined, and unintellectualized. His advice to other students while they're training: Stop thinking!

Your Anatomy and Motion

Your training in looseness, body unity, balance, and sensitivity takes advantage of a natural resource: your body. We all share certain physical attributes that guided chaos capitalizes on by emphasizing natural movement—motion that best suits the anatomical structure of whatever living thing we're talking about. Apes, whose physical structure most resembles ours, have no claws, horns, or giant canine teeth. What we have in common with apes are ropelike appendages that can grab, strike, rip, tear, crush, hammer, and strangle. Watch films of apes fighting. Without knives or guns, they achieve a ferocious lethality that involves no poses, X-blocks, reverse punches, or spinning wheel kicks. They have a loose, powerful, heavy way of moving that employs their entire bodies as coiled, whipping bludgeons. Any movement that goes against these attributes is unnatural motion.

The power in guided chaos comes from perfectly balanced mechanical alignment, gravity, and the plyometric rebound effect of relaxed muscles, not from raw muscular strength. Think of your bones as a collection of levers. With a lever, you can multiply your strength many times and move objects far larger and heavier than your own body. However, a lever is useless if it is not positioned properly. The same holds true for your bones because leverage applies to striking, balancing, yielding, or using any other combative motions.

For this reason, when defending yourself and fighting back, relax your muscles and suspend your body from your skeletal structure as much as possible. Like any bludgeoning weapon or striking tool (e.g., an ax or a hammer), once it's in motion, additional muscular input will not enhance its impact significantly. The looser the swing, the more the implement will make the most efficient use of its own mass.

To understand your muscles, think of them not so much as power plants but as giant elastic fibers, anchored to your bones by cables. When properly conditioned, these fibers allow the body to articulate, react, and change with lightning speed.

However, when you fight with constant maximum contraction—using all your strength—your muscles lose their elastic properties, which causes your joints to seize up like the pistons of an automobile engine with dirty oil. Mobility, articulation, and speed are severely compromised. This is the last thing you want to happen in a fight to the death. What does this teach us? Change the oil in your car and train in a loose, relaxed manner.

Now you may say, "I know where this is going because I do train to have a loose, snappy jab." This represents a limited understanding of what we mean by looseness (see chapter 3). Even if your punches are loose, you may tighten your whole body dramatically to initiate them, creating a rigid platform from which to launch them. This is not the ideal. Instead, you will be learning to initiate strikes using gravity, your own body's momentum, and that of your opponent. You can do this successfully only if you are supremely relaxed and your muscles are loose.

The human body is over 70 percent water. Make use of this fact. Water is heavy, dense, and infinitely malleable. A drop of water can stick to your skin and follow your every motion (sensitivity). Bundles of energy can cause water to gather into an ocean wave that hits like a mountain (body unity), yet splits easily when you dive through it (looseness). In an unconfined state, water has great mass yet no fixed center of gravity and is therefore impossible to pin down (balance). Water flows organically and can move from anywhere to anywhere (total freedom of action). These are the qualities (and not those of mechanical robots) the principles in part II will help you apply to your fighting.

CHAPTER THREE

LOOSENESS

The best defense against any type of strike—fist, kick, or gunshot—is not to be there when the strike arrives. This is a central tenet of guided chaos, but you cannot accomplish it without looseness—the ability to change direction with any part of your body with the tiniest impetus, with no conscious thought or physical restriction. To do so requires becoming relaxed, reactive, rooted, and yielding.

Relaxed Looseness

Muscular tension is so deeply ingrained in most people that they are astonished to learn it isn't natural. Watch the way animals fight, especially apes, who most resemble us anatomically. They are living embodiments of loose, powerful ferocity. In the heat of battle and at extreme speed, common alley cats bend and arch away from strikes like rubber, yet their teeth and claws are always ready, positioned, and in the attacker's face.

Animals don't need to make a moral or strategic choice when challenged. It's simply fight or flight for them. In contrast, the frozen terror and indecision humans experience during combat is actually a combination of these factors:

1. Moral and cultural breeding (discussed in chapter 1).
2. The brain searching its memory for appropriate physical defense responses.
3. The body's execution of those responses using muscular tension because it has been trained that way. This can also occur when a sport fighter trained to prefer grappling maneuvers over evasion and lethal striking tries to *control* a crazed assailant bent on taking his or her life.

The result of this combination is impeded movement. Tension lengthens your reaction time and cuts down your speed and power. It also makes your body easier to break. Thus, it is self-defeating to practice striking and blocking with full-force muscular contractions as if you were performing a 300-pound (136 kg) bench press. Ironically, practicing with such muscular tension is an error found in virtually all classical, hard-style martial arts training.

You can't achieve looseness without relaxation, and as most top-level sports training research reveals, relaxation aids physical and mental performance. Later in this chapter, we introduce drills to help you develop your ability to stay loose. It is important that you practice these drills with full seriousness because reacting with tension, especially in a life-or-death situation, is a very hard habit to break. In addition, physical tension encourages mental tension, which narrows your awareness dangerously. We want to be clear that when we mean eliminate tension, we're not talking about fear. As addressed in chapter 1, fear can be paralyzing—but it can also turbocharge your nervous system to perform nearly super-human feats of strength and agility.

In an effort to stabilize and strengthen our motions, we regularly use muscle groups that interfere with the motion we are trying to perform. That is, the muscles tend to work against one another. When the muscles work against each other, the body has a tendency to drag. For example, if you extend your arm to strike and you exert strong muscular force, you are restraining your joints. You begin to involve other muscles (called antagonistic muscles) to overcome this drag, so you strain even harder. This creates a vicious cycle. The more force you use, the tighter your joints, the less relaxed you are, and the slower you respond to your opponent's moves.

No matter how hard you think you're punching, you're not punching nearly as hard as you could be if you loosened your muscles and thereby limited the interaction with and among other muscle groups, allowing proper skeletal alignment, body mass, and gravity to do the work. This is what you'll learn to do from the drills and principles of guided chaos in this book. By remaining loose and pliable at all times, you automatically remove the resistance created by antagonistic muscles when you strike or are struck. This allows you to hit with uninhibited power as well as to absorb the strike of a stronger adversary. You'll do this by using your muscles as little as possible and relying on momentum, relaxation, and two concepts you'll learn more thoroughly later on: body unity and dropping energy.

All muscular movement is controlled by the mind. A loose, relaxed mind creates a loose, relaxed body—it's that simple. Relax the mind, and the body will relax. To relax your mind, you'll need to put your brain on autopilot. It must remain focused and aware, yet placid. To do this, you need to relieve your brain of the job of thinking while fighting and train it to simply sense and feel instead.

> When you practice patterned movements, you expect your opponent to move in certain ways. Trust us: Unlike in the movies, this rarely happens during an attack. Your brain, shocked at this discovery, may temporarily freeze, putting the brakes on your muscles and nervous system and increasing the strength you need to apply, which makes the situation worse.

Reactive Looseness

Being loose also means never being static. As long as you're either receiving energy (yielding) or transmitting energy (striking), you're in a continuous state of movement and flow. This characteristic of looseness is important to remember. In a fight, there is always enough energy coming from the opponent to propel you into a constant flow of motion. As soon as you stop, the opponent gets a fix on you. These behaviors obstruct the flow of energy:

When you think, you stop.
When you pose, you stop.
When you block or lock, you stop.
When you strain or grapple, you stop.
When you execute a technique, you stop because you're thinking.

You will learn to develop your looseness so that any input of energy from your opponent causes your entire body to respond, like a seesaw or revolving door.

You can be hurt or killed only if you can be hit. You must be able to disappear from where your attacker wants you to be and reappear where your attacker doesn't want or expect you to be. You must become like a phantom or mongoose. The mongoose is one of the few creatures that can stand directly in front of a poisonous snake and avoid being bit. It pops up and strikes from seemingly impossible angles, sensing and flowing with the snake's every move.

Learn to hit and articulate your body to strike wherever and whenever. However, avoid the limp-noodle looseness characteristic of many tai chi practitioners who lack true combat training (they may be loose in their forms but are stiff as boards in their push hands).

Their intention is sincere, since extreme looseness does protect you from hard impacts. Unfortunately, it can also leave you in a position where you can't get out of your own way to deliver a counterattack. The problem is that extreme looseness

1. can leave you unprotected if you don't keep some part of your body between your opponent's weapon and its target (more on this in chapter 7),
2. has no power if it's not connected to the ground (see the next section), and
3. can get your limbs twisted into positions that are impossible to launch counterattacks from (you can actually block yourself).

Instead of just limp looseness, you want a kind of steel-spring looseness that's exceptionally flexible and reactive, capable of slicing your attacker to ribbons on the rebound. Perhaps a better term than looseness is pliability. This kind of resilient energy has a name in tai chi: peng ching. It is often unfamiliar or overlooked, yet ironically, it's critical to making looseness a combative attribute.

Rooted Looseness

The other factor for making looseness powerful and combative is your root, your ability to transfer energy from your foot to any external body part through a balanced connection to the ground (see chapter 5 for more on rooting as it applies to balance). If you're unbalanced, you have no root. If you're stiff, you have no root. If you carry your body weight too high, you have no root.

To understand looseness without a root, imagine that your entire body is a whip—limp and flexible, just a hanging rope. Your root (foot) is the handle of the whip; your hand is the tip. When you learn to drop (chapter 6) and create an instant explosion of energy that bounces off the ground back up into your legs and body, it's your root that anchors and cracks the whip, even if the root or drop occurs for just a split second.

Imagine if someone cracked a real whip and let go of the handle precisely at the moment of impact. The wavelike power of the whip would completely disintegrate and hit you with all the force of overcooked spaghetti. It's the anchoring action of the handle that roots the transfer of power to the tip.

Beginning students tend to limit their looseness to their arms. Think of it this way: the crack of the whip has more power if the wave of looseness is allowed to traverse its entire length before reaching the tip. Limiting looseness to just your arms or shoulders or even your hips is akin to grabbing the whip in the middle and trying to snap it hard.

Looseness anchors at the foot, just as holding the handle of the whip anchors the rope. The hand is like the tip of the rope. The power of your strikes is directly related to how much body mass you can get moving loosely. When doing the Psycho-chimp and other looseness drills (pp. 61-71), initiate all your movements by stepping, dropping, or transferring weight in your feet and lower legs.

What does a strong root feel like? You can create an exaggerated sense of rooting when you do a dance that involves swinging your partner around, such as the Lindy, jitterbug, or hustle. You counterbalance your partner's swinging body weight by firmly anchoring your feet. At that moment, you feel as if your feet are nailed to the floor. When you release, letting your partner go into a spin or other movement, you feel a tremendous uncorking of energy. You need to develop that same rooted sensation in your feet throughout the entire range of your own combative movements. We'll work on developing this sensation of suspending and releasing in the more advanced drills in chapter 6.

Yielding, Looseness, and Pocketing

Achieving looseness requires your body to become totally receptive and yielding, and it requires you to assume that everyone is stronger than you are. This is not wimping out but is actually tactically superior in that this attitude will help you survive a strike. The principle of yielding, however, does not mean you become a punching bag or a leaf blowing in the wind. To learn yielding, you adopt the fluid nature of water. Water is never stopped, just redirected. If you plunge your fist into water, the water moves out of the way and engulfs your arm at the same time. It avoids you, yet sticks to you (think how this applies to grappling). You also cannot compress water. No matter how hard or softly you squeeze it, it instantly moves to an area of lower pressure. Nothing is as soft as water, yet, if it's completely contained, it can be harder than stone. It is at once extremely mobile and heavy. It can wash away whole towns and mountains. Your body is 70 percent water. Why fight nature? Use it.

To be loose, move your arms and body with the fluid nature of two king cobras—yielding, expanding, contracting, sliding, redirecting, engulfing, and nullifying. Just as the head of a serpent is always moving into position to strike, so should your hands always be seeking a path of destruction. If a python meets a stone head-on in its path, does it try to smash through it? Of course not. The snake isn't anatomically constructed to slam through rock. When its sensitive tongue encounters an obstacle, its entire body moves to accommodate the obstacle. The snake effortlessly and sinously writhes around and past it. Yet, when necessary, the snake can crush the life out of its prey by incrementally relaxing and taking up slack. Likewise, you are never blocked, merely redirected to a more advantageous position from which to strike or avoid an attack.

Reality is not a movie. You can't withstand a barrage of blows like John Wayne in an old western barroom brawl and remain standing. When an elbow is slammed into your neck, your neck breaks. When a fist is buried deep into your kidneys, you land in the hospital. Tightening your neck muscles won't stop a chop to the throat, nor will closing your eyelids stop an eye gouge. It's simply a joke to think the ability to do 500 sit-ups will protect your trunk. What muscles protect your ribcage?

To apply the principle of yielding to your body's survival chances, you have to do something called pocketing. The whole concept of pocketing is simple: Remove the target, and the target only, so the rest of you can remain close. That is, get the part of the body that's about to be hit out of the way of an opponent's strike by becoming sensitive to your opponent's intentions and relaxing the muscles. For example, if the target is your stomach, make it concave so it shrinks away from the blow; leave the rest of your body relatively where it is so you can counterattack simultaneously.

If your opponent's intended target suddenly becomes even 1 inch (2.5 cm) farther away than he or she expects, you will lessen the impact significantly. Whatever the target, pull it away, as if your opponent's fist was red hot or covered with a deadly virus. Get the imagery? Don't let your opponent even touch you with it. Self-defense is not about how tough you are; it's about survival. You don't want to get broken. But instead of relying on blocking, you're going to learn how to make opponents miss so you can stay close and deliver attacks while simultaneously avoiding theirs.

Accordingly, in practicing the drills in this chapter, you will learn to modify your whole body's shape like rubber so it molds to avoid blows. Your head will yield like a jack-in-the-box, and your midsection will stretch like Silly Putty. Paradoxically, you will later discover that yielding can also put you in prime positions to attack. Yielding invites the attacker in closer until, like a Venus flytrap, you spring the trap.

Yielding should be a kinesthetic response to stimuli. As soon as you feel so much as a hair of your body becoming compressed from an attacker or even the intent of an attack, you should already be moving. How do you know which part of you to yield? This is not something a rigid technique can teach. Rather, you will learn to use your awareness (see chapter 1) and hone your sensitivity (chapter 6). Like radar, you will learn to interpret the incoming attack's direction and speed before the strike makes deep penetration.

If you loosen your body to avoid a strike to the point where you can loosen no more, then you must step to a new root point. If you've exceeded your pocketing space limit, step in closer to the attacker either directly or to one side. In either case, the step should put you in a more advantageous position from which to deliver the coup de grâce. How do you know when to step? When you feel that you're losing your balance from excessive pressure (we discuss balance extensively in chapter 5). Cut your losses and move. Don't get in the habit of challenging your opponent or you will fall into the ego trap caused by strength

You must develop reactive looseness and extend it throughout your entire body. Don't limit it only to your arms. Looseness enables you to achieve angles of attack and defense that would otherwise be totally unavailable to you.

contests and ever-increasing rigidity. We will repeat this point endlessly: Never challenge your attacker's strength. You never know who you're dealing with. For a few seconds, a 120-pound (54 kg) insane person or a crackhead on Angel Dust can be stronger than a 200-pound (91 kg) bodybuilder. Yield and find an alternative attack entry. More on this later.

The following are a few examples of the principle of yielding. Understand these are only a few of many thousands of possible movements, which are limited only by your imagination. Master the principle, not the technique. The movements will vary from opponent to opponent due to different body types, physical abilities, and so on.

Yielding a Strike

Instead of blocking your opponent's motion, let him go where he wants to go—except that you're not going to be there when he arrives. Here, B is dealing with an attacker, A, who is trying to strike B in the chest or face. Rather than try to take the blow straight on, B yields, or contorts, his body to redirect the force of the strike, thus avoiding it (figure 3.1a). If B attempts to block the strike straight on, B must meet that force with equal or greater force. The strike may get through in some fashion. It will either go through B's block, or it will knock B's hand into his body, thus allowing time for A to gain an advantage. Or, if B's blocking arm is rigid, his whole body will be rigid, allowing a well-trained opponent to move B and throw a quick secondary strike. However, by redirecting the strike, turning his body, and pocketing the target area (figure 3.1b), B can control the direction of A's force with little or no effort.

For your opponent to hit you with power, you must "cooperate" to a certain extent. Typically, you harden your body and gird yourself against impacts. In trying to be tougher than your attacker, you become a rigid bull's eye. By yielding, however, you become uncooperative with your attacker. When a person throws a strike at you or grapples you, there is a certain expectation that you will be there when the strike lands or that you will grapple back. This gives your attacker's mind and body a point of reference from which to balance. Because most people, including fighters, never train to develop dynamic balance independent of their opponent's, they become vulnerable to attack. They need the resistance of your body to maintain their own balance and stay in the fight. By taking away reference points, you take away the attacker's balance, however slightly. If you have balance and your opponent doesn't, no matter how hard he can punch or kick, he can't strike with effective power. When his energy is neither rooted nor focused, his energy is negated.

> Yielding has a strange effect on your opponent. He expects to make contact and finds nothing. He will often fall over himself as if drawn by some invisible magnet.

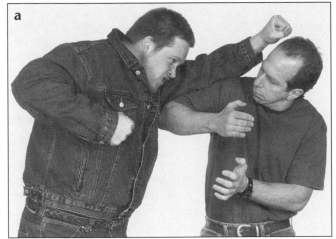 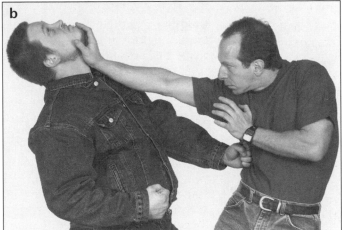

Figure 3.1

Spike-in-the-Sponge

When you are pushed or hit, you should imagine yourself as a sponge. No matter how hard you hit a sponge, it always returns to its original shape. Now, imagine yourself as

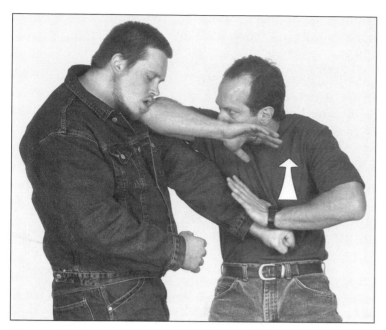

Figure 3.2

a sponge with a steel spike in its center. Notice how A falls into the pocket made by B's collapsing chest and then walks right into B's elbow (figure 3.2). A has been impaled by the spike-in-the-sponge, a key example of the guided chaos principle of pocketing.

Your vitals are the sponge, and your weapons (hands, elbows, and so on) are the spikes. The harder the opponent hits you or the more force he exerts against you, the more damage he does to himself. This is why some people who can break boards, bats, and bricks cannot fight to save their lives. They don't understand the dynamics and chaos of combat. The human body is not like a brick. It flexes, moves its position, and fights back. There's a night-and-day difference between striking objects and hitting people. Besides, do you really have time to prepare, wind up, and focus all your power into one killing blow when you're attacked? Do you think your attacker will stand there and wait for your blow, like in the movies?

There are other ways of gaining power. Being extremely loose and pliable makes you extremely hard and powerful for the split second of impact. This is the same principle behind the power of a whip—or a wrecking ball.

Pressure Responses

The following are some simple examples of what we mean by responding loosely. Remember, these are not techniques. When your body becomes familiar with the principle and you develop the feel that characterizes looseness, you will spontaneously invent your own movements.

Down Pressure on Your Arm

A's arm exerts down pressure on B's forearm at close range. B yields the forearm downward, simultaneously rolling the elbow of the same arm up and over, striking the head or shoulder or spearing straight into the gut (figure 3.3a). A's down pressure results in a seesaw action by B, who uses no strength whatsoever. The whole body rises and falls with the rise and fall of the elbow, and it all started with the impetus of A's down pressure.

Another example of a loose response to down pressure is remarkably simple; nevertheless, it would be impossible to perform with a tight body. B, yielding to A's down pressure, simply punches down into the top of A's groin (figure 3.3b), bounces off, and up-elbows into A's jaw like a rubber band (figure 3.3c).

Another possible reaction: B drops the down-pressured arm and turns his whole body away to the right like a windmill, driving his left opposite elbow into A's face. You can see that this bouncing strike principle becomes effective for delivering many strikes within one motion. You won't, however, have the required springiness unless you're loose.

You may say to yourself, *How am I going to remember all these moves*? We can't stress enough, if you're loose and sensitive and have learned and practiced applying the principles, you won't have to. You'll just fall into them and say, "Oh! Look what I just did!" or "He made me do it!" and you will be right. Techniques will emerge from the flow, not vice versa. In classical training, you practice 100 techniques and hope they'll work just as they did in class if reality rears its ugly head. You've already seen this doesn't work in the real world. Or you learn one technique, perfect it, and hope to apply it to every situation you run across. This isn't practical either. Would you bring a screwdriver to a job that requires a hammer?

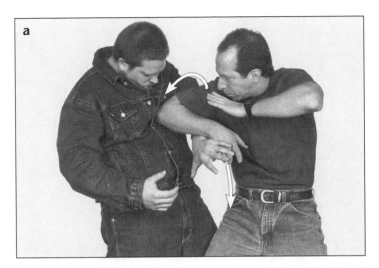

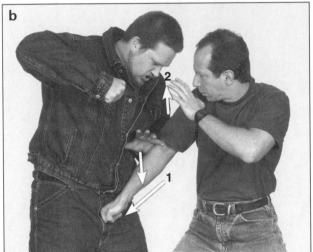 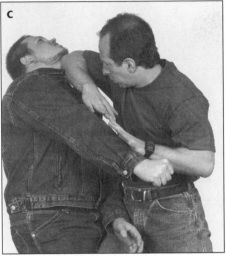

Figure 3.3

Up Pressure on Your Arm

B can simply slide in with a horizontal chop to the face (figure 3.4*a* on p. 58), or he can punch down by simply rolling his elbow up in a yielding response to A's rising pressure into the crook of his arm, thus giving B room to drive his fist in (figure 3.4*b*). Or B can circle over and underneath in yielding to A's up pressure and drive a spear hand up into A's throat (figure 3.4*c*). Or A's up pressure on B's forearm can cause B simply to rotate his shoulder, raising into an up-elbow strike under A's arm and up into his chin (figure 3.4*d*). The possibilities are endless, but they're all created by looseness.

Inward Pressure on Your Arm

A pushes in against B's arms to collapse them (figure 3.5*a* on p. 59). B lets A's hands go where they want to, which is right at B's throat, except that B won't be there when they arrive. Because of body unity (see chapter 4), when B yields to A's pressure, her entire body pivots out of the way and to the side of A. This actually brings B in closer where she can easily pivot like a windmill into an elbow strike to A's head (figure 3.5*b*).

In doing so, B has yielded her hands and forearms inward and rolled her elbow up, over, and down on A's head or shoulder joint. B has actually sucked A into the spike-in-the-sponge. Remember, with proper looseness, all these motions have a flip-floppy kind of feel, as if you were a drunken puppet—but with iron limbs.

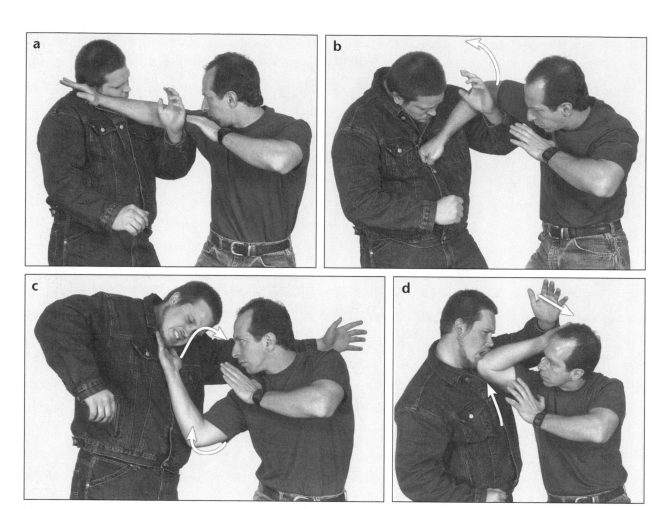

Figure 3.4

> The first law of war is the preservation of yourself and the destruction of your enemy.

Here's another example of flowing with the attacker's inward energy instead of against it: in figure 3.5c, B goes with the direction of A's energy and steps in, smashing either a punch or an elbow (figure 3.5d) into the nerves of A's biceps or a palm into the shoulder joint, separating it (figure 3.5e). This clears the offending arm, making room for B's arm to come slashing back with a chop to A's neck or temple (figure 3.5f). The chopping motion immediately follows the clearing motion with a plyometric or recoil effect. In other words, instead of forcing the body into two separate, full-muscular contractions, you rely on the natural elastic properties of muscle tissue to initiate and augment the return strike (the chop). This is further augmented by B shifting her weight from her right foot to her left and then returning to her right like a pendulum that has reached the end of its arc and now returns with the full, falling power of gravity. This is a crucial concept that lies at the root of guided chaos that you must understand and experiment with.

Outward Pressure on Your Arm

In an attempt to control the victim's blows, an attacker often will actually pull the victim into his midsection to smother his arms. In addition, sometimes an attempt to block a strike downward winds up pulling the strike in. If you're loose and sensitive enough, you flow with this energy and actually augment it by striking the attacker in the same direction he's pulling you. For example, B is now counterattacking by punching at A's throat. A, panicking, attempts to smother the blows by pulling B's fists into his chest (figure 3.6a). B, by being loose and sensitive, detects this change

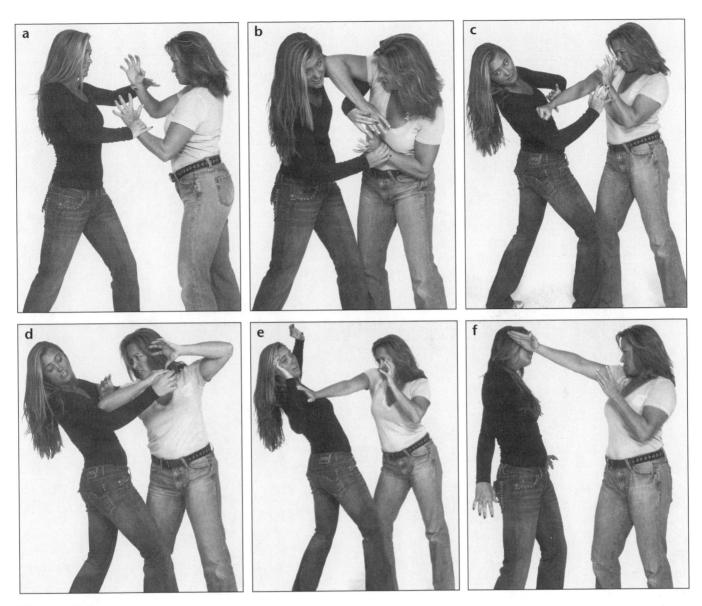

Figure 3.5

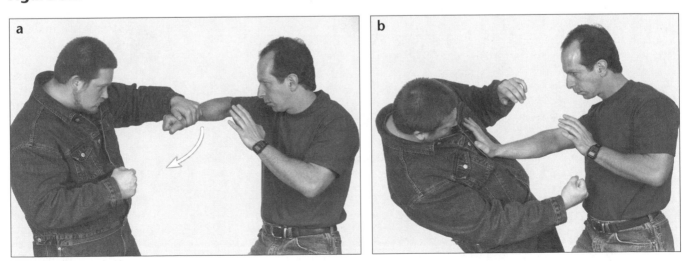

Figure 3.6

59

instantly and flows with it by stepping in and augmenting A's directional energy, striking to the chest with his palm (figure 3.6b). As much as possible, try not to pull back on the attacker's arm before you reverse direction on him. As you increase your sensitivity, you will learn to make the transition time between direction changes shorter and shorter until, in the end, your attacker feels nothing, and you stick and follow his motions like a ghost.

Elbow Pressure

B is in a right lead, standing a little too sideways, so A pushes against B's right elbow to keep him from turning back (figure 3.7a). Instead of resisting, B loosens the right shoulder completely and lets it go, yielding and turning away with A's push just enough to release the pressure (figure 3.7b). The speed with which B yields is directly proportional to the amount of force A exerts on the elbow. In fact, B reacts to this touch on his elbow the same way as if he had been touched with a red-hot frying pan. Notice also that A's pushing hand has inadvertently fallen into B's other hand. With a springlike action, B's whole body jerks away—perhaps only 1 inch (2.5 cm)—and then bounces back in with a loose, smashing chop to the throat (figure 3.7c). Another option that displays more economy of motion (see chapter 8) is for B to isolate his yielding to his right shoulder joint. This would retract his upper arm perhaps 2 inches (5 cm), creating a new entry angle for either a right chop to A's throat or (using rotational energy in response to A's push) a right hammer fist to A's right temple.

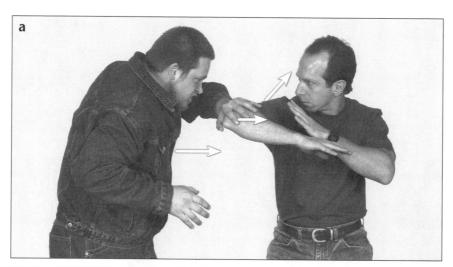

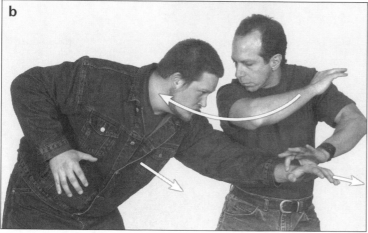

Figure 3.7

These are all examples of what you can accomplish with looseness. If they seem absurdly simple, it's because they are. If you're wondering if they work, they do. If you haven't trained yourself to be loose, however, even if you're highly trained in other ways, you won't be able to perform them. Here are some drills to develop your ability to be loose.

Looseness Drills

The point of these drills is to develop the overall body feel that characterizes looseness. If you focus on pummeling your target or your partner, you'll miss the whole point.

Relaxed Breathing

The key to developing looseness or pliability is relaxation, not only physical but also mental relaxation. Remember, the mind controls the body. When the mind is agitated, so is the body. When the mind is calm and focused, the body becomes more responsive to whatever the mind wants it to do. Conversely, if you practice with a loose, relaxed body, the training acts as a moving meditation, and the mind becomes relaxed. This drill helps you focus on relaxing your breathing, thereby relaxing your mind and body.

1. Stand in a relaxed stance, feet shoulder-width apart, and sink your weight into your legs. Keep your back straight, knees slightly bent, and arms hanging at your sides like wet noodles.
2. Empty your mind of all the day's tension. Relax your upper body and breathe through your nose deep into your belly, loosening your diaphragm. (Note: Breathing high in the chest, the way most people do, creates neurological tension and anxiety.)
3. Imagine your skin is inhaling also, absorbing fresh air and sunshine through every pore like a sponge. Feel this absorbed air and energy adding relaxation, gravity, and blood mass to your body and limply hanging arms.
4. Feel your stomach actually expand like a balloon with each inhalation of fresh, soothing air.

   Exhale by releasing your expanded stomach so air flows out naturally through your nose (don't force it out). Imagine all negative energy leaving with your expended breath. Feel fresh blood pumping into the vessels of your arms, adding weight and liquid relaxation.
5. Feel the movement of air across your skin. Imagine a gentle breeze swaying your body like a blade of grass.

Fold Like a Napkin

This kind of looseness is not combative because you are not going to purposely collapse in a fight. However, because the concept of completely relaxing local target areas of your body is so alien, we are going for total surrender in this drill.

1. Stand with your eyes closed.
2. Have one partner stand behind you and one in front.
3. Have your partners take turns slowly pushing you.
4. Let your body be so relaxed that as soon as you're pushed, you fold like a napkin and fall totally limp into the arms of the other partner. Let yourself go completely (obviously you'll need partners you can trust).

Dead-Fish Arms

So how do you know if you are relaxed? Try this:

1. Stand with your arms hanging at your sides.

2. Have another person take your arms by the wrists and raise them outward for you. Do not help in any way! You'll be amazed how difficult this is for most people. They try to raise their arms themselves. They simply can't let go.

3. Let your elbows hang loosely below your wrists and shoulders (since this is the "folding point" of the limb).

4. Let your arms flop to your sides like two dead fish when your partner suddenly releases your wrists.

5. Have your partner place his or her hands under your armpits and push straight up. Most people will be immovable because their shoulders are locked to their trunk. If you are truly loose, your shoulders will rise independent of the rest of your body, as if you were shrugging.

6. Let your arms and shoulders flop down like two heavy, wet noodles when the upward pressure is released.

Weaving Python

The sort of body isolation and pliability you demonstrate with this drill is vital to your survival. You must assume that every person who attacks you is far stronger than you, is deadly serious, and can hurt you wherever he strikes.

1. Stand with your arms hanging at your sides.

2. Have your partner place one hand about 6 inches (15 cm) away from the center of your chest, palm in. Your partner's other hand should be 6 inches (15 cm) away from the center of your back, also palm in.

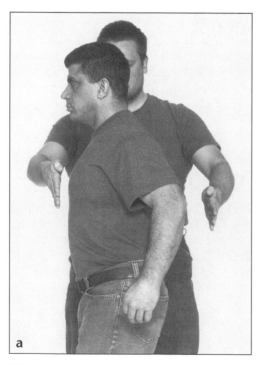 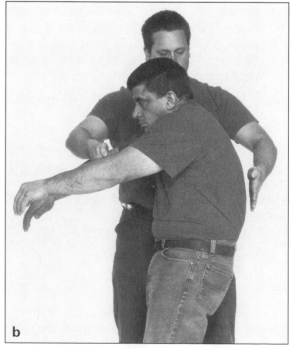

Figure 3.8

3. Without moving your feet or raising or turning your body, expand your chest directly outward so you can touch your partner's hand. This requires you to throw your shoulders and arms back, loosen your stomach and pectoral muscles, and bend your knees further to sink your weight backward into your hips and buttocks. This is a compensating move to keep you from falling on your face (figure 3.8a).

4. Reverse the movement and touch your partner's rear hand with the center of your back (figure 3.8b). You will have to cave in your chest and throw your shoulders and arms forward, loosening your back muscles. You'll also have to rotate your pelvis down and forward and sink your weight into your knees to avoid falling backward.

5. In one loose, continuous movement, like a python weaving backward and forward, touch one of your partner's hands and then the other repeatedly. Keep this motion completely horizontal. Your head should remain the same height above the floor. Your knees should remain bent and your feet flat on the floor.

What is the point of all this? If the two palms were knives, it would be immediately apparent. Try this with every part of your body. Note that the far more advanced exercise Washing the Body (chapter 6) also uses this concept.

The Hula

You want to keep your weight low and balanced, like a downhill skier or a middle linebacker, rather than high and precarious like a ballet dancer. This drill encourages you to keep your root mobile, like a big jungle cat or a tank on ball bearings.

1. Stand with your arms hanging at your sides.

2. Imagine that the air has weight, like seawater. Feel the currents drift across your skin. Feel that your arms, indeed your whole body, could easily float in the air through no effort of their own. Imagine, however, that your pelvis is attached by a steel cable to a 500-pound (227 kg) weight hanging below you.

3. Gently raise your arms in front of you, about as high and wide as your shoulders. Help raise them by straightening your knees slightly. While doing this, use only enough strength to keep them up. Keep your upper and lower arms totally flaccid without any muscle tension whatsoever.

4. Practice raising your arms up and down, back and forth, in a super-slow, graceful manner like a drunken hula dancer, keeping your feet well rooted to the ground. As if your whole body is moving in a current of water, your legs, hips, back, and shoulders drift with your arms as they move. Breathe slowly and deeply into your belly at the same time.

5. Perform this while walking around slowly with knees bent like an ice skater or Groucho Marx.

At first your arms may feel unnatural and heavy, but as you become more accustomed to this exercise, you will notice your arms beginning to feel weightless. Develop the sensation that your arms are suspended on a cushion of air, so light and responsive that a fly landing on them would cause them to move. Apply this sensation to your whole body. This is what it feels like to be loose. Remember, though, that a 500-pound (227 kg) weight is keeping your pelvis anchored low to the ground. Although your hips and knees can sway with the current easily, you are rooted to the ground through your feet like an oak tree. A common mistake, however, is to glue your feet to the ground and refuse to move them, even if you're losing your balance. This is both unnecessary and dangerous.

Figure 3.9

Turning

Perform this simple movement in a dreamlike, meditative manner, as if driven by ocean waves. Breathe deep into your belly. If some part of your body were to hit a pole as it moves, it would wrap around the pole like a heavy sausage chain.

1. Begin by performing the Relaxed Breathing drill (p. 61).

2. Use only enough muscle to completely shift your weight from one leg to the other. Empty your entire body of muscle tension as if you were asleep or drunk. Imagine your arms, shoulders, back, chest, waist, and hips are simply dead meat hanging from your skeleton.

3. As you slowly shift your weight completely from foot to foot without rising or leaning, let your body initiate a slow, twisting motion. Keep your whole body fairly low.

4. As you increase the twisting motion, let your arms leave your sides and begin limply swinging in the air from the centrifugal force. At the end of each weight shift, let your arms wrap around your body one way and then unwrap as you shift to the other leg (figure 3.9). Don't make your arms move. This is critical. Let the momentum of your body dictate their entire motion.

5. Increase the twisting slowly until, with your knees bent, your shoulders turn almost 90 degrees beyond your feet. At the end of each turn, your hips should be above the foot toward which you have turned. Thus, your hips travel a linear distance that is as far as your stance is wide. At no point in this exercise should your body rise. Keep your knees bent deeply. As you become more advanced, try shifting your weight so completely from leg to leg that you can actually lift the foot an inch (2.5 cm) off the ground at the end of each swing while casually balancing on the other. This should be accomplished smoothly without any jerking, leaning, hitching, or further weight shift, otherwise it will be clear that you are not balanced (see chapter 5).

Swimming

Now instead of just drifting with the waves, you will begin to glide and swim through them. The swimming analogy is useful in correcting an error beginning students of guided chaos often make. When blocking, beginners often actually pull a strike into the body in an effort to smother it. However, if you do this against a more experienced student or opponent, he will push your pull (see chapter 6) and use your energy to catapult a strike into you. In other words, when you pull his arm in, he'll add to your pulling energy by beating your energy back to its source—you—and actually strike with both, like a rubber band. When you swim, as you pull your arm back, do you pull the water into your chest? Of course not. You pull and then push the water past you. You do the same with an opponent's strike when you employ the swimming motion. This drill develops your ability to use your pulling energy to push your opponent's strike past you.

1. Do a swimming crawl stroke through the air as if it were made of water. Loosely articulate your shoulders, back, and waist to get the maximum extension; keep your body low with the knees bent (figure 3.10a) but don't lean.

2. Step forward with each stroke with the leg opposite the arm you're using.

3. Turn your feet as you accommodate the extra reach required to make the motion. Reach as far as you can with each stroke, but without leaning. As you swim, be sure to drive with the legs, completely shifting your weight from foot to foot as in the turning drill. However, keep the path your arms take as economical as possible. In other words,

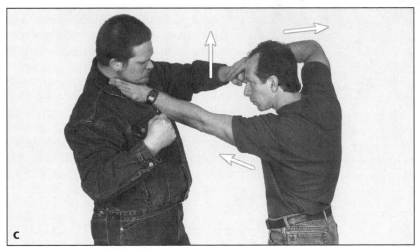

Figure 3.10

    don't windmill them. Try to cut through the water with a flat stroke; move your body and arms with as little resistance, or splash, and as much efficiency as you can.

4. Imagine you are sending a spearing strike into the attacker's eyes, skimming over his arms.

5. As your hands retract, sweep them down a few inches away from your pectorals and make tight circles as they extend back out. Once again, make your shoulders do the circling so your hands don't take on a wide, windmill-like path. Imagine you are clearing the attacker's arms.

    It's a lot harder to move a flat surface broadside through water than if you turn it edgewise. So, too, a wild, sloppy stroke will slow you down as you try to swim. The application is that in combat, you should swim through your opponent's defenses and knife through his resistance, rather than challenging either head-on.

For example, if an opponent exerts down pressure on your arm, yield with it and swim out of it, circling your arm down and then over for a dropping palm strike to the neck or a spear hand to the eyes. This is yielding with the same arm. As your arm circles down, the tight arc it makes across your pectorals will serve to cover you as it yields. If your whole body yields, it turns away like a propeller on one side and crashes in with borrowed energy on the opposite side (figure 3.10*b*). This is not something you plan; it just happens because you're loose and without thought, like a drunken puppet.

If your opponent is applying up pressure against your arm, guess what? That's right—backstroke out of it. As the pressured side of your body yields and turns away from the force, the other side turns in and delivers a devastating rising spear hand to the throat (figure 3.10*c*). Practice swimming backward and forward and at different angles. We want to keep repeating: Do not memorize this as a technique. Instead, become familiar with the principle of looseness and reciprocal motion.

Figure 3.11

Swimming Backstroke

Now in addition to working looseness, you're going to combine two strikes at once to develop the guided chaos subprinciple of multitasking. Looking over your right shoulder, begin doing a backstroke by elbowing a rear attacker in the face with your right arm). Simultaneously, drive a rising ridgehand into the groin of a frontal attacker. Without pausing, continue with a left elbow and right ridgehand (figure 3.11), and so on. In this picture, the defender has dropped his weight into both legs. This is one option. You should also practice this drill in a manner similar to turning; stand with your feet square to your partner in front of you and drive with your legs using a complete lateral foot-to-foot weight shift. Using this method, a left rear elbow strike would have you placing 99.9% of your weight on your left foot. In either case, make sure you are loosely rolling your shoulders and back to gain maximum elastic power. The quality of your movement should be springy and whipping, not stiff and staccato as is typical in many external styles.

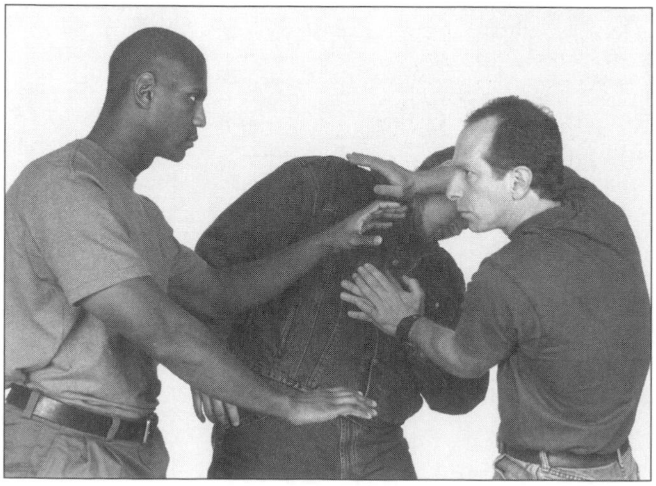

Swimming Sidestroke

Exactly as the name implies, practice doing the sidestroke. As with all swimming movements, fully turn and extend your back and shoulders. It helps to step forward with each stroke with the leg opposite the arm you're using. This helps to get your entire body weight moving behind each movement. This motion is useful for warding off strikes to your side, as from multiple attackers, and is similar to the CCUE. In figure 3.12, the defender on the right is warding off the attacker's arms with a sidestroke-like motion and will next extend his left arm in a spearing or thrusting chop to the approaching attacker's windpipe.

Figure 3.12

Solo Circle Flow

This drill is not a fighting technique. It's simply an exercise for emphasizing looseness and full body weight transfer. As you more thoroughly understand the movements in this drill, you can try the more advanced guided chaos solo exercises later in the book.

1. Using the same, slow, relaxed, side-to-side swaying motion used in the Turning drill (p. 64), make small circles—no wider than the perimeter of your body—in front of your body with your hands and arms (when deflecting strikes, it's a waste to protect empty space).

2. Synchronize the movement of your arms with the flowing, side-to-side weight transfer from leg to leg, so that as you move to the left, your right hand is pushing the air across the front of your body and down to the left from the top of its arc, and your left hand is doing a backhanded sweep to the left along the bottom of its arc (figure 3.13*a*).

3. As you transfer your weight and sway back to the right, reverse your arms and complete the other halves of their circles (figure 3.13*b*).

4. Drive with the legs as you flow loosely with your upper body from side to side. Make believe the air you're pushing weighs 1,000 pounds (454 kg), but use absolutely no tension. Try to develop a flowing, rolling sensation in your movements as if your body was being driven by ocean waves. This imagery promotes relaxation along with full body unity (chapter 4).

 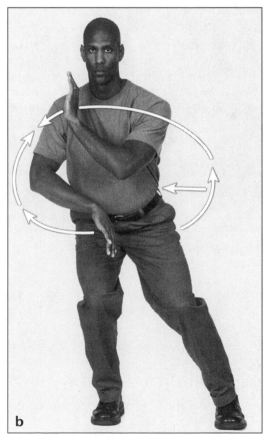

Figure 3.13

Sticks of Death

This drill requires great looseness, balance, and sensitivity so that you don't swing wildly at the sticks but instead glance off them as you use pocketing to avoid contact.

1. Have your partner stand behind a heavy bag or padded dummy, holding two, 4-foot-long (1.2 m) padded sticks like cue sticks against the dummy.
2. Stand 3 feet (.9 m) away from your partner. Your partner should randomly poke the sticks at you.
3. Evade, pocket, and redirect the sticks, sliding through them while simultaneously attacking the dummy's eyes and throat with both hands (figure 3.14). (Refer back to the Jack Benny stance in chapter 2.) The object is to get in to biting range, while simultaneously remaining unavailable to the sticks.

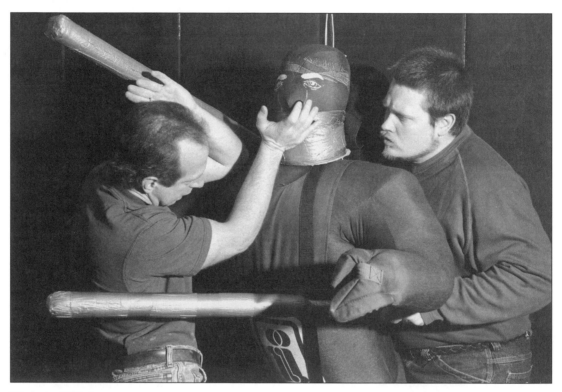

Figure 3.14

Sticky Fingers

Maybe this should be called stinky fingers. All kidding aside, your sense of smell is a superb example of heightened sensitivity in that it forces you to extend your awareness out beyond your skin. This drill is vital in re-learning the deeply ingrained, macho habit of overcoming strength with strength by trying to withstand incoming blows.

1. Have someone try to poke you randomly with both hands anywhere on your body at ever-increasing speed.
2. Don't back up or block. Bend, twist, pocket, and fold your body like rubber. It's like when you were five years old, and your older brother tried to tickle you to exhaustion.
3. Imagine some vile substance on the tips of his fingers to aid in your pocketing reaction. Revulsion is a good source of yielding energy. Some people put on old clothes and try to dot each other with paint.

Small Circle Dance

This may qualify as the strangest looking of all the drills. At all times while performing this drill, stay balanced, no matter how wild it gets. Try it with music. If you start looking like Elvis on acid, you're on the right track. This drill helps develop your ability to hit with several parts of your body simultaneously, without direct control from your rational brain.

Figure 3.15

1. Start with one part of your body, say, your hand, and begin making small, loose circles in the air with it.
2. Begin making circles in the opposite direction with your other hand. This trains your brain to handle various parts of your body in motion simultaneously. From here it gets crazy.
3. Begin making circles with one elbow, then add the other in the opposite direction.
4. Start circling with your knees. Add your hips, your head, back, buttocks, and shoulders. In short, try it simultaneously with as many parts of your body as you can manage, loosely, and in complete balance (figure 3.15).

What is the point of all this silliness? Looseness. Police reports show time and again that when a car full of people crashes, it's the drunken passengers, ironically, who walk away. They're too crocked to panic, and their bodies stay loose on impact. You also want to begin getting all parts of your body to work independently for random striking.

Psycho-Chimp

Second only to the previous drill in terms of wackiness, this exercise will have a very liberating result on your looseness and savagery.

1. Begin with a relaxed stance, feet about shoulder-width apart, knees slightly bent and loose, arms outstretched to the left. Your arms should feel like dead weight, with what seem like the finest strings barely holding them up by the wrists.
2. With a strong, dropping motion of your knees, let your arms fall and swing to the right, using only the turning momentum of your body, the drive of your legs, and the weight of your arms to propel them. Limit the use of your arm or shoulder muscles.
3. Without pausing, drop and swing your arms back in the other direction.
4. Keep going. As you continue to do this drill, your arms should maintain complete, dead-weight relaxation. They will begin to take on snapping, chaotic trajectories that get wilder and wilder.
5. Drop on each motion, like cracking a whip, with your entire body (the whip) and your connection with the ground (the handle). Step around as you drop.
6. Increase the speed gradually until you're going as fast as you can, and you begin to look like a psycho-chimp. Be free, but try not to hit yourself!
7. While maintaining looseness, modify your arms' trajectories (using your body's momentum, not your arm muscles) so they don't swing behind your body, which would be wasteful movement. Pocket and yield your body severely to keep from hitting yourself and to create more room for your arms to move. At the same time, modify the wildness so it occurs mostly in front of you.
8. Now, without stopping this swinging, dervishlike craziness, merely recognize the inherent strikes within the flow, without forcing them. Without much planning, have the

snapping motions turn into chops, spears, uppercuts, and other strikes we don't have names for.

If the wavelike energy you're creating is properly guided by your whole body weight, the power, speed, and savagery of your movement will be plainly evident. If your arms encounter each other, they will whip and coil like live snakes, yet avoid entangling each other because of your looseness.

Notice that as the arc of some whipping movements tightens, the speed increases. We call this slingshotting, a method for increasing the power behind strikes. For example, the arm, after connecting with a loose, rising backhand strike to the chin, will increase in speed greatly if its arc tightens as it loops all the way around into a hook punch to the ribs. This is akin to the speed of a spinning figure skater increasing as she pulls in her arms.

Gorilla Walk

You see we have a fondness for simian-named drills. Maybe it's because our primate relatives had a natural looseness and savagery that we've since lost. In this odd-looking drill, you're going to take deliberate, swinging steps and drop into them so heavily and loosely that all the loose flesh on your body (you know what we mean) reverberates and jiggles in waves like jello. When we say drop heavily, though, we're not talking about stamping your feet. To emphasize what we mean, stand on one leg with your other knee in the air and then just collapse into the other foot as if someone had just cut the tendons in your knees. As your foot hits the ground, feel the impact reverberate back up into your body as a wave that makes your back, arms, and shoulders jiggle and roll, like a drunken gorilla. This exercise is actually a precursor to feeling dropping energy, except that instead of channeling the rebound wave into strikes, we just want you to feel it interacting with your looseness. Continue stepping so you feel your entire body rolling loosely throughout the exercise.

Circle Clap

This drill is very important for developing a feeling of explosiveness at high speed while maintaining muscular relaxation.

1. Clap your hands as fast as you can. Your clapping speed and endurance will be dictated exclusively by your ability to relax your muscles.

2. Simultaneously, move your hands above your head and make a wide circle, down to your waist, back above your head, and in and out.

3. Now circle your hands side to side. Clap at any angle you can think of.

4. Do it on one leg and with your eyes closed as you twist and turn your body into bizarre contortions. Try generating the power for the claps not in your arms but in a vibration that wells up from your legs into your hips. Think of your whole body as spasming with your arms loosely attached. You will probably find that your hands are most comfortable about 2 inches (5 cm) apart.

5. When tension overcomes motion, stop, breathe, and visualize your exhalation spreading relaxation throughout your arms. Start again.

The reason you make the circles is that you want to maintain the relaxation no matter what your position. What is the application? Later, you will learn to deliver blows from anywhere to anywhere with no windup or room to move. In a fight, most people's muscles clamp up with supreme, adrenaline-fueled exertion. This renders the person frozen with tension as he fights the movements of his own body. With the Circle Clap drill, you reprogram your nervous system to tense only in tiny microbursts separated by total relaxation. This allows you to change direction at any time and thus flow with the fight. Try this drill again after you completely understand dropping (chapter 6).

TWO RULES TO LIVE BY: DON'T GO TO CRIME SCENE TWO; ATTACK THE ATTACKER

Jane (one of our students who had been out of training for over six years because of a car accident) saved her life in a horrific attack by sticking to two basic rules of self-defense. One day, when Jane was waiting to see her doctor, a man entered the waiting room and wanted to see the physician before Jane. Jane explained to the man that she was in a hurry, and he would have to wait. The man left the waiting room. Jane then went in to see the doctor.

After a while, Jane and her doctor heard screaming coming from somewhere in the building. The doctor told Jane that he would look into the matter and left the office. After a few minutes, there was still some commotion, and Jane decided to find out what had happened to the doctor. She entered the narrow hallway as the door closed behind her. Almost immediately, she was confronted by a vision of horror. Directly in front of her stood a man covered in blood. He pointed to the rear of the hallway and ordered her to go there. Now Jane had to make a life and death decision. She knew that one basic rule of survival when confronted by a potentially violent psychopath is never go with the person to a second location. Her wrists had been injured previously, and she realized that she might not be able to use them for her defense. But she knew what she must do to stay alive. Attack the attacker! Although she could not use her hands, she improvised. As the psycho stepped forward, she drop stepped into him, kneed him in the groin, and slammed him in the nose with her forehead. The attacker stopped in his tracks. He was stunned. Jane then "convinced" him to leave the hallway.

Her doctor emerged from an adjacent door. He was covered in blood with gaping wounds to his face, head, and hands. The psychopath had attacked him with a cleaver, and the doctor had fought him off. Inside the office was the body of a female doctor who wasn't so lucky. She had been hacked to death. This killer was later found to have brought other bladed weapons and a large suitcase, which was hidden in another part of the building. Jane had stopped the killer from killing her and her doctor, and who knows how many others.

Split-Brain Air Writing

Since you are learning to fight spontaneously with total freedom, your nervous system needs to be able to keep pace with your increasing sensitivity in order to handle uncoordinated movements by different parts of your body simultaneously. This bizarre exercise helps you develop a loose, relaxed brain.

1. With your right hand, write the letter *B* in the air. At the same time, write the same letter with your left hand, but flipped, as if it is a mirror image. Write a few more letters.
2. Now it gets fun. Simultaneously, write a different letter with each hand. Start at the same time and end at the same time with each hand.

It's not easy. Do a few of these until your head hurts and then stop. If you do this a few times every day, your brain will begin to adjust, and your fighting will become freer. You will develop the ability to hit one attacker with one kind of strike with one hand and another attacker with a different kind of strike with your other hand simultaneously. Fighting multiple opponents requires just this kind of split-brain awareness.

Learning guided chaos is like having a whole series of aha! experiences. Sudden realizations of how all the principles come together will happen with increasing frequency. Even though we've only gone through some drills to encourage looseness, you will be using what you've learned in this chapter to develop the principles explained in the remaining chapters in part II: body unity (chapter 4), balance (chapter 5), and sensitivity (chapter 6). It's important, therefore, to come back to these drills and imbue them with your heightened understanding as you advance. Moreover, many of the drills you will perform in upcoming chapters will continue to train and hone your looseness.

Preventing Common Mistakes

➤ Maintain a strong root at all times while doing looseness drills. The tendency is to stumble around like a drunkard with your new-found looseness.

➤ Step to a new root point only when your balance is overchallenged. Keep your feet connected to the ground like the roots of an oak, but everything from your ankles up should be like ribbons of spring steel. Even so, you're not glued to the ground. You should be able to glide to a new root point as easily and powerfully as a jungle cat.

➤ Make sure your arms move in sync with your body in solo circle flow. In other words, as you transfer weight to your right leg, your left hand sweeps to the right and down in an arc in front of your chin. It should have all your mass behind it. If your right hand swept to the left as your body moved to the right, all your momentum would be dissipated.

➤ Be aware that looseness doesn't mean you become a helpless noodle. Rather, you want to become like a whip. In chapter 7, you will learn to move in ways that help you instead of hurt you as you remain loose.

CHAPTER FOUR

BODY UNITY

Balance is the foundation of body unity, and body unity is your power source augmented by looseness and triggered by sensitivity. Simply put, body unity means that if any part of your body moves, no matter how slightly, then the rest of your body moves also. If you weigh 180 pounds (82 kg), then every movement, even a finger strike, should have at least 180 pounds of body mass momentum behind it. (We say "at least" because the phenomenon of dropping energy that you will learn fully in chapter 6 will increase this amount.)

We're not talking about mystical secrets to achieve body unity. In almost any sport, you've got to get your body behind the ball. Top athletes, with little strain, are able to do this with grace, balance, power, and accuracy. An athlete's body unity is manifest in a perfect, relaxed, mechanical alignment of all the skeletal joints. This is vital. Without it, you cannot develop relaxed power.

The movements in fighting, however, are far more varied and anarchic than those in sports, whether it be football, soccer, or wrestling. There are millions of tiny differences in the way tennis players serve, but the parameters and the end result are always the same: They must stand behind the baseline, toss the ball vertically, and hit it into a box with every fiber of their being. A street brawl has no such rules. Therefore, you must really understand what's going on behind attributes such as body unity, balance, looseness, and sensitivity in order to apply them to a combat situation of total chaos.

Introduction to Chi

In Eastern martial thought, the terms are different, but the goals are the same. The esoteric tai chi term for perfect alignment is translated as "moving the chi like a thread through the nine pearls." The nine pearls are the joints of the body: the ankle, knee, hip, waist, spine, shoulder, elbow, wrist, and fist. If we take out the obscure symbolism, what we're left with is simple physics. Chi is "threaded" through the joints, with each alignment augmenting and reinforcing the others with a smooth, unkinked flow of power from the floor to the hand (or whatever weapon you're using). "Great," you say, "but what is chi?" The simplest definition of chi is energy. We bring up the mysterious subject of chi here because it directly relates to all our principles, especially body unity, with its concept of delivering the most power with the greatest efficiency. But to speak of chi, we must first explain the concept of internal energy.

Internal Energy

One way of differentiating the styles of martial arts is to divide them into two categories depending on whether the source and application of available energy is external or internal. In an external art, the source of power is almost purely muscular: Strength and speed are emphasized through learning and repeatedly executing fixed drills in unvarying patterns. The full-power muscular contractions that are characteristic of external-style arts are typically marked by a battle cry, or kiai. External-style arts place a substantial amount of stress on your tissues, as is evidenced by the high incidence of tendon, ligament, and muscle injuries in external-style schools. These injuries often occur without even making contact with an adversary. Ideally, after decades of training (if his or her body holds out), the external-style martial artist sometimes develops an easy, effortless grace that requires little muscular exertion. This begs the question: If this is what you're really after, why not learn grace from the beginning? This is what we do in guided chaos by developing and training the attributes of body unity, balance, looseness, and sensitivity that typify grace.

Although our approach is different from all the others, you could consider guided chaos one of the internal-style arts, along with the traditional Chinese styles of tai chi, hsing I, and bagua. In an internal-style art, the mind and nervous system are relaxed and amplified with both static and moving meditation exercises. Internal-style energy methods emphasize perfect, relaxed, mechanical alignment of the bones and tendons to achieve the most efficient plyometric application of energy via an explosive nervous system instead of through rigid muscular force. This application is aided both by gravity and the exploitation of the enemy's muscular force. It's the same with body unity. Your body, even if you're a small person, has significant mass irrespective of its inherent strength. In other words, even if you can't punch your way out of a paper bag, if you simply dropped the dead weight of your body on another individual, the force generated would be substantial, especially if the contact point was something hard, like an elbow.

The goal in using your internal energy is to have the entire mass of your body perfectly aligned with all the bones in your body so that this mass is behind every movement assisted by gravity. This way you can strike, block, and so forth, and still maintain muscular relaxation because you are not forcing the motion but remaining loose. An example of perfect misalignment would be trying to push a car with your feet pointing in opposite directions, standing sideways, your head near your knees, using the backs of your fingertips. Even if you can bench-press 400 pounds (181.4 kilogams), if you are positioned this way, the car is not going to move, and you'll probably break your hands, too. "So," you might ask, "wouldn't the ideal combination be perfect alignment with massive muscular strength?" Yes, if you're pushing a car, because in such a case, the goal is to move one object (the car) in space from point A to point B in a straight line. You can commit all your force to one direction because you're not expecting the car to suddenly jump up and down or sideways. Unfortunately we're talking about combat, where there are no rules and where everything changes, including force, speed, angle of attack, opponents, weapons, and traction—millisecond by millisecond. In the famous film *Enter the Dragon,* a bad guy tries to impress Bruce Lee with his power by breaking boards with his hand. Lee, unimpressed, remains calm and says enigmatically, "Boards don't hit back!" In short, your assailant is not going to stand still while you wind up to take your best shot.

When the muscles of your arm strain to do heavy work, the triceps and biceps oppose each other to stabilize the joint. These muscles have what is called an antagonistic relationship. This hinders either one from accomplishing its respective task: extending and contracting the elbow joint. Using intense, continuous muscular effort anywhere in your body activates antagonistic muscles, making you rigid, hard, slow, and unresponsive—just what you don't want to be when fighting for your life. Most people (and many trained martial artists) get very hung up on this because they think pure strength is the end-all of fighting. Unfortunately, the simple reality is this: No matter how strong you are, there's always someone stronger.

Internal energy, however, is more than just perfect alignment, more than just having a long lever to, say, pry loose a boulder. Cultivating internal energy involves developing an explosive nervous system as a conduit for chi. You can achieve this through the unique principle of dropping (introduced in chapter 2 and detailed within the context of guided chaos in chapter 6). "Chi?" you ask. "Isn't that the supernatural force you see in movies that can hit people without physical contact?" Let's look at this concept more closely.

Chi and Combat

There are many intriguing accounts of the much-sought-after phenomenon of projecting chi outside your body without actual physical contact as a source of self-defense. Even though decades of day-long meditation may or may not actually make this possible, this expectation continues to foster the image of being able to develop superhuman powers with an average body. This only adds to the mystery, confusion, and eventual frustration over how to make ordinary self-defense work for you without getting caught up in the illusion of becoming a Jedi warrior overnight. You may think no one could be quite this gullible, but this expectation lives in many dedicated tai chi practitioners as a longed-for end result of their training. However, there is a danger in pining for the long-term development of an almost unattainable weapon when the short-term prospect of taking your life in your hands could be a much closer reality.

Since we've never seen a demonstration of chi projection outside of video games (and some of us have spent large sums of money in China looking for it; see p. 76), we can only speak of chi as it has been defined in other classic literature and experienced by us. Chi is not a myth. Nor is it mystical. The simplest definition of chi is "life energy." In classic Chinese literature, this energy can take many fascinating forms, which we won't go into here. For self-defense purposes, let's simply call it "internally applied grace and balance." A close reading of classic Chinese texts will yield a definition that can be understood in a firm, scientific light. The *T'ai Chi Boxing Chronicle* by Kuo Lien-Ying (1994 Berkely CA, North Atlantic Books) defines chi as the "circulating point of finesse within the body" (p. vi). What's unclear in the English translation is that chi is not some indefinable, supernatural force (although it can appear so); it's merely a code word for describing multiple, simultaneous attributes. Even the English word *finesse* can be hard to define. But don't worry; you won't need a crystal ball to get it. We define chi in terms of guided chaos as the constant powerful interaction between your ever-changing center of gravity, root, and contact point with the enemy, aided by looseness, body unity, and heightened sensitivity. (This is also close to the definition of proprioception, explained later).

Diligently practicing and applying all the principles of guided chaos will develop chi in you to the extent that others will not understand how you're doing what you're doing to them.

Another classic analogy for the flow of energy, or chi, through a unified body is to visualize your tendons and bones as a garden hose with water rushing through them. If the joints or muscles are not loosely, gracefully, and mechanically aligned, the hose becomes kinked, and the water does not flow. When you apply body unity to the definition of chi as a circulating point of finesse, you can see that this implies that chi also embodies automatic physical awareness and skill—awareness of your own body's position and movement as well as your opponent's—a phenomenon known as proprioception. This kinesthetic awareness requires a foundation of balance and sensitivity, which you will learn to develop in upcoming chapters.

Where is this rushing water, or chi, supposed to come from? It comes from a relaxed, unified body that knows how to react instantly to outside force. Outside force generated by your attacker should compress your whole body like a spring, provoking a reaction: an absorbing, yielding, and collecting of energy on the side of your body in contact with your opponent, and an explosive, steel spring–like releasing of the accumulated energy on the opposite (striking) side. When you're balanced, some part of your body will be rooting the energy (absorbing the energy in your feet like a coiled spring), and another body part—the hand, elbow, or other foot—will be delivering it.

Viewed from the outside, unified body movement is often undetectable because it might involve only internal energy changes or slight muscle and joint realignments. As you move toward mastery of this methodology, your large body movements and circular

> Body unity does not mean body rigidity. Effective, combative body unity requires the ability to change direction effortlessly and instantaneously while maintaining looseness. You cannot respond to change if all your force is stiffly committed to one direction. Think organically, not mechanically. Think tidal wave, not Tin Man.

In Search of Chi Projection

A group of John Perkins' friends spent thousands of dollars on a trip to China where they were invited by a particular school to witness a demonstration of authentic chi projection. When they finally met with the masters of this school, they were told they could not have chi projection demonstrated on them because it would kill them. The masters performed great pushing and throwing techniques, but not one would demonstrate chi projection.

redirections of strikes will become more and more economical. The sensation of body unity becomes obvious only to you or the person you are hitting. At this point, the energy is truly internal, and you may seem to move hardly at all. This occurs, for example, when some part of your body (like an elbow) is in contact with your opponent's trunk. Using dropping energy and body unity, you can achieve (with apologies to Bruce Lee's 1-inch punch) a no-inch punch, which can either send your attacker flying or cause internal damage, depending on how you deliver it. And this is with no winding up. To summarize, when you move to strike, your opponent should always feel as if he or she's getting hit with an object that weighs at least as much as your entire body, even if it's only your finger.

There is a more common term for body unity—grace. When a person moves with grace, he or she epitomizes coordination, finesse, balance, power, and body unity all coming together as one. In fact, maybe we could call grace a mystical Western principle!

Body Unity Drills

We need to be clear here: Having great muscular strength is always an advantage, but only if it's used properly. When fighters rely solely on muscle, they tend to destroy body unity, and thus power delivery becomes more and more inefficient. The goal is to apply full muscular power explosively and only for a millisecond in the same direction and at the precise apex of shifting body unity guided by sensitivity and aided by gravity. This prevents you from becoming overcommitted and unbalanced in any attack. Muscular strength is the icing on the cake and not the cake itself. If you don't understand what we're saying here, don't worry. This incredibly important concept will become completely clear after finishing part II.

In order to rearrange your priorities, body unity drills focus on training you to move with the intent of driving a thousand pounds with nothing but alignment and the barest application of muscle. In other words, you train by positioning your body to overcome that degree of resistance, but you actually use only enough muscular strength to move the weight of your own flesh. Why? Because you want to avoid the tightness that comes from straining. As you learned in chapter 3, you need to remain loose enough to react instantly to a change in your attacker's energy so that you can take advantage of your superior body position and amplify your opponent's energy to use against him.

Enhance body unity when striking by training so that when your knee stops bending (when dropping or stepping), your hand stops moving. This prevents you from leaning or overcommitting and ensures full body mass behind every strike. Another way to enhance body unity is to experience every strike you deliver as pressure building in your feet.

Body Writing

Many beginners have a lot of trouble understanding the concept of looseness combined with body unity. They wave their arms around as if they were disembodied serpents or the robot from *Lost in Space*. This exercise may help you begin to feel what body unity is.

1. Stand facing a wall and raise your arm as if to write on a blackboard (if you've got a real blackboard, use it).
2. With your right hand, sign your name in big letters at least 3 feet (.9 m) high. Notice your wrist and elbow do all the work.

3. Now do it again, but this time, lock your wrist, arm, elbow, and shoulder so they are absolutely immobile. So how are you supposed to write? By stepping, sinking, and turning your body from the waist down, you actually write with your legs.

4. Do the same thing with your other hand.

5. Repeat this drill, writing the whole alphabet, until you can achieve the same fluidity in your body writing as you have writing the normal way.

Granted, body unity should also involve free movement of your hand, wrist, elbow, and shoulder, but most people can do this anyway. It's the foot, leg, hip, waist, trunk, and back involvement that eludes most beginners. That's why it's helpful to do this drill, writing the whole alphabet, until you can achieve the same fluidity as you'd have writing the normal way.

TALES OF CHI
John Perkins

While teaching in a New York City school in 1980, I saw a demonstration given by a group of Japanese martial artists who claimed some amazing powers. I observed one practitioner kicking to the throats of three others, who were kneeling, without inflicting injury. I thought there must be something in the way the kick was performed and absorbed that would be significant. The problem arose when these practitioners stated that no one could hurt them because they had covered themselves with a protective shield of energy. Although they did not specifically call this energy chi, this was the implication. Demonstrations such as this are typical of those who claim to have supernatural chi. I then requested if I could simply poke each of the kneeling men in the trachea with my index finger. They looked at me with contempt but would not allow an "unbeliever" to try it out. Later, when I engaged in some not-so-gentle kumite (free sparring), I found them susceptible to being thrown, pushed, and struck.

I'm not saying that chi flow or iron-shirt techniques don't exist. In fact, I've seen ordinary people struck many times with bludgeons (including blackjacks and nightsticks) and have even broken my own heavyweight police baton over a few heads without stopping the attackers. I have seen other authentic demonstrations, but they have always involved some kind of absorption of energy. I have also seen many fakers, who used tricks analogous to those used in professional wrestling.

Yes, the professional boxer or highly skilled martial arts practitioner can toughen his or her body to what seems a supernatural degree. But as far as projecting a shield of energy around the body, all I can say is, try this acid test: Ask the claimant if he would allow you to poke him in the eye. See if he can bounce your finger off with pure energy.

Starting the Mower

This drill involves visualization of another common movement. It requires you to follow the principle of positioning your body to do 1,000 pounds (454 kg) of work with none of the exertion.

1. Imagine you're starting the world's most stubborn lawn mower. Without using any strength or tension, stand with your feet wide, bend your knees, turn, reach deeply to your left or right, and loosely grab the mower's starter cord. Keep your head and back relatively perpendicular to the ground. Turn as far as you can, shifting your weight to your forward leg (figure 4.1a on p. 78).

2. Moving slowly and loosely, breathing deeply, begin to pull until you have shifted all your weight to your rear leg. Your elbow should be behind you and your pulling hand should be near your shoulder (figure 4.1b).

Figure 4.1

3. Slowly reverse the movement, pushing the cord back to its source, while aligning your body as if the recalcitrant mower cord is pushing against your hand. Try to become aware of every joint used and feel how to align the bones for the most power.

4. Repeat several times, moving as slowly as possible with no muscular tension. This is not an isometric exercise, however, so don't flex while doing it. The trick is to train your legs and back to do all the work. Remember that your entire body starts and finishes the motion at the same time, so if your hand is still moving at the completion of the move, you're not unitized.

As you get more advanced, do a 100 percent weight shift from leg to leg so that at each end you're able to raise the unweighted foot off the ground and balance on the other one. Do this smoothly with no hitching or further movement. You want to be able to get 100 percent of your body mass shifting from root to root; each time you shift, balance effortlessly on your root, poised for complete and total release of your power into a new, balanced root at the slightest provocation.

Opening the Door

No, this is not some mysterious drill from the Twilight Zone. Anytime you open a door and walk through it, you have an opportunity to practice body unity. This works best on spring-loaded doors that close on their own.

1. When you open a door, don't lean or stretch to reach the knob. Walk up to it so that your arm, elbow, and shoulder remain in a low, relaxed position.

2. When you reach for the knob, don't yank with the biceps or shoulder. Step away from the door and rotate your body and feet to generate the necessary torque so you use only minimal finger strength to hold it (pull with your legs, not your hand). If you examine

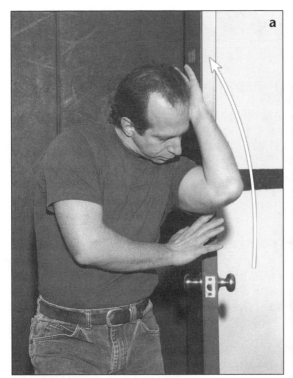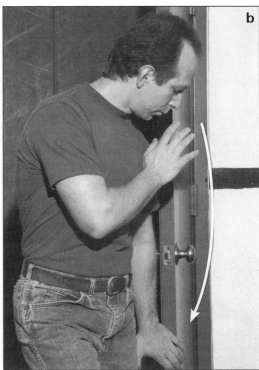

Figure 4.2

this motion, with the exception of your hand position, you'll see that we're asking you to move with the same mechanics you'd use if the door weighed 500 pounds (227 kg).

3. As you walk through the door, stay as close to it as possible. Release your arm and swing it through, yielding your upper body so the door won't touch any part of you.

4. As you swing your arm through, bring it up at the same time in an answer-the-phone motion to keep the door off you, yet whisker close (figure 4.2*a*).

5. The phone-answering motion should transition in one smooth movement into a reverse rocker (discussed in detail in chapter 9, p. 186) with your elbow or fingertips until you're clear of the door (figure 4.2*b*). Your fingertips should touch the door as lightly as a feather. This movement acts as a check to be sure the door (or an attacker's strike) is clear or, at least, not about to swing back on you. You can do this slowly to accentuate the feeling of powering the door with your whole body or at normal speed.

Free-Form Body Unity

This is a prelude to the **Polishing the Sphere drill in chapter 6.**

1. Stand in front of a full-length mirror.

2. Start by slowly moving your palm in front of you side to side. Do this by shifting your weight from leg to leg, similar to body writing.

3. Continue to move slowly while moving your palm anywhere and everywhere: up, down, diagonally, in, out, and behind you. Move your entire body with your hand no matter how small the movement; don't just wave your hand around. You may step anywhere necessary to accomplish this but try to do one other thing along with it: Wherever your hand goes, make sure you are always behind it. In other words, visualize that there is an enemy out there, and you always want to keep your palm between you and the enemy. This will be further explained later on under Moving Behind a Guard.

Unitized Long-Stepping

It helps while doing this exercise to visualize all of the following and use whatever works for you (depending on how old you are!): Groucho Marx running with a cigar, Mr. Natural striding down the road, or Olympic speed skater Apolo Anton Ohno burning up the ice. What we want you to do is practice walking slowly with long, balanced strides such that each step pauses briefly in the air before angling outward slightly and powerfully driving out the next step. Your head should be down and your back bent determinedly as if each turbocharged stride could pull a tractor or blast you through a brick wall. Simultaneously, swing your arms powerfully high in front and behind you to augment your steps, left arm forward with the right leg and vice versa. Get your back and shoulders into the motion. You should look like a videotape slow-mo of Ohno going for the gold.

Puppeteering

This drill teaches you to unitize **your** hands **and feet** and to hit as if you can feel your feet in your hands. It also increases balance and the ability to strike freely with hand/foot combinations simultaneously. (Note: this is different from the puppeteering concept described in chapter 9.)

1. Imagine there is a magic string connected from your right hand to your right foot. Raise your right hand and pull your foot into the air, balancing on your left and bending the knee. The foot movement should be exactly proportional to the hand movement (figure 4.3*a*).
2. Move the hand (and string and foot) up and down, side to side, and in circles. Do both tiny and large sweeping movements.
3. Repeat with the left hand and foot.
4. Transfer the imaginary string back to the right hand but keep the connection to the left foot. This subtly changes the way the foot responds to the hand rising, falling, and circling (figure 4.3*b*). Switch hands and feet.
5. Move the hand behind your back so that now the connected foot rises, circles, and moves to the rear (figure 4.3*c*). Switch hands and feet.
6. Perform all these with your eyes closed.

Figure 4.3

What you will rapidly begin to feel is a powerful, instinctive connection between your hands and feet so that you can chop and step or chop and kick with full body unity. This drill also helps you learn to change the striking angle and step or kick appropriately with lightning speed. This overcomes the common tendency to fight with sluggish, plodding footwork, using only arm power.

ELEVATOR ATTACK

Picture yourself traveling up in a freight elevator about 7 feet by 8 feet (about 2 by 2.4 m). You are with two well-dressed men. You are carrying a briefcase. Suddenly one of the men hits the emergency button while the other turns toward you with his right hand reaching behind his back. The man who has turned toward you now steps in your direction with his head slightly down and his eyes focused on you.

What is your next step?

a. Ask them what's going on.
b. Grab for your handgun or folding knife.
c. Step back with your briefcase raised to protect your face.
d. Step off line and attack the man approaching you using your briefcase as a shield.

The answer is *d*. Since the elevator was stopped for no apparent reason by one of the men, you should be ready for something out of the ordinary. The fact that the second man turned toward you with his hand behind him and stepped in your direction should have set off your alarm bells.

If you chose *b*, you most likely would not have had time to pull your weapon and prevent being stabbed or slashed repeatedly.

If you chose *a*, you might have been lucky enough to find out that these were salesmen who wanted to sell you some sharp knives and have a captive audience.

If you chose *c* you may have kept your face protected at the cost of stabs to various other body parts.

This experience actually happened to one of our students. Luckily, he attacked the attacker. The man approaching had a knife as did the first man, the one who had pushed the stop button. Our student stepped off line, sprang off the door of the elevator, and drop-kicked the approaching man. The student did not stop there. As the button man went into action, our student stopped him with a dropping side kick that struck above the knee. He next went into a hell-evator frenzy, using the walls as reinforcement and ricocheting from man to man with kicks, palm heels, chops, punches, and elbows. As soon as the student was able to get out of the elevator, he called the police. The emergency personnel who treated the two men thought that our student had hit them with a baseball bat—he had done that much damage.

Preventing Common Mistakes

➤ While performing body writing or any other body unity drills, the object is not to move your whole body together as one rigid object, like a statue. Instead, move your body as one unit in the same loose way the entire length of a whip lends its power to the snap of its tip.

➤ Starting the mower is not a muscular tension exercise like Sanchin kata. Remember, move with the intent of driving 1,000 pounds (454 kg) but without the exertion.

CHAPTER FIVE

BALANCE, ROOTING, AND FOOTWORK

When most people think of balance, they might imagine a tightrope walker or something similar. This type of balance is one-dimensional. The rope is always the balance point. In a fight, your balance point is always changing. Your foot positions move constantly, or you may be against a wall, on one knee, or on your back (yes, you still have to be balanced, even on your back), but even this is not the only kind of balance we're going to be talking about or having you practice.

Body unity and looseness are both fundamental components of balance because they help you develop grace as well as the ability to deliver tremendous energy by loosely controlling your body's mass. In guided chaos, we're not talking about developing everyday balance; rather, we're talking about hyperbalance, balance on steroids, balance that is fundamentally different in two unique ways:

1. It's dynamic. You can attack and defend in body positions and angles that other people just don't have because they don't learn and practice them. You can't train hyperbalance with a fixed drill or static exercise because all fights are chaotic; any attempt to adopt a stance, form, or technique under duress will meet with catastrophe. This is a fact, as explained in the introduction, that is confirmed by police reports (and by anyone, for that matter, who's been in a fight for his or her life). Balance must be dynamic.

2. It's cumulative. You must first feel a sense of balance in each part of your body in order to then get each part to act collectively in a powerful manner. Imagine each bone as a scale, or better yet, as a seesaw. If your attacker pushes down on one end of your forearm, let's say the hand, the other end of the forearm (the elbow) should swing up and hit the attacker in the jaw. The elbow's power is augmented by all the other bones in your body through body unity. Thus, balance also refers to the position of each bone in relation to the position of every other bone. It also refers to the ability of each bone (and the heavy, connected flesh) to deliver its delicately balanced momentum to each succeeding bone in turn.

To understand this further, imagine every one of your bones as a sledgehammer, finely balanced on the end of every other bone and connected by ball bearings like a big chain.

The ball bearings are all the joints in your fingers, hands, wrists, upper and lower arms, shoulders, every vertebra in your back, and every joint in your hips and legs. Your job is to whip them so that their individual momentum is cumulative, like a big wave. When the bones move counter to each other, there's no body unity, and those movements detract from the total amount of momentum, even if they're all loose. It would be like five people grabbing a whip at different points along its length and attempting to snap their individual sections with force.

With the progressive drills provided in this chapter, you will train your body to balance so that every part of it is counterbalanced and influenced by every other part, so that if one part moves, even the slightest bit, every other part moves also. For example, think about when you pass through a subway turnstile. If you walk through one slowly, the other side simultaneously rotates behind you. If you were to *run* through, the back side would whip around and smack you in the rear violently. This is also a simple example of yin and yang energy transformation. Briefly, yin and yang are two Chinese Taoist terms that define opposite energy states (e.g., hard and soft, or attacking and yielding). The side of the turnstile that moves away when you hit it is receiving energy and is thus in a yin state. The part of the turnstile that swings around and hits you in the rear is transmitting energy and is thus in a yang state. Understand that the balanced looseness of a turnstile happens in a single horizontal plane. Your joints are infinitely more mobile, moving in directions multiplied geometrically by all your other joints and by how each one influences the other. Now you can see why we talked so much about internal energy in the previous chapter: Balance is the axle that the wheel of internal energy turns around; external energy actually disrupts the individual and collective balance of your bones by committing you to rigid, full-force unidirectional movement.

When your body has momentum, it has latent energy without the input of muscular force. Guided chaos makes extensive use of this. But to generate momentum and get it to go where you want, you have to be both balanced and loose. The total momentum of a guided chaos strike will come from the weight of all the flesh and bones in motion, not from a continuous muscular contraction. This allows for two different kinds of loose, powerful strikes:

1. Whipping strikes. When used correctly, a whip conducts its energy instantly from the handle to the tip, where energy is amplified and focused. The tip can cut like a knife or smash like a wrecking ball depending on how it's delivered and how much mass it has. This occurs even though every other point of the whip's length is totally soft and flexible. If the whip strikes a solid object, like an iron pipe, the whip merely wraps around it. Every point of its length has a balanced energy relationship with every other, like a visible sine wave. This whipping motion is also perfectly suited for the human body.

2. Jackhammer strikes. In addition to circular whipping blows, balance and body unity can manifest in loose, linear, pile-driver-like strikes. As explained in chapter 4, having a relaxed body allows you to drive from your feet through your hands with uninhibited power. This is why each bone must be balanced in relation to every other bone. If the bones are not lined up, however, energy will be frittered away into space. Whipping and jackhammer strikes will both be augmented by dropping energy (chapter 6, p. 109).

> Balance acts as the axis between soft and hard, strike and yield, push and pull, and attack and defend, allowing for one to flow into the other with no discernible interruption, so one becomes indistinguishable from the other.

Your Balance Foundation

In guided chaos, you're going to be moving your body's mass so dynamically to avoid and deliver strikes that without hyperbalance you'd be spending half your time on your backside. To keep your balance, you must move your body mass around your center of gravity so it's constantly counterbalanced. No matter how you bend and gyrate, if you can move a compensating amount of mass in the opposite direction from the part of your body that's avoiding a strike so that your center of gravity remains directly above one or both feet, you will remain balanced.

For example, if your chest collapses to absorb a blow (see Yielding, Looseness, and Pocketing, p. 53), the target area moves outside your center of gravity. But because you're

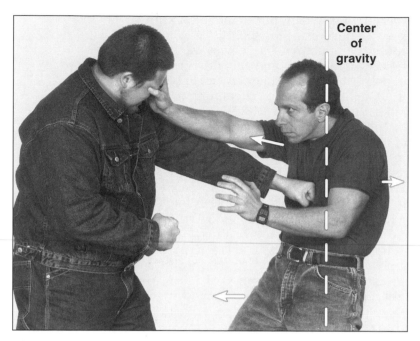

Figure 5.1

still balanced, it's possible to deliver a counterattack at the same time you're avoiding the attack. To remain balanced, your knees, hips, and shoulders need to compensate by bending forward (figure 5.1). This keeps your center of gravity in the same place and maintains your rooted connection to the ground (see the following section).

Rooting Your Feet

When we say rooting, we simply mean your body's completely relaxed, dead weight sinking into and balancing on one or both feet (with no leaning or bouncing). Rooting provides your body a firm foundation from which to fight. However, firm does not mean rigid. Even if you are standing completely still, the feeling you want in your body is one of complete liquid relaxation, like a buoy bobbing in the ocean. Even small waves are subtly flowed with. When large waves develop, you ride them and let them drive you into reciprocal action. Thus, rooting is never static. This is true whether you're balancing on one or both feet. You need to develop the dynamic, surefooted balance of a cat, so that no matter which way you're pushed or thrown, you always land on your feet in a pliable, balanced, and stable root from which to launch your attack.

Rooting can take two forms, and it's vital to understand and incorporate both of them. One is 50–50 or neutral balance and the other is single-leg balance. The idea of 50–50 refers to splitting your weight equally between your feet. This does not mean that you stand like a statue or doggedly maintain a stance under duress. Rather, you want to develop the sensation of taking incoming pressure from one or more attackers and sending it down deep into the ground at a point equidistant between your feet. Rather than loading up or leaning on one leg against an aggressor, try to maintain this 50–50 sensation so both legs compress against *each other* and focus the force down into a midway point in the ground beneath your center of gravity. Bend your knees and sink or screw your mass down into this center focal point and begin to load and coil your body like a spring. You can then explode and twist around this point, throwing the attacker with the rebounded force of his own incoming energy.

Do not interpret this fixed, two-legged root as an excuse for practicing rigid immobility. Rather, your body pegs, compresses, and releases like a trapped mongoose in a mere microsecond, with both feet rooted to the ground. This principle is especially useful when trapped between multiple, in-pressing attackers, where essentially the energy from one person is balanced and reflected against a second person, compressed into the ground via the 50–50 root, and then released into a third person. Again, note that if you try this with one leg loading more weight than the other, your root will collapse. By maintaining the 50–50 distribution and loading one foot against the other, you can absorb and redirect tremendous amounts of force. Also, do not confuse this with the classic error tai chi describes as being double weighted (explained elsewhere in this book). When you're double weighted, you're compressed force has nowhere else to go. This is true of many styles' two-footed, immovable roots. In guided chaos, however, energy is extremely volatile and always channeled and released instantaneously, even from a two-footed root.

The other type of rooting we call single-leg balance; it is just as critical to your understanding of guided chaos as 50–50 rooting. Although at first blush the principles may seem contradictory, they are in fact interrelated for two reasons:

1. They both involve loading and releasing energy instantaneously, like a pressure cooker, in accordance with yin and yang principles (more on this later).
2. Because they both redirect energy, they render your own root invisible to the opponent. This is why we say you want to develop a root that can't be found (more on this later). When you use one or the other depends on the situation and what you are feeling from the attacker. If you have neither the time nor the space to step out of the way, the 50–50 balance principle is a way of loading and releasing power while remaining unavailable to the enemy. If you have space to step, however, single-leg balance allows you to compress and uncork even more power.

In the constantly changing dynamics of a fight, if your weight ever sits in both your feet, it is only for a split second. This also applies as you step, gyrate, and contort your body to avoid or deliver strikes because you are coiling or loading your energy plyometrically onto one leg so you can explode and deliver onto the other leg. You will learn to compensate for your extreme looseness by gyrating, twisting, and writhing like a mongoose while balancing on one leg (which can instantly change to the other if needed) but without leaning, posing, or rising onto your heels or toes—all of which destroy balance and power.

Creating a Root That Can't Be Found

The type of root you must develop in guided chaos is quite different from what is typical in most martial arts, and it affects your footwork and how you step. What is interesting to note is that rooting and footwork are often properly developed in sports such as tennis and football, where power and mobility are paramount, but their expression in many martial systems is overstylized and rigid in order to fit some romanticized notion of fighting. Watch a tennis pro's feet as he anticipates the direction of his opponent's serve: He will move his feet and entire body mass wherever he needs as fast as he needs to deliver a powerful return with every body-unitized fiber of his being. He instantaneously plants his feet, drops his weight, and plyometrically explodes into whatever new position he needs to line up every joint of his body for the next shot.

What we mean by a root that can't be found is that your balance and thus your stepping become invisible and undetectable to your opponent, yet rock solid and totally mobile, fluid, and adaptable to you. You want to be able to fully plant your weight and plyometric body unity into one or both legs, yet never become stuck or overcommitted so that you can't step. By plyometric we mean engaging the full, elastic tension of the muscles and tendons, encouraging their natural reflexive rebounding nature that is expressed in the fright reaction and especially in dropping energy, which we get into later in the book. For now, what we mean by plyometric rooting is continually catching the rebound from shifts in your body's balance brought on by offensive and defensive movements and instantaneously pegging your weight into the ground. We say this so you don't make the following extremely common mistakes:

1. Planting both feet like a statue and thinking that you can weather any attack if you just stay glued to the ground
2. Bouncing around on the balls of your feet in a poor imitation of a boxer

In the first instance, you must learn that no matter how strong you are, there's always someone stronger. If you train in the myth that through certain exercises you can become immovable, you are actually setting up your nervous system for disaster. Try this: Plant yourself with your knees bent and your weight split evenly between your feet. Then, have an obviously stronger person walk quickly into you, pushing hard. If you try to stay rooted to the spot on both feet, you will easily become unbalanced and be driven backward. This may be a little disconcerting but remember that the pusher also has the benefit of momentum. This is the self-limiting byproduct of concentrating on developing one root split between both feet. Remember in part I of this book where we said that anyone (even smaller people), whether under the influence of drugs or extreme adrenaline, can become insanely powerful for brief periods, long enough to blow you off your feet or even tear the fingers off your hands? You can see it is always in your interest to develop a mobile root.

However, do not fall into the trap of mistake 2. To illustrate what happens if you fall into this trap, bounce around on your feet like a poor caricature of Muhammad Ali, throwing punches at your opponent within typical boxing range. Without warning, have your opponent dive on you like a middle linebacker. You will either be blown back stumbling or knocked off your feet. Not only can your opponent not find your root—you can't find it either! This is for the simple reason that you have none.

In order to develop the correct balance of rooting and moving, you first have to fully understand the limits of a static, two-legged root. What follows is a very simplified version of a more advanced contact flow exercise explained later in the book.

Practicing Fixed-Step Rooting

Stand facing your partner with your left feet either just touching or about a foot (30 cm) apart (depending on your reach). Make sure both your bodies are fully accessible to each other. While remaining in contact with each other's hands or arms, slowly strike or push each other. You can either slowly strike toward each other's bodies or attempt to push the other's arms or trunk, but never lose contact with your partner's skin. You can change the point of contact by sliding or replacing (for example, exchanging your hand for an elbow, triceps, or shoulder). This may have some similarity to simplified tai chi push hands or even sumo. The goal here, however, is not to win but to fully explore the limits of your balance. What you specifically want to see is how far you can completely transfer your total body weight from the forward to the rear leg and back again without stepping or losing your balance. Try to firmly but slowly unbalance each other by shifting completely to the front foot without lifting your rear foot. Flow with and avoid these attempts by fully shifting onto your rear foot, again without raising or moving your front foot. If you can retreat on one vector and then loosen, twist, pocket, and enter on another vector so that you can elude his pushes and drive him back, all the better. Stay low and do not rise.

As you get better, instead of pushing harder, experiment with getting sneakier so you can get progressively lighter. Feel his balance points and coax him into pushing when perhaps he should be yielding or pulling. Then reverse the energy and unbalance him. You will find that pushing harder actually over-commits you and disrupts your sensitivity and balance. This is a precursor to the discussion in the Sensitivity chapter coming later, but for now, the idea is to be able to recognize the slightest change in your partner's direction and pressure and allow it to motivate complete and total weight redistribution.

By engaging in this exercise frequently, you avoid the errors of standing rooted on both legs like a statue or bouncing around with no root at all. You will also begin to develop adaptability in your looseness and body unity but only within this limited context of forward and back weight shifting. This is critically important but do not become enamored of it. To truly develop a root that can't be found, you must also develop extreme single-leg balance and the ability to find and move to an infinite number of root points. The following drills do just that. But first, consider these key points.

Bending Your Knees

Bend your knees at all times. Since the knees are attached to the largest muscles in the body (the thighs), your knees must properly return energy without buckling, yet remain springy. The bend must be natural to allow for freedom of movement. In other words, don't use excessively low classical or posed stances that compromise your stability in any way (you martial artists know which ones we mean). If the stance wouldn't work for a National Football League middle linebacker or a professional tennis player, it won't work for you in a real or potential bloodbath. In the advanced version of some of these exercises, exaggerated low postures are used solely to develop strength and balance and are not fighting forms.

Once the fight begins, the amount of knee bend can vary. When you're under zero pressure, always return to neutral. As you turn your body, keep your knees pressing

"Let your body remain as supple as a blade of grass, yet as rooted as an oak." You may have heard this martial art maxim before—and it's true. Except that in guided chaos, the oak tree can walk and re-root in an instant.

inward slightly. Your stance becomes weak when one knee bends out farther than the stance requires. This also makes the knee susceptible to injury and attack. Moreover, the straight leg, prevalent in many styles of martial arts, is a mechanically poor position and a bad habit to fall into. Not only does it take away from your ability to balance yourself, but it also puts your leg in a position where it can be easily broken.

Balancing Your Breathing

Breathe deep into the belly through your nose using your diaphragm muscle (located under your rib cage). Your stomach should expand outward as you inhale. Breathing high in the chest (chest breathing) tends to raise your center of gravity, disrupting your balance. Chest breathing also neurologically increases your tension and anxiety.

Balancing Your Posture

Balance your posture so your bones are aligned. Your posture should not resemble a West Point cadet's, but rather an upright ape's. Your arms, when raised, should assume a relaxed, sunken position with the elbows down, as if you were riding a Harley Davidson motorcycle (figure 5.2).

Figure 5.2

Balance Drills

These exercises may seem unusual, but they share principals with many established fighting styles, including tai chi, bagua and Native American fighting arts. Nevertheless they are totally unique.

Ninja Walk

1. Stand with either foot forward, hands up in a relaxed fighting position, with your knees bent, elbows down and relaxed, back straight, and head up.

2. Slowly redistribute 99 percent of your weight over your forward leg, just enough to balance on it, yet keep your rear foot flat and barely on the floor (figure 5.3a on p. 88).

3. Keep your rear leg relatively straight and the foot flat. Point only the big toe of your rear leg up in the air without changing the angle of your foot. This will force you to keep your rear foot flat as you perform the following: Raise your entire body by straightening your supporting (front) leg, as if you were doing a one-legged squat. This one-legged squatting action will bring your rear foot off the ground an eighth of an inch. The purpose of raising the toe of the rear foot first is to make sure you come off the ground with a flat foot (i.e., parallel to the ground and without benefit of a heel-toe push off). Do this at an extremely slow speed. Do not raise your rear foot off the ground by merely curling your rear leg's knee. For the moment, your rear knee should actually remain fairly straight (figure 5.3b).

4. Once your rear foot is off the floor, bend your rear knee and point the toe of the raised foot toward the ground.

5. Tap slowly and lightly on the ground behind you twice with your toe. However, don't tap by straightening the knee of your rear leg. Rather, maintain the bend in the knee as it is. You will reach the floor with your toe by lowering your entire body as you perform a one-legged squat with your front leg (figure 5.3c). Don't cheat on this, or you'll defeat the whole purpose of the exercise. Depending on how low you are, the burn in your thighs can be tremendous. You can make this harder by bending the knee of the tapping leg more and maintaining that bend as your supporting leg's knee bends,

Figure 5.3

raising and lowering your entire body. Since the tapping leg's knee is bent more, your supporting leg's knee must bend more for the tapping foot to reach the ground.

6. Slowly bring the tapping leg forward and tap lightly two times on the ground in front of you with your heel. Be sure you're tapping by sinking and squatting down on your supporting leg. Do not bend the tapping leg's knee independently to make the foot reach the ground (figure 5.3d).

7. After slowly tapping twice with the heel in front of you, flatten the tapping foot and slowly place it on the ground. Slowly redistribute your weight so that 99 percent of it is on the new supporting leg. Do not rush this or throw yourself onto the new leg or you will completely defeat the exercise.

8. As before, slowly raise your entire body with your new supporting leg so that your rear leg comes off the ground with the foot flat and parallel to the ground without any kind of toe push off.

9. Repeat this process over and over in the same fashion, alternating legs so you are "walking" forward. One complete cycle should take no less than 40 seconds—the slower, the better. The key with this drill is not to build up forward momentum, where you could propel yourself from one step to another by pushing off your toes, but rather to slowly place each foot down, so you create the maximum stress, challenging your balance as you tap and change supporting legs.

Vacuum Walk

By doing this walk correctly, you **develop tremen**dous balance in areas where most people don't, and you will begin to glide low and powerfully across the ground like a cat. The Ninja Walk and the Vacuum Walk drills develop and strengthen the small stabilizing muscles in the hips necessary for powerful but subtle weight shifts that occur during a fight as you constantly struggle to regain your balance and step to your new root points on uncertain ground. This walk is vital for developing a root that can't be found as well as the rooted, one-legged, instant balance essential to dropping into awkward positions and redirecting kicks or delivering multiple counterkicks, Rockette style.

1. Begin with steps 1 through 3 of the ninja walk described previously.

2. Once again, raise your rear foot parallel to the floor. Remember—do not raise this foot independently. Don't bring the foot near the ground merely by bending and unbending the knee of the leg that is in the air.

3. While bending the knee of your supporting leg even farther so that your whole body sinks lower, bring your rear foot alongside the front, supporting foot but do not put it on the ground. While doing this, maintain the bottom of the foot at an eighth of an inch (less than 1 cm) above the ground and parallel to it (figure 5.4*a*).

4. From there, circle your raised leg from the front to the rear in the shape of an outward crescent, keeping the foot no more than an eighth of an inch off the ground at all times, as if you were vacuuming the floor.

5. Keep the entire bottom of the foot parallel to the floor, no matter where it moves. This requires you to constantly change the angle of your ankle as well as the bend in your supporting knee.

6. The slower you do all the movements, the better. Each foot circle should take no less than three seconds and should be no less than 2 feet (.6 m) in diameter (figure 5.4*b*).

7. Circle the leg slowly twice, then place it silently on the ground in front of you, redistributing all your weight onto that leg.

8. Repeat this process with your other leg. Continue to do this so you are slowly "walking" forward (or backward if you choose).

Completing the foot circles forces you to be sensitive to the surface of the ground as if you were battling in the dark or on uneven terrain. The leg muscle isolation strengthens your lower body, while your upper body stays loose. If you are doing this honestly, you won't be able to perform the vacuum walk drill for more than a few minutes. Here are a few more reminders:

- Keep your back straight and don't lean.
- Keep your head and hands up and in fighting position.
- Breathe slowly, deep into your belly.

Figure 5.4

Advanced Ninja and Vacuum Walks

You can increase the difficulty of the vacuum walk by doing the following:

- Lower your supporting leg and bend the knee of your circling leg so you have to sink your whole body further down to keep your foot an eighth of an inch (less than 1 cm) off the ground.

- Do both walks slowly up and down stairs (when doing the vacuum walk, circle your leg behind you to avoid hitting the step in front of you).
- Do the walks outdoors on large rocks with your eyes closed. The best place for this is in a dry streambed or along a rocky shoreline. Alternatively, you can try them on an old, round-rung ladder laid on the ground. Try using various parts of your foot to balance on (heel, midsole, ball of the foot). The ultimate challenge would be to use the ladder with your eyes closed. The mental concentration and muscular control required are considerable, but the development of your fighting root and stability will accelerate quickly. Try adding the Ninja and Vacuum walks to the end position of other exercises, such as Turning, Swimming, Solo Circle Flow, Rolling the Ball, and Starting the Mower. This ensures that each turn, cord pull, or stroke has a complete body-unitized weight shift and root transfer.

Crazy Walk

Now perform the Ninja and Vacuum walks together while purposely stepping to the oddest and most challenging positions possible. This is where you really begin to amplify the circuitry in your nervous system and increase your adaptability and versatility—the two primary objectives of guided chaos that prepare you for dealing with the random insanity of real violence. Remember: No real fight looks pretty.

Step deeply in front, behind, or to your side with your foot twisted in as difficult an angle as possible, including across the other leg. The key is to place the foot on the floor in its final position without twisting or sliding it once it's in contact with the ground. Continue to slowly and completely transfer and then isolate your balance onto the new leg; then s-l-o-w-l-y perform the squatting movement to raise and lower your body as you tap or circle your foot while you're in these bizarre positions. The burn in your thigh, hip, and back muscles will be intense.

Over the years, we have found that when students conscientiously perform just these exercises five minutes a day for a year, they will effectively develop superior balance and root equal to what might be achieved after 10 years of doing the tai chi form. This is because you're specifically working on the attributes the form is designed to develop, without spending years perfecting the exact movements, and you increase your adaptability by never stepping in fixed patterns. When you combine the walks with Polishing the Sphere (p. 131) and other random-flow drills described later, you teach your nervous system to be balanced as it becomes comfortable with spontaneous movement.

Guided Chaos Form

The name is actually an inside joke because guided chaos *has* no forms. This is merely a drill to improve your balance and body unity, though the uninitiated may think it somehow defines the art. Perform all the movements excruciatingly slow and you will develop extraordinary strength and balance.

1. Stand on your left foot with your right knee held high. Simultaneously send out a slow right front kick and a right chop to an imagined attacker's throat. They should both move in unison. Your left hand should be by your face to ward off strikes.
2. Without putting the right foot down, bring it and the right hand back to the starting position with the knee held high and then extend both for a simultaneous right roundhouse kick and right chop.
3. Retract both without putting the foot down and then do a right-side kick and right chop combo.
4. Retract both without putting the foot down and then do a right-back kick and right chop combo.

5. Retract both without putting the foot down and then do a right-back kick and double front palm strike combo. Rock forward so that your trunk is parallel to the ground and you look like a figure skater. This really challenges your balance and by now your legs are getting pretty shaky.

6. As you pull your legs and arms back in, go right into a high-forward right-knee smash (but sink on your left leg) as if pulling the enemy's head into the knee.

7. Without putting the foot down first, step forward, land, and deliver a right chop with the left hand protecting the face. Sink as you chop. This is the first time you have put the right foot on the ground.

8. Turning your waist and sinking a little deeper, throw out a left palm heel to the head with your right hand now guarding your face.

9. Rise up on your right foot with your left knee held high and do the entire sequence with left hand and foot combinations. Continue back and forth until tired. Breathe deeply and exhale on every strike. Visualize crushing the enemy. If you want be a complete psycho, combine with the following drill.

Wood Surfing

The benefits of doing this drill daily for a few minutes are substantial. You build up tremendous strength and sensitivity in all the tiny foot and lower leg muscles. At the same time, you form new neural connections in the motor reflex areas of your brain, raising awareness of your center of gravity.

1. Find a board, preferably a two-by-four, cut to a length a little wider than the width of your shoulders.

2. Make the board unstable. There are a million methods. The simplest is to wad up duct tape into balls and tape them to the bottom of each end of the board. A more elegant solution is to nail on strips of garden hose. You get the picture.

3. Stand on the board with your feet about shoulder-width apart; work to balance yourself without falling off. This is similar to Canadian log rolling.

4. If you feel yourself losing your balance, just step off the board. In this way, you teach yourself to step to a new root point without struggling excessively. Struggling can be a fatal tendency in classical training: A practitioner will strain to maintain his stance even after his balance is shot. You need to learn how to flow smoothly to a new balance point.

5. Try slowly turning at the waist, staying low, until your stability is compromised.

6. Twist the other way.

7. Try this while doing the Swimming, Solo Circle Flow, Ninja Walk, and Small Circle Dance drills from chapter 3, among others (figure 5.5).

8. Next, position the board 2 to 3 feet (.6 to .9 m) away from a pole or tree and slowly perform random anywhere strikes (chapter 2). Do them on one leg.

Figure 5.5

9. Vacuum and crazy walk on the board. Try the walks with your eyes closed while swimming.

There are even harder drills you can do while wood surfing that you will read about in chapter 7. For now, while balancing, visualize attack and avoidance as you move with your anywhere strikes. You should push the envelope with your twisting and writhing to hypersensitize your balance.

Box Step

This drill develops the box step, a key movement principle of guided chaos. With it, you develop a feel for your body's equilibrium while in motion; you learn to move your entire body in a balanced, coordinated manner, without retreating, leaning, or hopping, or without crossing your feet. The box step helps you elude attacks, stay close, and get behind the attacker. In guided chaos, feeling where your body is and how it's balanced is more important than adopting a stance or technique. This drill will train you to land positioned, balanced, and ready to strike, with no extra movement, especially in the dark and against multiple opponents. For a real-life example of how the training principles of balance and kinesthetic awareness can aid you in a fight for your life, see the Williams Brothers' Attack (p. 101).

1. Mark out a box on the ground, roughly 3 feet by 3 feet (.9 m square).
2. Stand in an L-shaped stance, with the heel of your right (forward) foot in one corner of the box and the left (rear) foot behind it and outside the box at about a 90-degree angle to the right foot (figure 5.6a).
3. From there, step with your rear foot clockwise to another corner of the box, landing in an L but with your left foot forward.
4. Continue stepping to a new corner with your rear foot, which, when it lands, becomes the new forward foot. You always step in the direction of the rear foot. If your right foot is forward, stepping with your rear (left) foot to the corner on your left is the easiest. A little tougher is stepping with your rear foot to the corner directly across the box. This requires you to turn 180 degrees in the air clockwise and land facing in the direction from which you came (figure 5.6b). Most difficult is bringing your rear (left) foot all the way to the corner of the box directly to your right. This means you have to turn your body 270 degrees in the air clockwise (figure 5.6c). With all these movements, you never cross your feet, and you never step behind yourself.
5. Continue to do this drill back and forth in both directions, stepping to any corner at random without pause.

If you feel your weight is off when you land, you are off balance, and you need to adjust in the air. This will present a challenge with the more difficult steps. To get your feet to land properly without twisting, you will have to get your hips moving early while you're still in the air.

Keep in mind the importance of how you step.

- When you step to your new position, don't hop or jump. Glide softly and smoothly, like a cat hugging the ground (or like Groucho Marx).
- Rise as little as possible, as if at the apex of your step you might hit your head on a very low ceiling.
- Be careful not to lean too far back or too far forward when landing in your new position.
- When you land, be sure your feet are in the final L-stance before each makes contact with the ground so you don't have to readjust or twist either foot in any way.
- Land the new front foot smack in the middle of the new corner.

 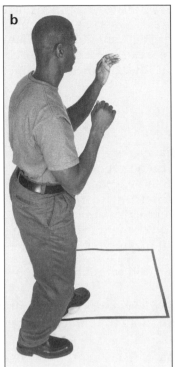 

Figure 5.6

This is the simplest way to do the box step. Once you are able to land without making a sound and can get your entire body balanced and positioned without readjustment at each corner, you can begin to add some of the following drills. These drills will also apply to sensitivity and other guided chaos principles, which you will learn about in later chapters.

Free-Striking Box Step

Perform the box drill, but each time you land, throw a strike. This drill trains you to land balanced and ready to throw a strike, and then immediately go into the next box step.

1. Begin with low kicks, such as short front kicks, roundhouses, side-kicks, knee kicks, whatever. The type of kick is not important.

2. Try the kicks using either your front or rear leg as soon as you land. This will require you to be in the dead center of your equilibrium; otherwise you'll lean, fall, and have no power.

3. If you do this drill with a few partners, each of them can be positioned outside a corner of the box with his or her own kicking shield, which you will kick after each box step (figure 5.7). Your partners will step in toward you from the opposite corners with their shields.

4. Try this using upper body strikes. Remember, the type of strike is unimportant, but you should try everything you can think of. Refer back to the Anywhere Strikes drills (I, II, and III) in chapter 2 (pp. 37-39) if you need some ideas.

5. Try this exercise holding light weights or a baseball bat. Using a sledgehammer is a real challenge.

Figure 5.7

An important principle related to this drill particularly and balance in general is containing the over-travel. To prevent overcommitment and loss of balance, strikes and kicks in guided chaos are delivered in such a away as to reflect and recycle the energy back to your root, where it can circle or snap back out plyometrically into another blow. This requires dropping (fully explained in chapter 6) and proper rooting and balance.

Battle-Ax Box Step

This drill purposely challenges your balance while teaching you not to tighten up on grabs (which is itself a unique concept; see chapter 9). The goal of this drill is to work up from a heavy stick to a sledgehammer. The key to handling a heavy sledgehammer like a paperweight is in flowing with its momentum, rather than fighting it. This way, you make gravity and inertia your allies. This is a process of self-discovery, however; no one can teach it to you. When you get it, the application to empty-handed fighting is obvious and powerful. It means you have mastered body unity as it applies to balance.

1. Perform the Box Step drill without pausing between steps. As soon as you land, begin a new step.

2. As you box-step, use a heavy stick, swinging it slowly above your head one revolution per step (figure 5.8*a*). Hold the end of the stick in both hands with the least amount of tension necessary.

3. Once you get good at this, begin using a sledgehammer. This will take some practice. First, center and balance your body with the added weight. Second, keep your hand and arm relaxed while you hold the handle. Ultimately, you should be able to hold

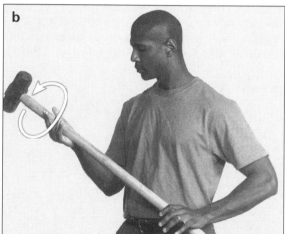

Figure 5.8

the sledgehammer with only the thumb and index finger of one hand. Third, generate the power to move the sledgehammer with the momentum of your body, not your muscles. To do so, you must also gently catch the hammer's motion between each step before changing the direction of the circular swing with your new step, without tightening up or throwing yourself off balance. Do this by imagining that the sledgehammer is a baby that's fallen out of a window.

4. During moments of weightlessness and transition between landings, try twirling the sledgehammer along its axis in your hand (figure 5.8*b*), spearing the hammer with either the handle or the head (figure 5.8*c*). Release and take up the slack by letting the hammer handle slide through your hand as you extend it. Let its momentum carry it just to the end of the handle until, like a relaxed pendulum, you swing it back and box-step to a new position.

5. Perform this drill for 5 to 10 minutes every few days to reap its benefits.

The Battle-Ax Box Step drill develops relaxation in your hands and power in your body; it gets you to step around and closer to your opponent to take his space (see Taking Your Opponent's Space, chapter 7) while avoiding being hit. With this drill you are obviously training for the largest possible moves. In reality, and when doing contact flow, all that may be necessary to gain a better entry angle or avoid strikes are tiny 1-inch (2.5 cm) box steps. But you will certainly develop tremendous unitized power no matter what their size. The box step also helps generate momentum for striking as a yielding response to pressure. How this applies to fighting will become clearer when you learn about sensitivity in chapter 6.

Whirling Dervish Box Step

The motion practiced in this drill is excellent for splitting multiple attackers if you're surrounded or for getting past your current attacker to the one behind you.

1. Box-step continuously so that you are whirling without pause, moving forward like a spinning running back in football, avoiding tacklers.

2. Strike as you turn, using your motion to augment the blows. For example, assume you're in a right lead. As you begin to box-step to the right by bringing your left foot forward, your right arm chops like a helicopter blade to the right while your left arm palm-heels straight forward.

3. As you continue to spin, this chop–palm strike combination is used every time you face in the direction of your forward movement (figure 5.9).

4. Don't make the mistake of moving high on your toes, like a twirling ballerina. When you spin, land, and strike, your body should feel mobile but heavy, like a tumbling boulder crushing trees as it rolls. Your arms stay loose, like flexible steel whips or lawnmower blades.

Try this exercise on uneven, rocky, or slippery terrain. Fights rarely take place on favorable ground, so training on flat dojo floors is deceiving because such surfaces don't challenge your balance. Indoors, you can tune up your balance by doing this drill over platforms such as those used in aerobic step training. Then, do the drill with your eyes closed. How do you keep from stumbling over obstacles? Practice. The battlefield is no different. Keep in mind that all your movements should be free, loose, relaxed, and heavy.

Figure 5.9

Footwork Drills

Now that you have become familiar with the sensation of complete body-unitized weight and root transfer, it is time to increase the versatility. Remember we said in the fixed-step rooting drill that you need to become aware of your personal balance, looseness, and weight-shifting limits while attacking and yielding within the confines of a fixed position—and then take them to the max. After much practice, the fixed-step rooting drill should almost look as if you're doing a Ninja Walk back and forth but without the tapping—in the sense that you achieve a decisive and purposeful 100 percent weight transfer from foot to foot so that the other foot is weightless. This has unbelievable benefits for increasing your power.

And now here is the paradox: After all your work developing a powerful, two-pointed root, we are now going to teach you to abandon it. The last thing we want you to do is fall in love with this new skill. The seductive tendency to just stay put in your front-to-back or side-to-side position is extremely dangerous because you never know who you're dealing with. You want to be able to have maximum power and weight shift not only in a fixed position, but in any position moving anywhere. The laws of physics dictate that the more you move mass, the more momentum you will have, even if it's just a tiny step. The fixed-step rooting drill was to maximize your power and elusiveness if for some reason you could not find room to move or step. It's also the prescription for people who have no balance, looseness, or body unity whatsoever. (For the ultimate in developing power without winding up, chambering, or even barely moving, see information on dropping energy in chapter 6.)

The following drills provide a systematic methodology for getting reluctant feet to move so that you will be able to use the same energy you developed in earlier drills but with even greater power and adaptability. These footwork drills have distinct patterns to get you comfortable with every kind of stepping you might encounter. But do not fall in love with them either. Once you get in the habit of stepping from anywhere to anywhere with full, body-unitized power, you will abandon them also. You would come back to them if your spontaneous footwork began to lose its body unity.

Rooted Multidirectional Step

This drill is really an offshoot of the Vacuum Walk, in that you keep all your weight on the rooted foot while the unweighted foot moves to the front, side, and back, barely tapping the floor.

1. As you root over your leg, keep your center of gravity over the center of your rooted foot.
2. Sink your weight, keeping the knee slightly bent over the rooted foot while controlling your balance.
3. As you become more proficient, start adding strikes as you move your foot. By not associating any particular strike with any particular step, you achieve the same kind of "split-brain" coordination developed in the Air Writing exercise (page 71). Start anywhere and begin to move the foot from the center and out to the front, back, or side, then back to the center, then out in another direction, and so on.

Key points: Keep the foot flat to the ground and resist the temptation to slide. You should be able to pick the foot up each time and place it on the ground. Start slowly and gradually increase your speed.

What you are doing in this and all the footwork drills is learning to load your coiled energy while balancing for a split second on one foot as your other foot probes for a new and superior root point, unfelt by the opponent. You then completely shift to this new root point, but again, only for a split second. The change in foot position may be large or a mere micro-adjustment. What you will find as you begin experimenting with contact flow later, is that the smallest root change can make an enormous difference in your ability to deliver strikes—or avoid them—unimpeded. Often, you will discover that a 1-inch (2.5 cm) foot reposition allows you to insert a strike that would've been impossible before. This may seem amazing, but subtlety creates a tremendous number of opportunities that are always missed when you rely on gross external muscular exertion, where it seems that all you can do is hit and retract. This is a key principle behind having a root that can't be found. Because you are so thoroughly developing your single-leg balance, the attacker will not perceive you subtly changing the angle of your attack or defense until it's too late.

Switch Feet

1. Begin with your right foot forward and your left foot back in a right lead boxing position.
2. Place your right foot alongside the left and then immediately step the left foot into the forward position so you are in a left lead.
3. Immediately place your left foot back alongside the right and then immediately step the right forward so you are again in a right lead.
4. Repeat the sequence continuously for two minutes, increasing your speed.

You might ask, "What is my weight distribution in these drills?" The answer is that every time you step, for a microsecond it is 100 percent on the new root—and then abandoned for the next. You never hang out or overcommit. You never leave your foot "in the bucket" (refer back to the rocket step). Your root is pegged, plyometrically spring-loaded—and then abandoned, depending on what you sense from the opponent.

Key points: The transition should be smooth, and there should be no hopping to the new root point. As you progress with this drill, you will want to add kicking to develop your balance. As you step, your feet must come off the ground. You should never pivot or slide on your feet, nor should you hop since this tends to raise your center of gravity too high, causing you to lose balance. Do not hitch, twist, or slide the foot in the slightest when preparing to step; be sure the foot is in its final position the instant it lands, also without any twisting or sliding. If you have to correct your foot position or angle while it's in contact with the ground, you will lose all benefits. The entire change of body and foot position is performed in the air so that you land silently, like a cat.

Box-Step Over the Line

In this exercise, you will be stepping laterally over an imaginary line while switching leads.

1. Begin with a left lead, then step with your right (rear) foot into a new lead but laterally across the line. Almost simultaneously step or leap with the formally front (left) foot laterally across the line into the rear position. The movement here is identical to what you have already done with the box step in that for a microsecond both feet are in the air.
2. Without pause, step or leap with the left (rear) foot laterally over the line and forward into a new left lead while almost simultaneously bringing the right foot laterally over the line into the rear position.
3. Repeat continuously for two minutes.

Stepping Over the Line

In this exercise, step backward and forward over an imaginary line with no pause while maintaining your lead. The motion is somewhat like a fencer's. After two minutes, switch your lead.

Stepping Off-Line Drill

In this drill, you step forward but at an oblique angle of about a 45 degrees to the right while maintaining your right lead. After a few of these switch leads. The fundamental key offensive and defensive movement of guided chaos is always to move in but at an angle to your opponent in order to throw a monkey wrench into his attack. This drill reinforces the attack the attacker principle outlined in part I. If you train to step back or to the side in any manner that moves you away from your attacker, he or she will eventually run you down. With all these drills, the intent is to get you used to stepping to a new position that is even closer to the attacker yet off line from the direction of the incoming strike.

Circle Box Step

In this drill, you maintain your lead but essentially step further to the side with your rear leg than with your front, essentially circling your attacker like a matador, keeping him or her in front of you. With a left lead, move your front foot just a few inches to the left while your right foot arcs behind to the left 12 inches (30 cm) or more. Typically, this movement would be accompanied by left horizontal chops to the throat, one for each step. From this position, you would never perform a regular step to the right since you would presumably be walking into the attacker's strength. To change leads, box step with your right (rear) foot to a forward position on the other side of your attacker's incoming force; continue playing the matador, making small adjustments to the right with the right lead foot and larger ones to the right with the rear (left) foot.

Hackey-Sack

This is another one of those bizarro drills that nevertheless yields amazing results in terms of balance and adaptability. What you're basically going to do is play ping-pong between your hands and feet. This drill becomes very free form, so don't get too caught up with the sequence we're about to describe once you get the idea.

1. Lift your right leg high enough in front of you so you can tap your toes with your outstretched right hand. Do the same with your left foot and hand.
2. Repeat with the left hand to right foot, then right hand to left foot.
3. Raise your right foot up obliquely so that the heel comes toward your crotch and tap the heel with your right hand. Do the same on the left side and then switch hands and feet as before.
4. Raise your right heel behind you toward your back, tapping it with your right hand. Do the same on the left and then repeat, switching hands and feet as before.
5. Now it gets crazy. Every time you raise your heel up and tap, swing it to the opposite position and tap again with the other hand before putting the foot down. For example, if your right heel comes up toward your crotch, tap it with the left hand, swing the heel out toward your side, and tap it with the right hand, and then place it down. Do the same with your heel coming up behind you: Swing it out and tap it with one hand, then immediately swing it in, tapping it with the other hand. Then try going directly from front to rear taps and vice versa without pausing.
6. At this point, you should be kicking, tapping, swinging quickly and freely, and looking like a mad hackey-sacker (this won't be the last drill that'll have onlookers staring!). Perform all this free form without pause while doing random box steps or Whirling Dervish box steps. What you are building is a synaptic familiarity with chaotic yet unitized movement: Your hands and feet are synchronized to move and hit as one in the midst of mayhem.

Guided Chaos Kicking

Although the close combat kicking described in chapter 2 is very nasty, it is merely a small component of guided chaos kicking methodology. This is because close combat kicking primarily addresses crude offensive aspects of kicking and defending against assaults. If, however, you are fighting someone who is also a skilled kicker (street or classically trained), you'll need to flow immediately into a guided chaos approach without thought. This is why we've saved this information for now. One thing you need to know is that if you are in love with spinning-wheel kicks and other flashy maneuvers, you'll be in for a rude awakening on the street.

In general, the same guided chaos principles that apply to the hands apply to the legs once contact is made. This will make far more sense after you have read, understood, and practiced contact flow in chapter 6. The reason we have placed the kicking section here is so you can see it all within the context of footwork. The difference is that you're not in a position to stick with your legs unless you are very close and kicking or responding to being kicked. Here's where your Vacuum Walk, Hackey-Sack, and Puppeteering drills apply. You can probe, stick, pulse, redirect, or tool destroy with your legs the same as with your arms (all these terms will be explained later). The Ninja Walk (p. 87) develops the one-legged balance required for multiple kicks. You can long step into the enemy's stance between his legs and disrupt his balance, sweeping out his legs with vacuuming. You can bend your knee into your opponent's back or side by rising on the toes of the bending leg. You can do a Mexican Hat Dance (p. 41) and smash your opponent's feet and shins. You can shove out your hip or backside to knock your opponent off balance and then throat strike.

When you're out of range and the opponent kicks, it shows your opponent is either inept or not serious, so simply walk away carefully. If you're out of range and need to move closer because you can't escape, follow his kick instantly, as if you're glued to it, and attack to smother any further kicks. You may get hit anyway, but it's better than staying outside in the ideal range for a long-distance kicker, such as a taekwondo expert. If your opponent jumps backward as if sparring, you should also jump back (if you can't get in on time) or run away. Force your opponent to charge you if he means business. When he does, jump toward him and stomp-step and drop-kick to the groin, while unleashing a barrage of full-power palm heels, eye gouges, and chops to the head and neck. This rapid-fire combination of stomping, low kicking, and palm heels sort of resembles a goose-stepping World War II German soldier (an unfortunate analogy). The enemy will be hard-pressed to get off any long kicks.

If you're already in range of a kick, take your opponent's space. Never give a good kicker what he wants: a cooperative target. He'll kick your head off if you stay outside. Most people hate to fight nose to nose, where our methodology gets the nastiest. Stomp his toes and crush his shins (you should be able to do this without looking down to see where his foot is). If your opponent is jammed, the kicking tool is eliminated. Jamming kicks with your knee rather than with your foot is more efficient because the knee is harder to turn aside and is closer to your center of gravity than the foot. It's also harder to get your foot into play when you're close, since it has farther to travel to intercept an attacker's kick.

At longer range you can also destroy his kick but always train using your shoes to make contact. Unless you're a lifelong Muay Thai fighter who's deadened his shins black by slamming tree trunks all day, your boots make the superior contact surface for all legwork.

Deliver the kick with no setting up, rising, or chambering of the knee. Simply shoot the foot out in a relaxed, low trajectory, straight from the floor. You will get it there faster. With a sturdy shoe on, that's all that matters. If you have a split second, drop-kick while stepping in but off line slightly. Another approach if you're in kicking range is simply to kick immediately. No matter what kick your attacker uses, kick straight ahead into the groin area. Notice the simplicity: He kicks with his leg, and his leg is attached to his pelvis. No matter what part of you he aims at, the base of his kick comes from the same, now-unguarded point of origin.

If he round-kicks, you'll hit his groin first and short-circuit his kick (figure 5.10*a*). Same for an ax, crescent, or side kick. If he tries a spinning kick, you'll hit him in the butt, knocking him down. If he tries a front kick, you'll intercept it. Now, all the principles you've studied come into play: While sticking loosely to his leg with your foot, using your body's mass and balance rather than your muscle, guide his leg to a new root point for yourself, either outside or inside (figure 5.10*b*). This is almost always a bad place for the opponent, since his root, if he ever had one, is committed to his kick. If you deny him a place to land, he is likely to stumble. Worse, since his supporting leg is unprotected and his balance disturbed, you have the opportunity to break his leg with yours by dropping and driving your knee into the back of his leg, sweeping his leg out with a motion similar to the vacuum walk, and stepping on his Achilles tendon. If your groin kick intercepts his kick but glances off without sticking, continue through (see Skimming Energy, chapter 6) and attack the supporting leg. When intercepting or kicking his shins, use multihitting and ricocheting principles. Your relaxed knee loosely but powerfully swings your foot into his leg. Your foot then bounces off and hits the same or a different spot on the same or different leg multiple times. You can do this with or without bouncing your kicking foot off the floor. You can also use your hip and backside as sticking and pulsing tools. You can also front heel kick his shins or knees with your knee pointed either in or outwards (notice the similarity to the Hackey Sack drill).

By adding dropping energy, you increase the delivery speed of your kicks. If you're a downhill skier, you know that down-unweighting creates the fastest type of turn By instantly dropping your weight (as if your knees were trying to beat your feet in a race to the floor), you can shoot out a close-range kick to the shins with no chambering, stepping, hopping, telegraphing, or any other kind of preparation.

This gives you a precious millisecond's advantage. Moreover, you can fire the kick with either leg, weight bearing or not. This is because your body becomes weightless when you drop. Accordingly, you can rapid-fire one dropkick after another, since no chamber is necessary. When you drop-kick on the supporting leg, you catch yourself by falling into the other or both legs. When you drop-kick on the non-weight-bearing leg, you can catch yourself by falling into either or both legs. Try these variations against a pole or low, heavy bag. Once again, the dropkick is an incredibly fast, highly effective close-range kick that you can do in the context of the Mexican Hat Dance.

It is vitally important to experiment with all of these while doing contact flow (coming up in chapter 6).

Figure 5.10

THE WILLIAMS BROTHERS' ATTACK

John Perkins

No match in a ring or martial arts school is as deadly as real-life armed and unarmed murder attempts by one or more would-be street assassins. Nearly all attacks on police officers are potentially lethal. Anyone who would attack a person in uniform, knowing beforehand that he or she has a weapon, has to be at least slightly psychotic. Anytime a grown person assaults another person in the real world, you should consider it an attempted execution. Why? Because you don't know what's in the mind of a stranger or mob that wants to do you harm. Will the attacker stop at the point of rendering you unconscious or maiming or paralyzing you? Will the attacker stop only when you're dead? If you are a police officer armed with a handgun, any fight you lose could be your last. When you're down, your assailant could take your weapon and finish you. When you're in the ring, even though there's a tiny chance you could be maimed, paralyzed, or killed, the combatants are known. There are referees, doctors, spectators, and most important, rules.

I was walking foot patrol one weekday evening. I had just finished my glass check, where I had looked over all the churches, schools, and stores for broken glass or any other signs of forced entry. I usually did this in the middle of my tour and again at the end. It was a summer night, and people were out enjoying the weather. However, some blocks in the commercial area were deserted. As I passed a gas station that was closed for the night, I noticed the outline of a man that seemed to disappear into the shadow of the building. I followed, tracking him by sound only because it was too dark to see. I had no time for my eyes to adjust to the darkness.

As I got a few feet into the rear of the garage, I could still hear the man I was following. Then, out of nowhere, I suddenly saw stars. I had been struck from behind with a terrific concussive force, and my head was thrown forward until it slammed into the wall of the garage. I fought to maintain consciousness, and as I did, the strangest thing seemed to happen: Heavy sandbags were being dropped on top of me from above with crushing force, and I couldn't get away. Then I realized that the sandbags were actually men jumping down on top of me. I didn't know how many there were, but I knew I might be killed.

I later found out that they had jumped off the back of a flatbed truck, which was parked in the rear. Their eyes had had time to adjust to the dark, but mine hadn't. Of course, I know now that you should never follow someone into the dark, even if the person isn't aware of your presence. You might surprise a gang of five and have them attack you all at once. Later, I puzzled over why these men would continue to attack me so brutally instead of just hitting and running. Most thieves usually take off when a cop arrives on the scene. These guys were hell-bent on destroying me.

They were all dropping on me, and I was getting pummeled from all directions in the dark. Luckily, at that time I knew how to yield with punches, and even back then, I had the rudiments of what was to become the box step and contact flow programmed inside me. My balance training came into play in the biggest way. My gun was unavailable to me at this point, due to the retention device I used and the barrage of blows I had to contend with. Under the worst conditions, in the dark on uncertain ground, with an unknown number of attackers coming from all directions, it was my ability to retain my balance with full body unity and looseness in the midst of chaos that kept me from going down.

My return attack was explosive and devastating. I struck outward with palm-heel, hammer-fist, and side-of-hand strikes (the Whirling Dervish Box Step); at the same time, I began stomping blindly and with full force (the Mexican Hat Dance). This seemed to free up my left side so I could get to my nightstick. As I drew the stick with my left hand from the ring on the left side of my gun belt, I remembered to grab it in an underhand position so I could strike with the tip of the handle as I drew it straight upward and forward. This first blow hit pay dirt. I felt the impact as it caught one of the attackers solidly in the jaw. Once I had gotten my nightstick into action, I was able to hit with more power.

(continued)

The Williams Brothers' Attack, *continued*

If I hadn't already been used to getting hit and yielding prior to this melee, that first kick to the back of my head would have been the beginning of the end. Maybe they would've been merciful and just left me there, but my survival response was in full swing, and swing, swing, swing is what I did with the nightstick (the Battle-Ax Box Step).

Training took over when the assailants seemed to rain down from the sky. I remembered to flow with the blows and made myself a moving target by swaying and striking all at once. Dropping my weight also saved me at the onset of the attack. By dropping into my blows and stomping my feet, I kept my balance and my footing, and I attacked simultaneously. It was fortuitous that I had known how to hit with my bare hands hard enough so I could finally get to my night stick. I was also lucky that only one of the assailants had a weapon. This was a wrench about a foot long, but I don't think he was able to hit me solidly with it because there was such ferocious and wild movement in all directions. He also may have been afraid he would hit one of his accomplices.

As I was delivering mostly two-handed jabs and butt strikes with my stick, I was perplexed as to why these guys kept on attacking. I knew they were getting seriously injured, but they just kept at me. I finally finished off the last attacker with a blow to the nose with the side of my stick. My eyesight was getting sharper, and when I finally took out my flashlight, I could see the mess around me. The groaning was loud. I couldn't believe I had been able to hold onto my stick with all the blood on it. The solution to the mystery as to why they never ran off after ambushing me was that three of them were brothers, and the other three were friends. They weren't about to leave someone behind.

Preventing Common Mistakes

➤ Don't lean while Ninja walking and vacuum walking. Keep your head up.

➤ Don't tap the floor in the Ninja Walk by bending the knee of your tapping leg. Rather, raise and lower your whole body by bending your supporting leg as if doing a one-legged squat. As your rear foot comes off the ground, be sure it is absolutely flat to prevent cheating and using a toe push off as a crutch.

➤ Don't hop while box stepping. Glide.

➤ Don't twist your foot into position when you land in the box step. It should already be in its final position relative to the floor.

CHAPTER SIX

SENSITIVITY

Sensitivity, looseness, body unity, and balance are the "big four" of our guided chaos methodology. They all work together to produce the devastating fifth principle: combat adaptability. But aside from the other important subprinciples in this book, if even one of the prime four is missing from the mix, you have nothing. Although we've mentioned sensitivity before, we've held off explaining it completely until now because the depth and power of this principle would be meaningless without first understanding the other three. It is also the prime mover of all the other principles.

Sensitivity is the ability to detect and create changes in energy, whether in type, amount, or direction, and to do so without conscious thought. This requires using a part of your brain and nervous system that you never have to think about. Something that is actually faster and more sensitive than eye–hand coordination: your sense of touch.

As you probably know, eye–hand coordination is the skill you use to whack a baseball, catch a pass, or block a punch. In terms of response time in an attack, however, it's too slow. What are we talking about? For the answer, we need to conduct a little experiment.

Get into a traditional boxer's stance, with your hands up and about 6 to 12 inches (15.2 to 30.5 cm) apart. Have your training partner pick a mutually agreed-on spot on your chest that he will try to touch. Your job is to block him. Your partner should stand the same distance away that he would be if he were sparring with you. He, of course, should move as fast as possible to touch that spot, and you should move as quickly as you can to block it (figure 6.1 on p. 104).

Guess what? Even though you know where he's going, if he's reasonably fast, you will never block him, try as you might. This is because eye–hand coordination requires your thinking brain to calculate the interception, a process that is way too slow for life and death combat. Our point here is that any form of fighting that relies on eye–hand coordination exclusively for self-defense is at an inherent disadvantage. Think about this carefully. This includes almost all styles of fighting (especially sparring) that rely on distance, space, and visual timing; however, there are some notable exceptions. The following styles have a distinct fighting advantage because they all, to some greater or lesser degree, address the subject of sensitivity: wrestling, wing chun, judo, aikido, ultimate fighting, and the tactile, internal "soft" martial arts styles such as tai chi, bagua, hsing I, and guided chaos. All these styles involve constant, close physical contact with the opponent. The difference is that in guided chaos, we place far greater importance on developing sensitivity from the very beginning.

Figure 6.1

Sensing Energy

Our focus in this book is on fighting to save your life, not gladiator nonsense. This may dictate some notable philosophical alterations in your self-defense strategy. It also bodes well for maintaining a personal philosophy of nonviolence. Why? Because unless you're cornered, if you have enough space to spar, you have enough space to run. Typically, if your attacker stays at a sparring distance, he's not really serious about hurting you. If your attacker backs up, you back up—and leave the area. Real mayhem begins only when you are in close physical contact with your attacker. This is where most of the damage is dished out and, coincidentally, where most traditional training breaks down.

This is because in a controlled environment like sparring or boxing, there are rules that govern the action. Strikes come at a cadence of one, retract, one, retract, and so on. Even in a flurry, each strike is separate from the one before and the one after. Strikes to the back of the head are prohibited. And how do most flurries end? With a clinch. Then the fight stops. This is not reality.

Let's return to the previous experiment but with a slight modification. Set up like before, only this time, gently rest your fingertips on your partner's hands, as if you were playing an expensive piano. Close your eyes; take a slow, deep breath; and try to completely relax your muscles. Clear your mind and think of nothing. All you want to do is react to the slightest change in pressure against your fingertips and nothing else. You might think, *This is ridiculous. What fight looks like this?* But consider the fact that no real fight begins, nobody hurts anybody, until the opponents actually make skin contact. Until you reach that point, running away is your first and best option. When both of you come close enough so that with arms fully extended you touch only at the fingertips, tactile sensitivity begins (note that this is also the beginning of your personal comfort zone and sphere of influence).

Now, moving as explosively as possible, have your partner again try to touch the spot on your chest while you attempt to block him. Keep your eyes closed. (What? You've never been attacked in the dark?) With practice, if you can relax enough, you'll find that your partner can't do it, not even once. With your eyes open it's not even close.

No amount of practice will enable you to stop an attacker at close range if you break off tactile contact and rely solely on eye–hand coordination. Why? The attacker is always one step ahead of you in terms of nerve impulses. When you use tactile sensitivity, however, you're relying on your sense of touch, which is hardwired into the primitive centers of your brain. You're bypassing the whole eye–hand coordination system wherein you see the punch, the image is sent to your brain, and your higher brain processes it, calculates an interception angle, and sends a signal to your muscles to carry out the defense. With tactile sensitivity, you react at a gross animal level, the same way a cat responds to danger or your eyelids respond to dust (sounds like the fright reaction again, doesn't it?) There's no reactive middleman. This is what you're going to exploit, develop, and amplify for self-defense.

Tactile Sensitivity and Sticking

In guided chaos, tactile sensitivity is concerned with achieving constant contact, or sticking, with your opponent with any part of your body that stands between your opponent's strike and its intended target. This could be almost anywhere, depending on the situation. Regardless, you never lose contact with your opponent. Your skin will become your eyes. This contact should be feather-light pressure at the beginner level, progressing through body hair sensitivity, to body heat or even energy field sensitivity at the master level.

We make the point of saying any part of your body because different styles of fighting may use different reference points of contact exclusively. In wing chun and tai chi, the reference points tend to be the hands, wrists, and forearms. Wrestlers have an advantage because they're used to sticking with their entire bodies. They have developed a certain level of sensitivity over their whole skin surface. Similarly, in guided chaos, we believe the entire body is the battleground, so we teach from the beginning that the contact reference points are anywhere on the body. The big difference between wrestling and guided chaos, however, is in how we respond to pressure.

The Disengagement Principle

In wrestling, most training is focused on overpowering, controlling, and submitting your opponent. Even though the best wrestlers have developed an elusive, slippery quality, their primary objective is still to pin the other fighter. In guided chaos, by contrast, we stress sensitivity and loose, balanced responsiveness over your entire body in order to be both unavailable and unavoidable. Delivering crushing strikes is paramount. Everything else is of less importance. With increasing sensitivity, you actually react subconsciously to your opponent's intentions of movement before he moves because his energy precedes him. How do you do this? By attempting a paradox: You want to be as disengaged as possible from your opponent, yet still be engaged.

We call this the disengagement principle. You stay as close to an attacker as you can without actually exerting any pressure. Like radar, you only maintain sufficient contact to know where he is, where he's going, and where you are in relation to him. That's it. When you become extremely sensitive, the enemy appears on your radar screen while you disappear from his. When an attacker strikes, he should never reach you, but when he retreats, he can never get away from you. You are flowing with him, following his every move, while you simultaneously mount your attacks. There's a great advantage to this.

When you are involved in a death match with someone twice your strength, you will fail if you attempt to engage the attacker, that is, to match his or her strength. No matter how strong you are, there's always someone stronger. This is true whether you can do 200 knuckle push-ups or break two bricks in the air. When you attempt to overpower a stronger opponent, your antagonistic muscles come into play; you become rigid, hard, and inflexible, and you are likely to be crushed or snapped like a dry twig. In addition, by resisting forcefully, you actually present your opponent with a road map of your intentions. If you attempt this strategy with an experienced grappler, you are actually playing into his game and giving him exactly what he wants: a handle with which to control you. With sensitivity, you're playing a different game. He can't grapple what's not there, especially while being hit in the eyes and throat. This is evidenced even in the untrained. As any cop will tell you, it is extremely difficult (not to mention dangerous) to cuff an unwilling, adrenaline-fueled psychopath. This person will writhe and twist out of your grasp like an enraged mongoose, often requiring five or more backup officers to pile on to get control. You see videos of this all the time on YouTube.

You want to stick—but not get stuck. You stick barely enough to sense your opponent's intentions, but lightly enough to avoid entanglement or grappling. If you grapple, you're stuck.

What Sensitivity Feels Like

To survive the onslaught of a more powerful opponent, you need to be so light, soft, flexible, and sensitive that to your opponent, you feel like a phantom or a cloud, dissolving like the liquid-metal Terminator, materializing only for the millisecond needed for your strike's impact. You should be like a wet dishrag that is soft and malleable until it's whipped and snapped. At the point of impact, the formerly limp dishrag takes on the solidity of steel and the sharpness of a knife.

To use a different analogy, you should feel to your opponent as if all your limbs are made of steel springs, connected by ball bearings and lubricated with super silicon. When your opponent exerts the slightest pressure on you, you disappear yet remain in contact no matter how he or she moves. This is the defensive aspect of extreme sensitivity, but don't interpret it as an admonition to be passive. When you hit, you feel like a tire iron, but when you absorb an attack, you feel like a turnstile. The opponent should feel as if he has fallen into a Cuisinart or a pinball machine rigged with knives and sledgehammers. At the same time, you never oppose your opponent's energy: Neither you nor your opponent should feel any resistance at any time (except when you pulse, which we'll explain later in this chapter). He basically gets sucked into every shot.

Or think of yourself as a block of ice thrown at the enemy. He can either move the ice, shatter his arm, or shatter the ice. Now, take that block of ice and replace it with a bucket of water and throw *that* at the enemy. His job is to block all the water. The result, of course, is that he gets soaked. How do you block water? Liquids merely seek the path of least resistance. A bonus is that water has both offensive and defensive attributes: It mindlessly slips through obstacles to attack, and it effortlessly sticks to your opponent's skin, following his or her every move and avoiding harm by virtue of its malleability.

Sensitivity and the disengagement principle offer you an alternative beyond yielding (see chapter 3). When you become supersensitive, you can let the opponent's energy slide right past you while still maintaining contact. This is analogous to a farmer trying to catch a greased pig. The instant your hands (or any other sticking surfaces of your body) sense an increase in incoming force, they simply let the offending limb slip by. By keeping your body loose and yielding, you ensure that the target won't be there when the strike arrives. Meanwhile, your hands are still in contact with your opponent's arms, but further up and closer in. This offers an opportunity to move in to yet a closer reference point on your opponent's body or to strike.

Comparing a fight to skiing down a mogul-filled trail that's as steep as a wall at 20 miles per hour (32.2 km per hour) can help you grasp the need for the sensitivity principle. If you've skied moguls, you know it can feel like being a passenger in a multiple car wreck. In fact, it feels like you're being assaulted. Now, the sport of skiing is jam-packed with techniques. However, as you're flying down a hill, if you keep your head down and try to concentrate on the correct technique for the mogul that's directly beneath you, the one that's slamming your knees into your face, you will never be able to deal with the 200 more bumps coming up that are poised to break you in half. If your brain is turned inward and focused on technique, you won't be getting the whole picture. You need to look outward and focus on the run ahead of you; otherwise, your nervous system will be overwhelmed by the deliberations of your brain, instead of being allowed to focus on feeling the terrain. It's the same with fighting. Sensitivity means to lose yourself and follow the opponent. You simply feel your opponent's motion. If you think only of what martial arts technique to use right now against your opponent's punch, you'll never feel the intent of the 200 strikes that are right behind it, and your opponent will break you into a thousand pieces.

As is said in tai chi, you should be so sensitive and responsive that a fly landing anywhere on your body will set your whole body in motion. "Well then," you may say, "to be so immaterial to my opponent, why don't I just remain completely disengaged, dancing beyond his reach?" Because then your opponent would also be beyond your reach. That would be fine if you have the speed and space to run away. Unfortunately, if you're cornered, unless you're the Roadrunner, escape is usually unavailable. We're not talking about sparring here. We're talking about life and death. You want to mold

> With increasing sensitivity you eliminate the middleman of your reactive intellectual mind, which acts as a drag on your response time.

to your attacker, be all over him or her, yet be completely unavailable. You *need* to be at close range to cause damage to your assailant and yet stay alive yourself, but you're not going to grapple. You will find that as you train, your definition of force will change. What the average person might call a light touch, you will call a shove. This means you are developing your sensitivity. If you overcommit to a block or forced strike in which you try to blast through your opponent's defense when there is no opening, you'll be stuck—you won't be able to react. You've committed yourself to one direction and can't recover in time to deal with your opponent's next strike. Because you've committed yourself, you won't recognize openings or be able to take advantage of them. This is why you stay soft—until you actually make contact with your own strike.

> In guided chaos, we like to say you're both unavailable and unavoidable.

You're not training sensitivity to become yieldingly passive like limp spaghetti. You're developing sensitivity to change (direction, force, or yin versus yang). These changes will then be amplified by you into deadly force. By being sensitive and remaining connected to your opponent, you follow his every move. When you move into some wild contortions in response to your opponent's energy, it will be impossible for you to deliver a rooted, powerful strike unless you also have hyperbalance that instantly readjusts with the same rapidity and fluidity as your sensitivity.

When you have developed your balance and sensitivity, you can deliver any strike from any position with devastating consequences. Learning to punch and kick by themselves is actually the easy part.

Now that you have built your foundation of looseness, body unity, and balance with the prior chapters, you are ready to see how sensitivity can also help you create energy.

Creating Energy

As both Eastern mystics and contemporary physicists will tell you, everything consists of energy. A punch, pull, kick, or block is an embodiment of bioelectric synaptic energy. Even your opponent's intent is latent, or potential, energy. Your nervous system is both a receptor and initiator of kinetic energy. This receiving and initiating of kinetic energy is enhanced by heightened sensitivity.

In guided chaos, we propose to become experts at the manipulation of raw movement, or energy, both in its delivery and reception. The principle of sensitivity has the effect of liberating you from concentrating on obscure techniques and configurations, allowing you to focus on feel. Feel is subconscious, and you are the only one who can develop it. Once you have it, the type of strike you use or that is used against you is irrelevant. Your feel will dictate what is appropriate, not your brain (your thinking brain, that is).

Yin-Yang Generator

As you learned in chapter 5, the principal of yin and yang delineates the universe in terms of opposites that can either be sharply separated or intermixed. Hard and soft, up and down, in and out, push and pull, attack and yield—these qualities need to be understood separately yet blended and applied simultaneously to achieve the unmatched power that is available to the practitioner of an internal art. There are many more qualities defining yin and yang, including male and female, heaven and earth, hot and cold, and so on, but these are not central to our discussion. Without getting philosophical (and to avoid the often intentional mystification and confusion associated with this vital topic), simply train yourself to be aware of and do the following: Push the opponent's pulling energy and pull the opponent's pushing energy.

Doing so has the effect of augmenting your opponent's energy and putting it at your disposal. We can categorize the push as yang energy and the pull as yin energy. This concept is not really so esoteric. When you push a child on a playground swing, you feel the right movement. Although you don't actually pull the swing back toward you once it's in full motion, you do retreat to stay out of its way. At this point only tiny, perfectly timed pushes are necessary to make the swing go higher. Given the swing's full arc, a six-year-old on a swing can knock a grown man's head off if his timing is wrong. But what does this have to do with fighting? With guided chaos, we're going to turn you into a yin-yang generator.

Consider what your stereo amplifier does to the signal it receives from an old phonograph. A vinyl record's grooves consist of millions of tiny wiggles—tiny, frozen, physical waves of energy that are an exact duplicate of the music it copied. The needle follows these grooves exactly and converts them to tiny waves of electrical energy. Your stereo amplifier takes these tiny waves of energy and amplifies them dramatically, but it doesn't alter the information they contain in any way. It doesn't oppose the waves. It follows them exactly and adds to their energy, using household current. Differences in volume and frequency are translated into powerful waves of magnetism that have gigantic peaks and troughs—opposites—that your speakers turn into loud, pulsing music.

These opposites are exactly analogous to the movements of your assailant as he or she struggles against you. You're going to follow these opposites—or yin-yang, push-pull movements—and amplify them using inertia, sensitive muscle contractions . . . and gravity. Using your loose, balanced, body-unified connection with the ground as your electricity, you're going to generate additional energy.

As you flow with your opponent's intention (remember, intention is a form of energy), learn to pull with one side of your body while you push with the other side. Your opponent's energy drives you like a seesaw. Your sensitivity tells you when pull becomes push. This simultaneous pushing and pulling could be a ripping or yielding action with your left side in response to an incoming attack and a reciprocating punch with your right side. This seesaw action can occur at any angle or along any direction and reverse itself at any time. What's important is that this push-pull relationship happens simultaneously—not first one and then the other—and that your body remains relaxed and whiplike, or like a steel spring, and is always perfectly balanced, like a gyroscope. The classic tai chi texts refer to this as having one side empty, one side filled and not being double-weighted. The theory is, if you're pushing rigidly with your whole body displaying yang, or hard, energy, you will have no counterbalance. Therefore, you would be relying exclusively on muscular force.

To become a yin-yang generator, you must learn to recognize and separate the fullness from the emptiness, the tension from the relaxation, the yin from the yang. This is so the yielding reception of your opponent's energy has someplace to go. When your balance and root are strong, this energy flows through your yielding side into your feet and bounces back out through your attacking side.

In accordance with the principles of body unity, do not isolate the push-pull action to just your hands. Move your entire body with this quality, even if the attack or defense is the subtlest of movements. Separating the yin from the yang (recognizing the pressured side from the unpressured side) can occur in the entire body or in just one part. When your weight is balanced momentarily on one foot and the power is poised to fly into the other foot, you're using push and pull physics. When you're hand receives downward pressure and your elbow flies up into an attacker's throat as an instant response, you're using push-pull physics. Your level of sensitivity dictates how soon and how small an amount of stimulus you require to set this reaction in motion. With these principles under your direction, you will eventually be able to redirect your opponent without effort. You need to have superior sensitivity to detect exactly when a push becomes a pull, and vice versa. When you can do this, you are separating the yin from the yang. The drills at the end of this chapter will help you learn and practice this separation.

With a kinesthetic understanding of the yin-yang generator, you can begin to develop an explosive, slingshot kind of energy that is amplified by your focused fear (chapter 2, Focus Your Fear drill, p. 25). In tai chi, this may be called borrowing jing, but we'd like to use a more modern explanation of this slingshot phenomenon using space-age science.

Because of the tremendous distances involved in space travel, the National Aeronautics and Space Administration (NASA) relies on the laws of physics to generate more speed in a spacecraft than its own propulsion could ever generate. To get probes, such as Voyager or Galileo, way out into the solar system, NASA aims them at a nearer planet or the sun first. As the probe approaches the planet, the planet's gravity draws the ship in even faster, in effect accelerating it as it falls toward the planet. Then, with a slight deviation in course, the probe is directed to narrowly miss the planet, whip around it, and slingshot away at tremendous velocity. The space probe borrows the planet's gravity for energy while using none of its own. Sound familiar? This is what happens when you learn to push your opponent's pull and pull his push.

Here are some actual physical examples of yin-yang energy generation. If you think of every joint in your body as being finely balanced, a breath of air can cause it to swing one way or the other:

- A touch on your elbow rotates your fist into the opponent's face.
- A touch on your hand swings your elbow down on your opponent's neck.
- A push on one shoulder shoots your other arm out.
- A strike to your chest collapses your chest like a sponge but shoots both your arms out into your opponent's eyes.
- A slight challenge to your root shifts you onto one leg momentarily, which swings your entire body weight into the returning blow.

These changes in balance are instantaneous. The energy is delivered in the transition from one relaxed point of balance to the next. There should be no pause in the flow between them.

Don't think of these balance points as slow or weak. Turning your body into a yin-yang generator is like becoming a ferocious, spring-loaded trap that instantly resets itself. Where does this explosive spring-loading come from, and how do you keep it from making you tense, causing muscular exertion? The next section provides the answer.

Dropping Energy

We've introduced some of the basics of dropping energy in chapter 2, but now that you have an applied understanding of looseness, body unity, balance, and sensitivity under your belt, you will be better able to understand the full depth of how dropping energy can be used to defend yourself. Dropping is an instantaneous explosion or wave of energy you can use for striking, deflecting, uprooting, regaining balance, and augmenting virtually any other movement.

Simply put, dropping energy refers to a spasmodic lowering of the entire body weight into a current or new root. Whatever your body weight is, it becomes a formidable weapon when you get it moving all at once in accordance with gravity. The sensation of dropping is similar to having your legs kicked out from under you, stumbling off a curb, or falling asleep at the wheel of your car and then jerking awake. If you're a downhill skier, the sensation of dropping is like the down-unweighting used for making the fastest possible edge change in a turn. The feeling is similar to a sneeze or cough in that your whole body spasms and drops. The energy is explosive but involuntary. You want to be able to control it at will, directing it to any weapon. When fueled by your fear and permitted to flow by your relaxation, the damage dished out by dropping can be devastating.

Dropping consists of three parts that all happen simultaneously:

1. Stand with your knees slightly bent, then try to bend them more so quickly that for a split second your whole body becomes weightless, so that a slip of paper could actually be inserted between your feet and the ground. Most beginners make the mistake of actually jumping up first, which entirely misses the point.

2. Halt the drop with a snap to start the shock wave of energy. When you drop, your body's momentum tries to continue going lower but is suddenly stopped. The energy reflects or rebounds off the ground and travels back up your body looking for an exit point. It's similar to a sneeze except that instead of coming out your nose, the energy is focused to come out as a strike. You don't want to drop more than a couple of inches at most. Think of it as snapping a wet towel or cracking a whip; you're essentially trying to catch the bounce your body makes as it's stopped.

In dropping you make gravity your friend. As you drop, you create a shock wave of energy that travels down your body, rebounds explosively off the ground, and races back up your legs to be channeled any way you desire.

Figure 6.2

Dropping is an instantaneous act of total relaxation of your whole body. Just let go. You can drop into both legs or into one. You can be standing on one leg and drop into the same leg or into the other leg. It all depends on what your sensitivity and balance dictate in the fight.

3. Channel the energy through looseness (chapter 3) and body unity (chapter 4) to any weapon you desire (figure 6.2). You can just as easily drop and hit off one leg as off both legs. Don't lean, though, or your energy will be dissipated by your struggle to regain your balance.

What you achieve with dropping is creating a root no one can find. In other words, the enemy can't get a handle on you. This is because your instant balance allows you to step, root, and re-root as fast as you can drop and re-drop. You can switch legs and stances in one, instantaneous drop (this facilitates kicking with either leg powerfully) or drop and root on one leg. The phenomenon of instant balance occurs instantaneously whenever you drop correctly. For example, you could be in the middle of wobbling, and a drop would fix it. If you're off balance, dropping roots you, giving you an opportunity to strike with power. Anytime you drop, you temporarily peg your balance to a spot and then instantly abandon it as soon as you step and drop again via the rebound effect of dropping. This creates the potential for delivering machine-gun sequences of strikes, something we'll get into with ricocheting energy.

There are some vaguely similar concepts in tai chi, but they are rarely taught this way. Even so, in most cases, they don't crystallize the essence of the power of dropping and its simplicity. There are also some individuals who have discovered it on their own. If you carefully watch films of the famous Cassius Clay–Sonny Liston fight, you will see that the infamous mystery knockout punch was actually a drop, which is why it didn't look very powerful. There was no windup: There wasn't time. The legendary old-time boxer Jack Dempsey did a crude form of dropping; he hit on his way down during the drop instead of on the rebound, basically falling into his punches with his full body weight behind them. Both methods are used in guided chaos, however, the rebound method we've been describing has the added advantage of spring-loading you for subsequent strikes, which is why we prefer it. Close combat often uses the down method, which is why we like to say guided chaos principles (via rebound dropping) supercharge ordinary close combat.

Dropping as a Source of Power

There are many advantages to using dropping as a source of power:

- It requires no continuous muscle tension or great strength.
- It requires no windup or chamber.
- It's perfect for fighting nose-to-nose, where the most mayhem occurs and where there's no room to pull back and chamber a strike.
- It delivers more energy in less time.
- It can be delivered at almost any angle, including upward.
- It doesn't drive or push the opponent back like a regular strike, pissing him off and allowing him to regroup.
- It penetrates deeply into the target, causing far more internal damage.
- It extends the reach of either a punch or kick.
- It doesn't disrupt your relaxation, sensitivity, or balance; instead, it augments them.
- It creates a chain reaction for exploding into additional strikes.

Dropping actually satisfies all the requirements of separating yin and yang: It completely relaxes and collapses the body, forming a yang wave of energy that falls into the now-emptied and relaxed lower regions of the body, ricochets off the floor, shoots back up through the joints of the body, and explodes out through the strike. For the tai chi practitioners among us, dropping energy is one way of "seeking the straight line from the circular," the essence being that as you circularly evade and redirect blows you can absorb the energy into your root and bounce it directly off the ground via dropping.

The injuries you inflict as a result of a dropping strike are different from those you might inflict with a conventional strike. The opponent may not appear to move at all, but the dropping energy reverberates inside his body like an implosion. This is due to its suddenness. You want to time your strike so you halt your drop and hit simultaneously. You want your arms loose and flaccid, with no muscular tension whatsoever. Drop-striking becomes even more devastating when someone is falling into your strike because you yielded to theirs. The effect is multiplied, depending on your opponent's incoming speed.

Some manuals, like the *T'ai Chi Classics* (Liao 1990), call this type of dropping energy cold power because the explosive, snappy action generates shock waves that blast into the opponent's body, penetrating without actually moving him much. It does catastrophic internal damage, however. Contrast this with long power that projects the opponent a distance away. For our purposes, we don't want to launch the attacker away, where he can regroup and attack again. Instead, we want to disable him where he stands. Remember, the way you train is the way you fight. In tai chi, if you always use long power during push hands (a tai chi training exercise), you'll probably also do it in a life-and-death situation.

What's the logic behind dropping? It eliminates winding up, chambering, or drawing back.. These are wasted motions. When you draw back to throw a punch, no matter how quick you are, you won't be able to get the strike off if your attacker is staying close to you or charging like an animal. When throwing a punch, the only motion that matters is the forward motion. Now you may be asking, "If I can't wind up to strike, then how am I supposed to hit? Not drawing back seems to be a contradiction." This is because the principle is paradoxical when compared with everything most of us have ever been taught about punching and kicking.

If you're relaxed and balanced, you can hit with enormous power with no windup by using the principle of dropping. With a no-inch punch, your acceleration is virtually instantaneous. This is strategically efficient for two reasons:

- If you draw back to strike, you create a natural opening for your attacker that can't be defended.
- If you're already sticking to follow the attacker's every motion, dropping allows you to attack and defend simultaneously because you never lose contact with your opponent. For example, if your hand is already near the opponent's face and dropping would allow you to hit with effective power, why draw back only to have to bring your hand forward again? In fact, in the time it takes you to pull back on a strike, not only could you have thrown a strike at your opponent, but you could have struck your opponent twice: once on the extension and once on the return.

> If you're not balanced, dropping energy is frittered away and misdirected into space as you try to regain your balance. Correct this situation by observing the principle of body unity.

Bruce Lee taught that punches should be felt, not seen. Whether or not he was the first to espouse this idea is unknown. Nevertheless, it's a very sound principle of fighting, which the looseness of dropping energy encourages. First, the strike is like steam—vaporous, illusive, unknown. Then it becomes like water—fluid, continuous, ever changing. Finally, on impact, it becomes like ice—crushing, destroying—and then immediately returns to steam. Dropping repeats the cycle over and over again.

Due to the dynamics of combat, however, it's not always physically possible to drop on every strike you deliver because you're continually loading and reloading your body weight. However, in your practice, you should try to drop as often as you can. Also, when you practice dropping within contact flow (explained later), your dropping speed should be the same as that of the rest of the flow.

Stealth Energy

Stealth energy is a term given to sensitivity so high you're in contact with your opponent's intent only. When your opponent's sensitivity is untrained, you do not appear on his radar screen, even though he is clearly on yours. Thus, his body's targets are defenseless, as if you were a stealth bomber preparing to drop its payload.

John Perkins can actually sense the heat of his attacker's skin. By training free-form creativity for most of his life (in between his hundreds of real fights), he has explored and programmed into his subconscious virtually every possible human combative motion, something that would have been impossible had he sought to deliver choreographed techniques at every opportunity. Thus, he has the ability to stick to your motion, often without even touching you. For most of us, this is a lofty goal, but it is definitely achievable with practice and is not the stuff of myth. Training to be so light and responsive that you actually avoid bending the hairs on your arm (except when landing with a strike) is one approach. Another is to visualize that you're sticking to a fatter version of your opponent, a Michelin Man existing beyond the skin of your partner. This keeps you from bearing down on him and allows higher contact flow speeds without causing injury. Dropping allows you take the same energy that would penetrate his body and recycle it back into your root for another drop. You bang against the ground instead of his body. This has the outward appearance of you smashing an invisible barrier right at the surface of his skin. Against heavy bags or a real attacker you just take the same energy you've practiced with and let it penetrate to the bone.

Pulsing Energy

Pulsing is any movement you make with any part of your body that adds energy to your contact with the intent of eliciting a response that can be exploited. In other words, it's a fake out. It may be a push, pull, tug, nudge, hip check, rocker (see chapter 7), or the like. For the sake of clarity, we will call all tugging and pulling actions inward pulses.

Now you may be thinking, *Isn't guided chaos about not adding energy, about being unavailable and sensitive to your opponent's intentions*? That's exactly right. The purpose of pulsing is not to overpower your opponent with a titanic push or tug-of-war: You're merely instigating a reaction in your opponent that you can flow off of. This is an important distinction to understand. You're not trying to engage and grapple with him. You're messing around with his balance and sensitivity, and thus trying to get him to grapple and engage you. When he does this, he uses more energy that you can turn back at him using push-pull principles. When you get your opponent to react to a pulse, you can also lead his energy away and slide into the opening. The sensation of pulsing is elastic and bouncy, kind of like a rubber ball bouncing rapidly between two walls or like the feeling of quickly tugging and releasing a bungee cord. The amount of energy imparted can be very subtle. Remember, however, that even though the pulse may be small, you should still have your entire rooted body behind it. You just don't use any muscle. This is so your countermove is fully balanced and spring-loaded.

A pulse can be as light as a touch; an inward pulse can be as delicate as plucking a guitar string. How much energy you use depends on what your sensitivity tells you about your opponent's structure and what it will take to trap him. You then take the opponent's reactive energy and amplify it against him. This is, in effect, what you're doing when you pulse an opponent. When your opponent reacts, he loads your spring, quite unconsciously, setting in motion a devastating slingshot or boomerang effect. In addition, by dropping as you pulse, you supercharge your next strike. To summarize: With pulsing, you instigate, your opponent reacts, and you amplify his reaction by using the yin-yang generator principle and by dropping.

An interesting byproduct of the disengagement principle is that you can often get an opponent to pulse *himself*. In an effort to find you, they wind up pushing and over-committing when they finally do make contact. You anticipate this, flow off of it, and they get sucked into their mistake.

One very important clarification must be made here because of an error we often see in classes: Pulsing is *not* a defensive tool and is not used to stop, block, or suppress an opponent (compare with destructions, coming up soon). Pulsing is a trap you set; it is delivered and exploited in a microsecond. Beginners often misinterpret pulsing as pushing and use it to block, setting back their development by years. They think they're pulsing when they're actually doing Sumo and using it as a crutch.

The difference between the yin-yang generator principle and pulsing is that in the former you are passively following the opponent and then amplifying his energy. In other words, if he's pushing, you actually pull his push so that he never feels any resistance until it's too late. This is a good way to ensnare them into arm breaks or blows with your other arm. If they're pulling (for example, trying to smother your hands against their body), you push their pull and pound them in the ribs without ever giving any resistance to their original pull. ("You want my hand? Here, take it!") In pulsing, you're *actively provoking* a reaction that you then flow off of. This is always in the opposite direction. Even if your opponent doesn't react strongly, a pulse gets the attacker to tighten and freeze for an instant, effectively taking all the slack out of his limb so it can be used as rudder to uproot his whole body or else be tool replaced (see tool replacement, p. 118) for a clean shot.

Until now, the following has been a closely guarded secret: Moe of the Three Stooges was actually a guided chaos master. Picture him with his outstretched arm, saying to Curly, "Hit this!" Imagine Moe's fist flying around in the opposite direction in an impressive display of pulsing before crashing into Curly's head. Nyuk nyuk! Seriously, though, the wide, circular swing Moe took would not be in keeping with the economical, tight circles that come from moving behind a guard (chapter 7). Well, maybe he was only a white belt.

Here's a more realistic example: Let's say you pulse an opponent's arm by pushing with your elbow (figure 6.3*a*). He panics, and his immediate, unconscious reaction is to tense up, pushing you back. This loads your spring. Your arm and shoulder, supercharged by his energy, move in a tight circle in the opposite direction, and you palm-heel him in the face (figure 6.3*b*).

Figure 6.3

Or, suppose you inward-pulse him by tugging on his forearm with your hand (figure 6.3c). He tightens and yanks back, in effect pulling a chop into his throat (figure 6.3d). This will cause an involuntary, outward deflection on his part, allowing you to pull his push. When you run this through your yin-yang generator, his attempt to block your chop to his throat gets his arm extended out, perhaps leading to a break. This little exchange, as you can see, has a Ping-Pong sort of quality, where one event (your inward pulse) starts a whole chain reaction.

Pulsing can get very nasty very quickly, because once you set the chain reaction in motion, it can feel to your opponent as if he's been thrown into a giant pinball machine. If he's not sensitive, balanced, and yielding like you, it will seem that every move he makes is wrong, putting him in even more mayhem.

A pulse can also be something as simple as a hand squeeze or pinch. This could be all you need to provoke a reaction. Just remember that when you pulse, you become the spark of an energy generator. It's easy to get off balance due to the forces you'll be creating. Learning to pulse is easier than learning hyperbalance, so be sure your training emphasizes the latter. Don't cheat yourself on the basics.

By the way, a feint is actually a pulse: Although you make no contact with it, a feint adds energy to the mix. Feints provoke a reaction in the opponent that you can take advantage of. For example, if B feints a chop straight into A's throat and circles into an overhand palm strike, A, moving to cut off the chop, overcommits to his centerline, leaving his outside line open to the palm strike.

Once you understand pulsing, you can use as much force as you want, as long as it's rooted, dropping, nonmuscular force. But force is often not necessary and sometimes wasteful. Stealth energy is of much higher value because the opponent can't even follow you. It's important to aspire to this level. Then you can sprinkle in some pulses randomly, without thought, and the combined effect will be overpowering.

Destruction Energy

When pulsing is performed at maximum speed and power, it becomes a destruction. You drop and splash your opponent's limb, damaging it but never just blocking, pushing, or suppressing its motion (see Skimming and Splashing Energy, coming up). Again this is because you have to be absolutely ruthless about not wrestling with the enemy. This is also because you want your destructions to lead to ricocheting energy.

Ricocheting Energy

Ricocheting occurs when you're moving at high speed and loading the spring almost instantaneously. You strike and bounce off your opponent's body into a different target, like a bullet ricocheting off concrete into an escaping felon (remember the scene from *Robocop*?). The point here is that the bullet changes direction without using any of its own energy, just what it receives from bouncing off the wall. Again, this effect can be amplified by dropping.

Ricocheting occurs whenever you strike some portion of your opponent's body, and the resulting recoil bounces you into additional strikes that you augment by dropping. The potential for ricocheting is always there when you strike. The problem is, if you're not loose and sensitive to the energy, it won't happen. Remember, don't tighten up and bear down on your opponent when you strike; this commits you to one direction only. Ricocheting energy and destructions become even more devastating when you regularly perform slambag drills (coming up later) because of the tendon strength and crushing power developed in your hands.

Sliding Energy

In the process of being as disengaged as possible while still being engaged, you attempt to slither through openings like a snake, not blast through them like a bull. This sliding energy requires great balance, sensitivity, and articulation because you will be moving at

A helpful visualization for sliding energy or sticking in general is to imagine your hands are hockey pucks and the entire surface of your partner's body is an air hockey table. Your hands skim just above the surface of his skin on a layer of compressed air. This helps you to stick but not get stuck.

many angles as you simultaneously stick and slide through the opponent's defenses. For example, suppose B is sticking to A's hands (figure 6.4*a*), and A decides to blast through B's guard to push or strike. B simply lets A go where he wants by letting A's arms slide right past his hands. By moving just his body out of the way but sticking with his hands, B remains in contact, yet makes his targets unavailable (figure 6.4*b*). B maintains strong structure the whole time by keeping his elbows low but does not use any force.

We also call this kind of energy forearm surfing. Using sliding energy, treat your opponent's forearms like ocean waves and your hands as the surfers. Since you could never hope to overpower a wall of water that weighs perhaps 20 tons (18.1 metric tons), you have to learn to ride the wave's surface. Similarly, as your opponent's arms move, slide your hands along their surface, moving to the elbow to stop an elbow strike or to the wrist to stop a chop or punch. You then ricochet off his attack. Remember to move your body and shift your footwork as necessary to maintain body unity and keep yourself behind a guard (chapter 7). To maintain a balance of yin-yang energy, keep sliding back to the middle of the forearm until your opponent's energy tips you off.

Figure 6.4

Sticking Energy

In guided chaos we don't block. We destroy or make them miss.

Sticking energy is an extremely subtle opposite of sliding energy and is actually a form of pulsing. (This is not to be confused with plain sticking, which is simply maintaining tactile contact with the opponent.) As you let the opponent's body slide through your hands, you can at any time press into his flesh slightly with your fingers, nails, or the V formed by your thumb and forefinger. Create an extremely brief and elastic adhesion by stretching his skin. Instantaneously rebound off this into a strike or other move. At no time do you grab onto your opponent or squeeze with your hand in any way. This is difficult, of course, if either one of you is sweaty. Sticking energy takes a lot of practice but is extremely sneaky.

Skimming Energy

Actually, you've already practiced skimming energy with the Sticks of Death drill (chapter 3, p. 68). Skimming energy refers to the glancing action a strike or deflection may take, similar to a flat stone skimming the surface of a pond. The stone will stop and sink rapidly if its angle is too steep. Similarly, if you become too engaged with an opponent, a skimming strike will get bogged down and will not have a clean bouncing action. If the opponent strikes to your face, skim by shooting your own strike in at an angle that glances off and deflects your opponent's attack and connects simultaneously. For example, A punches at B's head. B shoots a spear hand at A's face, which deflects A's strike and skims off into A's eyes (figure 6.5). Skimming differs from ricocheting in that the strike trajectory remains relatively unchanged. It also differs from sliding energy because you are skimming past your opponent; in sliding, you allow your opponent to slide past you.

Figure 6.5

A little move we call the rising ram is another example of skimming energy. While fighting A, B's lead arm winds up in an extended low position, pointing toward the ground. As B raises the arm it is blocked by A's hand or forearm. The instant the top of B's arm contacts the bottom of A's arm, the relaxed, rising motion of B's arm turns into a forward, sliding strike aided by B dropping, turning, and stepping forward slightly. It's almost like shoving your whole arm through a greased mail slot. This is a good example of highly tuned sensitivity, because if B is tight and tries to fight upward through A's block with brute force, he'll miss the opportunity for an easy, sneaky, and decisive blow forward into A's lower torso or groin. Although we've given this strike a name out of convenience, we can apply the principle behind the rising ram to almost any strike at almost any angle.

Splashing Energy

Splashing energy is an interesting principle, in that it relates the human body to water. Because the body is mostly liquid, it has a lot of give to it, so you must hit another's body differently than you would a brick. To make liquid act like a solid for a split second, you have to splash it. If you punch the surface of a pool, your hand will knife right in, but if you smack it as fast and snappy as you can with an open hand, you create much more disruption.

For various strikes, you can actually cause more trauma with a splashing action than with a strict reverse punch. You cause shock waves that travel deep into the tissue. The other advantage of splashing is that it doesn't overcommit you to the strike. Your aim is to penetrate the target to the depth of perhaps two inches (5.1 cm) and then completely relax the hand. This allows you to resume sticking to the exact spot you struck the instant after you make contact. This is an enormously important concept that keeps you balanced and ready to defend yourself further.

Suspending and Releasing Energy

Suspending and releasing energy involves the synthesis of balance and sensitivity; it requires you to determine unconsciously the exact moment when the opponent is between pushing and pulling, striking and retracting, yin and yang. In that split second of frozen time, your opponent is suspended and helpless. Pulsing is also a form of suspending and releasing energy.

What you're doing while sticking is encouraging this suspension with the tiniest pulse so you are set up to release or catch your opponent's reaction and do with it whatever you wish. This is analogous to pushing a child on a playground swing: For that split second of suspension at the end of each arc, all the latent energy in the swing is frozen. Before the swing begins to move again, it can be moved in virtually any direction without the resistance momentum would give it. This is also like a tight end in football tearing down the field and then leaping into the air to catch a pass. Although he may weigh 220 pounds (99.8 kg) and be able to squat 500 pounds (226.8 kg), for that suspended moment in time, a child could throw him on his head. This is when the most dangerous injuries in football occur, with very large men getting spun in the air by defensive collisions and landing on their necks.

You can create an exaggerated sense of suspending and releasing when you do a dance, like the Lindy or jitterbug, which involves swinging your partner around. You counterbalance your partner's body weight by firmly anchoring your feet. Then you release, letting him or her go into a spin or another move. You need to develop that same rooted sensation of suspending and releasing in your feet throughout the entire range of your combative movements. You let the pressure between you and your opponent build to whatever degree you want, and then release it so your opponent practically knocks himself out running into your fist. The suspension can be anything from a featherlight touch to your full body weight, poised to release like an atomic mouse trap. A full-body-weight suspension can also immobilize the enemy for a split second.

Isolation Energy

Isolation energy is another very subtle, advanced principle. An example is placing your palm on someone's arm while his or her eyes are closed and being able to walk around him or her, rising and sinking, all without that person being aware of any change in your pressure or direction. This kind of sensitivity allows you to confuse the other's nervous system and set up for strikes without triggering an alarm reaction on his or her part. You can use this point of contact as a fulcrum around which you may rotate to any new attack angle. For example, if your palm contacts your opponent's forearm so lightly that he or she

Figure 6.6

can barely feel it in the heat of battle, you can step or move your body just enough to change your attack angle.

Here, A's forearm is in between B's palm and B's intended target, which is A's face (figure 6.6a). By using isolation energy, B is able to subtly move his upper body and shoulder just enough to create a new entry angle, allowing him to launch a chop to A's throat through this opening (figure 6.6b). This whole scenario takes place in a fraction of a second. There's no obvious posing or setting up going on.

Transferring Energy

Your sensitivity is heightened, and you're sticking, when all of a sudden, your radar picks up your opponent's intention to strike with his fist. Instead of only yielding or pocketing, you pass off his incoming force to another part of your body better positioned to exploit the energy. We call this tool replacing, or transferring energy. For example, your hand is on his forearm (figure 6.7a). As soon as you feel his forearm tighten as if preparing for a strike, pass it off, using no strength on your part, to your other hand (figure 6.7b).

This action is similar to a waterwheel passing water to the next paddle as it rotates or two gears turning with their teeth intermeshed. It's also like climbing a rope, hand over hand. It's important not to grab or wrench your opponent's forearm because this would tighten you up, destroy your sensitivity, and alert your opponent to your intention. If you're skilled enough, you can pulse, which gets your opponent to push harder (remember that the average person tightens up when pressed, in effect fighting fire with fire). Once he does this, you can clear or break his extended arm, opening up new angles of attack.

Since the tool replacing described here is from hand to hand, we like to call it passing the apples. This implies that neither hand is going to keep the apple; rather, you're only transferring it to its final destination. You can rapidly pulse and pass the apple many times a second. This pulse-and-pass combo is extremely effective and feels to your opponent as if he's been tossed into the Cuisinart again.

Tool replacement is a flexible and powerful principle. You can essentially make a tool replacement between any two parts of your body: for example, replace your hand with the elbow of the same arm (figure 6.8a) or of the other arm (figure 6.8b); replace your elbow (using a rocker position; see chapter 7) with the hand of the other arm (figures 6.9a and 6.9b). You can also replace your elbow with your chest. This last example is particularly interesting, because your chest, acting as a checking tool, frees *both* your arms to strike (figure 6.10).

One little tip about passing your opponent from the hand to the elbow of the same arm: Because you're constantly trying to take your opponent's space, try to have the elbow reconnect farther up the limb you're passing. If your left hand is on his right forearm and he's pressing hard, you can step in slightly, pocket, and pass his right arm by reconnecting

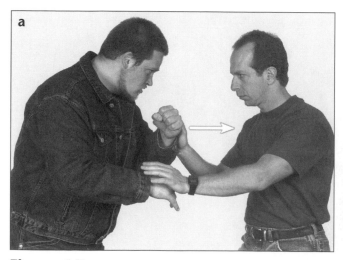
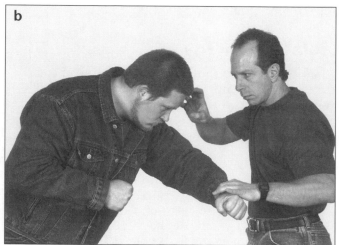

Figure 6.7

to it with your elbow at a point somewhere around his triceps. With this done, you've gotten his right arm completely cleared and out of the picture, you've closed the gap, and your left hand is free to chop, spear, or claw his face. In the meantime, your right hand has received the apple by hyperextending his right arm. By the way, this elbow replacement could also be a simple destruction to his shoulder joint, powered by his pressure.

Figure 6.8

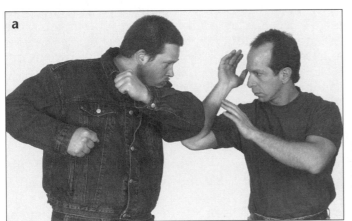

Figure 6.9

Figure 6.10

Releasing Tension and Taking Up Slack

When you're sticking to the opponent, let his limbs slip by while maintaining contact (sliding energy). This can result from a missed push or an attempt at retreat. What concerns you is when to stop giving slack and start taking up tension. Do so at a moment and from a position that is advantageous. At that point, drop rapidly and pulse, then wait for his reaction. For example, you are pulling a shoulder; he resists. Just as you would with a fishing reel, you release tension and let his arm slide out through your hand to his wrist. You then drop, root, and snap in for a strike. The reverse also works: If your opponent is loose without defending himself, creep in and take up slack like a boa constrictor by skimming, sliding, or tool replacing.

Recognizing Energy

After reading about the different energy principles, you may recognize that you've already felt them at one time or another by accident. These accidents can be the turning points of a fight. You may have deduced that they're all interrelated and seem to happen naturally. That's the idea. If you're moving in accordance with physics your natural animal reflexes often rise to the surface. It's very hard to dissect spontaneous energy and movement. We've simply tried to define the effects of certain kinds of motion and categorize them so that as you begin to do the drills that follow, you'll recognize and encourage all these accidents to happen more frequently.

Hitting Is a Part of Sensitivity

This may seem too esoteric a concept to comprehend at this point in your training, but we're presenting it here nevertheless so it becomes locked in your brain: As your sensitivity evolves you will actually pick up the entire structure of the enemy's defense by the way your strikes impact his body. Whether your strike is blocked or hits home, your subconscious will process data automatically on his root, balance, weaknesses, strengths, and openings based on the solidity, alignment, and *feel* of the target struck. Rather than a passive, touchy-feely *defensive* phenomenon, your sensitivity will actually become the byproduct of a brutally combative and aggressive *offense*. You'll know what he's doing by the way your shots feel on impact. Reread this section every 6 months and you'll begin to see what we mean.

Sensitivity Drills

The energy drills presented later in this chapter will help you develop sensitivity simultaneously with other attributes. For now, though, here are three very odd drills that develop sensitivity exclusively. You may think they're too wacky to be any good, but that's their strength: They force you to move in ways you'd never think of, and they require great concentration.

Coin Dance

The positions you get yourself into during this dance can be bizarre, but so are the positions you need to assume in a fight. This drill heightens your sensitivity by helping you focus on being relaxed and loose.

1. Place a penny on the tip of each index finger.
2. Have your partner carefully place the tips of his or her index fingers on yours, so you are holding the two coins between you.
3. Moving extremely slowly, begin to make large random circles with your arms without dropping the coins. Only the extreme tips of your index fingers should be holding the

coins. To do so will require both of you to forget everything else and really tune in to and follow the motion of the other partner.

4. In the beginning, you'll drop the coin frequently. But as you learn to stay focused, loose, and relaxed, you can actually strike at each other like two sloths slugging it out. There's no leader or follower, so don't cooperate with each other. Do not try to push back to stop a strike—get out of the way. The fragility of your fingers encourages this. Obviously, you would never block a strike with your fingers, which is why we're overemphasizing their use as sensing tools in this drill. When you have a ferociously powerful adversary, any part of your body is subject to breakage, so try to react with your entire body as you would with your fingers. Feel and move into areas of lower pressure and lesser structure so you can strike with unobstructed power. Remove your own targets so you don't get broken. Try to strike with your elbows at odd angles (your anywhere striking practice helps here). To increase the difficulty, both of you can move your arms in and out, high and low, and spin your bodies 360 degrees so, at some point, you actually have your back to your partner. Just don't drop the coins. If you have a third person available, add one more coin and join fingers so that you have three people attempting to sense each other's movements. Also, try holding the coins between your and your partners' respective elbows.

Coin Chase

To make things wilder and faster, hold a coin between your palm and your partner's. Both your and your partner's hands should stay flat at all times with no cupping. Now you can both go crazy running, spinning, jumping, and whipping your palms—but don't drop the coin. You must learn to sense your partner's movements. Yield when your partner pushes and follow when he or she retreats.

Back Walk

This drill goes counter to most martial arts training because you're not trying to overpower your opponent; instead, you're trying to listen to your opponent's movements with your whole body.

1. Stand back-to-back with your partner with your shoulder blades touching and knees slightly bent.
2. One of you becomes the leader and the other the follower. The leader tries to disconnect from the follower (not too quickly at first or you'll both be on your backsides) by walking forward, rising, sinking, and twisting.
3. No matter what happens, maintain contact between your shoulder blades at all times.

When you get better at this, you can dispense with the leader-follower scenario and try to freely chase and avoid each other. Your job is to completely eliminate any buildup of pressure between you, so if your partner suddenly stops running and comes toward you, you can immediately sense the change and reverse course. At the same time, don't lose your partner. Beware: This drill puts a tremendous load on your quadriceps. Practice this drill regularly, and you'll develop legs like tree trunks.

Dropping Drills

Beginners often misinterpret dropping as simply falling or bending the knees. But as we've said, the motion is more of a spasmodic, jerking action similar to the snap of a whip. To promote this feeling, notice what your body does the next time you sneeze. Your whole body spasms and then relaxes. How do you know if you are dropping correctly? Place your palm on a brick wall about chest high with only enough pressure to bend a blade of grass. Now drop strongly and direct the rebound energy out of your palm without ever breaking contact with the wall. If your relaxation is high and your timing is right, the shock wave that ricochets back into you will feel like it could dislocate your shoulder. If you didn't use a brick wall there will now be a hole in the wall. If your timing is off or you maintain too much pressure, all you'll be doing is pushing. If your balance is poor, you'll stumble backward. If at any point you didn't have your palm flat against the wall, you're wasting your time. What follows is a comprehensive program to develop the critical guided chaos principle of dropping. With consistent practice you will achieve remarkable results.

The first two drills may help you understand and approximate dropping's unusual snapping action. In addition to these exercises, go back to the Pyscho Chimp and Circle Clap drills in chapter 3 as well as the anywhere strikes drills in chapter 2 and add dropping to them. Note: Dropping drills can be very taxing on your knees and ligaments, so be careful if you have any joint problems.

Stumble Steps

Here's an artificial way of simulating the sensation of dropping:

1. Stand with your feet shoulder-width apart, knees slightly bent.
2. Close your eyes and have a partner suddenly push you from behind with moderate force. The shove should be enough to make you stumble and lose your balance.
3. Catch yourself by landing on one or both feet as abruptly as possible. If you're standing on a wooden floor, you should actually feel it give slightly beneath you. All the dinnerware in the house should rattle. This doesn't mean you should purposely kick the floor, however. The energy comes from the sudden collecting of your balance. This, timed with a forward punch or palm strike delivered simultaneously on landing, is the essence of dropping power.
4. Try to duplicate the sensation without being pushed. Just fall forward and drop on your own.
5. Eventually, you'll be able to do this drill with a partner slamming you with a kicking shield while your eyes are closed. Drop, catch your balance, and instantly launch into a barrage of chops and palms to the shield.

Stair Steps

Here's another way of simulating the dropping sensation:

1. Stand on the bottom step of a sturdy flight of stairs.
2. Balance on one leg and extend the other leg out in preparation for walking down to the next step.
3. Collapse your supporting leg abruptly as if someone has kicked out your knee. Don't try to brake yourself; instead, just let yourself go, falling hard into the other leg as you land on the floor, heel first. Do not absorb the impact by bending the landing knee but actually keep it only slightly bent and immobile. You have only fallen perhaps 10 inches (25.4 cm), but your whole body weight should hit the floor like a ton of bricks.
4. If you are sure you can do this without falling down the stairs and killing yourself—and have healthy knees—start at the top of the stairs and work your way down. Pause momentarily and then crash down to the next step. This exaggerates the feeling of dropping; when you drop for real, however, you will sink only about 1 inch (about 2.5 cm).

Seven-Step Dropping Drill

Here's a series of progressive exercises that you can practice on your own. As you drop, you must land with your foot flat and your center of gravity rooted over the foot you drop on.

1. Stand with your hands out in front of your arms at shoulder height, slightly bent and with your wrists relaxed. This position looks exactly like the first move in the tai chi form. As you drop and catch yourself, perform a double palm heel strike, focusing on timing your strikes with your drop. Your arms should feel the contraction of the muscles as your hands snap into the palm heel strikes. Your hands should strike outward in front of you with no more than 3 to 4 inches (7.6 to 10.1 cm) of movement. Start off slowly, focusing on developing the timing, and then gradually pick up speed. Resist the temptation to launch with your legs by jumping up in the air first. This is a common mistake and will not add one iota of power to your strikes.

   When you drop, ensure that all motion in your body ceases and hold your position for two full seconds. You should feel yourself rooting to the ground with each drop, knees bent, ensuring that you do not hop forward or lean in any one direction as you drop straight down. This will ensure that as you strike, you are able to do so with maximum muscle contraction and balance. Make sure as you recover for your next drop that you return to the original position, totally relaxed. Repeat this over and over for two minutes or until the point of fatigue.

2. This time, repeat all the actions in step 1; however, once you drop, ensure that all motion in your body ceases and hold your position for only one full second. In doing so, you will begin to cut down on the amount of time it takes between your strikes while ensuring that you'll be able to strike with maximum contraction and balance. Repeat this over and over for one minute or until the point of fatigue.

3. This time, once you drop, ensure that all motion in your body ceases and hold your position for half a second. This will cut down even more on the amount of time it takes between your strikes to gather yourself. The focus is on striking with maximum contraction and balance.

4. Stand with your hands out in front of your arms at shoulder height and slightly bent, wrists relaxed. As you drop and catch yourself, perform a side chop or shuto strike, focusing on timing your strike with your drop. Your arms should feel the contraction of the muscles as your hands snap into the strike. Again, your hands should strike outward in front of you with no more that 3 to 4 inches (7.6 to 10.1 cm) of movement. Ensure that your hands are already in the proper position to make the strike work as if you were striking for real; focus on hitting with the side of the hand, not the fingers. Now, you want to drop and strike as fast as you can, making sure you remain balanced as you strike and stay relaxed in between strikes. Do not lean forward or hop as you strike. Make sure that you are striking as you catch yourself when dropping. You are trying to sense and catch the plyometric wave or bounce that occurs on each drop to help launch you into the next one.

5. Repeat step 4, but this time, drop on one leg, alternating your feet. Do not lean forward or to the side and do not hop as you strike. Make sure your center of gravity is directly over the rooted leg. Once you gain proficiency at this, begin dropping with every possible weapon you can imagine.

6. Repeat step 5, striking and moving in every possible direction with every possible weapon within your sphere of influence. Maintain your body unity as you step. Then begin the guided chaos exercise called polishing the sphere (coming up later), intermixing it with drop hitting.

7. Drop until you can't drop anymore and repeat several times a week until dropping is infused into every fiber of your being. You should feel this mostly in your legs; later, you will want to practice dropping against a heavy bag, then on the wobble board, then on the board against the heavy bag, then on one leg, and so on. Practice this drill until you can hit like a machine gun.

Middle-Linebacker Hitting

Remember this exercise from chapter 2? Well, now that you fully understand dropping it's time to do it again:

1. With your hands in front of you, step in place as fast as you can.
2. Here's where we modify it: With each step, shoot out a palm-heel strike with the alternate hand. In other words, as your right foot lands, hit with the left palm heel and vice versa.
3. Make your steps smaller and smaller and faster and faster until your feet are barely leaving the ground. You could call this the supersonic shuffle. At the same time, try to keep your palm strikes in sync with your steps.
4. Try this against a heavy bag. Then try coordinating palm strikes with steps on the same side (e.g., left-hand step, left palm strike).

The point of this drill is to get you to drop on every strike. By stepping, you force this to happen. By taking smaller and faster steps, you increase your coordination and the ability to marshal all your power instantaneously and loosely, without muscling up.

TV-Cut

The beauty of the television as a training tool is that picture edits, without music or sound, have no rhythm whatsoever—as in a real fight. MTV works best because of its fast-paced programming and quick cuts. This is a highly effective drill that builds incredible reflexes, quickness, looseness, relaxation and dropping ability.

1. Make sure you're thoroughly warmed up first or you can easily tear a muscle or tendon.
2. Tune the TV to any program with fast-paced programming and quick cuts. Stand in a relaxed ready position in front of the TV with the volume off.
3. Begin by performing one type of dropping strike every time the picture changes. Explode out as fast as you can and retract the strike even faster.
4. Once your mind and body become extremely quiet and focused, work on spontaneously changing the strikes without thought. Use kicks also.

Ball Compression

This develops the no-inch punch from extremely close range, where most fighting ends up. The beauty of these strikes is that they require no chambering or pulling back of any kind. This drill develops body unity, balance, focus, relaxation, and most important, full-power dropping.

1. Take an old tennis ball and find a fat tree trunk or telephone pole.
2. Select any tool, for example, a palm strike, and place the ball in your hand against the tree (figure 6.11).
3. Orient your body using the principles of body unity into some rather strangely angled strike, such as might occur in a melee. You could even stand on one leg.
4. Hold the configuration, breathe deep into your belly, and relax your entire body—muscles, joints, and mind—while palming the ball against the tree as lightly as possible.
5. Now, as if you sneezed or coughed from the soles of your feet through all the joints of your body and out your hand, drop so the tennis ball is instantaneously and explosively compressed.
6. Change the angle and location of the strike and repeat.

Figure 6.11

7. Then change the tool (the palm is the easiest; chops are a lot harder). Try using your fist, elbow, shoulder, knee, and foot.

Remember to be relaxed, balanced, and sensitive when you practice this drill. If you are not completely relaxed, you will have no power. Muscle tension will have you fighting your own body's mass. Even if you are unusually strong, you will not compress the ball as much as when you drop correctly. If you aren't completely balanced, you will actually blast yourself away from the tree. If you aren't completely sensitive, the ball will shoot out of your hand due to the tree's curved surface. If you aren't properly aligned, your power will be nil.

If you practice this drill five minutes a day, you will increase the availability and effectiveness of your dropping strikes. When you do use dropping strikes against an opponent, the shock waves will reverberate inside the assailant without actually moving him. Because of splashing energy, they cause internal damage from their concussive force. This is effective when you're grappling with a larger opponent, especially when your strikes are slipped inside the opponent's arms and are directed against the five vital zones: eyes, throat, spine, groin, and kidneys.

Slambag Training

This comprehensive training regimen teaches you to both drop and splash while tremendously increasing hitting and crushing power. For this training, you'll need to make or purchase an empty beanbag from a martial arts supplier and fill it with from 2 to 10 pounds (1.0 to 4.5 kg) of beans or shot. Attackproof.com makes them specifically for this purpose. The slambag with its smooth, seamless leather skin and specially selected bean fill offers maximum potential for improvement balanced with minimum risk of injury for most people. With other bags and bean or shot fills, care must be taken to minimize the potential for injury through abrasion or through use of a fill that is too hard or heavy for your current level of development. Steel shot especially can lead to arthritis in your fingers.

Slambag training is very different from iron palm training. This is because rather than merely conditioning the hand for striking, slambag training allows you to improve your dropping power, splashing energy, timing, coordination, body unity, speed, and tendon strength, in addition to gradually and safely conditioning your striking surfaces for impact.

When using the slambag, keep the following in mind:

- Pay attention to your body. Although muscle soreness is an appropriate temporary result of diligent training, any numbness or tingling sensation in the hand, pain in the joints or bones, or damage to the skin should be an immediate cause for concern. Stop the training session immediately if you experience any of these. You may need to get a less abrasive bag; use softer, lighter, and less dense fill; or lighten up on the intensity and duration of your slambag sessions. Ideally, you should get equipment that allows you to work with full intensity (i.e., full-power striking) for at least five minutes at a time with no serious discomfort beyond muscle soreness.

- Always try to strike and penetrate the bag directly through its center, perpendicularly to its flat surface. Do not strike the bag off center, which would cause it to flip-flop around your weapon. Do not strike the bag at a glancing angle or into the side (along the seam). Adjust your entire body to line your weapon up to strike the bag at the correct angle. This gives you a feel for body unity in striking.

- Keep your whole body—including the striking arm—completely relaxed and loose as you move to hit. Do not consciously tighten up even as you hit. The plyometric effect of proper dropping will give you the instantaneous structure you need automatically. You do not need to consciously add tension. Do not wind up. Move your whole body directly to the hit from wherever it is.

- Use dropping energy to penetrate the airborne bag so abruptly that it feels like a solid object (as if you were doing a belly flop into water from a 100-foot (30.5-m) cliff—no, don't try that; just imagine). When you use splashing energy, you should feel as if the bag sticks to your relaxed striking surface for a brief moment after you penetrate it, even without grabbing it. If you're simply pushing or knocking the bag away, you're not dropping or splashing.

Solo Training

Here's a progression to use when training with the slambag by yourself. To begin, simply toss the bag in front of you with your left hand, then step in and slam-catch it with a dropping, right-palm strike. Then toss with the right and hit with the left. Remember to observe the ideas described above (hit through the center of the bag, hit perpendicularly to the flat of the bag, stay loose, drop and splash to penetrate and stick to the bag before seizing it with the fingers).

Using two kinds of tosses will allow you to vary up the focus of your training:

1. The pizza toss: Visualize a pizza chef tossing his disc of dough while keeping it spinning constantly. Tossing the bag in the same way enables you to control the angle of the surface the bag presents to you; it also ensures that the distribution of the fill inside the bag will be relatively uniform when you hit it, due to the centrifugal force generated by the spinning. You can use a vertical spin to simulate hitting someone straight in the face, for example, or a horizontal spin to simulate hitting straight down at the head of someone shooting in for a tackle. Of course, try all angles and adjust your body accordingly.

2. The flip toss: Toss the bag so that it flips end over end like a burger being flipped on a grill. This toss challenges your timing as you seek to hit the bag just as its flat side is presented to your striking surface. The faster and farther you flip the bag, the more difficult this becomes.

To emphasize looseness and sensitivity, follow the momentum of the captured bag after you grab it. Allow it to pull your whole body into a loose swing that launches it into the next toss.

To emphasize tendon strength development, freeze yourself and the bag in space for a second just as you grab it. You should feel a burst of energy in your muscles and tendons (particularly in your striking arm) when you do this. Feel that for a second, then release it and loosely swing into the next toss.

To force you to shorten up your hitting, toss and slam-catch the bag with the same hand. Remember to move your whole body to align with and drop into the bag.

Now toss the bag in ways other than right in front of you. You can toss it farther out, forcing you to long-step or gorilla-walk to it. Toss it to the side or even behind you. You can toss it very close to your own body, forcing you to shorten your hits, pocket, and adjust to get good hits (just be sure not to slam the bag into your body!).

Now that you've mastered the basic slam catch with the palm, start working on your high-speed tendon strength, looseness, and speed by doubling up. Hit the bag twice with the same hand before catching it. Start with an easy, slow pizza toss right in front of you. You'll have to drop, penetrate, and splash well on your first hit to ensure that you don't swat the bag away before you're able to bounce loosely into the second hit. The withdrawal from the first hit is like when you open your hands while clapping. Because you're dropping on both hits, you don't need more than an inch of clearance. After the second hit, stick and catch.

Making the double hit sing from all angles and distances? Good. Now make the first hit in the double hit a chop instead of a palm strike. Keep your thumb up, fingers straight and together, and hit with the base of the edge of the palm. Start out with downward chops to an easy, horizontal pizza toss. Chop straight through the center of the bag (you should be able to see the crease your chop leaves in the bag as you withdraw your hand), then drop again and slam-catch with the same hand. Horizontal chops to vertical pizza tosses are harder, but you'll get the feel of it. Remember to stay loose and adjust your whole body for the hit.

Now, triple the palm strikes, and do double chops into a slam catch on the third drop to challenge your speed. Make sure the strikes don't turn into mere taps. Each penetration should make the bag feel solid. Don't be surprised if in your efforts to do this properly, your feet naturally start dropping foot to foot (practically vibrating against the floor) at very high speed. That means you're getting it.

The possibilities for solo slambag practice are endless. You don't always have to catch the bag. You can just toss it up and hit it at all different angles, letting it fall to the ground after the hit. If you're dropping and splashing properly, the bag should not fall very far from where you hit it—maybe a few yards at most. Your goal is not to launch the bag across the room, but rather to slam it hard, sending your striking energy *into* the bag rather than pushing on its surface. An interesting variation is to do a horizontal pizza toss right in front of you, then wait until it's descending to hit it.

> The key to developing your sensitivity when training alone is to imagine that you are engaged with a real opponent

- Accelerate your hit downward quickly and loosely enough that it still feels like a rock when you hit it.

- Let a close vertical pizza toss descend past your hip before you hit it. See how your body has to move and drop to get the angle to hit it well. Imagine how this and variations might relate to stopping someone trying to tackle you (you slam your fingers into his eye sockets from underneath like a bowling ball).

- Slam-catch the bag, then immediately release it and smash or chop it down into the floor.

- Try using elbow strikes. Observe how moving your whole body becomes even more important. If you try to generate the necessary suddenness to splash the bag with your elbow by moving just your arm, you'll practically rip your shoulder out—and won't get a good hit anyway!

- Use fists, hammer fists, forearms, wrists, ridgehands, whatever you want (we do not recommend using your head, but it is your head to use as you see fit).

- Double-drop using both hands instead of just one. Do a slow, vertical pizza toss out in front of you; drop in and palm-strike it in midair with one hand, then slam-catch with the other. Make sure both hits are good, with the correct angles. Then vary the angles and weapons, coming from one or both sides of the bag. Slam the bag back and forth between two weapons. No one said this was easy. Stay loose and experiment.

- Try clapping the bag: Hit it from both sides at once with your palms. Double this, hitting the bag twice before you catch it between your hands. Vary the angles. Then try hitting with your hands off center in order to slam-twist the bag. For example, when you're doing a vertical pizza toss, the hand hitting forward hits at a slight upward angle while the hand hitting the other side pulls slightly downward. Imagine how this relates to simultaneously hitting a person's neck or base of the skull in one direction while hitting the upper skull in the other direction (something that is easily done when you take an opponent's space and tool-replace to the chest). Vary it at different angles and by using different weapons. Try an elbow with a palm, a palm with a ridgehand, an ox-jaw hand with a forearm—whatever you want. Vary the angles, vary the tosses, double it up. Try some variation of slam clapping on the first drop, and on the second drop, gouge the fingers of one hand deep into the bag.

- Step in different directions as you drop. Box-step. Do the Hackey-Sack drill with your nonstriking hand. Stand on one leg. Get on a wobble board. Catch the slambag with one hand and hit a heavy bag with the other on the same drop. Polish the Sphere and Wash the Body (coming up soon) as you work the slambag. Get two slambags and work them simultaneously.

The possibilities are endless. Just a note: Do not overdo it. In your training session, stop when your arms start getting fatigued and you begin to lose your dexterity with the bag. Your hands especially will begin to cramp. When first starting out, work the slambag only once or twice each week. Just as in weight training, your muscles get broken down and then need rest time to build back up stronger than before. Your tendons also need to adapt to the slambag training. Don't burn them out without giving them a chance to adapt and rebuild.

All the slambag exercises involve hitting the bag in midair or while holding it in your hand. We do not recommend placing the bag on a solid surface and hitting it. Not only does this eliminate the dynamism and hence most of the benefits to be gained from the training, but striking unyielding surfaces (even through softer objects) often leads to joint and nerve problems.

Although we do not consider using traditional liniments necessary or useful, we do recommend that you wash your hands thoroughly with soap and water after a slambag session. This helps to soothe and relax your hands, and it also prevents your hands from smelling like a dead cow for the rest of the day (assuming you have a leather slambag).

Partner Training

Throw the bag at each other. Use different kinds of tosses (pizza tosses, flip tosses, your own versions) at all different heights and angles, lobs and line drives, directly toward the body and away from the body. Hit and catch in different ways, for example, with a slam catch, a downward hit, a double hit, and so on. Stay loose, line up your whole body, and drop and splash through the center of the bag from the best angles. Don't just play catch with the bag (although that's fun, too). Throwing the bag can be a good tendon strengthener on its own.

Perform the Close Combat Universal Entry from chapter 2 but treat the incoming, thrown slambag to your face as the assailant's punch. Your parry hand slam-catches the bag while the chopping hand hits the air above it.

If you are practicing in a group, keep the bag moving and try to trick each other with no-look passes. Just try not to nail each other in the face and groin if you want to be friends at the end of the day. Get multiple bags moving simultaneously.

Energy Drills

Energy drills are absolutely critical to developing a natural synthesis of all the guided chaos principles in a free-form and spontaneous manner working by yourself. While doing these drills, remain loose, unified, balanced, and sensitive to the energy, no matter how much you contort, articulate, or pocket. Perform these flow exercises with an attitude of play and improvisation. Work to develop a sensation of natural movement that is effortless and powerful, yet virtually random—where you're free yet properly positioned to strike and deflect. Your movements should augment and support each other without thinking about what you're doing.

Moving spontaneously is a purely subconscious, kinesthetic skill. Anyone can develop it because it relies on mastering looseness, body unity, and balance, not on mechanical techniques. The only thing you need to learn is how to develop and use your spontaneous movement so it's unified and powerful enough for mortal combat. Otherwise, you'll wind up looking like a marionette on angel dust. These exercises are not only an excellent form of low-impact aerobics, but they're also a form of moving meditation. If you combine them with proper breathing—so that all yang, or outward, movements involve exhalation and all yin, or yielding, movements use inhalation deep into your belly—you'll achieve a level of relaxation and chi development equal to what you might find after decades of doing forms.

Rolling the Energy Ball/Striking Sequence

Yielding and redirecting, pushing and pulling, taking and giving away, twisting and tearing all happen at the same time. The relationship of opposite energies gives enormous power to guided chaos, and eventually you need to practice these relationships in a completely un-patterned way. That will be accomplished when you learn polishing the sphere, washing the body and contact flow. Before then, rolling the energy ball helps you develop that push-pull feeling, in which your body moves with wave-like unity.

1. Imagine you have in your hands an invisible energy ball. It has no weight, but it has a volume that can change from the size of a pea to that of a beach ball. As you roll it around in your hands, imagine it maintains its roundness with an outward pressure something like the feeling of repulsion you get when you try to bring two magnets together.

2. Take the energy ball in both hands and make it the size of a basketball.

3. Using the same side-to-side weight shift that you practiced in the Turning drill in chapter 3 (p. 64), carry the ball with your body. As you move to the right, your right arm is on top (figure 6.12a on p. 130). When you reach the limit of how far you can move sideways, roll the ball so that as you carry it back to the left, your left arm is on top (figure 6.12b). The top arm leads with the elbow, so it helps to visualize an elbow striking with each sideways carry; your lower hand clears, redirects, or shoves the opponent.

4. Drive your hands around the ball by turning your back and hips. Get your shoulders into it, as if the ball weighed 80 pounds (36.3 kg), but without any tension. Carry the ball by transferring your weight from foot to foot completely, but don't lean sideways as you shift from leg to leg.

5. Keep your upper body perpendicular to the ground, like a buoy floating in the ocean. This emphasizes that all power comes from your legs while all the joints and muscles in your upper body remain loose, like ball bearings.

6. Now, roll the energy ball clockwise, counterclockwise, horizontally, diagonally, and all around—a full arm's length, in front of your face, in front of your stomach, by your hips, and then so close to you that you must actually pocket to get out of its way (figure 6.12c). You will find that your hands move quite unconsciously in a yin-yang relationship to each other as they roll the ball. As one hand moves up, the other moves down. When one moves out, the other moves in. No matter where one hand goes, the other, mirroring it, is never far behind. This is a critical relationship principle, essential to all movements in guided chaos. The application to self-defense is that while one hand strikes, the other deflects (figure 6.12d), and while one hand rips, the other hand tears. The center of the ball is the pivot point around which your blocks and strikes effortlessly roll. It's also useful to think of whichever hand is closer to your body as the backup, or checking, hand, ready to deal with whatever gets past the front hand. Thus, the checking hand is frequently employed to pass the apples.

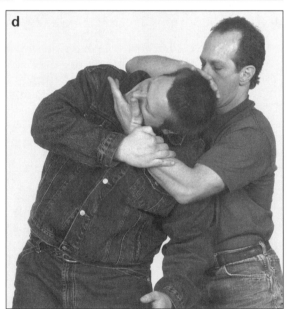

Figure 6.12

The ball itself represents your opponent's energy, which you never oppose. You roll around your opponent's attacking limbs and body, staying whisker close, yet unavailable. When you combine the effect of your opponent's energy being amplified by the yin-yang generator and your body unity loosely flip-flopping your arms between their opposite positions, the end result is that your rolling hands become like the blades of a blender: Anything that gets between them will get torn apart or crushed—using little of their own energy. To be sure you're balanced, try rolling the ball while doing a Ninja or Vacuum Walk at each end of the 100% weight shift.

7. Now we will bring this abstract drill down to earth and combine it with close combat. At the end of each weight shift, you will carry the ball at shoulder height but instead of rounding out the ball shape, you will deliver a chop to the side, so that a weight shift to the right ends in a right chop to the throat. End with a left chop when you move left. Now forget the ball and simply weight shift and drive out slow, menacing chops.

8. To heighten your balance and the sense of down dropping, stand completely on one leg by raising the knee of the leg that will be stepping into the strike as high as you can and then glide onto it, sink, and deliver the chop. For a left chop, you'd be standing on your right leg facing left, your left knee high in the air, your right hand protecting your face to ward off strikes, and your left elbow bent and held shoulder high, pointing like a spear out to the left. Glide with your left foot and step to the left, simultaneously and proportionately unfurling your left chop to the throat with your left shoulder held high to protect your throat. Tuck your head and peer out from behind the shoulder. As your foot descends it should follow an arc to the ground (don't just fall onto it; it should be a controlled, balanced descent, something like what you feel in the Vacuum Walk). Your chop should hit its apex at the exact instant you finish your weight shift on to your left foot. When the knee stops bending, the hand stops moving. At this point your weight distribution should be about 80% on your left foot and 20% on your right. Now sink a little lower and send out a right palm, rotating slightly at the waist. As you do this, your left hand comes to your face to ward off strikes. Feel the power from the legs. You should feel like you could chop down an oak tree. Now balance completely on your left foot, turn to the right, raise your right knee high, and step and glide into a right chop and left palm. Continue going back and forth for several minutes. This drill also greatly increases your body unity.

Polishing the Sphere I

Polishing the Sphere, along with Washing the Body, are the two most important solo drills for developing guided chaos attributes. This drill, when done regularly, will improve your looseness and body unity tremendously, resulting in greater power. More important, it increases your creativity and, thus, your adaptability. If you remember the personal comfort zone (PCZ) from part I, you'll see that the sphere of influence is actually its aggressive counterpart. The PCZ was an area as large as you could reach with fully extended arms or legs; you try to maintain your PCZ defensively and keep threats away through awareness and avoidance. If despite your best efforts an aggressor enters your PCZ, then that person has crossed the Rubicon and is now within your sphere of influence. Anything that enters your sphere of influence will be destroyed. The sphere of influence concept dictates that you cannot fight an enemy beyond your reach, but neither can your enemy reach you. When you engage the enemy, you take your sphere with you. Do not overextend or overcommit. These exercises help define that sphere for you.

1. Breathe deeply into your belly, expelling all tension as you exhale.
2. With your shoulders relaxed and your knees slightly bent like a sleepy ape, visualize all muscular tension draining out of your fingertips and into the ground. Your joints should be totally free and relaxed.
3. Imagine yourself standing inside a large glass sphere with a perimeter as far as you can comfortably reach with the palms of your outstretched arms.
4. Slowly and methodically move your body to polish the entire inside of the sphere with random, circular or brush stroke movements of all sizes and in all directions. For example, you polish a 12-inch (30.5-cm) section of the sphere in front of your face clockwise with your left hand; at the same time, with your right hand, you polish a 6-foot (1.8-m) arc directly overhead, to your side, behind you, or beneath you counterclockwise. Your entire body rises, falls, and turns side to side with the circles and arcs you make, no matter how small they are. Drive with your legs to reach the perimeter of the sphere and to make the circles just as you did with Body Writing in chapter 4.

You don't want to stand stiff as a post with your arms rotating at the shoulders like two propellers. In baseball, you can't hit a home run swinging the bat only with your wrists. Likewise, during this drill, you've got to stride, drop, and turn your feet, knees, back, hips, torso, shoulders, and arms. A tennis professional chasing down an opponent's ground stroke is not going to stand like a statue and flick at the ball with her wrist to smash it back. She has to reach, plant, drop, and align her body. When one part of you moves, your entire body must back it up.

Polishing the Sphere II

Perform Polishing the Sphere **I as before; however, this time** polish using any and every part of your body as the polishing implement. Polish with your head, feet, back, chest, hips, buttocks, elbows, forearms, shoulders, and knees. Use everything in any order you wish. Do small circles, large circles, arcs, brush strokes, horizontals, verticals and diagonals, whatever, driven by your whole body. This time the perimeter of the sphere is as far away as you can comfortably reach with whatever part of your body that's doing the polishing, using a maximum, balanced, full-body stretch. For example, by squatting with your knees deeply bent and your back parallel to the ground, you should almost be able to polish the floor with your elbow. This, then, would be the perimeter of the sphere for this tool at this angle. Use big and small circles, arcs, and brush strokes. Drive with your legs and turn with your body.

Polishing the Sphere III

Now polish as high, low, and wide as possible while standing on one leg (figure 6.13). Close your eyes. Try using the flat of one foot to polish the sphere both in front and behind you at various heights. Ideally, you should polish using both arms and one leg simultaneously, along with as many other body parts as you can put in play. The object is to challenge your balance as drastically as possible, even if it's only your pinkies that are doing the polishing. These motions mimic the kind of chaotic positions you might find yourself in during a fight. For the ultimate challenge, do all of this while doing the Wood Surfing drill (chapter 5, p. 91).

Figure 6.13

Washing the Body

Washing the Body is the single most important **drill for develo**ping **the four** main principles on your own. Unlike Polishing the Sphere, it greatly increases your sensitivity. The goal is to turn you into a human sponge with spikes. Remember Weaving Python (chapter 3, p. 62), where you alternately collapsed and expanded your chest and back in response to your partner's palms? Similarly, with this drill, you can practice the limits of your looseness, but you'll be doing it with every part of your body and by yourself.

1. Shrink the energy ball to the size of a pea.
2. As your hands roll the pea, again notice the yin-yang relationship between their movements. Roll the pea between your hands, and between your hand and your forearm, elbow (figure 6.14*a*), shoulder, chest, waist (figure 6.14*b*), and head (figure 6.14*c*). Use the lightest pressure possible. Feel every contour of your body.
3. Perform this motion as if you were washing your hands over your body with a slippery soap. This is where the drill becomes a little schizophrenic. As you wash, simultaneously avoid and pursue yourself. Simultaneously attack and yield by pocketing—moving those areas of your body that are being washed away from those that are doing the washing. At the same time, the attacking, or washing, areas *chase* them. For example, as your palm washes your elbow, your elbow moves away while maintaining a featherlight pressure on your hand the whole time. Your whole body turns away with the

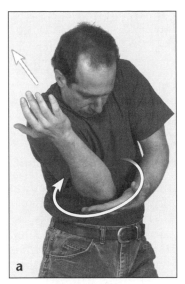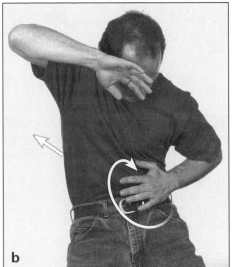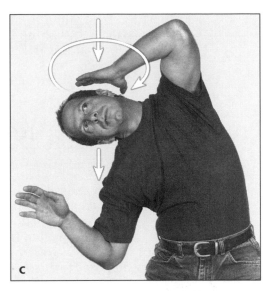

Figure 6.14

elbow. As the elbow avoids the buildup of pressure by the hand, it tries to circle back on the hand at a different angle. Your whole body circles back with it. The hand, sensing this change, yields and moves away, while also maintaining a featherlight pressure on the elbow. Remember, due to body unity, even if you are rolling a pea with your hands, your shoulders and back rise and fall to move your hands around the pea. In addition, your feet and legs stride and reposition to get the best body unity. You want to move with the *intent* of driving 1,000 pounds (453.6 kg), but not the force. This will make your mechanics perfect in a real fight so that, for the millisecond you drop and deliver the goods, the power will be there. Otherwise, stay completely relaxed. If your opponent resists, your mechanics will remain perfect as you instantly flip-flop and pull his push like a spring-loaded mousetrap.

4. Try rising and falling, carrying the pea all the way to the ground. Continue washing while lying on the ground. Wash any part of your body that could be struck or grabbed in a fight—in other words, everything. Try hitting your own head from all angles. Twist and contort your whole body like a beached catfish. Rolling on and off the floor develops total looseness, grace, and balance even when ground fighting (see chapter 10).

5. Try throwing yourself into locks and grabs. You will learn to flow with the locking energy so that others will find it impossible to lock or grab you.

Along with helping to keep your joints as loose as ball bearings, with your flesh simply hanging off your bones, the washing action embodies the principle of being as disengaged as possible yet still engaged. You roll the pea around (or in this case, your skin) with zero resistance. Be sure that you are never pressing hard against your skin like in Sanchin-kata or some other isometric exercise. You glide over your skin, barely touching it, like the puck on an air hockey table. Eventually you will actually be able to feel the heat of your own body and detect its presence without actually touching it. Think carefully on the implications of this: If you can detect and react to your *own* movements this way, imagine the effect it will have if you use it on the enemy? When you begin contact flow later, you will want to carry over the exact same sensation you experienced with washing the body. Do not revert to grabbing, grappling, or pushing him like a sumo wrestler.

You can wash (attack) your own ribs with your elbow, then yield, pocket, and check or clear it with the other hand. Meanwhile, don't forget to root and pulse yourself (again, as if you're your own worst enemy), attempting to create suspend-and-release situations you can simultaneously escape from. Remember, the extremes of your looseness and the rolling of your hands are actually balanced energy opposites. The ferocious power of guided chaos comes from flip-flopping between these opposite positions at a hair-trigger's notice by dropping.

Try combining all the energy drills: Polishing the Sphere (I, II, III), Rolling the Energy Ball, and Washing the Body. For the ultimate challenge, flow from one to the other while Wood Surfing (p. 91). In the end, your nervous system won't be able to tell the difference between attacking yourself and attacking someone else. So go ahead—beat yourself up. The benefits are immense.

Relationship of Human Energy to Movement (RHEM)

When you combine slow, deep breathing; the box step, the Ninja Walk, and the Vacuum Walk (chapter 5); and Polishing the Sphere (I, II, III) and Washing the Body, you are performing the Relationship of Human Energy to Movement drill (RHEM). RHEM looks like a tai chi form, but the methodology is different. With a form, you try to imbue patterned movements with qualities that are energetic and combative. After many years, the form is supposed to dissolve, and its essence become available to you if you get into an altercation.

RHEM is a more potent form of learning because instead of training fixed, patterned movements, you're teaching your subconscious to become comfortable with spontaneous, random motion—the kind you would use in a real fight. As we've alluded to previously, you give your nervous system what it needs from the beginning for combative development instead of programming it for hesitation. You develop creativity, governed only by guided chaos principles.

You perform the movements very slowly, doing the same things you would do in a real fight, and concentrate on looseness, body unity, balance, and sensitivity. As you perform the exercises, you will cultivate chi because you will be integrating internal energy (breathing, visualization, and a calm, focused mind), with physically coordinated, balanced, and aligned body movements. You may recall that we support the definition of chi as the "circulating point of finesse in the body" (Lien-Ying 1994, page vi). You will derive many of the benefits of cultivating chi without locking that finesse into choreographed forms. Then the chi can really flow spontaneously, the way you actually need it.

1. Breathe deeply, slowly, and evenly. Continue to breathe this way throughout the entire movement, exhaling as you move outward and downward.

2. Rise high onto one leg as you inhale deeply, simultaneously raising your other knee as high as you can. As you slowly exhale, slowly step to a new root point, anywhere you like. When you get familiar with RHEM, slowly step to the most challenging spot you can find. There should be a long period where you're suspended and balanced on one leg before your foot actually touches the ground and settles in. Observe all the principles of weight transfer you've practiced in the Ninja Walk and the Vacuum Walk drills (see chapter 5, pp. 87 and 88).

3. As you inhale and rise and then exhale and step to a new root point, simultaneously and slowly do either Polishing the Sphere I, II, or III or Washing the Body. Then, as you settle into your root point, slowly perform one strike of any kind or kick (it doesn't matter which). To maintain body unity, do these three things simultaneously: complete the strike, finish sinking into your new root, and exhale once. The slower you can do all these, the better.

4. Without pause, slowly inhale deep into your belly; rise a bit and begin to transfer to the new root point while washing or polishing. Suspend yourself here for a split second and then exhale, ending in a different strike. Don't forget to try kicks, knee strikes, elbows, and head butts—everything.

5. You can perform this drill with a group where one experienced person is the leader and everyone else tries to follow along as he makes it up. Obviously he will have to move very slowly. The benefits for combat are far greater than the tai chi form because you develop the ability to improvise while holding to the four internal principles (balance, body unity, looseness, and sensitivity). Additionally, you develop your proprioception,

because by attempting to follow your leader's movements you become very aware of both your structure and your leader's and how they align in space. This gives your nervous system and subconscious mind a big workout. Just imagine how much input you will process subconsciously when you make contact in contact flow!

If you do this exercise every day for 15 minutes, the improvements in power, balance, and looseness will be remarkable. You will imprint your subconscious with the necessary dynamics of combat instead of fixed choreography. In addition, you'll derive all the benefits of moving meditation: inner and outer harmony, stress reduction, and low-impact aerobic conditioning.

- Be aware of the rising and falling, which emphasize body unity and the separation of the yin and yang within dropping energy. The polishing the sphere and washing the body movements program your nervous system to become spontaneously evasive as it simultaneously attacks. This gets you as disengaged as possible, yet still engaged.
- Feel the exhalation and let the continuous, slow dropping drive you through the entire movement. Remember, gravity is your friend. Don't resist it. Learn to use it.
- Become familiar with the sensation of swinging your entire body's mass through every movement.
- Keep your hands in sync with your legs. When your legs stop moving, so do your hands, regardless of the relationship between them.
- Throughout the entire exercise, visualize the enemy as you focus your fear, mold to him, and destroy him. Visualize your targets. Begin making all the movements in washing and polishing combative and deadly.

This is not a form. Creativity is king.

Contact Flow

Let's face it: Although training on your own will enhance mastering principles, to get good at fighting with people, you have to either fight or train with another person. There are at least a million ways a person can move, and you need a way to become comfortable with all of them but without memorizing any of them.

The only way you can effectively practice all the principles in this book simultaneously is in a totally unchoreographed, completely spontaneous interchange through which you train with another person while experiencing minimum risk of injury. Contact flow is potentially very dangerous. It's essentially free fighting, and absolutely anything goes—but be careful about injuring your partner if you want to continue to have someone to train with. It's about creativity, adaptability, improvisation, energy, and movement—not about scoring points.

There's nothing highly complicated about this exercise, no obscure mystical secrets. You're simply learning how to deal with another person's motion. That's it.

Now you may be saying to yourself, *If two-person training is so critical, then what value is there in training on my own?* The answer is that both types of training complement each other. Each time you train, you get a little bit better, even if you can't discern any immediate progress in your ability. When you train on your own, you not only reinforce the basic principles but also discover and develop what works for you. This allows you to bring more things to the table the next time you contact flow with a partner. Also, if you practice diligently on your own, you won't regress if you later have little access to a partner. Because you're reprogramming your neural pathways, it's important to do drills that involve the four basic principles for at least a little time every day. When you're alone, you can examine your development closely.

The last thing you want to do when performing contact flow is think, plan, or try to win. Instead, you simply feel. Your biggest enemy is your brain. Your subconscious, the

Contact Flow is the most advanced of all the drills, combining everything you've learned and will learn. Nevertheless, it's something you practice with a partner from the very beginning; it will be the foundation of all your future training.

same part of you that carries out the billions of operations that keep you alive and upright without your thinking about them, is the part of you that will be guiding your movement. By using visualization when you perform the solo drills, the principles slowly will creep in by themselves. So relax and be free. When you're done, you can analyze what you did and refer back to the book all you like. But remember, while you do this drill, empty your mind. After all, how much analyzing are you going to do during a fight? This drill helps you prepare to adapt your movements to any situation you might find yourself in.

1. Face your partner in a basic Jack Benny stance (sideways, so you don't expose too much target area). Before beginning every Contact Flow drill session, note the distance between you immediately and recognize that, if your partner's safely beyond your personal comfort zone, you should run or back away.

2. If your partner is within your personal comfort zone, reach out with your sensitivity to make contact with his intent before you even touch him. This way, your body is already in motion by the time the action begins. Slowly reach for your partner to slowly strike and stick, simultaneously. When you first approach your partner, don't be casual. Even though your speed and pressure are limited, you want to visualize destroying the enemy: breaking, penetrating, and tearing the enemy limb from limb. Move, as Bruce Lee said in the film, *Enter the Dragon*, with "emotional content," not anger. This ferocious mindset should characterize all your movement and imbue every fiber of your being. It should be expressed in the latent power of your body unity and the wicked elusiveness of your looseness. You are right on top of your partner, unavailable and unavoidable.

3. Begin contact flow by doing two things simultaneously: Step off line and attack the attacker. As you recall from part I, step in but obliquely, not off to the side. You can actually begin with a slow fright reaction, eye or throat spear, chin jab, or the stomp-step-kick sequence from chapter 2. This is basic close combat. You can also do the close combat universal entry (CCUE), which is highly efficient. Once contact is made, however, full guided chaos begins.

4. Stick to your opponent as closely as possible, but keep the contact as light as a feather, except, of course, when you're hitting or gouging him. Slide and skim over the surface of his skin without ever getting caught. You both want to strike each other and avoid being struck, without ever losing contact with each other, all at the same time. Twist, bend, and pocket like two weasels.

5. When moving, use whatever you want on each other: elbows, palm strikes, chops, breaks, punches, gouges, pinches, kicks, head butts, you name it. If you know a technique from some other art, try it. Interestingly, what you will find is that you will rarely be able to pull off any set techniques. This is because if your logical mind plans them, it not only makes you tight and slow, it practically air-mails your intentions to your partner (that is, if he or she has any sensitivity). If you're working the principles correctly, it should be virtually impossible for your partner to grapple or lock you, regardless of your speed. Don't cooperate. One of you is not defense and the other offense. There are no points, pauses, breaks, or restarting. You stop when you both feel like it. You are, in essence, fighting.

In order to improve when doing contact flow you have to be absolutely ruthless with yourself: Refuse to either push or be pushed (except when pulsing).

After much practice, you will plan nothing. Everything will happen seemingly by accident. You'll have no idea what you're doing or what you'll try next. All you will be doing is feeling your own and your opponent's movement.

There are various kinds of flow you can play with later, but in its basic form, stick to this principle: Keep the energy level consistent with regard to speed and pressure. Even when you drop, do that at the same speed and pressure as the rest of the flow. There are important reasons for this: In guided chaos we do not allow ourselves to be controlled, grabbed, or grappled by anyone. We also do not seek control. We seek destruction. This is a completely different methodology that is foreign to most styles. It is intrinsic to being both unavailable and unavoidable. Here's the deal: If your opponent decides to use force and speed it actually makes it *easier* for you to annihilate him. This is because he practically airmails you his intentions. He also learns nothing from the drill. We want to increase your adaptability and versatility versus other humans regardless of their size and strength, and so we are forcing you to rely on increased looseness and sensitivity for your offense and defense. This also means that until you completely understand sensitivity, you should refrain from pulsing while performing contact flow. As described earlier, pulsing is a learning trap for beginners (and even intermediates) because they completely misinterpret what it's for.

Throughout the drill, maintain a relatively slow, constant speed, proportionate with one another. Move with your whole body with the intent of driving 1,000 pounds (453.6 kg) but without the force or tension. Speed will come later as you learn to move in the most efficient, natural, and powerful manner you can. You'll find it's much easier for your brain to work toward developing a feel while doing contact flow than to analyze, plan, and execute prescribed techniques.

Another reason to go slowly at first is that all human beings have virtually the same top muscle speed, no matter how much it's trained. Put a straight razor in the hands of a sedentary woman and tell her you're holding her children hostage, and she'll cut you up faster than lightning, black belt or no black belt. Therefore, if you or your partner should suddenly accelerate to 10 times practice speed to score a point, it's stupid and unrealistic. In a real psychotic bloodbath, you'll both be going at maximum adrenaline velocity anyway, which is virtually the same speed. If you could go twice as fast as that, you would be Superman and wouldn't need any martial art! Think of contact flow as some alternate universe where the top speed you and your partner can move is, say, 2 miles per hour (3.3 km per hour). This way, in order to hit or avoid being hit, you have to rely completely on looseness and adaptability. You can't speed up, and you can't push. If you feel an opening and sense a target but you can't reach it in time because you're moving slowly, too bad. As you get more sensitive, you'll get better tactical position earlier. If your openings are blocked, find another way around the block without pushing through. Learn how to explore and discover all your movement options. If you push, your skills will go backward for two reasons: First, you're cheating, and second, the increased energy of a push is nothing but a contained speed increase. Your partner is required to speed up in response to your pressure increase because he or she should at all times be following the principle of refusing to accept pressure. If your partner doesn't speed up, then you're both pushing because you're both containing your speed; you might as well quit now because you're wasting your time. Go ahead and push to your heart's content, but only if you want to play football or do sumo. In a real fight, you'd be crushed by a stronger attacker because you'd be playing the enemy's game!

If your partner speeds up, it's you, ironically, who'll benefit because you'll get a chance to see how calm, loose, and adaptive you are while your opponent foolishly exercises his ego and wastes his time and energy. Moreover, if you get competitive or angry, you'll learn nothing and become rigid. That would be very bad. In a real fight situation, if either extreme fear or anger paralyzes you, your emotions will have inhibited your sensitivity and power. There's no ego here. Your attacker is not a person—just energy and motion you have been training to deal with. Contact flow, and all its variations, will teach you to channel your adrenaline into an unrestricted flow of sheer animal power like nothing else.

Train for life-and-death combat, be real with yourself, and worry about looking cool later. As you progress, you can eventually do contact flow as fast as you want. You can pulse and drop with full power. But in the beginning, go slowly so your nervous system won't become overloaded. Keep your speeds proportionate so your subconscious can digest the kinesthetic data it's experiencing and explore all options. Remember: Guided chaos is extremely dangerous, so use common sense at all times.

We can't emphasize enough that it's senseless to get competitive and try to score on your partner by overpowering him or her. This is not why you're training. Remember that no matter how strong you are, there's always someone stronger, perhaps even twice as strong as you. This is not to say you can't experiment with excessive speed and strength. It's just that as you get better, you won't need it, and if your partner is far more balanced, loose, and sensitive than you, you'll be annihilated, no matter how fast or strong you are.

How do you improve at this drill? There's no mystery—just lots of practice, with as many different partners as you can find. If you have friends who are schooled in different defense styles, performing contact flow with them can provide a gold mine of experience. Most schools train students to move in characteristic ways. But because you're not locked into any one way of moving, you react to the motion and nothing else.

Once you've finished practicing, think about what you experienced:

- How did your partner feel? How did you feel?
- Did you turn your brain off to avoid thinking about what you were doing?
- Did you observe the principles? Which ones?
- Did you feel rooted? Balanced? Did you step when you needed to?
- Did you challenge your opponent's strength or did you flow with him or her like a ghost?
- Were your mind and breathing slow, calm, and relaxed?
- Did your body have unified motion?
- Did your body feel relaxed yet springy, like a metal whip?
- Were you leaning?
- Did you stand sideways to your opponent or did you face him or her squarely, creating a giant target?
- Was your sticking pressure light, like a butterfly's, or were you pushing your partner to force openings?
- Did you stick consistently without grabbing?
- Did you drop at every opportunity?
- Could you clearly separate the sensations of yin and yang in your body, so your opponent's energy was reflected and magnified back?
- Did you keep your elbows down?
- Did you stick with whatever part of your body was necessary or did you limit yourself by sticking only with your hands?
- Did you slide, skim, fold, pocket, weasel, step, and tool replace to stay as close as possible while both eluding and delivering devastating strikes?
- Did you make him miss instead of blocking?
- Did you hit with as many different kinds of weapons as possible?
- Did you try to hit with more than one weapon at a time (multitasking)?
- Did you multi-hit or ricochet (coming up later)?
- Did you use your feet like your hands?

There's much to reflect on, including some additional principles in the following chapters that you will also apply to this drill. Just don't think while you're training. If you've read all this without actually experiencing contact flow, you may think it's wacky, New Age junk. All we can say is, try it, practice it diligently, and you'll be shocked how much faster you'll learn how to protect yourself than you would by doing 100 knuckle push-ups, board breaking, forms, splits, sparring, and fighting by the numbers.

Contact Flow Variations

Most beginners rely too much on their hands for sticking and sensitivity. To break this habit, perform contact flow but stick using only your elbows. You must learn that they can be nearly as versatile as your hands. After that, try doing contact flow with just your shoulders. That's right. Stick as if you had no hands, forearms, or elbows. How much subtlety and sensitivity can you develop? Explore all the deflecting and striking angles, using only your shoulders as weapons. Note that this doesn't mean you should be shoving each other around like bulls or sumo wrestlers. Instead, your goal is to develop extreme shoulder looseness and isolation so the joints become as disembodied and articulate as your hands (this will also come in to play later in some choke, knife, and gun defenses). They should slide and circle into attacks and deflections. To add the ultimate challenge, do contact flow with your eyes closed. After understanding and practicing the information in chapter 10, add ground fighting.

Once you become comfortable with the concept of contact flow, try it while wood-surfing. First try it with both you and your partner on boards, then with only one of you on a board and the other person standing on the ground, creating an obvious balance mismatch. This forces the person standing on the board to further develop his or her hyperbalance. This is equivalent to fighting someone on the edge of a cliff. To make it even more difficult, stand on one leg with your eyes closed.

As you contact-flow with every movement and in any position, remember to learn to feel the separation of yin and yang. What part of me is relaxed, and what part is tensed? Where is the energy building? Where does it want to go? Where am I resisting its trajectory? How can I let go enough to guide it without exertion and without planning?

1. **Super-slow flow.** This is contact flow performed as slowly as possible. An outside observer should barely see any movement. Both training partners must move as if they were the hands of a clock (no, not the second hand!) and refuse to speed up or add energy no matter what.

   The easiest way to begin this exercise is in a neutral position, facing each other in L stances with arms touching. From here, to do the exercise correctly, your mind must enter a tranquil, meditative alpha state where you think and plan nothing, but you remain completely open to all sensation. You are in the moment. Do not have any desire to win or score. The movement that results may be so subtle as to be almost completely internal, consisting of minute realignments and tiny shifts of weight. What usually happens is that within a minute, one person or the other will end up in an unbalanced position where he or she must speed up to adjust and recover. Instead of doing this, the one who has to adjust simply says, "You got me," and the exercise restarts from a neutral position.

   As a beginner, if you can achieve even a few seconds of true alpha state in a minute of practice, consider it a success. As you improve, you'll be able to clear your mind for longer periods and achieve extremely high levels of subconscious learning. By moving this slowly with no conscious mental interference, your subconscious naturally picks up loads of detail about your and your training partner's balance, positioning, and subtle muscular control and movement. This kind of training is the door to the most subtle, esoteric aspects of guided chaos and the highest levels of proprioception.

2. **Fixed-step flow.** This variation is useful in the beginning of your training and is good to revisit periodically. Both training partners begin facing each other in L stances with arms touching (lead foot pointing at the opponent and the rear foot perpendicular with the heels about shoulder width so that two lines going through the feet converge to form an L). Your bodies are bladed toward each other to minimize frontal striking targets, but this will change as you twist and pocket. From here, begin to flow at slow to medium speed without moving your feet at all. The feet must remain cemented to the floor. This allows you to explore the huge amount of mobility available within your body as long as you remain loose and balanced. Note how much space you can create by shifting your weight back, sinking, pocketing, and turning. Note how much space you can take up by shifting your weight forward, sinking, and penetrating. Any stiffness, lack of balance, or conscious intention to perform a specific movement will result in the closing off of much of the available mobility; instead of being able to move your entire body from the ankles up, your mobility will be pinched off somewhere (e.g., in the shoulder that exhibits the intention to hit).

   Experiment with 100 percent weight shifts from foot to foot (as in the body unity exercises in chapter 4) to exploit the absolute limits of your rooting, balance, body unity, yielding, pocketing, and looseness. This is the prescription for practitioners who are either too high and floaty on their toes or too rigid in the knees, hips, and waist. In the former, they simply have no root; in the latter, they will be shattered by a stronger opponent. Conversely, experiment with minimal defensive motion, economically eluding blows with as little movement as possible. Elude on one vector and enter on another. You'll discover how a weight shift of less than half an inch (1.25 cm) completely changes the entire situation and can turn the tables instantly—even before you move your feet. Once you can completely exploit the limits of fixed front-to-back and side-to-side shifting, it is time to work on a mobile root and add stepping.

3. **Balance flow.** Use various methods to challenge your balance during contact flow. Stand on wobble boards or uneven, slanted, wet, icy, or soft surfaces. John Perkins used to train students on rocks along the shore and in riverbeds. Stand on one leg, feeling the range of motion and energy initiation available from rooting through different points on the sole of the foot. The ultimate is doing flow on an old, round-rung ladder. Wear a weighted backpack to throw off your balance. Get creative—challenge your balance!

4. **Stalker flow.** This exercise requires an odd number of training partners, three or more. While the pair or pairs of training partners practice contact flow, the stalker sneaks up on one of the training partners and executes a sneak attack at whatever speed the contact flow is being performed. The attacked partner must react to the sneak attack (a slow fright reaction is usually appropriate) and flow with the stalker. The attacked person's former partner now becomes the stalker.

5. **Melee flow.** This contact flow variation requires three or more training partners. It's every one for himself or herself (although briefly ganging up on one unfortunate victim is . . . human). This exercise becomes more and more fun the bigger the group gets. In a large group, everyone should strive to continually move through the center of the melee without using force, lest the melee soon disperse as everyone naturally moves out to safety. If you're ever caught up in a real riot or mass attack situation, the skill you develop by moving into the middle of the training melee will help you move out of the real melee, which should be your goal. When practicing this exercise, be sure to always protect your head, keep your body soft to absorb impact, keep moving in order to give no one a bead on your back, and never fixate for more than a brief moment on any one person or location. Be sure to constantly drop and stomp your feet, both to maintain balance in the chaos and to crack shins and crush insteps. These actions are critical to survival in a maelstrom. Keep the action slow enough that the least experienced person in the group does not become overwhelmed. If you have a large group of experienced training partners who have the control necessary to move relatively quickly without injuring each other, things can get pretty chaotic! Try the exercise on a field of wobble boards or BOSUs (balance trainers) to add an additional balance challenge.

6. **Set-up attack flow.** This contact flow variation, usually performed at higher speeds (once everyone involved has the requisite levels of looseness, sensitivity, control, and trust in each other), involves beginning the flow from a disadvantaged position. For example, a trainee may stand with his or her eyes closed. The training partner will attack from an unexpected angle. The trainee must flow with the attack and work from there. Or they can both be back-to-back with eyes closed and start with one partner saying Go! It could begin with an attempted takedown with eyes closed. Other set-up attacks might begin with the trainee in a seated or lying position, with the goal to get up and move to a predetermined location (i.e., get away). You could begin with your eyes closed, and two or more attackers attempt to kidnap you and throw you in a van. This contact flow variation improves the trainee's spontaneity and ability to adapt to bad situations.

7. **Timed flow.** This high-speed contact flow variation uses a predetermined time limit (typically 5 to 10 seconds) counted out by an uninvolved observer. The goal of the trainees is to land as many "decisive" blows as possible within the timeframe while avoiding getting struck. No score is kept. Obviously, a higher level of skill and control is necessary to participate in this sort of training. If one of the trainees clearly outclasses the other in terms of skill, the less experienced trainee's goal can be to simply stay in the flow for the whole duration while minimizing damage to himself or herself. This is an excellent exercise for improving one's fighting spirit and scrappiness. In this manner, a trainee can take on a roomful of attackers sequentially.

8. **Leg flow.** This drill will be described in great detail in chapter 10, Ground Fighting. For now, begin to visualize all the attributes of guided chaos and contact flow being applied to your feet and legs while you are rolling and skittering on the ground. Tool replacement, pulsing, and the disengagement principle will all come into play, so stay tuned! Use your legs and feet in the same way as your hands to feel, pulse, intercept, and destroy. There is much more information in the section Using Anywhere Kicks on the Ground in the Ground Fighting chapter. You should also try to use all the skills developed in the Hackey Sack, Mexican Hat Dance, Puppeteering, and guided chaos kicking sections of this book while doing standing contact flow.

9. **Striking intervals.** This contact flow variation partially compensates for the one shortcoming in the contact flow exercise: the proscription against striking your training partner in all areas with full speed and penetration. Obviously, no matter how skilled you and your training partner are, and no matter how loose, you cannot actually strike your training partner in the head and neck (nor eyes and groin for that matter) with full speed and penetration. (Even during high-speed flow, if you understand dropping, you can apply full-power dropping without penetrating deeply by striking a virtual "fatter version" of your partner. By the way, this is not pulling your strikes. You are simply cracking the whip of your dropping strike a few inches (centimeters) short so the full power goes back down into your root. This may seem esoteric at first but will become easier as your understanding of dropping matures.)

    In striking intervals contact flow, a third-party observer watching a pair practice contact flow calls out "Go!" every few seconds. At the command, both training partners immediately attack heavy bags or dummies positioned nearby with a flurry of full-power strikes, then quickly go back to doing contact flow with each other at whatever speed was agreed to. Kicking shields or focus mitts held by other training partners who move around can substitute for the heavy bags or dummies. Another variation is for a training partner wearing a pair of focus mitts to flow with another trainee wearing no mitts. Every few seconds, especially right after disrupting the trainee's balance with a violent shove, the person with the focus mitts holds them up; the trainee immediately hits them with full speed and full power, and then goes back to flowing.

10. **Weapons flow.** This would be an exercise you come back to after reading and practicing the drills in the Ground Fighting and Weapons Fighting chapters. You begin with one or more partners; everyone has his or her eyes closed in a room filled with environmental weapons, such as padded sticks, rubber knives, boxes, books , garbage cans, you name it. At the signal "Go!" it's everyone for himself or herself, evading, attacking and using whatever is at hand as weapons. If none is available, you fight empty handed. All the previous contact flow concepts still apply. You can also create teams to train defensive cooperation tactics, like circling the wagons and seeking cover.

Common Faults Practicing Two-Person Contact Flow

Since contact flow is your most important training tool, it's important to approach it constructively. Actually "common faults" is too judgmental a term because contact flow drilling should be, above all, a method of experimentation. You're not looking for perfect execution or, for example, the exact position of the left pinkie. You're not looking to score points. You're training to become an expert at relaxed, spontaneous, and powerful movement, with the accent on spontaneous.

1. When you do contact flow, don't think, plan, or try to win.

2. When you first approach your partner in contact flow, don't be casual and don't cooperate. One person is not offense and the other defense. You're fighting to save your life. Your first move is to simultaneously attack and avoid, as in the CCUE. Reach out with your sensitivity to make contact with your opponent's intent before you even touch him or her. This way, your body is already in motion by the time the action begins.

3. Keep your elbows down (in general, not as a rule).

4. Don't lean.

5. Never oppose your opponent's energy: Neither your opponent nor you should feel any resistance at any time. Don't power through blocks; go around them or entice them away via pulsing. Do not use pulsing to block, push, grapple, or in any way suppress your partner's motion. Pulsing is not a defensive tool; it's offensive. When pulsing is done at maximum speed and power, it can be used as a destruction.

6. Stick but don't get stuck. Stick closely enough to sense your opponent's intentions, but lightly enough to avoid entanglement or grappling. You're not developing sensitivity to become passive like limp spaghetti. You're developing sensitivity to change direction, force, and yin versus yang. You can then amplify these changes into deadly force.

7. To develop in your training, be ruthless with your sensitivity practice. Never challenge, accept, or oppose your opponent's force. Don't bite on your opponent's pressure. Don't play into the game of pressing back. Instead, disappear and return your opponent's energy reversed and amplified from a different direction. Again, this has nothing to do with pulsing.

8. Don't think about anything at all when practicing. Just feel. Later, during a quiet moment, relax your mind and visualize the sensations each of the following ways of moving would trigger:

   • Refuse to either accept or give pressure, except when pulsing or destroying.

   • Use pulsing as an offensive trap you set to instigate a reaction. Pulsing is not a defensive tool.

   • Never challenge your enemy's energy.

   • Don't linger. Don't fixate. Keep moving; don't stop the flow.

   • When sticking, don't follow an opponent's limbs out farther than the perimeter of his or your body. If he or she blocks wide, simply slide straight in. Once you become aware of this, you won't believe how many openings it creates. Of course, the same thing applies in reverse. If you swing your arms wildly in order to attack or block, your defense will have as many holes as Swiss cheese.

9. Don't reach across your body if your body is not turning with it. If you do, you're violating yin and yang principles by adopting a double-yang position. For example, if you're in a left lead and you reach all the way across your centerline to the left with your right hand to intercept a strike, you'll wind up folded like a pretzel. Such a movement unbalances you because both sides are sending energy out and neither is receiving. This leaves you open to being tied up, locked, and uprooted, as well as hit. It also violates body unity and moving behind a guard (see chapter 7).

10. Don't hang out with an arm in a horizontal position (or any posed position for that matter). It's all right if it occurs temporarily within the movement of sticking or striking, but it leaves your midsection unprotected by your elbows. Your wrist and forearm also become susceptible to crushing, jujitsu-style breaks. Finally, it violates guard and home principles (coming up soon). You will see that your guard moves and changes with the flow.

11. Except within a strike, fright reaction, or a drac (chapter 8, p. 178), don't raise your elbow above shoulder level. Doing so leaves everything too open and makes you unbalanced. There are times when it may become the only strike or interception available, but in general, the hand is much more efficient.

12. Don't block. Make your opponent miss.

13. Don't back up when fighting a kicker. A really excellent kicker loves it if you do this and will take your head off. Always take his or her space. Don't have a guided chaos upper body and a karate lower body.

14. Train your legs to be as sensitive and versatile as your arms.

15. Use your shoes as contact surfaces, not your shins (unless you've been bashing banana trees your whole life). You can also use your knees.

16. No matter what kind of kick your opponent tries, kick to the groin.

17. Practice biting, ripping, and tearing within flow; also practice head butts at safe speeds.

18. Drop on everything.

19. Develop more lateral movement with zoning and box stepping. Generally maintain a sideways L stance.

20. Always step off line and in.

21. Step and hit simultaneously. If you need to step, then step fully. Avoid the floating sensation of being on your toes, heels, or halfway between roots. Don't lunge and leave your back foot in the bucket. Do not step with just one foot. Make all your stepping a 1-2 affair.

22. Don't move unnecessarily unless forced to do so by your opponent or because you feel an opening in his structure.

23. Don't clamp down when using grabbing as a pulse. Let the strength of your pulse remain constant and loose; as it slides down the limb, let it snag itself on bony protrusions. If your opponent pulls back, snap in. If your opponent pushes back and attacks, pass the apple.

24. Don't fall into patterns. Be creative, inventing your own strikes. For example, try backhanded eye pokes; they're very sneaky (figure 6.15).

25. To break a tie-up, drop, turn, and step in, using your whole body. Don't muscle it. Smash and spear with your elbows. Try to keep your fingers on top of your opponent's arms as you stick. Stick with your elbows to free your hands.

Figure 6.15

26. Stick with your shoulders to free your elbows (after tool-replacing inside).

27. If your opponent merely backs up, follow him or her and keep hitting. Never give your opponent an inch to breathe. (If your attacker falls or becomes disabled, however, run away.)

28. Drop and pocket at the same time you absorb the strike.

29. Use your legs to pulse, too.

30. Don't simply feel with your hands or your upper body. Feel every point of contact as a pressure change in your feet. Use this awareness to move your center off line and find the perfect weight distribution and rooting. This will allow you to deliver maximum power at the perfect angle of attack as well as avoid incoming attacks.

31. Don't just play sumo with your contact flow partner. Hook your proprioception into his so you can feel his root and manipulate his intentions before he's even aware of them.

Advanced Sensitivity Concepts: The Esoteric Side

Until now, we have discussed sensitivity in terms of the tactile awareness of external stimuli. There are other aspects of sensitivity, however, and deeper ways of understanding it.

Sensitivity in guided chaos is divided into three aspects:

1. External tactile sensitivity. This is the sensitivity we have already discussed at length. It involves the sensing and perceiving of external stimuli via tactile means. This is how your subconscious can know by feel exactly how others are moving.

2. Internal sensitivity. Proprioception. Proprioception is the unconscious perception of movement and spatial orientation arising from stimuli within the body itself. Proprioception is the ability to accurately feel the exact position and tension state of all parts of your own body (body awareness). People often take proprioception for granted, but it is actually a critical attribute that varies widely between individuals and can be easily improved in most people.

Most of the guided chaos solo exercises you have already practiced actually train your proprioception. Proprioception is an essential part of developing the other principles of balance, looseness, and body unity. How loose you can get depends on how precisely you can feel the tension states of all parts of your body. Your body unity depends on your ability to feel the relationships between different parts of your body and how they move with each other. Dynamic balance is basically proprioception applied to controlling your center of gravity in any circumstance. The more accurate and precise the feedback your subconscious gets from your body, the better the subconscious can adjust the body to maintain balance. Therefore, internal sensitivity to your own body is critical to your fighting ability. An example of this is learning to become acutely aware of pressure changes in your feet as you flow with the attacker's energy. This awareness helps dictate possible root changes on your part to maximize avoiding or delivering power.

Another example is always attempting to feel your feet in your hands. With every contact with the enemy, you should feel a direct line of body-unitized power all the way from your root, through the bones, to the contact point. This is much more subtle and all encompassing than the boxer's maxim of punching from your feet, and it requires awareness of all tense and relaxed muscles in the body as well as the alignment of the bones they control.

3. External subcortical visual sensitivity. We have already established that conscious visual perception is too slow and too easily tricked to effectively guide your actions in close quarters combat. Therefore, we showed you how to develop subconscious external tactile sensitivity. However, external tactile sensitivity on its own cannot help in situations when you are not in physical contact with the enemy. Fortunately, another kind of sensitivity can help in these situations.

The mode of visual perception that most of us are accustomed to using may be characterized as conscious cortical perception. The images we normally perceive and act on have already been organized, recognized, and labeled by the visual cortex of the brain. We are consciously aware of what we're looking at. It takes time for information to be transmitted from the retinas of the eyes to the visual cortex of the brain (located at the upper rear of the brain), for the visual cortex to organize the information into the image we consciously see, and then for us to consciously determine a response to the image. This perception pathway is far too slow to deal with the split-second changes that occur in close quarters combat.

However, we've all had the experience of experiencing a blink reflex or even a complete startle response triggered by a sudden visual cue without any conscious recognition. If a small fly or some other object suddenly moves quickly near your eyes, you typically become consciously aware of what it was only after your body has reacted—if you become consciously aware of it at all. The object (or more correctly, the movement or change of the object) is being subconsciously perceived and acted on via different neural pathways, ones that occur below the level of the visual cortex, or subcortically.

Retinal information actually goes to several areas of the brain stem before being transmitted to the visual cortex. These areas are responsible for various optical reflexes, as well as for prioritization and emotional attribution of the received information. It is these areas, as well as those involved in external tactile sensitivity, that are involved in subcortical visual sensitivity.

Subcortical visual sensitivity is an advanced attribute applicable only after a high level of tactile sensitivity has been achieved; it involves training to associate preconscious visual cues with tactile responsiveness. You can detect a movement before you're consciously aware of "seeing" it (i.e., before it is processed in the visual cortex of the brain); that movement can be detected and treated as a tactile stimulus in terms of subconscious reaction. This is why you want to do most of your contact flow practice with your eyes open, even though practicing with your eyes closed would seem to more thoroughly emphasize tactile awareness. If you are seeing what is going on during contact flow with relaxed, impartial, unattached observation—not consciously looking at anything, but simply allowing your eyes to take in the information—over time, your subconscious mind can build associations between the movement it sees and what your body feels. It can then subconsciously act on subcortical visual stimuli almost as quickly and precisely as if those visual stimuli were tactile. This is what we mean by extending or reaching out with your sensitivity. If this sounds weird, don't worry—it is! However, it becomes clearer when you work with a guided chaos practitioner who can use subcortical visual sensitivity. He or she will seem to feel your motion and adapt instantly to it even before physical contact is established. Even then, this attribute is used primarily to safely guide the practitioner into a position where physical contact can be established, allowing the tactile sensitivity to take over.

The Art of Perception: It's All Mental

Guided chaos masters like to point out that beyond a certain point of physical development, advancing in guided chaos is more a mental challenge than a physical one. How you mentally perceive and interpret what your senses tell you—and how you comprehend the movement of your own body and those of others—are what will change the most and will most affect your combat abilities once your physical prowess has advanced sufficiently.

Even though you can never have enough balance, and you can always improve, it does not take long for most people who do the guided chaos exercises to achieve a level of physical balance far superior to that of most normal people. The same goes for the physical aspects (e.g., muscle development and coordination) of the other basic principles. In combat, all things being equal, even small advantages in the basic principles by one combatant over the other can pay big dividends. However, mental internalization and deeper understanding of the basic principles begin the road to mastery.

Everyone perceives and internalizes things differently. Imagine trying to explain to someone else exactly how you perceive the color red. A similar situation exists in the internal martial arts. What can be suggested and passed on from teacher to student in long-term, hands-on training is difficult to put into writing in a way that makes sense. (This is one reason for the often impenetrably esoteric and flowery writings that come out of China about internal martial arts such as tai chi. The writers are struggling to convey internal feelings and perceptions that are truly unique to each individual, although all these individuals want to achieve the same external effects. Then, of course, the writings are translated by people who may not know much about martial arts.)

In the following sections, we'll attempt to offer several ideas (and even a drill or two) to jump-start your journey toward thinking differently about movement and combat.

Unifying Proprioception, Body Unity, and Intention: Moving From the Feet

All active motion should be initiated by a change in how the feet interact with the ground. One foot can push harder than the other, causing some weight to transfer from the harder-pushing foot to the other. Different parts of the foot can push against the ground in different ways. For example, even when you're standing on one foot, pushing more with the ball of the foot than with the heel is enough of a change to cause a great deal of motion in the rest of the body. There are infinite points on the soles of your feet that can push against the ground in different ways, in different directions, and in different combinations.

The looser your body is, the better it will carry through all the energy generated by each change of pressure of your feet against the ground. Any stiffness will stifle the energy transfer and flow of movement.

The basic Turning drill (see chapter 5, p. 64) is a good way to get a feel for this. Forget any idea of how this drill is supposed to look or what you're supposed to do. Simply move your limp body back and forth by pushing harder against the floor with one foot, then with the other. Keep your body from your ankles up completely loose, passively letting your body move with changes in pressure against the ground. Start out by letting your body settle between each weight shift, allowing your body to move as freely as possible before coming to rest.

Once you have the feeling of letting your body move with each change of foot pressure, the next time don't let your body settle. As your body moves with one pressure change, change the pressure in your feet again before the body stops moving. As you continue doing this, and changing your foot pressure in a variety of ways, your completely passive body should begin to move randomly until you're doing a passive version of polishing the sphere. Each successive energy wave from each change of foot pressure collides with and augments the waves still traveling through the body from the previous changes, creating unpredictable but increasingly powerful, flowing full-body movement. Concentrate only on the connections of the feet against the ground and the pressure changes they make, allowing the rest of your body to just go where it will. Strive to fine-tune your proprioception so that you can feel even the slight deformation of your feet against the ground as you distribute more or less weight to different parts.

All active intention should come from the feet, pushing against the ground. No intention should come from anywhere else.

By *intention*, we mean initial motivation to action. If you want to react to an attack, and your brain decides to initiate the action anywhere other than in your feet, you'll be easily stopped and knocked off balance. For example, many people initiate the motion of a punch from the shoulder, hip, or head. If you do this, not only will you telegraph your motion but the enemy need only shoulder-stop you (slam a palm strike into the shoulder of the punching arm) to stop your attack, jolt your whole body, and take over control of your balance. However, if your initiation is only in your feet pressing against the ground, and your loose body simply carries the wave of energy from that pressure change from the foot-ground connection up through your body into the punch, the shoulder stop will not unbalance you; because your whole body is involved, the wave of energy will be redirected to the other side of your body, which will proceed to hit the enemy. You're giving your opponent no intention to block.

Having no intention in the upper body means that you don't want anything in particular to happen (e.g., you're not thinking, *I want to punch him there, now!*). As soon as you want something specific to happen, your mind and therefore your intention goes to where you want it to happen, and you present your intention and the key to your balance to the enemy. However, if your intention remains in your feet, and you simply add energy to position your center of gravity according to the dictates of your sensitivity and its bead on the enemy's center of gravity, your body remains without intention and therefore able to adapt naturally to anything the enemy does without conscious thought.

The key to having intention in your feet is staying low and rooted throughout all movement and stepping, letting all your vitality and strength sink into your feet so that your feet are full and heavy while the rest of your body is empty and flaccid. If you rise up during a movement, losing the fullness and weight of the feet, you will lose your rooted connection to the ground, and nothing will work. If you stay rooted and full with your feet and empty in the rest of your body, it is practically impossible to overcommit and throw yourself off balance. Pressure from your rooted feet will never throw your center of gravity beyond your base. In contrast, movement initiated by intention in your upper body can easily throw your balance beyond the base provided by your feet because your feet, which root your balance, don't get a say in the matter!

If you move with intention solely from your feet while remaining rooted, it is practically impossible for the enemy to control your balance unless he controls your center directly. He cannot force you off balance through your periphery because it is empty of intention, giving him nothing to push against; your center of gravity remains under the control of your root. If you feel him getting close to controlling your center directly, changing the pressure in your feet to move your center even one inch is enough to make you safe again—unless he's better at the whole game, does not overcommit to anything, and is sensitive enough to follow your change.

Remember that a person can stop your motion, jam you up, and force you off balance only if he has a direct line with his pressure through your center, no matter where he's pushing from. For example, if he pushes on your arm directly into your center, he'll be able to stop that arm and your whole body from moving and force you off balance. Many students try to move the pushed arm to shed the opponent's push. This simply won't work if the pusher is at all sensitive, because all the pusher has to do is follow the obviously moving limb and keep the pressure toward the center; the pusher can even abandon the limb and take up the slack closer to the center itself. However, if you keep the limb where it is and simply use the pressure of your feet to move your center only 1 inch (2.5 centimeters) and take all intention out of your body, you'll immediately regain control of your center and allow your body to slip in and destroy the pusher, unless the pusher is sensitive enough to change immediately. This requires an entirely different level of sensitivity from that required to follow a moving arm because, in this case, the point of contact does not move until the movement of the center has already put the pusher in checkmate. A less sensitive pusher may not even detect a change until suddenly he's being hit from all directions while his push slides harmlessly off your body. Compare this concept with isolation energy (discussed earlier) and moving behind the guard (chapter 7).

This is only a first step to moving with full body unity and ghostliness: where every contact with the enemy is either too light for him to perceive or heavy enough to get him off balance and damage him. Once you attain the proprioception and relaxation under pressure to move exclusively from your root, which results in body unity, you can start to break the rules and isolate movements of your limbs and body apart from your root. You can disconnect and isolate when that helps, and reconnect where appropriate. Within your flow of motion, you can isolate and change something before reconnecting to destroy, which really confuses things for an opponent who does not yet understand such things. This requires a higher level of sensitivity and proprioception. When appropriate, you can strategically add intention and fullness—but not overcommitment—back into your upper body to bait and deceive the enemy. This is part of pulsing. The key is that you have complete control over your movements and can empty instantly when needed so you don't get stuck. This is different from the actions of a less experienced student, who simply does not yet know how to empty his or her upper body and fill his or her feet.

Psycho Tango

This solo drill can help you begin to isolate upper and lower body movements in an effective, deceptive way.

1. Root on your left leg, sinking low so that all your weight flows into the ground through your left foot. Keep your arms relaxed, with your hands in front of your throat.

2. Begin to tap a steady, rhythmic pattern (about two taps per second) with your right foot against the ground. Tap your foot against the ground in front of you, then back to the center, then out to the right side, then back to the center, then behind you, then back to the center, and then repeat. Make sure the entire sole of your foot touches the ground at the same moment with each tap—don't tap just your heel or toe, and don't roll your foot. Make sure your toes remain pointed straight forward. Make sure your body does not bounce at all—you should be completely rooted and steady on your left leg. Watch yourself in a mirror. You should not be able to discern any movement in your body from the waist up as you perform the tapping pattern. Concentrate on executing this pattern absolutely precisely, with a perfectly steady rhythm.

3. Maintain the precise rhythmic pattern with the lower body and begin polishing the sphere and washing the body from the waist up. The polishing and washing with your upper body should be completely random, without any rhythm or pattern. The random, arrhythmic movement of your upper body should be completely divorced

from the patterned, rhythmic movement of your lower body. This is more difficult than it sounds. Watch yourself closely to ensure that your upper body is not subtlety following the rhythm of your lower body.

4. Speed up the motion of your upper body, keeping it completely unpatterned and arrhythmic; maintain the precise tempo, rhythm, and pattern of your lower body.

5. Slow down the motion of your upper body, keeping it completely unpatterned and arrhythmic; continue to maintain the precise tempo, rhythm, and pattern of the lower body.

6. To make things more difficult, wash your head and hips while ensuring your right foot still taps in the exact same places in the exact same pattern, rhythm, and tempo.

7. Repeat the drill, rooting on the right leg and tapping with the left. Compare with the Split-Brain Air Writing drill in chapter 4.

Unifying Internal and External Sensitivity: Plugging In to the Enemy

Don't think of your training partner as an enemy or opponent. Instead, imagine that your partner's body is actually part of your own. When you make contact with his or her body, don't think of the situation as trying to feel what someone else is doing. Instead, feeling your partner's body is exactly the same as feeling your own body internally. It's as if you're plugging your proprioception into your partner's body (or, alternately, you're tapping into his or her proprioception) so that you feel everything going on inside your partner's body just as you feel everything going on inside of yours. You're extending your proprioception into your partner's body, making it part of your own. You never accidentally hit yourself in the head with your own arm, do you? Therefore, how could your proprioception allow your third and fourth arms (your partner's arms) to hit you? Experiment with mind games such as this.

The Four Feelings

Know yourself, know your enemies, know what your enemies know about you, and know your vulnerabilities. To paraphrase Sun Tzu in *The Art of War*,

Know your enemy and know yourself, and in 100 battles you will not be defeated.

Proprioception is the "know yourself" part. The more precisely you can subconsciously feel all the details of your own body and movement, the better.

External sensitivity (tactile and subcortical visual) is the "know your enemy" part. The more precisely you can subconsciously feel all the details of your opponents' bodies and movement, feel their intentions and balance more precisely and more quickly than even they can, the better.

Being subconsciously aware of what you are allowing your opponents to feel is the "knowing what your enemies know about you" part. Having good proprioception and external sensitivity will do you little good if you constantly give away your intentions to your opponents through excess contact. The pinnacle of ghostly movement is allowing your enemy to feel nothing except lack of balance and damage. Any contact heavy enough for him to perceive, and that does not damage him or immediately upset his balance, is contact his sensitivity can use to gather information about your movement. If you understand what you are allowing him to feel, you can use such contact deceptively as pulsing. By doing so, you allow him to feel something other than what actually is, which is facilitated by isolation energy (described earlier).

Being subconsciously self-aware is the "know your vulnerabilities" part. You must be aware of your vulnerabilities moment by moment, given your position, intentions, and balance relative to your opponent. This enables your body to move to cut off all possible vulnerabilities as quickly as possible by moving your body and your opponent's as necessary. You can then deal with and defeat what *could* be rather than simply what *is*. As John Perkins says, "An ounce of prevention is worth a pound of pain!"

In guided chaos, you must deal with what actually *is* true and what actually *could* be true, not what you want to be true. This is one of the important differences between guided chaos and conventional, patterned-movement martial arts.

What follows is an example of a ferocious altercation where form went right out the window. It is the same kind of situation you may come up against some day—with one big difference. In this case, the defending partners were police officers who were trying to subdue a psychotic attacker without the use of lethal force. In the end they all piled on at once and only then was Perkins able to subdue the maniac with a sleeper hold (which was legal at the time). Even if they had decided the situation warranted it, the ongoing chaos would have prevented them from using their guns because of the risk of shooting a fellow officer. As a a policeman following correct protocol, Perkins could not end the fight immediately with deadly strikes to the eyes and throat, even though the opportunities were there. As a civilian, you're under no such obligation if you think you're going to die. Your attacker certainly isn't.

MIKE THE SAILOR
John Perkins

Headquarters called us and said we had a 14B—a person with mental illness in need of assistance. The department rule on 14B calls at that time was to unload your weapon before you engaged the suspect. The reasoning for this came from years of experience: The last thing you needed was a person with an emotional disability getting your gun during a struggle. (I don't believe this is as likely today because the new holsters are much better at retaining weapons.)

We arrived at a small apartment. My partner, two other officers, and I began interviewing a young man and his mother. The mother was very distraught and crying. She told me they were originally from Europe, and her son was a sailor. He had been giving her a very hard time, and she felt he might become dangerous. The son seemed pretty calm to us. The mother then told us that her son would not take his medication. Now we felt a little more uneasy.

My partner and I separated the son and his mother into different rooms. While two officers were interviewing "mom" in the kitchen, we were speaking with Mike (a fictitious name) in the bedroom. The young man was approximately 23 years old. He stood 5 feet, 10 inches (1.8 m) tall and weighed 190 to 200 pounds (86.2 to 90.7 kg). He was powerfully built with a great deal of natural strength. We spoke with Mike for a few more minutes until his mother began to yell and make a scene. My partner (who was the senior member of our radio car team) told me to keep an eye on Mike for a few seconds so he could see what was going on.

As soon as my partner left the room, Mike started chuckling. I looked at his face and saw that he was not in the same mood as before. He then stated in a thick accent that he could have easily killed my partner. I guess he hadn't been impressed with Bill's size, 6 feet, 5 inches (1.96 m) tall and about 240 pounds (108.9 kg). Maybe the outcry from Mike's mother and the fact that Bill had stood with his chest in Mike's face precipitated the change in Mike's behavior.

I looked at Mike's hands to see if he had a weapon we might have overlooked. He was bare-handed. Mike then stepped a little closer to me and said that he knew karate. My back was facing an old wooden closet door. This door had panels three-quarters to two inches (1.9 to 5.1 cm) thick, made of solid maple. As he finished speaking, he flinched on his right side. That's when I knew he was going to try to hit me. What I didn't know was how. I jumped and yielded to my right just in time to see his right hand, with his fingers fully extended, fly past the left side of my face as he lunged forward. He had tried to take out my eyes. Instead, Mike's hand struck the closet door and broke through a three-quarter-inch-thick (1.9-cm-thick) section of wood, whereupon his pinkie came off.

(continued)

Mike the Sailor, *continued*

When I saw this, I realized I'd have to fight for my life. After Mike pulled his hand out of the door, he spun around to find me. I had box-stepped and landed behind him. As he started to turn, I hit him on the side of his head with a right palm-heel strike. It was a solid shot. This unbalanced him for a split second, and he bounced into the closet door. I knew instantly that, given the amount of force I had used, he would not easily succumb to kicks and punches.

My blackjack was in the side leg pocket of my uniform pants, but before I could pull it out, he was on me. I drove him away with a dropping, two-handed palm-heel shove. (I later found out from the hospital that this shove had broken two of his ribs.) I felt the power of his body at that instant and realized that, given his mental state, I was no physical match for him. I knew that my fellow officers were only seconds away and that I had to hold out until they arrived. As I moved backward, I found that the bed was now at my right side. I dragged the bed for an instant and tried to place it between Mike and me as I attempted to get through the doorway. Somehow I lifted the bed up and pushed it forward, sending Mike backward. At this point, my buddies came crashing in behind me to get at the enraged Mike. They got around and over the bed and, with blackjacks and sticks flying, attempted to subdue him.

Mike proved to be even stronger than I imagined. With strength powered by his mental illness, he was able to disarm two of the officers and began kicking them and striking them with a nightstick. I recognized that even if my gun had been loaded, it would be too dangerous to shoot because of the chance of hitting an officer. I then leaped in, and through the barrage of hits and kicks from Mike and the officers, I got onto Mike's back. Just before jumping in, I made the conscious decision not to strike Mike in the eyes or throat. Mercy, and the hated paperwork I would have to do if I blinded or killed him, guided my actions. I quickly applied a sleeper hold, which was legal at the time. This was dangerous because he was trying to take my eyes out with his thumb. I placed my head close to Mike's back and squeezed, and in a matter of seconds, he went limp. We handcuffed him and tied his upper torso and arms with the bed sheet. We took Mike and his mangled hand to the hospital, where after a long struggle, he was finally sedated and repaired.

Preventing Common Mistakes

➤ You can't be stiff and drop effectively. Dropping is a brief, instantaneous act of complete bodily relaxation that essentially loads your spring, so you can't be totally limp either when you rebound and strike.

➤ Pocketing requires counterbalancing other portions of your body. For example, when pocketing your chest, don't lean forward, stick out your chin, sit back on your heels, or stick your butt out. Any of these actions can throw you off balance. Instead, drop your hips straight down and rock the bottom of your pelvis down and forward. Keep your head in line with your pelvis (unless it's your head you're pocketing), which allows you to respond quickly.

➤ When polishing the sphere, don't stand stiffly with your arms rotating at the shoulders like two propellers. Just as with the body unity drills in chapter 4 (Body Writing and Starting the Mower, pp. 76-77), you want to get your entire mass behind every nuance of the circles you make, even if they're just an inch (2.5 cm) in diameter. Your entire body rises, falls, and turns side to side with the circles you make, no matter how small they are.

➤ When washing the body, don't just rub yourself. Try to move those areas of your body that are being washed away from those that are doing the washing. At any time, the areas that are moving away can turn around and chase the others.

PART

III

GUIDED CHAOS FOR SUPERIOR SELF-DEFENSE

Now that you have an understanding of the principles of guided chaos, we can begin to discuss more specific strategies and tactics that will help you use the principles to move freely as well as efficiently, effectively, and combatively. Although all fights are chaotic, the human body tends to move in characteristic ways when attacking and defending. Part III addresses these tendencies by showing how the guided chaos principles flow into related subprinciples that deal effectively with the particulars of combat. We have waited until now to go into these subprinciples because, to the uninitiated, they may seem like techniques. Rather, they are merely snapshots in a continuous flow that give clues to dealing with chaos. Before we explore part III's subprinciples, however, let's review the larger concepts you picked up in part II:

- The state of natural awareness is a combination of looseness, body unity, balance, and sensitivity functioning as one, not as independent parts of the whole.
- You cannot have looseness without balance. You'll simply be knocked over or twisted into a pretzel.
- You have to develop sensitivity to know when to yield or step around a strike to move to a new, balanced position.
- When you're better balanced, your opponent can't move you; yet because of body unity, you can move your opponent at will.
- If your opponent pushes you, he'll find himself off balance, pushing against nothing because you're loose and balanced, yet you're constantly all over him, sticking like jelly.

- Because you're sensitive, you've already moved as little or as much as neccessary to strike your opponent with deadly force from bizarre angles, seemingly out of nowhere.

- When you're sensitive, balanced, and loose, you can be both as hard as you want to be and as soft—at the same time.

- With extreme sensitivity and balance, you can move like the wind, strike with the authority of lightning, then leave like the wind. Your strikes should be felt, not seen.

- By dropping and driving from your feet through your legs, turning at the waist, and extending the power loosely through your arm, you're able to hit with immense power yet with little effort.

- You're able to do this because you have learned not to exert negative tension with antagonistic muscle groups. Without strain, power flows uninhibitedly.

When attacked, you're able to negate the opponent's force by yielding and redirecting. You can even borrow your opponent's power and use it against him or her. In all this, you're developing your mind and body to function and fight from every possible angle, instantly inventing and creating your defense as you need it. When all four principles come together, you become an enigma and embody the fifth principle: spontaneous freedom of action and reaction, the principle we call adaptability. In part III we show comprehensively how to achieve it.

CHAPTER SEVEN

APPLYING THE PRINCIPLES TO MOTION

The subprinciples discussed in this chapter are not some great secrets of the universe; they merely reflect the way the human body naturally moves. We emphasize natural movement because wild animals don't have a cognitive mind fighting for control over their nervous systems as we do. For example, you can't teach a tiger to fight "better." It's always performing at maximum for its species. Similarly, there are ways of attacking and defending that are naturally efficient for the human body. Part II explained these in terms of looseness, body unity, balance, and sensitivity. Now, to help you understand how to apply these principles to specific attack and defense scenarios, we have divided the material into two sections: the body as a shield and the body as a weapon.

The Body as a Shield

You've already learned in close combat that blocking as a fixed technique is wasteful, slow, and inefficient. Moreover, the understanding of skimming energy that you picked up in chapter 6 shows you that it's far better to deflect an incoming strike incidentally, on the way to delivering your own. You facilitate this by being aware of the natural deflecting attributes obtained by the way you position certain parts of your anatomy. We explore these movements and positions in the following sections.

Moving Behind a Guard

Ironically, when most people move, they leave vital areas wide open all the time. Beginners in guided chaos especially, in an effort to be loose and avoid strikes, will often twist themselves into positions that leave them even more vulnerable. They also have an excessively loose reaction to incoming pressure that creates additional openings. The solution is to always move behind a guard. Keep something between you and the attacker at all times as you stick to him or her. This is so simple we're almost embarrassed to teach it; nevertheless, as obvious as it sounds, it is rarely observed. Sticking lightly is not the same as blocking. Instead of just picking off hits, mold to your opponent's weapons, continuously sealing off your targets. When you practice the contact flow drill, you learn to stick with your opponent's every move while still keeping something practical—like a hand or elbow, not a toe, pinky, or nose—in front of the nearest threatened vital area: your face, neck (front and rear), torso, and groin. What most people don't realize is that as they move and stick, the relative alignment of weapon, guard, and target constantly changes and must be readjusted; otherwise, they'll be sticking to the wrong side of the weapon! When you have just a blocking mentality, this constant readjustment process never occurs, and you're always one step behind the attacker—waiting to block.

While maintaining contact, you can cover your face and neck with your hand or forearm (and sometimes your elbow), your torso with your elbow (and sometimes your hand), and your groin with the angle of your hips or knees. Keep the area you're protecting as unexposed as possible. Remember that by standing sideways, you reduce the size of the target area and allow your lead leg to guard your groin.

> Don't move the attacker's strike. Move your *body* so it stays behind your guard (contact point with the enemy).

If you watch how people move, they often pull strikes into their bodies in an unconscious (or, in the case of some extremely popular styles, conscious and purposeful) attempt to smother or grapple the attack. Doing so will actually make you stick to the wrong side of your opponent's weapon, eliminate your guard, and encourage your opponent to drive in farther! Is this really a tactic you want to employ against larger, stronger, and more dangerous individuals? You want to be unavailable yet unavoidable. Every second you grapple with or are otherwise locked to a stronger opponent exposes you to more danger. You always want to work the paradox of being as disengaged as possible yet still engaged, remaining in contact yet being free to move.

A simple way to practice this is to look in the mirror and move your hand randomly in circles and arcs in front of your body with the palm always facing away from your body (this is a precursor to the advanced Polishing the Sphere exercise). As you move your hand, try to imagine a line between the back of your hand and your face; constantly move and align your body to keep your face behind your hand (but not 2 inches [5 cm] away). We mean a reasonable but defendable distance so there's room to deflect an incoming strike. You should almost look like you're playing follow the leader with your hand. Now do the same thing with the point of your elbow. Move it around in front of you, side to side and up and down, but keep your face and throat tucked behind it in the drac position described in chapter 8. This is simple stuff, but even skilled fighters use techniques that allow the enemy to engage and grapple them directly! This is insanity. Remember the key guided chaos principle that under the influence of adrenaline or drugs, anyone can be dangerous, and any fight can result in your death. Ingrain this deep into your brain: If you can't run, be as disengaged as possible yet still be engaged.

Now, using both arms, randomly move your forearms, palms, elbows, and shoulders. The key point of this drill is that however you move, your vital areas should be covered as much as possible by whatever body part is practical. There is no rule or form to this. To keep this drill simple in the beginning, one or both palms should remain in front of your eyes and throat (facing out) in the direction you're moving, and your elbows should be within 12 inches (30 cm) of your kidneys. The elbow of the lead arm should be down no matter which direction you're facing.

As a variation, do the same drill but move so the elbow of your lead arm sticks out in front of your face with that arm bent and held horizontally so you look like Count Dracula hiding behind his cape. Keep the palm of your rear hand facing forward, near your solar plexus. As you turn and face a different direction, your hands reverse, with your new lead arm doing the drac elbow and the other palm guarding your solar plexus (figure 7.1). Try having your lead elbow move randomly from a vertical to a horizontal or an inverted position (see the Elbow Strikes section in chapter 2, pp. 21). Finally, be aware that although you are consciously choosing positions in this drill, when you flow with a partner, it will be your partner's motions that determine the shape of your guard. Just be sure it's an effective one.

Try to apply moving behind a guard as you're practicing polishing the sphere and washing the body. Granted, there's no actual opponent to shield yourself from. Nevertheless, even though you're moving freely and creatively in these drills, you want to move with the intention that you're also protecting your vital areas. This significantly changes the character of your movements and helps to ingrain them into your nervous system.

Yielding to Your Advantage

"OK," you say, "so I'm loose, balanced, and sensitive, but when my opponent punches through my hand, and my hand punches me in the face because it yielded like you said, I get a little confused as well as bloody. What's wrong?" The answer is so simple it may sound like a joke, but there's a principle involved: Yield in ways that are helpful and not hurtful to you. And, of course, still maintain balance. In the previous example, by sticking with your hand, you've only got it half right. Instead of yielding your deflection so your opponent's fist drives your own hand into your face, move the target (your face) behind your guard (your hand) so hat you're letting the strike go where it wants, except you won't be there when it arrives. Let him win. You simultaneously slide or skim along the arm and slam your opponent with your own strike, maintaining contact the whole time. *Don't deflect your opponent. Make him or her miss. Don't move the strike—remove the target.* This is accomplished by pocketing, turning, stepping, or all three.

Figure 7.1

Your guard is not a static thing, and your arms should still stick, following the opponent's body within the flow until you find an opening to hit through. Moving behind a guard also dictates that the guard—the arms in this case—never move beyond the perimeter of your body. You need to protect only you, not the air around you.

If your opponent swings wildly to hit you or get away, slide into the centerline opening this creates and attack. This is not a mental strategy. You will simply feel a crack in his defense and fall through it automatically, like water draining through a bucketful of holes.

When do you change your guard or contact point? All the time. Never be locked into any defensive position. Your contact points change continuously as you seal openings and search for the same in the enemy. An analogy might be to compare contact flow to shaping clay on a potter's wheel. As the object spins, you have to be sensitive to its shape, constantly changing contact points and sliding over the clay without overcommitting and grappling with it.

The Formless Stance

Don't equate formless with powerless. To generate the most power by separating the yin from the yang, your body needs to adapt to whatever is coming at it, allowing it to move between extremes. Your stance, therefore, should be dictated by function. It needs to provide efficient cover as well as the ability to move freely in any direction.

Neutral Balance   When you stand motionless in the formless stance, you attempt to distribute your weight evenly between both feet, creating neutral balance and thus a strong root. You should feel like a buoy in the ocean. However, since you're in constant motion, you'll never have perfect, 50–50 weight distribution, so you should not try to force yourself to adopt or revert to it. This is why it is vital to develop single-leg balance because you need to be able to change your root continuously from foot to foot under dynamic stress. All the while, you need to remain comfortable with delivering strikes with dropping energy and plyometrically loading your coiled body unity so that it explodes with full-body mass into the new, completely balanced root, which is yet again instantly abandoned for a new, more powerful root. Do not stubbornly cling to a fixed root. A mere quarter-inch (.6 cm) microadjustment in your foot position makes a colossal difference in your defense. Go with the energy, and like a sprung mousetrap, pour yourself into the new root. When you have a root that can't be found, you can move in any direction, redistribute your weight, and yield or change positions at any time without ever having the need to dance on your toes. Focus on adaptability, not choreography.

Leaning Versus Yielding
Leaning is a reactive handicap common in many classical fighting stances. It indicates poor balance and makes it harder to respond to incoming strikes. Keep your feet as flat to the ground as possible (refer to the Ninja Walk and Vacuum Walk, pp. 87-88). This is easier to do if your lower back remains relatively straight as it comes to rest in the neutral position; a straight lower back prevents you from leaning forward on your toes or backward on your heels. When you yield and pocket you move just the target area out of the way while moving the rest of your body a compensating amount to retain balance. This maintains your ability to step freely if necessary. Leaning in any direction hinders this and rocks you off the flats of your feet.

Efficient Guarding
Seek to root yourself so you face your opponent sideways, and your profile becomes narrow enough to protect with one arm. Your lead hand covers your face with your palm facing out to ward off head shots. Your lead forearm protects your chest, and your lead elbow covers your kidneys and ribs. As you stick to your opponent, move behind your guard by keeping your targets diametrically opposite his weapons. This further reduces the area you need to defend. Contrast with blocking, which attempts to move the incoming strike off-line.

Stand with your feet in an L stance so your lead foot always points toward the enemy, and your rear foot points to the side. If your opponent tries to circle you, simply pivot slightly on your front foot, keeping it pointed at him so you retain a narrow profile. He'll have to travel five times farther than you to get around your lead. Follow these guidelines for creating an efficient defense:

There are a million counters made possible by taking your opponent's space, but all you need to know is that if you remain loose and sensitive, you will simply flow into the openings without effort.

- Even though you're sticking to the opponent, don't chase his arms beyond what's necessary. It may take only 1 inch (2.5 cm) of deflection or redirection at an early stage of a strike to protect a wide swath of your body.

- As soon as you gain 1 inch of deflection or redirection from yielding, turning, or tool replacing, slide, fold, skim, ricochet, or weasel your strike into the opening.

- When you turn your body, turn fully so you present your other side to your opponent. This is an example of separating the yin from the yang. Don't hang out in between—the target it creates is equivalent to the broadside of a barn. This is a common beginner's mistake.

- If you only turn your upper body, with your right hand, shoulder, and left foot forward, you'll be poised for a split second, suspended like a wrecking ball or a rubber band, before you release and fly back the other way to a normal lead. As you return with your wound-up energy, you can deliver a strike out of both lead positions like a whip. Or you can simply box step out of it into a new lead.

Taking Your Opponent's Space

Taking your opponent's space is something you try to do continuously in guided chaos. It doesn't mean, however, that you bully your opponent. That would run counter to everything we've discussed so far. What you want to do is enter but remain unavailable. This is a paradox that may seem difficult to understand without showing some parallels in nature.

Think of water flowing through holes in a bucket. Similarly, you flow through the holes in your opponent's defense. But you'll only be able to find them if you're loose and sensitive. This means moving in where there's no pressure. If you're not loose, you may not recognize an opening even when it's right in front of your face.

For example, A is firmly controlling B's hands with his hands. A's hands are on top of them and forcing them inside. If B isn't loose, he'll perceive that there's no way he can throw a punch at A's face because he thinks he's blocked. Typically, B will reason that the only way out is to draw his arm back. If B is loose, however, he'll sense that the hand-to-hand reference point is actually a pivot point, much like a door hinge. He'll perceive that there's actually nothing standing between his elbow and A's head—if he merely relaxes his shoulder and box-steps in on either side.

This actually brings B in closer, yet takes him away from A's hands. This is an example of taking an opponent's space. Now, suppose as B box-steps around, he's stopped by A's elbow in the side of his chest (figure 7.2a). Once again, if B is tight, he'll perceive an obstruction and (wastefully) either back off or attempt to muscle through. If, however, B is sensitive, A's elbow will feel like a red-hot poker, and B will pocket his chest out of the way, allowing him to box step slightly into A's rear without interference (figure 7.2b). Now that B is closer, he can drive his knee into the side of A's knee, further taking A's space as well as causing significant pain.

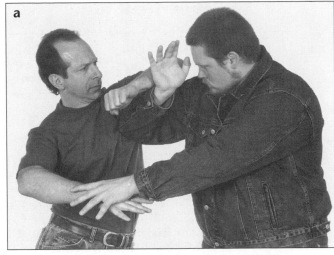

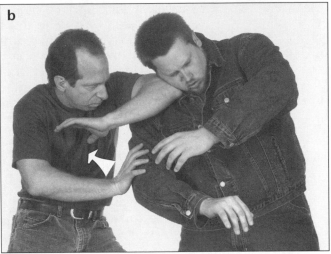

Figure 7.2

Any time you fold a limb under pressure to bring you closer to your opponent, you're taking his space. If A pushes up on B's forearm, B merely folds in underneath with a spearing, up-elbow strike as he steps in (figure 7.3). All B is doing is folding into an area of lower pressure that also happens to be closer to his attacker. In addition, as B steps in, he long steps deeply between A's legs, severely disrupting A's balance and leaving him wide open for strikes, not the least of which could be a knee to the groin.

In the animal kingdom you'll find boa constrictors can kill animals far larger than themselves. Do they crush them with brute strength? Of course not. They loosely wrap themselves around their victims and let the victims flail to exhaustion. Meanwhile, the boa uses its own mass and relaxed skeletal structure to hold its position. When the prey exhales, the boa tightens its coils, taking up slack. The animal struggles, tires, and the boa takes up more slack, eventually crushing its prey when the animal can no longer expand its lungs to breathe. So, too, you should relax, allow your opponent to panic, and then guide his energy just out of your way as you slide in closer.

Long-stepping into the enemy's stance (between his legs) to sweep or hip bump also qualifies as taking space.

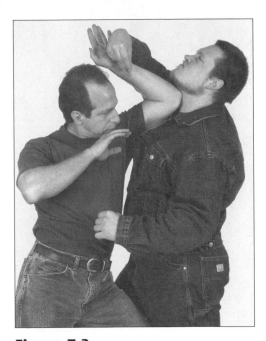

Figure 7.3

Overbending

In the act of yielding, don't let your elbow bend totally or you'll wind up crimping yourself. This is a mechanically weak position that your opponent can easily lock. You shouldn't need to overbend your elbow because the yielding should be taken up as your shoulder joint rotates, your trunk pockets, and your waist and feet rotate or re-root. Also, overbending your elbow can leave it trapped against your body.

Riding the Harley

If you're relaxed and loose, standing formless, motionless, and aware, with your back straight, arms up, and hands facing out (on the handlebars), you might look as if you're riding a motorcycle (although slightly sidesaddle). Most important, your elbows are down in the home position (see figure 5.2, p. 87).

Structurally, you're stronger with your elbows near your body's center of gravity—a point halfway between your hip bones and below and behind your navel—with your weight sunk. Many beginners keep their elbows aloft, flapping them like bird wings. When your elbows are low and protecting your ribs, they can swing like pendulums in either direction, efficiently deflecting or destroying strikes to your midsection and leaving your hands free. This position, combined with the awareness that the elbow can stick, deflect, strike, and flow as naturally as the hand, often allows you to evade a strike to your head and ribs simultaneously with only one arm. This is because when you stand with your side turned to your opponent, thus presenting a smaller target, your elbow covers your lower torso by swinging left and right (see next section), and your hand covers your head and neck area.

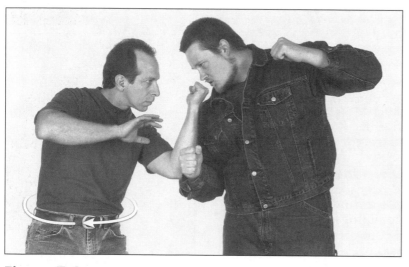

Figure 7.4

When your elbows come near your sides, either from pushing, pulling, or yielding to your opponent's pushing or pulling, you should get even looser than you already are so your elbows don't get trapped against your sides. Your body should turn, your sides pocket, and your shoulders articulate. As your elbows pass the home position, they gain energy from your center of gravity due to the slingshot effect of dropping.

For example, in figure 7.4, B has deflected a shot to the ribs with his elbow, using a rocker motion.

As B's elbow swings through the home position, it gains energy like a roller coaster, shooting his arm up into a shovel punch. It is important to feel the effect of relaxed acceleration through this movement instead of forced muscling.

The Rocker

Use your palms, the edges of your hands, and your inner and outer forearms, elbows, shoulders, and hips as primary sticking surfaces.

With guided chaos, there are no prescribed techniques because your attacker's motion dictates what form your defense and offense will take, guided only by the principles. However, in order to illustrate a typical adaptation, we're going to break down how you might move with a particular part of your body (in this case the elbow) in a given situation. So for the sake of illustration, we'll call the following a rocker. This would be an effective movement that might arise from combining the principles of yielding, pulsing, tool replacing, and moving behind a guard. It also capitalizes on the elbow home position.

With your elbows down and relaxed, your whole arm can rock like a pendulum from side to side from your shoulder, sweeping across your lower midsection. Envision your shoulder as the fulcrum and your upper and lower arm as the pendulum, roughly maintaining a V position as your elbow swings through the widest portion of an arc near your waist. This protects an area from one side of your ribcage to the other. At each end of the arc, your body turns also, so you have a pendulum swinging from a horizontally rotating base. If it swings inward, we'll call it a rocker. If it swings outward, we'll call it a reverse rocker. These rockers are positions you might adopt as a result of tool replacements from the hand.

Whether you'd do one or the other depends on the direction of the force applied to the arm. If the strike to your trunk takes an inside line, the rocker uses the outer ridge of your forearm down to the elbow as a sticking, deflecting, or destroying surface. You pocket simultaneously, so there's little chance of getting hit (figure 7.5a). The rocker can also be a smash that destroys the attacking limb (see Tool Destruction in chapter 8, p. 177). If the strike to your trunk is coming from the outside, the reverse rocker deflects it, using your lower triceps area (figure 7.5b).

A variation of the reverse rocker is to use your hand as the clearing tool, bypassing your elbow entirely (figure 7.5c). This is a delicate, sensitive maneuver because your hand is structurally weak in this position. Ironically, that's its advantage. Your arm and body act as a finely balanced pendulum in this maneuver because if your opponent exerts the slightest resistance, he loads your spring, and you can come smashing back with a variety of strikes. Furthermore, because this kind of reverse rocker is so subtle, your opponent often doesn't notice it. Using just your fingertips, you suspend and release to clear his arm perhaps half an inch (1.3 cm) before you explode through the tiny opening straight forward with a punch to the throat or solar plexus. This rocker is a natural position if you're relaxed, loose, and rooted with your elbows down in the home position, moving behind a guard. The beauty of the rockers is in how their wedge shape works with tool replacement.

Reverse rockers are good for fending off attacks to the ribs as well as for wedges that create openings inside. Here, with A in close, B circles his elbow over A's forearm and reverse-rockers it outside slightly (figure 7.6), creating an inside line to punch through. This could be a short shot to the ribs or a punch straight down to the groin.

The rocker and reverse rocker are energy opposites: one arm rockers, deflecting an inside attack inward (yang), while the other arm reverse-rockers, pulling the attacker's other arm outside (yin).

Triangle Defense

This is a typical expression of moving behind a guard. The name is derived from the shape created by keeping a forearm in front of your head and neck, your head tucked low behind your shoulder, and your elbow always threatening to extend into your opponent's face at close range, like a spear or a spike, and forming the point of a triangle or wedge. You can create the triangle by positioning your elbow either horizontally or vertically (figures

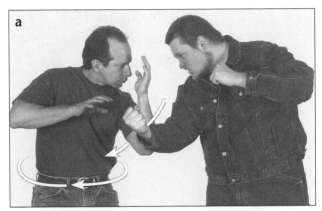

Figure 7.5

Figure 7.6

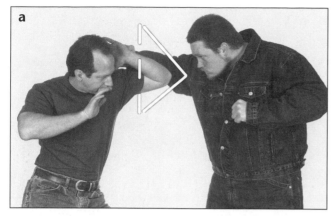

Figure 7.7

7.7, *a-b*) Compare this with the drac. Remember, this is not a position you pose with. You come to it because the opponent's energy led you to it through sensitivity. Normally, your elbows are down low, protecting your flanks, but if you feel an attack on your head coming, you nest your head within your defensive triangle.

As you're standing sideways in an L position (exposing the least amount of your body to attack), think of the triangle as the prow of a ship. It slips through water, diverting it to either side. Can you imagine a boat trying to move through the ocean broadside? Well, that's how dangerous and inefficient it is for you to stand square to your opponent.

The triangle is never static. You're constantly moving behind your guard, so the guard also moves. Usually, what your opponent feels is that he can't hit you (because you divert his attacks to either side), and he feels threatened by the possibility of an elbow spear or smash to his hands or face in his centerline any time he presses in on you. Like a finely balanced sledgehammer, your arm can roll either way, with the elbow occupying centerline and the middle of the forearm acting like the balance point. A breath of air should be enough to set it in motion. Of course, your feet and body must move to set up the right range. Your hand should maintain light contact, while your body drives inside; your elbow folds left, right, or up underneath into areas of low pressure resistance. You can even fake the up elbow as a pulse to get a reaction, then circle over for a down-elbow strike. When combined with the hello handposition (see next section) and high sensitivity, the triangle makes a formidable defense.

Hello Hand Position

When your opponent's hands are on top of or outside yours, and you feel the pressure of his hands release without his stepping back, usually it's because he intends to retract his arm and take a high, outside line to attack you (like with a big ol' Hollywood roundhouse punch). If you're moving behind a guard as you stick, your hand will come up and fill the area he's vacating by the side of your face with a move that looks like you're waving hello to someone standing on that side. After your palm makes contact, you can easily skim it right into a strike to the face (figure 7.8). At the very least, it'll serve as a block (check his punch at the forearm, not the biceps where he may have enough leverage to blow through it). But ideally, when you feel his energy coming through against the hello hand position, rotate your body like a revolving door away from the pressure and smash him in the face with the other hand.

Most important, avoid using the back of your hand to make contact or block. Face your palm outward, as if you were saying hello to someone on that side. This is a much stronger position structurally than the back of the hand, which can easily be bent, breaking the wrist, or merely blasted through with a strong roundhouse punch. Which would you rather catch

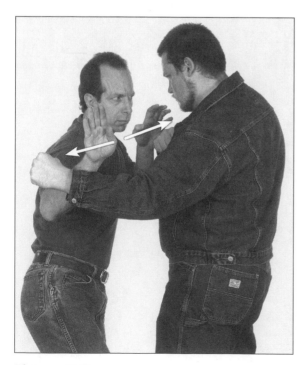

Figure 7.8

a fastball with, your palm or the back of your hand? Which would you rather push a stalled car with?

There's also a tendency in the beginning to block hooks to your head with either a high elbow or a traditional boxer's fist by the temple. The elbow may work, but what if your opponent's arm is longer than yours? It will just snake around your elbow and find your head anyway (figure 7.9). Furthermore, this approach leaves your kidneys wide open. The hello hand position prevents this situation entirely because your elbow is in the home position, protecting your midsection. It might only have to drop a few inches (centimeters). The boxer's block, with the palm toward the face and only an inch (2.5 cm) away, was meant to be used only with big, soft boxing gloves, which act as cushions. Without the gloves, your own hands would smash you in the head as the opponent's punch comes barreling through. Moreover, in a real-life attack, there's nothing to prevent your attacker from punching you in the back of the head (a move that is illegal in boxing).

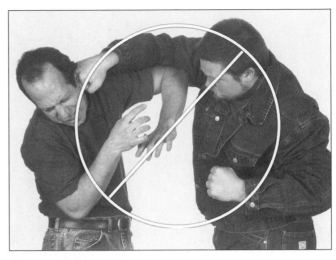

Figure 7.9

In addition, the high elbow block mentioned earlier could work very well—if it's not used as a block. Instead, dive straight forward with it and smash your opponent in the face like a spear. Now *that's* taking his space! His strike will be deflected incidentally (as in figure 7.7b on p. 160).

The hello hand position and the triangle defense underscore a very important subprinciple of moving behind a guard: The guard must be structurally strong. This may sound obvious, but often even well-trained people use naturally weak parts of their bodies or hold their arms in weak positions as they try to fend off strikes. Instead of yielding, some styles train a reliance on highly developed neck muscles to protect the head and neck from impact. Others have the mistaken belief that tightly closed eyelids protect you from eye gouges. But the prime example, as mentioned before, is using the back of the hand as a blocking surface. It has no strength in this position and, in fact, is very easy to lock up and break. The back of the hand is suitable only as a sensitive antenna, and even then, you should use it only for an instant.

In guided chaos we don't block. We either destroy, ricochet, or make them miss.

Hello Hand Position–Triangle Combo

When you combine the hello hand position with the triangle defense, you've got two natural motions that work together to turn away attacks. For example, A has his hands on top of and in control of B's hands, pushing down and in. Because the backs of the hands are structurally weak (figure 7.10a on p. 162), B needs to move them to get to better-sticking surfaces. This is because from here, A can do almost anything: punch straight to B's face, hook to B's ear, and so on. B needs to cut off this whole line of attack in a way that doesn't require muscling A's hands off. By being balanced, loose, and sensitive, B can turn in either direction to take both of A's hands out of the attacking centerline and move them outside using their own energy. For example, if B turns to the right, he does a hello hand position with his right hand and a smashing down elbow with his left (figure 7.10b). Box stepping aids this. The hello hand tool replaces the sticking surface of B's right hand from the back of the hand to the palm, which forces A's left hand outside. B's down-elbow strike tool-replaces the sticking surface from the top of B's left hand to the bottom of his left elbow. This elbow comes over A's right hand and either strikes A's upper arm or the side of his face.

What are the energies that prompted these movements, and why aren't they a technique? The elbow strike was actually motivated by a loose, seesaw response to the mere weight of A's right hand on the top of B's left. Notice, too, that turning right has brought B's left side closer to A, driving A's right arm down and out of B's centerline. By being loose and thus turning fully, B's left elbow now occupies the centerline (instead of A's

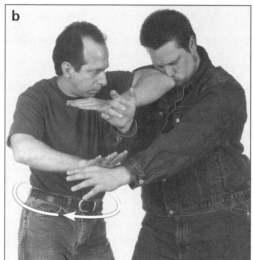

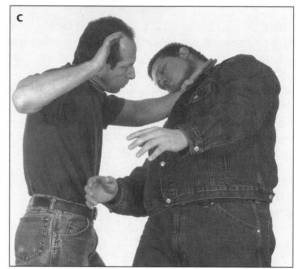

Figure 7.10

arm), and his left side is facing A. Also, turning to the right has allowed B's right hand to simply yield to the pressure from A's left hand and thus rise up into the hello hand position, keeping A's left arm outside.

All B has done is respond to stimuli. Now for the coup de grâce: Following the principles of suspend and release, looseness, and multihitting, B immediately turns back to his left like a spring-loaded door hinge. B's left inward elbow strike turns into a left outward chop to A's throat, and his right outward hello hand turns into a right inward palm heel (figure 7.10*c*). In this example, B has not only been moving behind a guard, but bringing a weapon on line as well. These two principles, moving behind a guard, and bringing a weapon on line (coming up) should always be at work simultaneously. This is a prime example of combat efficiency.

We have painstakingly broken this movement down so you can see the simple physics behind it. In reality, though, you shouldn't get too hung up on each part of the movement; the whole feel of this thing is actually like a gorilla swinging its body back and forth with its arms flying. Program that into your brain instead.

Flipper

The flipper is insurance against having a wrist broken. While sticking to an opponent, if his hand slides down over yours, and your hand bends downward and inward in an attempt to yield, your hand easily can be broken by an aikido-type wrist lock (figure 7.11*a*). This is an example of moving in ways that hurt rather than help you. You can prevent this potential mishap by being sensitive to the attempt and then flipping your hand up in a hello gesture (figure 7.11*b*).

This stops the sliding action leading to your opponent's wrist lock. It also gives you yet another springboard from which to launch either a rolling elbow (triggered in a seesaw fashion by the application of pressure against the flipper) or an inward pulse toward you with the back of your hand acting as a hook, which then spring-loads a palm strike forward in response to your opponent's pulling.

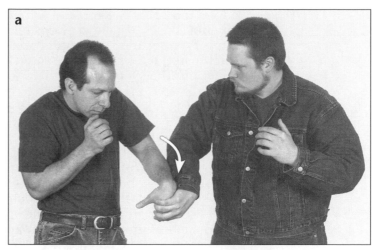

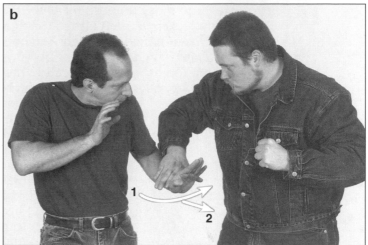

Figure 7.11

The Body as a Weapon

Without fangs or claws, the human body nevertheless has some formidable natural weapons. Any system that disregards their importance for some politically correct purpose does its followers a disservice. All these strikes are for close fighting, where the most damage is dished out. It's important in your training, from solo anywhere striking to two-person contact flow, to incorporate the following weapons at all times.

- Head butts from every possible angle
- Biting (don't break the skin in practice)
- Heel stomps (see Mexican Hat Dance, p. 41)
- Spitting into the eyes (as a visualization, of course)
- Pinching, clawing, and ripping loose skin (within reason)
- Fish-hooking
- Neck-breaking (be extremely careful)
- Eye gouging (within reason)
- Hair-pulling
- Crushing the testicles (within reason)

Note that most if not all of these are outlawed in professional sport fighting.

Always Bring a Weapon on Line

This is the partner principle to always move behind a guard. Never just yield without also delivering a strike in return. Ideally, you want to deliver a strike at the same moment and within the same motion as the yield or guard. Though not always possible, it is tactically efficient, and there are more opportunities for it then you know. As you move and elude strikes in contact flow, *don't just curl up passively,* taking your weapons off line or worse, blocking yourself. Always use the energy to turn, skim, slide, or fold in a weapon like a sprung mouse trap or revolving door. As you yield, guide your own chaos so that a weapon is always coming online, and you're in position to strike. By working primarily with chops, palms, and elbows you will see that they all easily flow into each other. Even while sticking, your weapons should always be formed and on line. How? If you're sticking with your palm, it's already weaponized. Move it sideways and you have chops and ridge-hands. Fold the arm and you have elbow strikes. Dig in your fingers and you have rips and gouges. When you focus on traditional punching (as opposed to hammer fists) or any of the exotic blocks and strikes from kung fu like phoenix eye fists, chicken beaks, and the like, it takes longer to actually form the weapons. Even if it's milliseconds, this is precious time you can't afford to waste in a fight for your life. Keep it simple and live.

Fighting As If You Have Four Hands

You want to think of your elbows as an extra pair of hands, sensing and deflecting in a state of constant flow and movement. Rather than using your hands exclusively to clear an opponent's arms, work from your elbows as much as possible. By doing so, you free up your hands while allowing yourself the same degree of combativeness.

When extending the elbow or doing a tool replacement from the hand to the elbow, don't lean forward or hyperextend your arm to control the other person's motion. Step in. Your elbow shouldn't stretch away from your body as if it's a flapping wing. This will only place your body off balance. Remember that your elbows, no matter how loose they are, must move proportionately with the rest of your body (body unity). In other words, if you rocker your left arm to the right (inward), your hips, back, and legs turn that way also. Even though you align your body to push forcefully, you use little muscle, only the power generated by dropping. As you're moving and sensing your opponent's intentions, the motion of your body creates a moving platform that keeps your elbows in proximity to your opponent's weapons. Don't reach for them. He'll be reaching for you, and then your elbows will meet his weapons, either directly or from folding due to pressure on your hands.

Place the elbow of your rocker against your opponent's outer elbow; you don't need to use any muscular tension to do this—just rooting and body unity. This will pin his arm momentarily and prevent him from striking you with it. More important, it pulses him because he'll want to get it off him. From here you can either clear (destroy) with the elbow rocker, pass (pulse) the arm to your other hand, or slide a chop in with the same arm. You can also reach underneath your own elbow (figure 7.12*a*), clear, and chop (figure 7.12*b*).

If your opponent offers resistance to the rocker inward pulse (i.e., pushes back), simply reverse-rocker outward with your fingers, letting his resistance spring-load you. This opens an inside line where you can snap back and strike through with the same or other arm. Execute this movement smoothly in one fluid motion so that it appears seamless to your opponent.

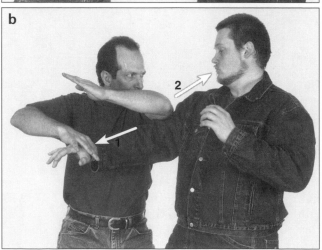

Figure 7.12

You can wrench with your elbows with incredible power as long as they remain close to your body (as long as they're not touching your flanks or you may have difficulty bringing them online. Remember you may need to pocket so you can get your own strikes out). The action of the elbow can also be subtle. Depending on its position, it can pulse, spear, or strike in virtually any direction creating limitless opportunities. It's up to you to explore them.

- Getting hit with an elbow is like getting hit with a baseball bat.
- Keeping your elbows close to but not touching your sides when moving helps protect your ribs.

- Keeping your elbows close to you doesn't preclude you from throwing spearing downward elbow strikes. You don't have to wind up—simply drop your body. If the attacker has gotten his arms around your waist or lower for a take-down, his spine should be perfectly positioned for one of these downward spearing elbow strikes.

- To loosen your elbows even more, you must loosen your shoulders. By doing this, you give your elbows an extra 3 to 5 inches (about 8 to 13 cm) in range and mobility.

- Stab the elbow against the soft parts of your opponent's body with an abrupt, thrusting motion. This spearing (accompanied by dropping) makes your attacker feel he's been jabbed with a crowbar.

- When used in conjunction with taking your opponent's space and dropping, your elbow can uproot your opponent while it slashes back and forth in a rocker motion, continually moving through the home position to gain power.

- In line with the principles of the triangle defense, when you're in close and sticking your elbow in your opponent's face, your elbow should have the same sensitivity as your hand. If it's pushed or pulled, it can yield with a small circle and come right back in your opponent's face like a rubber band. You can also retract the shoulder, which frees the elbow. You can use the elbow to pulse his arm slightly in any direction so you can move it in a small circle and wedge it into an opening from another direction. Thus, the elbow can slither in with the same sensitivity as the hand.

The best way to practice using your elbow is with the Anywhere Striking drills (chapter 2) against a pole and with the elbow contact flow option. When striking a pole, also practice pulsing (inward, outward, and side to side) from every possible angle.

Open Hand Versus Fist

As you learned in chapter 2, open-handed strikes using your palm and the side of your hand are better than using your fists for striking hard targets such as heads and jaws. Try smashing a brick wall with a palm strike or a chop. Hard. Now try this with a clenched fist. No? Good thinking. If you applied the same force on both strikes, your hand would be broken.

The palm can deliver more force than a punch because there are fewer bones interspersed with tendons acting as shock absorbers. With the palm strike, you have an almost direct connection to the forearm because the hand essentially sits on top of it. A fist needs to compress through all the joints of the fingers and the hand like an accordion before it can deliver a solid blow. Also, to make a proper fist, you need lots of practice. You must learn to align your wrist bones and make your hand tight; employing antagonistic muscles throughout your arm or it will break on impact. This is why boxers tape their wrists, a luxury you can't afford. Forming a proper punch slows you down, decreases your sensitivity, and makes the rest of you rigid. Note that none of this applies to hammer fists, which is why we love them.

By considering the palm or chop your primary hand position, you're already set up properly for using skimming energy. Like a flat stone skimming the surface of a pond, the palm and chop combination skips in more easily over blocks than a fist.

You should only punch against soft targets. When striking, keep your arm and fist loose until the moment of impact. At this point, close your hand as if grabbing a bar and then instantaneously relax it. Combined with dropping, the effect of the hand's relaxing and tightening is like the crack of a whip: The fist remains fluid and loose until the wave of energy reaches it, whereupon it solidifies into steel.

There is another use for fists that involves destroying incoming limbs like a lumberjack cutting down trees. In guided chaos we call this combat boxing, but it requires extensive slambag training and is beyond the scope of this book.

Always Form Weapons

As you've learned, open-hand strikes are more versatile (and sensitive) than fists. It is no coincidence that your main weapons tend to be palm strikes, chops, and elbow strikes. You will see that it's generally easier to form them in the midst of contact flow than punches because they transition so easily from sensitive sticking tools to strikes. They also flow naturally from one to the other: Palm strikes and chops collapse to elbow strikes, and elbow strikes unfold to chops and palms. Try to always form weapons as you stick so that you're not just playing touchy-feely games with your partner.

Skipping Hands

Punching makiwara boards half your life is a waste of time. As far as sensitivity goes, developing your hands by making them tough as stone also makes them dumb as doorknobs. With skipping hands, you'll be able to play the attacker's body like a piano, something you'd find difficult with arthritic joints.

When sticking with your hand, try to use two points of contact: the tips of your fingers and the heel of your palm. Think of them as having a yin and yang relationship: Your fingers act as delicate probes, and the heel of your palm acts as a structurally strong guard. When the opponent's pressure builds beyond what your fingertips can handle (which isn't much), they tool-replace to the heel of the palm of the same hand.

As you already know, the reason you stick with your fingers is so you can remain disengaged. It's easier, and you've got more clearance to throw a strike than when your hand is clamped to the opponent's body. In addition, if your fingertips sense so much as a muscle twitching in your opponent's forearms, you'll know something's coming. The reason your fingers don't get broken is because you're reacting to the slightest change in pressure as if you had touched a hot frying pan.

It may help to think of the hand as a smaller version of the rocker: With the slightest increase in the opponent's energy, the hand rockers from the fingers to the heel of the palm, allowing your opponent's arms to be redirected. With your elbow down low in the home position, and your body lining up behind it and your palm, you can exert tremendous pulsing power that you can flow off of. This is all in accordance with moving behind a guard.

From the heel of your palm, you can tool-replace back to your fingertips with a walking, or skipping, action. This allows you to alternately scoot and check along the surface of an attacking limb as you redirect it. This is a very sneaky, effective concept you should play with while doing contact flow. Although a little different in principle, the effect is the same as with sliding energy by allowing the attacking limb to slide past. For example, B's fingertips are delicately poised on A's forearms, with the heel of the palm barely touching (figure 7.13*a*). B picks up that a muscle is tensing slightly a millisecond before A launches a strike. B's fingers rocker, or skip, to the heel position with the elbow low and supported by the alignment of B's whole body and both legs (figure 7.13*b*).

This position is structurally powerful, requiring little muscular exertion. This momentarily pulses or destroys A's attack as well as occupies the line A was going to enter. If A attempts to slide around this position, B forearm-surfs and takes A's space, in effect, letting A slide into an even more disadvantageous position (figure 7.13*c*). B's hand actually skips, or scuttles rapidly like a crab, along the outside surface of A's arm as it runs from heel to fingertips, heel to fingertips, letting A's arm go by. B's hand has thus skipped from an initial contact point on the forearm to the outside of A's elbow, which is a better reference point. From the palm position, B can let A's elbow fall into the groove between thumb and index finger for more control (figure 7.13*c*). If A attempts to power through the heel of B's palm, B does a reverse rocker with his fingers, clearing A's arm in the same direction it wants to go (figure 7.13*d*). B slides right into a strike that A practically fell into with his chin.

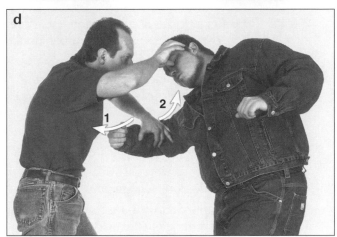

Figure 7.13

Ripping and Tearing, Crushing and Breaking

As you become more comfortable whipping your body around with full body unity, you'll find that strikes often come about because the attacker's body simply gets in the way.

After a strike, you may find that your body's turning and contorting momentum makes your arms fly apart of their own accord. You can learn to use this by grabbing with both hands onto different parts of the attacker's body. What you will find is that you begin to create situations where you're literally tearing your assailant limb from limb but using virtually no muscle strength. This works best when the two areas you grab are obviously not designed to be pulled in opposite directions. For example, in the course of practicing contact flow, you may find yourself pulling your partner's face to the left with your left arm in a backhanded grab (twisting his head clockwise if viewed from above) and pulling his right arm out to your right with a two-fingered grab with your right hand (perhaps because you were redirecting his punch). If this was a fight for your life, and you felt like you were going to die, you could easily see how the assailant's neck might break. Similarly, in the process of rolling the ball, you might find yourself pushing the back of your partner's head forward to the right with your left hand while pushing his left shoulder to your left (or clockwise if viewed from above) with your right hand. You would do this almost as if you were trying to make them meet in the middle. As in the previous example, if this was a real fight to save your life (or a loved one's), the assailant's neck would be crushed. You use plyometric rebound energy to spring from crushing to tearing and back again. There are an infinite number of handles on the body that can be used to rip it apart. This would be difficult to accomplish without sensing and flowing with the enemy's motion. Slambag training greatly increases this ability.

THE POWER OF THE PINKIE
John Perkins

In the chaos of a fight, any part of the body can become a nasty weapon. In one incident as a police officer, I was fighting a raving wild man with psychiatric problems on a stairwell. He had me so tied up I couldn't punch, fire my gun, or swing my nightstick. The only thing I could get free was my pinkie, and I drilled it into the corner of my attacker's eye. Once the man started going into convulsions, the fight was over.

Preventing Common Mistakes

➤ Being loose doesn't mean your defense should collapse when you yield. Train yourself to be loose while moving behind a guard and bringing a weapon on line at all times.

➤ Moving behind a guard is not merely a defense. Within the triangle principle, pressure anywhere against your hand or forearm is a stimulus for folding and striking simultaneously, using your elbow like a seesaw. Conversely, pressure on your elbow unbends it, turns your body, and drives a palm or hammerfist into the attacker.

➤ Don't stick with the backs of your hands. They'll be overpowered, locked, and maybe broken.

➤ Don't rocker just with your elbow. This skill requires a loose shoulder, rotating waist, pocketing ribcage, and turning feet.

➤ Don't stand square to your opponent. It creates too much target area to defend economically. Instead, stand sideways behind your guards. When you turn your body, box-step and turn 180 degrees so you present your other side, which is now also behind a guard, to your opponent,.

➤ When you turn, you can just make it a simple twist of your upper body. Your legs can remain in a reversed stance (e.g., right hand, right elbow, and right shoulder forward, with your left foot in the lead position). This is because you're only positioned there for a split second—suspended like a rubber band or a wrecking ball—before you release and fly back the other way to a normal lead. Or you can just box step out of it into a new lead.

➤ Use yielding as an opportunity to get in, not run away. Take his space. Don't box-step to the side and away from your opponent. Box-step to the side and in, or better yet, move behind your opponent to throttle him.

➤ When yielding, don't totally fold your elbow joint, or you'll get your arm broken. Your yielding should be taken up by other areas of your body, such as your shoulder or waist as you turn away. Also don't fold your arms against your body or they will become restricted. Pocket to create breathing space so they can move and hit.

➤ Try not to block. As you stick, keep your targets diametrically opposite the enemy's weapons with your guard directly between them. As the enemy's weapons reposition or strike, move your guard with them as little but as efficiently as possible to stay between them *but don't force his weapons offline.* Instead, move your targets so they remain offline and unavailable behind your guard. Make them miss. This has the effect of sucking the opponent's strike (and balance) down a black hole where it can be slid, skimmed, destroyed, broken, turned, tool replaced, or weaseled against for your simultaneous counter attack.

CHAPTER EIGHT

ECONOMY OF MOVEMENT

Within guided chaos are many powerful ways to economically cover your target areas as well as to deliver the most damage with the least movement. The elbow home position and the triangle defense discussed in chapter 7 are examples of the former. In addition, you already know that chambering, or setting up, is a wasted attacking movement.

Defensive Economy

To begin, let's address a common beginner's problem: Windmilling the arms in an effort to stay loose. The answer is to follow the economy of movement principle: Move your body and feet more so you have to move your arms and hands less.

When you're balanced enough to step and move your body more, you accomplish four critical goals:

- You move your guard less, thus hiding your footwork and intent to counter.
- You remove vital targets from direct attack.
- You generate tremendous counterattacking energy through body unity.
- You are ready to attack, as your arms are close to centerline in the home position.

If you keep your body static like a statue but swing your arms independently like propellers, your balance will be off, your power weak, your targets open, and your arms can be twisted, pinned, or generally taken out of the fight. This result is even more evident when you develop looseness without moving behind a guard.

Practice maximum motions to discover your balance limits. Then pare them down so you move only as much as needed. Don't defend beyond the perimeter of your vital areas. Better yet, don't intercept even 1 inch (2.5 cm) beyond an imaginary cylinder formed by the width of the weapon and its attack path toward its target. In other words, if the attacker is punching at your face, you only have to be concerned with intercepting an area that is 4 inches (10 cm) wide (the diameter of his fist) and about 2.5 feet (.8 m) long (the distance to your face). This will keep you from performing wide superfluous movements that will only take you out of a fight. Be sure, however, to move enough so that you can survive. If you have to move radically, you will have already played with your limits.

Riding the Vortex

How do you deal with a wild, chaotic fighter moving at top speed? If you stick or grab stubbornly to fixed contact points, your nervous system will become overloaded, you'll become tense, your defense will collapse, and you'll get sucked into a vortex of destruction, susceptible to locks, grappling, and worse.

Remember, if you have room to retreat, you have room to run.

You need to become even less engaged, while still remaining in contact. Here is where you must amplify your sensitivity. Imagine that your opponent is the Tasmanian Devil. As in the cartoon, his moving limbs form the surface of a spinning tornado. Even though the area between his arms is mostly air, his speed creates the illusion of solidity. As such, treat the perimeter of Taz's tornado as you would skin and glide across its surface. Do not attempt to penetrate it directly. Flow with it as if it were one solid object. We call this riding the vortex. For those spared in childhood from this cartoon character, visualize a potter molding clay on a rapidly spinning wheel. Without losing contact, the potter deftly alters the shape of his creation as it flies through his or her fingers. The potter is at once engaged, yet disengaged. Similarly, you can use sliding energy (p. 114), forearm surfing (p. 115), releasing tension, and taking up slack (p. 120) to control your opponent's motion.

Riding the Lightning

When striking, view your entry as a bolt of lightning flashing from the void. When you know and can feel the shape of the enemy's movement, you can feel the path of least resistance and splash or destroy his weapons, then skim or ricochet into penetrating strikes, like lightning skipping from cloud to tree to house to ground. This cuts down excess motion (like chambering) and prevents your enemy from recovering. With heightened sensitivity, you can instantly feel every open target of your enemy from just one contact point. This is what allows advanced practitioners to hit people multiple times within one movement. By exploiting dropping and ricocheting energy, you can develop tremendous power without the superfluous motion of chambering or winding up. As your opponents' bodies are penetrated, you take up the slack and bounce off their tension, continuously loading and reloading your spring. As an enemy's strike comes toward you, drop and destroy it with your palm or hammerfist (slambag training really helps here). Instantly skim in and spear your enemy's throat, bounce off and punch his temple, fold in and chop his throat, or fold in and elbow his jaw. Any of these four options and more is possible depending on what you feel from your enemy's vortex.

Zoning

How do cats and dogs confront danger? They either run or fight. When they fight, they dive in with their teeth for the kill. Rarely, however, do they go straight in. They penetrate at a slight angle, far enough to get past their enemy's teeth and claws, but close enough to get a death grip on the enemy's throat. They go in because backing up can be fatal. It's easy to trip and fall. When you dive in, you move in at a slight angle; we call this zoning. You can then actually avoid big, looping blows as well as close-in strikes—as long as you remain loose, flexible, and relaxed.

If you're fighting, it's assumed you have no other recourse. In guided chaos, you rarely back up. When you need to relieve pressure, you zone by stepping in and to your opponent's side, staying close. This is the purpose of box stepping. By pocketing and passing the apples, you get your opponent's energy to bypass you. Thus, you attack and defend simultaneously. When you box-step, your outside foot goes directly to the side of or behind your opponent's. You tool-replace and pocket to keep your opponent's limbs from impeding your progress. In addition, your chest or shoulder can become a checking tool replacement, leaving your arms free to hit (figure 8.1).

An important point about zoning and any other stepping move is that you should almost always hit simultaneously as you step. This economically unifies your body and power, giving your opponent more to deal with. Although in guided chaos it's a basic principle not to use both hands on only one of the opponent's hands, zoning gives you the opportunity to violate this principle for a purpose. Usually, whenever you try two hands on one, if your opponent is sensitive enough, he will immediately hit you with his free hand. Since zoning effectively takes you out of reach of his far hand, you can safely use two hands on one for a variety of breaks, strikes, and so forth.

The Three-Part Insurance Policy

We have broken down a typical guided chaos defensive response into its isolated components so you can see how three principles operate at once without blocking. When working together they protect you in three ways:

1. Yielding by pocketing (shown in isolation in figure 8.2*a* on p. 172)
2. Turning (shown in isolation in figure 8.2*b*)
3. Box stepping (shown in isolation in figure 8.2*c*)

Yielding and pocketing the intended target area minimizes the impact. But they are effective only up to a point. You can only pocket so much. If the enemy is too close or his arm is too long, you will be penetrated regardless (figure 8.2*d*). This

Figure 8.1

is counteracted by turning as well as pocketing (figure 8.2*e*). Turning cuts off the attack angle and sluices out the attacking limb.

Box stepping not only ensures that a very large attacker is bypassed, it also puts you in a better position to counterattack which is closer yet further off-line. Box stepping can be as subtle as an inch change in position or as dramatic as a step behind the attacker (figure 8.2*f*). When you employ pocketing, turning, and box stepping simultaneously, you maximize your unavailability (figure 8.2*g*).

We have only shown you the defensive application of the three-part insurance policy for clarity. In reality, you always attack and defend simultaneously. From your initial point of contact (figure 8.2*h*) you can fold and elbow strike (figure 8.2*i*), slide (figure 8.2*j*) in preparation for a tool-replace strike (figure 8.2*k*), or skim (figure 8.2*l*).

There are other offensive options based on your unavailability. Because you made him "miss" (as opposed to blocking), the attacker's limb gets strung out where you can easily break it by pressing your chest against the elbow and snapping (figure 8.2*f*). The enemy ended up here because you "pulled his push" and overextended his missed strike. His overcommitment was swallowed up by the yin energy of your pocketing, turning, and box-stepping. This break happens simultaneously with a face rip off the skim (compare this to the motion in the Swimming drill on page 64). Then, when the attacker panics and tries to pull his arm out, you follow it back like a big rubber band and blast him with your counterattack (figure 8.2*m*).

Make sure you don't trap your inside elbow as you yield and turn. Roll your elbow over so it doesn't get stuck between your chest and his arm. Pocketing the chest gives the elbow the breathing space it needs to get out. This ensures that you always have a weapon online, like a chop or elbow strike with your inside arm, depending on the distance.

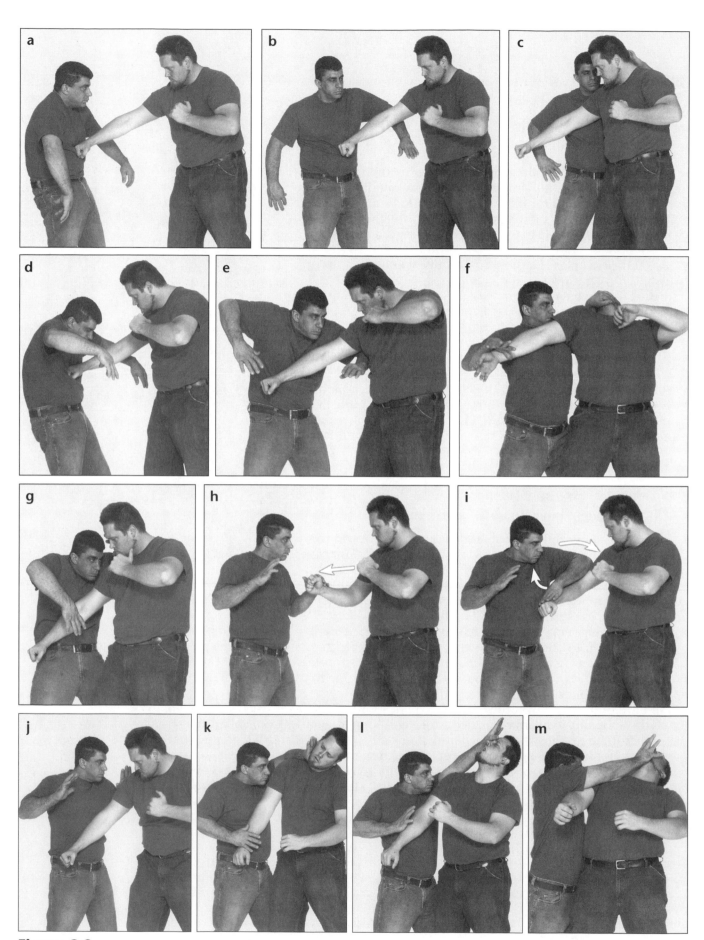

Figure 8.2

Dropping to Deflect

As part of moving behind a guard, remember that most of the deadly damage an assailant can inflict is against your head, neck, solar plexus, and kidneys. Dropping destructions against incoming strikes to these areas as you pocket helps protect them. This is vital, because the dropping gives you power, rooting, and stability at the moment you need it most, and your looseness evades the strikes. This enables you to take your opponent's space while defending and attacking simultaneously.

By dropping a split second before you yield, you create a situation in which you can loosely but powerfully destroy a strike, yet slide in and counterattack, all in the same motion. The yielding and articulating allows you to slither in and strike simultaneously, but it's impossible to pull this off without dropping. Dropping anchors you to your root so you avoid the floating and light-footed sensation of instability common to beginning students who are learning to yield.

Another advantage to dropping as you yield is that your explosion of energy loads your own spring, because you bounce off the attacker's strike. This acts as a pulse, which makes the attacker push even harder to knock your hands off. But it's too late for him. You pull his push and crush him or fold around and impale him (see Spike-in-the-Sponge, chapter 3).

As long as we're in the defensive category, it would be neglectful not to mention such fighting fundamentals as tucking your chin (except when yielding your head) and keeping your teeth together.

All strikes, pulses, and destructions are merely motions within the flow. As soon as you separate them out in your brain and think, *Now I will strike,* or *Now I will pulse,* you become rigid, slower, weaker, overcommitted, less sensitive, and less balanced.

Offensive Economy

We're now in the category of economical attacking principles. The first one is unique to guided chaos, and it depends totally on your ability to develop looseness. If you refer back to the Circle Clap drill in chapter 3, you'll know exactly what we're talking about.

Multihitting

The goal of multihitting is to insert as many strikes within one flow of movement as possible. This is tactically efficient, so you can mete out maximum damage in the least time. However, do not force superfluous or awkward blows into the mix. What you should find is that the enemy's targets are just conveniently in the way of your body as it moves from a yang state to a yin state, and vice versa. All your strikes should be empty and unformed until contact (remember, don't clench your fist until impact—this prevents stiffness). Here are some examples of multihitting, some of which you have already practiced in your Anywhere Strikes I, II, and III drills in chapter 2.

- When you palm to the chest, slide a spear hand into the throat.
- When you step straight in with a palm strike to the head or chest, continue the motion without stopping so that, immediately after contact, your elbow folds and blasts up into the attacker's chin. You must simultaneously step in and take the attacker's space to do this.
- If you deliver a right palm or slapping strike along a more circular path (like a right hook to the head in boxing), continue rotating your body to the left, fold your elbow slightly, and within the same motion, slam your attacker with a horizontal right elbow to the side of the head.
- When you turn out with an elbow strike to the side of the head, continue turning so it becomes a chop to the same spot. This can be linked to the move described in the previous bullet.
- If you explode with a palm strike to the face, claw the eyes or clear an obstructing arm as you retract.
- If you're punching into the stomach, you can slide into an uppercut.

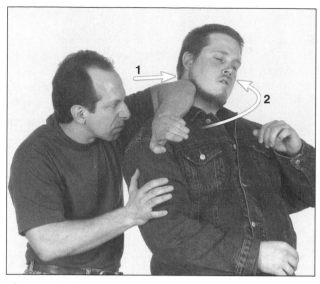

Figure 8.3

- When you use ricocheting (chapter 6), you can bounce the opponent's head between a hooked, backhanded chop and an elbow from the same arm repeatedly, like a yo-yo (figure 8.3).
- If you've just punched with a right into and past the assailant's midsection so that your right arm is backhand to the left of his body, why waste time chambering the arm to strike again? As you retract the arm, do it with a slashing, backhanded chop, hammer fist, or forearm against his side.

To make things more interesting, you can combine all of these. For example, the palm-elbow combination can happen on the way in, and the elbow-chop combination can happen on the way out. So with a simple, swinging, yang-yin motion, you have delivered four blows with one arm in the time it takes most people to throw one.

To make things even more interesting, note that these combinations have occurred within the motion of only one side of your body. If you think of yourself as a gorilla, swinging your arms loosely from side to side, you can double the number of strikes by performing this motion with your right arm moving in and out, immediately followed by your left arm moving in and out and back again. That's eight strikes in the time it takes most people to launch two. Combine these with a couple of drops, and your opponent will think he's back in the Cuisinart again! If this all sounds familiar, it's because you've already practiced a more basic version with the Anywhere Strikes III drill in chapter 2.

There are an infinite number of combinations possible with multihitting, but you won't need to memorize them because your looseness and sensitivity will create them spontaneously. As we've asserted throughout this book, focus on acquiring the feel of the principles, and the strikes will come automatically. Try to have your blows bounce from one to another as if your opponent had fallen into a giant pinball machine. With enough looseness and dropping, you can actually ricochet repeatedly between hooks to the head and the ribs. Boxers can't do this because they don't train to recognize or exploit ricocheting, splashing, or skimming sensations (wearing boxing gloves doesn't help either) that allow you to remain loose and multihit.

The energy behind shortening the weapon is like having to hold a hot potato in your hands and carry it from the oven to the table without dropping it on the floor. You must rapidly engage and disengage the potato to maintain control over its motion.

Vibrating

An extension of multihitting, vibrating occurs when you deliver no-inch punches so rapidly that the striking weapon seems to vibrate with energy. This linear ricocheting energy is like doing a drum solo or blasting with a jackhammer. An example is if you bounced five palm strikes off an attacker's head or chest in one second, dropping with each shot (recall the Circle Clap drill, p. 70). Still another example of vibrating is a movement coming from Native American martial arts called shaking the tree. The vibrating energy spasms your entire body as you take your opponent in both hands and shake him or her violently. You do this loosely, powerfully, and quickly, so that at any moment you can explode off the shake into a barrage of multihitting elbows.

Taking Something With You

If your punch goes past your opponent's face (or any other part of the body), why not strike on the return (e.g., while retracting your arm as with a chop or a claw)? This concept—taking something with you—is an important, economical corollary to multihitting and something you've already practiced with the swimming drills in chapter 3. After every strike, if possible, take a piece of the opponent with you as you retract your weapon. Here are a few examples:

- After you turn through your punch, as you pull your arm back, grab the back of the opponent's elbow, opening his ribs to a strike from your other arm, which is simultaneously moving toward those ribs.

- Grab an ear, eye socket, or the side of your opponent's head and wrench it sideways after a palm strike (while pulling his lead arm in the opposite direction).

- Grab his wrist or some hair, pulling his head past you into an elbow smash as if you were clearing your way through bushes in the jungle.

- Palm-heel under his chin on the way up, rake his eyes, or rip at his shirt on the way down, then spring up into another palm heel.

- If you're falling, rip at something on the way down to ground fighting (see chapter 10).

Figure 8.4

Typically, your opponent is still trying to push you away as you withdraw a strike, so you'll end up pulling his push. It's important to combine this with splashing and passing the apples to create and briefly maintain an opening. For example, B chops at A with his right (figure 8.4a). A's block misses, but his energy continues to carry the blocking arm outward (remember, we're talking about responses that last only a few hundredths of a second). B's right arm is already retracting after the chop, but on the way back, it takes A's right hand with it, using a delicate two-fingered grab. Almost instantly, B's left hand or elbow splashes or destroys A's right elbow to the inside, clearing the line (figure 8.4b).

Shortening the Weapon

Shortening the weapon is a subtle but powerful principle of economy that affects virtually all your movement. The reason we've waited until now to explain it is that without first understanding sensitivity and looseness, this principle would be meaningless.

You're already familiar with the concepts of sensitivity and of being as disengaged as possible, yet still engaged. We're now going to take it a step further to make your sensitivity more ballistic. By mixing in constant pulsing, skimming, and ricocheting energies, we now want you to experience contact with your attacker a little differently.

Imagine that your training partner's skin is red hot. If you touch your partner for longer than a fraction of a second, you'll burn yourself. At the same time, you'll need to remain close enough to sense your partner's motion. This paradox sets up your nervous system for explosive movement because you are constantly loading your own spring.

This approach trains you to instantly open new entry angles and protects you from grappling. Any time you contact your opponent, shrink from the touch and then reacquire him, over and over at high speed. This can be extremely subtle as compared with vibrating energy and multihitting. To an observer, in fact, it might look like you've never broken contact at all. What this movement does, however, is keep you from becoming overly engaged with your attacker, except when you have clean openings that you skim, slide, or stealth your way through. This forces you to probe for different entry angles. It also has another dramatic effect: Your opponent has a hard time getting a fix on you because *you* know what you're doing, but he hasn't a clue. As his frustration quickly mounts, he desperately tries to hit and grab you, but this only increases your reactivity. As his energy rises, you react as if his skin were getting hotter and hotter, which loads your spring even further. Eventually, he overcommits, and you explode into action.

Consider shortening the weapon as something you need to apply to all your motion. For example, B palm-heels at A, who manages to block it. When B first senses contact with the block, her nervous system should react as if she had just touched a red-hot frying pan (figure 8.5a). This causes her to shorten her weapon, pulling her shoulder up and back while she continues to step in, taking her opponent's space. Simultaneously, B readjusts, turning her torso and shoulder slightly and firing the same or a slightly different weapon (like a spear hand) at a slightly different angle (figure 8.5b). In the meantime, A is still reacting to the feel of the block she just made, because she expected the contact with B to last longer and be more substantial. As if sucked away by a vacuum, B is no longer there. This begins to establish a pattern of overcommitment on the part of A, who searches for something to get a grip on.

If you throw in pulsing and dropping, shortening the weapon becomes very nasty.

When shortening the weapon, however, you don't pull your hand back dramatically as if winding up. Instead, the shortening should be whatever the maximum range of your shoulder joint is. Shortening the weapon can also be a completely internal movement, in the sense that your nerves, muscles, and tendons reverse suddenly without you actually moving your arm. This makes you even harder to read. Ideally, you should be able to strike your opponent's arm with power and then instantly relax so your fingertips stick to the target with feather-light pressure, never once breaking contact (compare with skimming and splashing, p. 116).

An extremely important point about shortening the weapon is to never let anyone get control of your elbow. Your elbow is one of your body's most critical control points. If your opponent possesses any sensitivity at all and gets an opportunity to grab, pull, or press your elbow, you could be in great peril. Therefore, at the slightest touch on your elbow, shorten the weapon and get it the heck out of there immediately (this motion is practiced in the Row the Boat drill coming up). Do a small circle and then whip back with a chop to the throat.

By the way, you can take advantage of the reverse scenario: Take control of your opponent's body while forearm surfing to slide to the back of the elbow. With just two fingers, you can pinch the joint at the brachial nerve, wait for your opponent to panic, and either pass the arm off to your other hand or hit directly with the same hand.

Figure 8.5

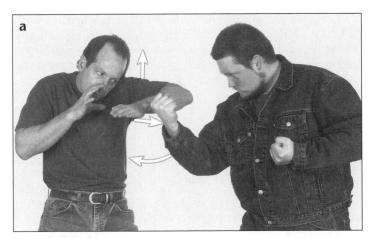
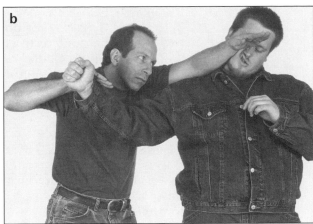

Figure 8.6

In guided chaos, it is vital to develop a full, isolated range of motion for every possible angle in the shoulder joint so that you look as if you are shrugging up, down, backward, and forward. When you accomplish this, your hands can be in contact with your opponent's limbs and remain relatively motionless, yet have a multitude of different attack angles available because of the dynamic, isolated movement of your shoulders. For example, B is in contact with A, whose arm is in the way of a direct strike (figure 8.6a). B raises his whole shoulder joint while leaving the rest of his body still so that a new angle opens up, which he can strike through (figure 8.6b). Practice shortening the weapon with the Row the Boat drill and the Contact Flow Shoulder Option drill (chapter 6).

Attacking the Attacker

You already know about this from part I: To attack the attacker, you must get past his guard as efficiently as possible, clearing a line of entry to his vital areas. The crudest way to do this is with the CCUE; however, this won't work against a much stronger enemy. You already know you should never force your way in, nor should you try to forcibly move a block to get to a vital area because it's typically a waste of energy against a stronger opponent. Instead, use as much of the opponent's energy and as little of your own as possible. When your guided chaos skills are honed, you'll be able to use stealth energy and ghost your way in virtually untouched, yet still maintain contact. This is the highest level of the art. Until then, you can clear the line with skills you already know, such as passing the apples, pulsing, and taking something with you. In this section, you'll learn a few more ways to clear the line.

Tool Destruction

You also already know about tool destructions from part II. Although this initially sounds as if you're forcing your way in, the reality of tool destruction in guided chaos is that you're actually going to be using your attacker's energy. You're already familiar with tool destruction if you've used rockers to smash incoming punches with your elbow. Since rockers involve a loose turning of your body, it's the force of the incoming strike that does the damage. Your sensitivity initiates a seesaw rocker to perform tool destruction. For example, your fingertips, perched on the arm of the attacker, sense the intention of a strike. When the strike comes, your arm folds rapidly at the elbow into a rocker as your midsection pockets and turns. Instead of the rocker simply redirecting the strike, the rapid folding of your elbow caused by the incoming force of the opponent's blow smashes the rocker elbow into his shoulder joint or jaw hinge. The power is augmented by the turning and dropping of your whole body. This has a popping quality, quick as lightning, while your rear hand accepts the passed apple (the attacker's fist) and clears it. The ricochet off the destruction immediately launches you into further strikes with both hands. This can't be done if you linger or grapple with the opponent's arm in any way. (Note that tool destruction is also discussed in chapter 9 as a sensitive reaction to grabs.) A full-power pulse can become a tool destruction, as can riding the lightning. In both cases, you smash the enemy's strike with a punch, palm, hammerfist, or elbow and ricochet into a strike of your own.

Checking

Checking refers to a short, snappy pulse that pops an opponent's tool slightly off line. Checking is not blocking. Usually done with the palm, checking can be used to initiate an attack, create an opening, maintain an opening (by knocking an arm out of the way), or ensure that an opponent's attack, like an elbow to your stomach, never reaches its target. This is merely a safeguard you can combine with pocketing. Checking and its more aggressive cousin, tool destruction, are both far more effective with dropping.

Don't overcommit with a follow-through motion in a check or tool destruction. Splash your opponent's striking arm and shorten your weapon so you can take his space without being thrown off balance. Your splashing hand penetrates only a maximum of a few inches beyond the point of contact. If your check or tool destruction knocks the opponent's arms away and wide, you still need to be sure he's not going to come back and nail you as you step in to take his space. If you pass the apple by guiding his arm and elbow past you, a check with your other hand makes sure his arm stays out of your line for the split second you need to enter and attack. You can also ricochet off the check. Palm-strike or splash the elbow and dive through the opening into another strike. Just remember that when you enter, get as close to your opponent as possible. Checking, tool destruction, and the like are all fine if the enemy is somewhere around your size and strength. Understand however that at the highest levels of the art, you want to keep your interaction with the enemy limited to just two kinds of contact: near-invisible sticking and the striking of lethal targets. This level makes any other kind of contact unnecessary and more risky, especially when fighting monsters.

Dog-Dig Entry

The dog-dig entry qualifies as one of the simplest and most effective entries you can do. Skip in and kick the assailant's shins while rapidly rolling your hands in a dog-paddling or dog-digging motion. Just as you would enter using a swimming sidestroke or CCUE, smack his lead hand out of the way and either gouge out his eyes, chin-jab his head, or spear his throat repeatedly like a buzz saw.

If he resists the first clearing dog-dig motion, make sure the second, third, and fourth are right behind it. If he pulls back against the dog-dig, use his energy to pull your strikes into his face. If he pushes them away with superior force, skim over them or circle in the opposite direction and use rising spear hands to the throat. By rolling with his energy, not against it, you avoid tightness and wasted motion. If you don't like the dog-dig analogy, you can visualize yourself as a foaming wildcat and claw, gouge, and shred your way to his vitals.

The Drac Entry

When you're relatively close to your opponent, jump in sideways with your lead arm's elbow extended out horizontally in front of your face so that you're peering out from behind it like Count Dracula. Keep your rear checking hand underneath, near the center of your chest. At the same time you make contact with this front-spearing elbow, knock your attacker's lead hand away to your inside with your rear checking hand in a clearing move (figure 8.7a). Instantly unbend your Dracula arm as you turn into your attacker with a dropping, backhanded chop to the side of his head (figure 8.7b), followed immediately in the same turning motion with a palm-heel from your checking hand. Your attacker will either eat the elbow when you whip it out or succumb to the chop because

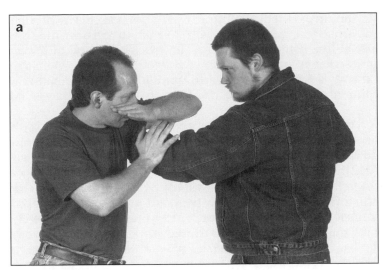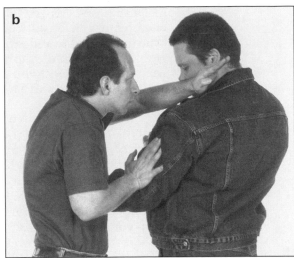

Figure 8.7

your clearing hand was hidden from view by your Dracula elbow. You can substitute a straight, spearing strike to the eyes with your lead arm for the Dracula elbow if you want. The spear hand has the advantage of skimming off and deflecting an incoming strike as it simultaneously hits its target. Note the similarity of this move to the swimming sidestroke and the CCUE.

Timing, Distance, and "Bringing the Chaos"

In this art, you don't want to just *deal* with chaos, you want to "bring the chaos" to your enemy. We mean several things by this. The entire paradigm of avoiding fixed and recognizable patterns in your training has equal importance with regard to timing your movements. In all your contact flow, washing the body, and polishing the sphere exercises it is vital to eliminate all regular cadences, rhythms, and feints and introduce as much chaos as possible. This consists of broken, irregular, and erratic timing, timing that might even be viewed by many as inelegant or even spastic or spasmodic. This does *not* mean uncoordinated or without body unity. You still must have highly trained single-leg balance to make it all work. You simply want to offer *nothing* that the enemy can latch onto in terms of timing your strikes.

Other than pulsing, in guided chaos we don't feint or fake. Feints and fakes fall within the realm of sparring, and as we've said repeatedly, if you have enough room (and time) to spar, you have enough room (and time) to run. Instead, by virtue of your sensitivity, you develop something that looks like feinting but is far more direct, efficient, and devastating—the ability to make midcourse corrections. Shortening the weapon is just part of this. Before contact is made in guided chaos, you always move in at oblique angles, like a mongoose. You are always moving offline even when the enemy is nearly on top of you (as with the CCUE). This is the case even in hair-trigger maneuvers like the fright reaction because dropping essentially moves you from where the enemy *thought* you were to a place with more power and balance. Yielding and pocketing simultaneously increases your unavailability.

As you deliver your strikes, if you feel that something is in the way you instantly make midcourse corrections without retracting the weapon. You continue on in to the same or different vital target. You practice this by always performing contact flow with *ruthless intent* (more on this in the Afterword). Every motion is focused on getting *in* and tearing the enemy limb from limb and utterly destroying him. There is no dancing or backing up. If something's in the way you simply go around it without retreating. This may involve skimming, sliding, folding, turning, transferring, shortening or simply weaseling. Obviously this requires highly trained looseness as well as balance.

By the way, your sensitivity should also tell you intuitively if you can blast through the enemy's defenses using destructions. You will be able to instantly assess his size, density, strength, and structure at first contact (or earlier). This is essential because you never want to challenge your attacker as a matter of habit. Sometimes destructions are helpful (especially if you are already a formidably powerful individual) but remember it is always deadlier, cleaner, and more efficient to hit your targets unimpeded like a guided missile or a cobra.

You have to be in it to win it. Endeavor in contact flow to get as close as possible and still remain unavailable. Even at slow speeds you can work on "cleaving" the enemy's neck with your entire descending arm like a guillotine with full body unity while simultaneously smashing him in the kidney with the other. Rip at the face, bite, head butt, and elbow with full intent and alignment but at slow speeds so your training partner isn't injured. Be very careful with this. As you improve you will be able to go faster with more force but you never actually need to damage your partner because when you learn how to really drop you will know exactly how much power can be delivered. You can even drop with full power but send the energy back into your root instead of your partner. You need to be very high level with this, but the idea is to feel the "bounce" off your partner's target that is just at skin level without penetrating. You feel what you *would have* hit him with if this was an actual fight because the full energy, as mentioned before, goes back into the floor and is felt as intense, rapid pressure in the feet. When you work with John Perkins or his top students, you often feel like you're going to die and are surprised and relieved that you didn't, because you can literally feel the energy that would've annihilated you whirl around and pass you without penetrating.

Economy of Movement Drills

Many of the principles in this chapter can be practiced only during contact flow. They're simply too subtle to be extracted out into separate drills. You can, however, practice shortening the weapon with a drill you already know.

Modified Anywhere Strikes

If you review the Anywhere Strikes drills in chapter 2, you can modify them by imagining that the pole or swinging, heavy bag you're hitting is red hot. Strike from every possible angle, remain close, but don't get burned. You have to hit, instantly relax, and lightly stick. You can also practice isolating your shoulder by shortening the weapon and only moving your shoulder joint. Thus, the rest of your body remains motionless while your shoulder pulls your hand or any other weapon away from the pole by stretching backward dramatically. You can also enhance this movement with Row the Boat.

Row the Boat

Aside from gaining new entry angles for the hand, this motion is also useful for pulsing, raising, and clearing the opponent's arms when you're nose to nose.

1. Touch your hands together in front of you as if you're grabbing oars.
2. Keeping your hands relatively stationary, pull both arms back simultaneously by shrugging your shoulders backward.
3. Roll your shoulders in a circle as far forward, upward, backward, and downward as you can, initiating a rolling movement in your arms. By rolling the shoulders, covert entry angles are created while your hands are allowed to remain relatively motionless, sticking to the attacker's limbs and safely guarding your centerline. Because this motion

activates some of the strongest muscles in your body, it is used for clearing chokes and strangles—and knives and guns placed against your head, as you will see in Chapter 12.

4. Roll each shoulder independently: When one is up, the other is down; when one is forward, the other back. If you combine this with weight shifting, you will find yourself morphing into the Rolling the Energy Ball drill.

Preventing Common Mistakes

➤ When zoning, don't step away from your opponent. Instead, step to the side and in.

➤ During contact flow, don't tense up when your partner goes at high speed. Relax and ride the vortex.

➤ Don't try to do each part of three-part insurance policy separately or you will be crushed. Perform them simultaneously.

➤ Multihitting is not like a combination in boxing. In multihitting, move your whole body in loosely for a punch; body parts, like your elbow, simply seem to fall into line during the same motion and strike the opponent as well. This also happens as you pull your arm back. Mulithitting should have a relaxed, bouncing quality, like doing a drum solo. It can be a result of folding and unfolding your arm and skimming your strikes.

➤ If you force your movements, they will fail.

➤ If a movement doesn't feel natural, or as if it could spring out subconsciously, it will fail.

➤ Never force your way in, nor forcibly push or pull a block to get to a vital area. Use as much of the opponent's energy and as little of your own as possible. This doesn't mean you shouldn't use every ounce of power you have to destroy the enemy. It simply means never *oppose* the enemy's energy. Flow with it, amplify it, and return it. Slither in like a snake, skim in like a flat stone, or ricochet in like a bullet.

➤ Checking and tool destruction are useless without dropping.

➤ Don't overcommit to a check or tool destruction. Splash his weapon so you can take its space without throwing yourself off balance. Your splashing hand should penetrate only a few inches, at maximum, beyond the point of contact.

CHAPTER NINE

GRABS AND LOCKS

Grabs and locks are excellent tools for explaining guided chaos principles for two reasons:

1. They represent opposing forces and condensed combat on a small scale.
2. They are revered by many and thus are ripe for debunking.

Grabs

Because we never want to be overcommitted and thus involve antagonistic muscles, limiting our ability to flow, an effective grab should be an instantaneous, elastic maneuver. In guided chaos, you never grab to restrain someone, and if you really clamped down with intent to control, you wouldn't be sensitive enough to deal with the other's response. If your attacker is stronger than you and adrenaline fueled, you'll be thrown like a toy. Moreover, don't count on being able to grab at an attacker moving at high speed. It is nearly impossible. Instead, use grabs as a probing tool to instigate a reaction from your opponent that you can flow off of. Grabs need to be subtle to remain undetected and to pass the apples or tool-replace. In general, only take a grab you can accomplish with two fingers (the thumb and index or middle finger). But let's be clear about this: You can grab with as much power as you want, but it must come from your root and must be quick, reactive, and *immediately* abandoned. Don't wrestle. Striking should always be your priority.

You don't need to use a grab to bring an opponent closer. Doing so always runs the risk of using antagonistic muscles, leading to a tug-of-war. By being mobile and stealthy you can take his space without him knowing it. By pulsing you can get him to come to you while reeling him in.

If you use a grab as a pulse, drop with your whole body weight for a split second, and then release the grab. Applied this way, a grab can unbalance your opponent or create an opening. It's often useful to grab an elbow and move it just enough so you can punch right into the spot the elbow just occupied. Your grabbing hand then becomes a target that your punching hand can lock onto. A good example of all of this is puppeteering (not to be confused with the hand and foot drill called Puppeteering).

Puppeteering involves lightly applying a two-fingered grab (with your thumb and middle or index finger) on each of your opponent's wrists and merely following his limbs around without adding any energy of your own. This causes a very curious thing to happen. The opponent panics because he hasn't the slightest idea what you're doing, and all he wants is to hit or wrestle—anything to get you off him. Puppeteering is a subtle variation on pulsing because it instigates a reaction.

It's doubly annoying to your attacker because you're following him around and can thus easily redirect a strike. You're connected to a control point—as if you were a matador leading a 2,000-pound (.91-metric-ton) bull around by a nose hair. Keep your elbows loose, relaxed, and near the home position to keep yourself structurally strong. As soon as your opponent commits or overextends, release, tool-replace, and attack. You can use his first arm strike to block his second by redirecting the first into the path of the second. But the key here is his reaction. Whatever move he makes, flow with him and hit him. Hold on only as long as you need to get a reaction.

If your opponent yanks away, follow him, release, and hit. If he strikes, step in, pull his push, extend his arm, check or destroy it with your chest or other arm, then let go with your grabbing hand and strike. The grab can thus be doubly unnerving if used as a pulse because the opponent doesn't know if you're going to hit with the grabbing hand if he pulls out or hit with your free hand if he pushes through (if he pulls out you can hit with the free hand anyway!). If he attempts to pull his hand away behind his back, follow his movement and break his wrist.

Locks

As any cop can tell you, in a real fight, when everyone is moving at maximum speed, it's virtually impossible to apply a lock if you're looking for one. Once adrenaline kicks in, locks, even applied by experts, become less effective (see chapter 1). The reason you see locks working in UFC competitions is primarily because half the time they're trying to lock *each other*; maiming and killing is not allowed. The other half of the time they're looking for knockouts that require full-power punches to areas that aren't necessarily lethal. Look back at the UFC fouls in the book's introduction. Using all of them viciously precludes any locking. Also, grappling involves committing and fixating your arms on restraining moves, leaving them static and susceptible to counter-locks; this becomes a vicious cycle in the sporting arena. The one good thing about UFC is that the locks are being done with full speed and power—short of *intentionally* snapping the bones (the rules forbid it and encourage tapping out). In many dojos, they're worked and reworked cooperatively, flowing from one to the next with the choreography of a dance. When you train in guided chaos, you *never* cooperate, even in the beginning.

In general, we don't advocate locks because they fixate you. However, sometimes locks can be used effectively, but they should be fast, snapping actions that last a millisecond before you flow out and into a strike. Police officers generally have to lock people without breaking their arms, which is why their jobs are so dangerous. It would be better if the perpetrator could be softened up before the lock was applied, but nowadays that's viewed as brutality, even if more people are injured because the bad guy wasn't stopped immediately. If there isn't sufficient backup to pile on, a solitary officer then may have to resort to using excessive violence anyway, including emptying his gun. Which is better?

You may know of or have been shown how to apply a particular lock from some other art, but in guided chaos, it's up to you to discover *when* to apply it. This will be dictated by the flow and energy of the movement. If you don't train this way from the start, you'll be lost.

For example, if your opponent punches, you stick and yield, breaking his arm as you pull his push, extend his punching arm, and apply a rising palm to the elbow (figure

> Never look for a lock; either they happen or they don't.

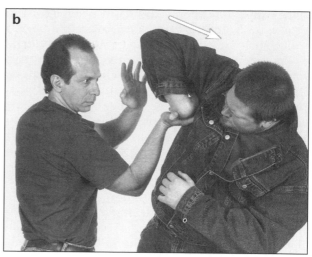

Figure 9.1

9.1*a*). But suppose your opponent is sensitive, picks up on his overcommitment to the punch, and retracts. You might follow him and tuck his wrist under his armpit (figure 9.1*b*), thereby breaking his wrist.

If there's resistance to the lock, that's fine: He's loading your spring. Don't bear down and hang on. Abandon the lock and release the energy. If you fall into a two-hands-on-one situation, and he fails to do the flipper (chapter 7), his yielding will result in a crushed wrist when you apply inward pressure. Of course he could also punch you in the face with his free hand, which is another reason not to lock in the first place.

Don't fall in love with locks. They are restraining maneuvers that act as drags on your flow. They make you move as if you were mired in mud. If you bear down on a lock, you employ antagonistic muscles that can start wrestling matches, possibly with opponents twice your size. Bad move unless you're a punk just horsing around for a youtube video, which means you're a jackass. It's better to deliver a lock like it's a strike and snap his bones like lightning. That's what you do when you're fighting to save your life.

The Vise

A different type of lock is the vise—a quick, springy action you suspend and release. While fighting, if A's limb gets caught between B's limb and B's trunk, B can quickly drop and clamp down with the elbow (figure 9.2*a*). This abruptly disrupts A's balance, causing him to resist forcibly with upward pressure. This is great because the vice has acted as a

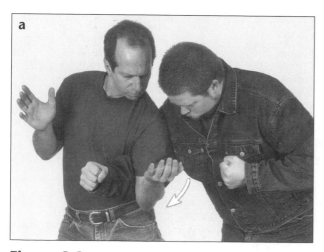

Figure 9.2

pulse or springboard to further hits. From here, B instantly springs up into a chop to the throat. B simultaneously passes the arm he has in a vise to his other hand (figure 9.2*b*).

If B had not been loose but only had clamped down with the vise and held it with all his might, he would have become as fixated and vulnerable as A. This is an obvious display of strength, and its direction gives the opponent a virtual road map of your intentions. This is also the antithesis of stealth energy, guaranteeing an unsuccessful counterattack on your part.

The Cross-Tie

The cross-tie is an opportunistic lock that occurs frequently when you train with someone unskilled in guided chaos. It occurs when one punch is pulsed, passed, deflected, or thrown down and into the path that an anticipated second punch would take (figure 9.3*a*). In the process of rolling the ball or passing the apples during contact flow, the hand that was doing the deflecting circles under and cross-grabs the second punch while your other hand cross-grabs the first (figure 9.3*b*). Because your opponent's hands are crossed and yours aren't, and since his momentum carried him to this position, you can easily twist his arms up while continuing to roll. Just remember that your body's turning drives the cross-tie, not your arm muscles.

What's interesting is that once your opponent's tied up, you can let go—and strike—because he will actually tense and resist against himself, causing an instant opening to his torso or head (figure 9.3*c*). Or you can just twist, drop, and break. If he resists strongly,

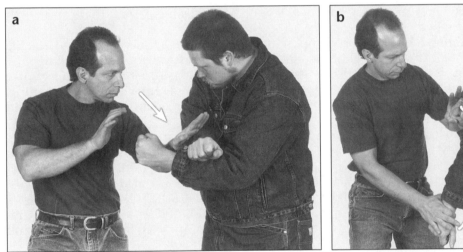
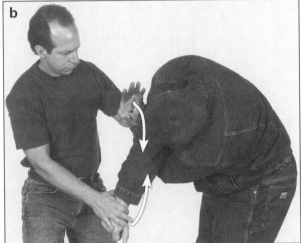
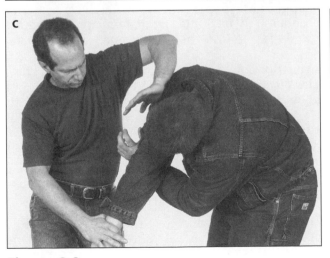
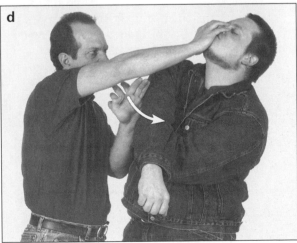

Figure 9.3

just roll back with him in the other direction, release one or both grabs, and hit, using his resistance to propel your strike. It's usually easier to let go with the hand that's holding his lower arm (because it's trapped by his own upper arm) and hit. You can also instigate a cross-tie by actually knocking or throwing one arm into the other, then grabbing and twisting. Sometimes it helps to pop-check and destroy his elbow with your palm to keep him in the cross-tie a split second longer to ensure your opening (figure 9.3*d*).

You can avoid being caught in a cross-tie yourself by staying sideways to your opponent, turning when pushed, and not presenting him with two outstretched arms. If you are caught in a cross-tie, step and shoot the arm that is on top in the direction it is being pulled. Because you are going with the energy, this will release the lock. Instantly fly back with an axe hand to the neck.

Resisting Grabs and Locks

Since you should imagine your enemy's skin as either red hot or covered with some foul-smelling slime, being touched, much less grabbed by him, should put your sensitivity on high alert. This mental image will condition you to avoid entanglement. Resist the temptation to grab back with your other hand. This gives you no advantage; instead, it leaves you with both hands involved and no guard available. At best, you end up in a stalemate. If your opponent's stronger, you lose, and now he has a handle with which to crush you. How do you condition your nervous system to both disengage from potential grabs and re-engage to keep contact? Practice. It helps to visualize the hot potato analogy described elsewhere: Treat your opponent's body like a steaming spud that can neither be held nor dropped.

If you're grabbed anyway, his clamping down should be as successful as squeezing an angry alley cat or a handful of mercury: The more pressure your opponent applies, the faster it squirts out through his fingers. Your sensitivity, since it's confined, acts like an incompressible liquid, exploding toward freedom through any convenient opening. Since the move is rapid, you must shift your balance and readapt just as rapidly, with your entire body moving in concert.

By using body unity principles, you'll generate more releasing power by repositioning your whole body to free the grabbed arm than if you strain with your arm's muscular strength. While you drive with your body, your arms can move wildly in any direction to free themselves, as long as it's in the direction of a strike to a vital area. In other words, it makes no sense to release straight up, down, or far out to the side. This makes you a sitting duck. The releasing movement by its very nature should be a direct blow to your attacker, satisfying the principles of economy of motion, moving behind a guard, and bringing weapons online.

If you're grabbed, your free hand should always go right for the attacker's eyes or throat. It's amazing how so many techniques rely on some elaborate maneuver against the grabbing arm when all you need to do is stab into the jugular notch or eye socket with your free hand.

Avoid excessive contact from the start and shoot your hand forward through his grasp and into his face. Just say to yourself, *Don't touch me, you vile dog* and you'll be in the right frame of mind. Drop/destroy his hand out of the way or evade the grab and strike with the same hand or both.

Despite all this, you may be successfully grabbed anyway. Read the following material with an eye toward developing the underlying feel of the movements described without necessarily obsessing over their specific components.

Answer the Phone

This is an extremely common, multipurpose movement related to the triangle defense. It can shield against strikes, punches, rakes, chokes, or other harassment to the head. Due to its extremely dynamic use of body unity, it's also a terrific grab breaker. For example, B is in a left lead, properly standing sideways to A to create a smaller target. A grabs B's left wrist to get control (figure 9.4a). B can stab A in the eyes with his right, but if A is ready for that, B can answer the phone by relaxing and circling his shoulder down, inward, and up, raising his whole left arm from the shoulder. As B brings the arm up, he keeps it near his side to gain the mechanical advantage of being close to his center of gravity (figure 9.4b). The action is like scraping your ribs with the inside of your palm, forearm, and elbow. As you can see, this involves turning to the right from the waist, stepping in closer with the left foot to take A's space (A's grab was pulling B in anyway), and pocketing the left side of the ribcage in case of an attack to the kidneys (this movement also makes room for B's arm to slide past). B moves his hand, palm inward, close by and then past his ear as if raising a receiver to listen (figure 9.4c). Raising the arm this way forms a protective wedge around the side of the head, which can also ward off strikes to the rear. It also tool-replaces the attack or grab from B's wrist or forearm to B's shoulder, freeing B's arm. Compare with the fright reaction.

Because A's grab pulled B in, B followed the energy and took A's space, moving behind the guard provided by the answer-the-phone motion. This, combined with B turning away from A as he raises the phone, generates tremendous torque against A's wrist, breaking the grab. After B answers-the-phone, he turns back to the left, whipping a chop or elbow to the left side of A's neck through the huge opening answering the phone just made (figure 9.4d).

After answering the phone, B delivers the chop as if saying, "Here, it's for you!" This action is one continuous movement, like swimming. It's also a swinging, yin-yang type of motion, because B twists one way and then immediately whips the other way. This allows for a palm strike with B's other hand.

Figure 9.4

Answering the phone is also a good response any time an opponent's arm contacts your arm between the elbow and shoulder, because he's too high on your arm for you to roll your elbow over (and he's too close for comfort to your face). It's also great for warding off a flurry of strikes to your head by multiple attackers. Under these circumstances, answering the phone looks like you're fighting a swarm of bees.

Swarm of Bees

If you were being dive-bombed by a swarm of angry bees, would you drop into a deep karate stance and throw reverse punches or perhaps use an esoteric tai chi technique such as grasping the sparrow's tail? Of course not. While guarding your face, you'd whip your hands around as fast and lightly as possible with great sensitivity to avoid being stung. This is natural. However, if you examine these movements, you'll notice they look like multiple answer the phones, combined with short swimming and chopping movements. Do the same to protect yourself from flurries to the head.

Breaking the Double Grab

Common errors people make trying to break grabs include:

- letting it happen in the first place by having a grappling mentality,
- grabbing back, and
- trying to break the grab by either opposing it or moving against the weakest joint as a rule.

The best response is to stay within the principles and flow in the same direction as the energy the enemy is applying. If you do this from the start, it is virtually impossible to be grabbed, locked, or tied up.

For a single grab, forget about fancy counterlocks, wrist twists, and other nonsense. Simply spear the enemy in the eyes or throat with your other hand, stomp his toes, or kick his shins. Stabbing in the eyes and throat should always be your first move if you're afraid of dying.

However, if both your arms are grabbed you have an excellent opportunity to display the principles in action. You can certainly still kick, but since by virtue of the grab you are receiving sensory input directly to the arms first, your reaction will be more immediate there than with kicking (of course if you visually pick up that you're *about* to be grabbed, your instant response could be a whip chop to the throat, Y-strike, or low shin kick).

Because grabs, locks, and ties can be applied in virtually any direction, all of the methods of release are too numerous to be detailed in this book. Just to give you an idea, however, say both your arms are grabbed despite applying what you've learned so far in this chapter. If they are being pulled into the enemy, your looseness just flows into the next available weapon—your elbows. Turn your body and take your attacker's space by stepping in deeply. Loosen your arm and shoulder muscles, firing one or both elbows sequentially with a rocker motion at one or more of the following targets: the face, upper arm, chest, or uppermost restraining hand (figure 9.5). A nice, multihitting follow-up is to slide straight up and chin-jab with your palm. This also works against a single grab.

After you smash your attacker's top restraining arm with your elbow, don't try to pry or wrestle it off. If you simply turn, step, and drop with your whole body, you'll have all the mechanical advantage you need. Multihit, bouncing your elbows from the restraining arm to the face and back again; use both elbows, one right after the other. You can also spear your elbows into the attacker's chest.

Figure 9.5

Regardless of the technique described above, the *key* principle is to always flow *with* the grabber's energy. If the enemy is facing you and he has grabbed your left wrist with his right arm and is pulling it to your right, do not think you are being sensitive and loose by simply collapsing your left elbow into his chest or face (a common mistake). You would still be opposing him because he's pulling *sideways* and you're trying to hit straight ahead (even though you're folding). Instead, punch or shoot your arm out in the exact same vector as he's pulling. This briefly releases the tension, causing him to go "uh-oh" and try to pull you back in the opposite direction, which is exactly what you want. Snap the arm back and, augmented by the enemy's energy, smash him in the face or ribs (depending on the angle of return) with an elbow, chop him in the side of the neck, or blast him with a palm heel with the other hand.

Both movements (the tension release and the snap-back) are performed with full body unity, meaning you step away and back in as you release and strike. This adds enormously to the power and occurs lightning fast, with no pause in between, aided by dropping. Notice that at no time (either with the tension release or the snap-back) are you opposing his energy.

Tool Destruction

Smashing a rocker into your opponent's grabbing hand to liberate your own is tool destruction, as is slamming the knuckles or forearm of an incoming punch with your elbow. Tool destruction is a common martial arts term for attacking the attacker's limbs. What is uncommon is how we use it. Instead of trying to pick an incoming strike out of the air like a baseball or a scud missile, guided chaos tool destruction often results from either folding or turning your body away from pressure. In the latter case, you should use the principles of taking your attacker's space, body unity, the triangle defense, and the box step to turn your whole body and step into a horizontal palm smash at a grabbing arm (figure 9.6*a*, arrow 1). Within the same movement, your elbow should slash his face—provided the grab was held high enough (arrow 2)—and your now-freed hand should chin jab (arrow 3). Instantly, using multihitting, your elbow slashes back in the opposite direction (arrow 4), followed immediately by a backhanded chop with the same arm (arrow 5) and another inside palm strike or claw with your freed arm (figure 9.6*b*). This whole sequence occurs in less than a second. This works against both regular and cross-grabs. When executed, it looks like an ax tearing through balsa wood. Remember, though, to turn with each movement so you're only presenting your side to your opponent.

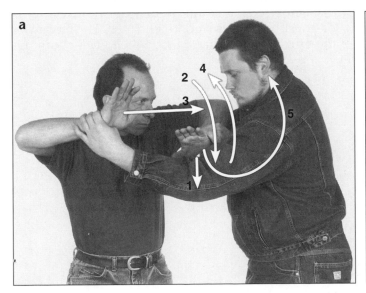 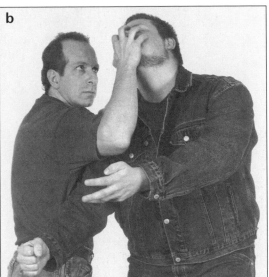

Figure 9.6

Grip Exercises

Your hands can really benefit from a strength-building regimen. If you think about it, other than our teeth (which are feeble compared with those of most predators), the only raw weapons we have (other than bludgeoning surfaces like knees, feet, and elbows) are our fingers. Lacking claws, we nevertheless have great power in our fingers, relative to the rest of our bodies. This pays off whenever you rip, tear, gouge, and pinch. Grip strength is essential when you're totally tied up, and your hands are against your opponent's skin. The amount of pain an iron-like rip can deliver is sometimes sufficient to create room for further strikes.

The trick in gripping is not to hang on. Your hand should have a snapping, biting quality that instantly relaxes to avoid sustained tightness, allowing you to find other targets. That said, one of the best exercises for developing your grip (as well as hitting) is the entire slambag drill series in chapter 6. The following drills develop the grip exclusively.

Finger Creep

The purpose of this exercise is to strengthen the muscles that contract the fingers, which are different from the ones that turn the wrist.

1. Take a full-length broom. Hold the stick at the top with the fingers of one hand so that the bristles hang just above the floor.
2. Using only your fingertips, walk your fingers down the handle so you're raising the broom off the floor while your arm stays at the same height.
3. Pull the broom up till you reach the bottom and start over.

You can weight the broom to make this harder by slipping 2-pound (1 kg) barbell plates over the broomstick.

Grab to Destroy

Grabs should be lightning fast destructions and rips. Peel off fingers and snap them (do not hold them—this fixates you). To save your life, grab bone protrusions and cavities and wrench them quickly till the part breaks. Within contact flow, experiment with finding every bony protrusion of the body that can be dug into and wrenched. Do this with the tenacity of a rock climber looking for finger holds on a smooth cliff face. The finger tips should be fully bent to the base of the fingers (almost like a fist), which gives enormous strength to the grab. Just a few of the possible handles:

- The hair
- The nostrils
- The nose ridge
- The ear
- The ear hole
- The eye socket
- The eye brow ridge
- The cheek bone
- The jaw (front, side, and underneath)
- The larynx
- The clavicle, collarbone, or jugular notch
- The rear base of the skull
- The skull protrusion behind the ear

- Upper vertebra protrusions (depending on body type)
- Any loose fold of skin: cheek, neck, lower edge of pectoral near the armpit, or loose skin over side of ribs (depending on body type)

Sand Bucket

You've probably heard that the crushing force of an alligator's jaws are immense, but that an average person can hold the gator's mouth shut. To avoid the gator's dilemma, you need to work the muscles that open your hand, not only the ones that close it. When opening and closing strengths are balanced, they actually augment each other. You need a bucket of sand to do this drill.

1. Form your hand into an eagle's beak. The tips of your fingers should be pressed together and even with the end of your thumb.
2. Spear your hand into the sand and then twist it two or three times to drill it in.
3. While continuing to push down, spread your fingers as far as they will go, angling your hand for the most resistance against the sand with all your fingers, including your pinkie and thumb.
4. Repeat steps 2 and 3 at least 10 times per hand, and then try the reverse: Spread your palm wide on top of the sand, push down, and try to crush a handful of it into a diamond like Superman. Do this 15 times or until your forearms feel as if they're going to explode.

Tendon Strengtheners

The following exercises develop tendon strength, which is far more important for fighting than muscular strength. When you're moving loosely and powerfully at high speed, your large, strong muscles that have been trained purely for strength and size tend to be slow and highly injury prone. This is why strict bodybuilders can't play in the National Football League. Their tendons would simply blow apart. Tendons connect muscle to bone and need to be strengthened carefully along their entire range of movement. Some of the drills are extremely slow and others extremely fast. This combination trains the tendons (and the muscles they are connected to) to withstand the ballistics of wild and chaotic combat conditions.

Two-Minute Push-Up

High-speed looseness doesn't require big, bulging muscles; instead, it requires tough, elastic tendons with strong bone attachments that resist tearing.

1. Perform a push-up very slowly, working to increase the time it takes for you to go down and come back up.
2. Continue until you can take two minutes to go down and two to come up. This will take some significant training.

Iso-Strike

These are slow, isometric tension exercises that build strength throughout the length of a combative movement, rather than only through the limited range of resistance found in most weight training.

Figure 9.7

1. Begin with your right arm wrapped tightly around your body in an exaggerated starting position for a backhanded chop.
2. Stand against a wall and exert strong tension against it in a slow, controlled effort to uncoil your strike (figure 9.7).
3. Inch by inch, reposition your feet so you experience resistance against every part of the chop's movement throughout your body from your hand all the way down to your feet until the chop is fully extended.
4. Don't forget to drop in slow motion as well.
5. Try this with every type of strike you can think of, continually repositioning your body to offer the maximum isometric resistance throughout the entire range of movement.

Speed Flow

As well as working your tendons, these exercises promote high-speed muscle strength, which is different from brute strength.

1. Make slow, circular, horizontal chopping motions with your hand and arm. Your forearm should be parallel to the floor. Use a subtle dropping motion with your knees as the chop comes out. Do this for 30 seconds.
2. Increase to three-quarter speed for 30 seconds.
3. Then go to full speed for as long as you can maintain full looseness and relaxation. Whip your arm, making the air move.
4. When you begin to fight against the cramping and stiffening of your own muscles, stop.
5. Repeat with your other arm.

Apply this same procedure of speeding up the flow in increments to the following:

Figure 9.8

- Dog-dig: Use a repetitive digging motion. This is useful for clearing limbs or batting away a knife in a last-ditch effort as you backpedal. This movement is similar to that of a cat rapidly clawing at an enemy in a circular, buzz-saw motion. Try this motion toward your side, where it would then look like a swimming sidestroke.
- Stacked spears: Chop straight out in front of you with both hands alternately so your upper hand comes out and then returns underneath in a rapid, circular motion (figure 9.8). Once you tire, reverse the motion.
- Answer the phone and chop combo: Do both motions with one arm and then switch. Performing this as rapidly as possible takes on the appearance of fighting off a swarm of angry bees. Don't overextend on the chop; it should snap out and back like a whip.
- Hammer-fists: Pound your fists in the air alternately at high speed like you're doing a drum solo. Do them to the front, the side, anywhere you can think of.
- Free flow: Psycho-chimp and do the small circle dance at maximum velocity. Be careful not to hit yourself!

ATTACKED AT WORK

I'm a steel worker in New York City working the high iron in Manhattan. I was being messed with early in the morning by this man about 6 feet 2 inches (180 cm) tall and around 230 pounds (104 kg). He thought he was being cute and grabbed my wooden folding ruler I carry in my tool belt. I was tired and weighted down with heavy tools and a safety harness.

Now, mind you, it is about 7:00 a.m. and there are about 20 guys waiting for the elevator to take us up to the 17th floor to start the day. This guy opened my ruler and started poking me with it. It blew my mind that a 40-year-old man would be inclined to act this way. It's scary how ignorant people can be.

As he poked me with my ruler it snapped in half. Now I had no ruler to do my job. At that moment, he was standing to my side, and I threw a low side kick to his knee. This all happened very quickly, but for some reason I pulled back on the kick because I just thought it was overkill. I then snatched my broken ruler out of his hand.

He got angry, snuck up behind me, and immediately threw me into some sort of a choke hold. Without hesitation or thought, I loosened, dropped into a fright reaction, and spun directly into him, palm-heeling to the side of his head. I then followed with a right palm strike but missed him because he had already been launched backward to the ground about 6 feet from me. He had no intention of fighting any longer.

I felt my body knew just how much force to use. It was as if I was on autopilot and just acted, not so much reacted. Also, it shocked me that a guy my size could send a guy twice as big (who also does the same hard work) flying off his feet.

It all happened so quickly, and to be honest, I didn't even feel it when I struck him. The man had sheer terror in his face. He then started apologizing and trying to make up for what he had done. I just told him to stay away from me. I honestly felt sorry for having to do what I did, but I believe it was justifiable since he could've choked me out.

Preventing Common Mistakes

- ➤ In general, don't take any grab you can't do with two fingers.
- ➤ Don't clamp down while puppeteering. Your hand and arm should be able to loosely rotate around and follow the trapped wrist, allowing the opponent to move as he wishes, without letting go.
- ➤ Don't think your grab has to pull the opponent toward you. Pulling the attacker toward you runs the risk of using antagonistic muscles and getting into a tug-of-war. Instead, use a grab as an energy gauge and distance finder; then step toward the attacker.
- ➤ Never look for a lock; either they happen or they don't.
- ➤ Treat your attacker's skin as if it is covered with a foul-smelling slime. If you do, the attacker will have a hard time grabbing you in the first place.
- ➤ Generate more releasing power against a grab by repositioning your whole body and dropping to free a grabbed arm. This works better than straining with all your arm strength. Better yet, don't monkey around. Just spear the attacker in the eyes or throat with your fingers.
- ➤ Don't release straight up, down, or far out to the side. Your releasing movement should be in the direction of a straight blow to your attacker's nearest vital area or limb. Always bring a weapon on line.
- ➤ Resist the temptation to grab back with your other hand.
- ➤ Don't just wave your arms around in the speed-flow drill. Move your whole body, drop, and pocket so you don't hit yourself.

CHAPTER TEN

GROUND FIGHTING

Despite your training, and whether you like it or not, you may find yourself defending your life on the ground. The reason we've saved this subject until now is that ground fighting employs all the previous principles except that now you have to translate them to a new dimension where they become even more savage. These principles are very different from the way most other martial arts handle grappling. The ground fighting concepts of guided chaos represent some of the art's most devastating aspects. Developed by John Perkins in his early bouts with his father and uncles, refined in the bloodbaths he survived as a cop, and confirmed by his later forensic homicide research, they reflect a great deal of Native American martial arts influence in that they are based on freedom of movement and an "anything goes" adaptability.

There are some arts in vogue now that actually prefer to take the fight to the ground and emphasize this in their training. Fans of the UFC and no-holds-barred matches (which is a misnomer because there are strict rules to prevent serious injury) contend you should practice grappling because more often than not you end up there. Although highly skilled in modified Native American ground-fighting techniques, John Perkins has gone to the ground in less than 10 percent of the over 100 serious, violent, armed, and unarmed confrontations he has been involved in. Intending to go to the ground as a form of self-defense is a potentially fatal way of thinking for at least six reasons:

1. By violating the principle of challenging no one, you eliminate the simplest and most effective form of self-defense there is: running away.

2. On the ground, your advantages of upright balance and rooting become negated—bad news if your attacker outweighs you by 100 pounds (45.4 kg) or more.

3. The real world is not a martial arts school classroom with soft mats. In a dogfight, the last thing you want to do is smash your head, tailbone, or neck on a car bumper, concrete sidewalk, fire hydrant, or broken glass to gain a so-called ground advantage!

4. Weapons, such as knives, eliminate most grappling techniques. Try wrestling with an opponent wielding a Magic Marker at breakneck speed and see how long you can avoid being turned into a piece of graffiti.

5. You might be fighting multiple opponents. With standard grappling, you can fight only one assailant at a time. Meanwhile, that attacker's buddies will stomp you into dog food.

6. The entire notion of controlling or submitting a dangerous opponent, essentially attaching your body to his to incapacitate him, runs totally contrary to the very definition of survival. Every second you are tied to your enemy exposes you to more danger.

People ask, "But isn't grappling better than punching? Everybody knows a wrestler can beat a boxer." To answer this, read the following excerpt from a letter the president of the International Combat Martial Arts Federation, professor Bradley J. Steiner, sent to his associates:

During WWII, with the exception of Jack Dempsey, virtually every single unarmed and hand-to-hand combat instructor for the United States, Canadian, French, and British forces had a formidable and core background in wrestling, judo, ju-jutsu—yet every single one of those instructors deliberately minimized, played down, and de-emphasized all grappling in favor of basic, simple blows, when preparing men for war. Why? Well, why do you think? Some of these experts, like Pat (Dermot) O'Neil and William Ewart Fairbairn, were literally the first Caucasian ju-jutsu/judo black belts in the world at that time! They were ranked fifth-degree black belt, and second-degree black belt, respectively. Fairbairn had personally participated in more than 600 deadly encounters (armed and unarmed) prior to WWII, when he was Commissioner of the Shanghai Municipal Police! Don't you think that man knew what real combat required?

Also consider this from Colonel Rex Applegate, the former director of close combat training at the Military Intelligence Training Center, who accumulated his experience during wartime and trained over 10,000 military and intelligence personnel for the Office of Strategic Services (OSS) (which eventually became the CIA): "Blows should always be used in preference to throws" (*Kill or Get Killed* by Colonel Rex Applegate, Paladin Press, 1976, p. 29).

If you've read through the book this far, you already know that if you use only strength, speed, and standard wrestling, boxing, or no-holds-barred fighting skills, your odds of disabling a larger opponent who has the same skills are virtually nil. Unless you're extremely fast or lucky, you'll be crushed, mangled, and torn limb from limb. However, the extremely nasty tactics of guided chaos and close combat can negate an opponent's superior skills and physical strength. Why? Even past ultimate champion Royce Gracie would find it difficult to fight with a finger buried in his eye (and why he did it himself on his opponent in one of his early televised bouts when he got into trouble). This is why these tactics are forbidden in UFC competitions.

You may wonder what might prevent your attacker from using these tactics, too. Nothing, except that you will be better at them. The ability to deliver and defend against these tactics for survival is based solely on looseness, body unity, balance, and sensitivity—aspects virtually no one else teaches, especially on the ground.

Going to the ground to grapple could mean going to your grave. If your opponent falls to the ground, don't follow him. Run away.

Guided Chaos Ground Fighting Versus Conventional Grappling

One of the more intriguing aspects of guided chaos for beginners and outside observers is Master Perkins' modified Native American ground fighting. Not only have most people never seen or experienced authentic Native American martial arts (because of the dearth of practitioners alive today and the even smaller number interested in sharing their skills with the public), but most martial artists and combative sports fans cannot even conceive of an effective method of fighting on the ground that differs significantly from the grappling methods (wrestling, jujitsu, etc.) so universally practiced today. To even suggest that a very different method may be equally or even more effective for real violence immediately evokes skepticism, so conditioned are most people to consider ground fighting as synonymous with wrestling or grappling.

Let's take an analytical look at what guided chaos modified Native American ground fighting actually is, why it is, and how and why it differs from conventional ground fighting (grappling) methods.

Disengagement Versus Engagement

Guided chaos ground fighting, unlike grappling, emphasizes disengagement rather than engagement with the enemy. *Engagement* means the merging of two bodies into a single system of forces for more than a split second's duration. Put more simply, conventional grappling methods emphasize engagement with the adversary so that the practitioner seeks to tie up with the adversary in order to apply his or her techniques. The grounded grappler on the offensive seeks to minimize the distance between his or her body and the opponent's, thereby gaining maximum control over and awareness of all of the opponent's movements, maximizing opportunities to apply attached joint locking or breaking and choking or strangling techniques. Minimizing the space available to the opponent minimizes the opponent's opportunities to strike the grappler (using conventional strikes, at least) and allows the grappler to use full body weight and the strength of core muscles against the isolated, weaker joints of the opponent, provided the grappler has sufficient sensitivity, agility, endurance, and knowledge to make the techniques work against his or her opponent. Even when conventional striking methods are integrated into grappling, as in the popular ground and pound strategy of MMA competitions, the striking is usually performed from prescribed positions of maximum engagement (e.g., punches from the mount position or knee strikes from the side control position) so as to maintain control over the opponent's movements while creating just enough space for the grappler to strike.

Guided chaos ground fighting, on the other hand, implores you to remain as disengaged as possible. Rather than tying up with the enemy, you strive to maintain freedom of movement rather than commit your body to striving against the movements of a single adversary. Contact with the enemy, rather than being tight and constant as in conventional grappling, is fleeting and minimal, consisting primarily of kicks, strikes, slams, gouges, rips, and quick wrenches. The principle of disengagement allows you to use an element relatively unavailable to the conventional grappler: mobility.

Ground Mobility

Although a good grappler is mobile relative to his or her opponent because the grappler is able to climb rapidly all over and around the opponent's body, the engaged aspect of grappling prevents the grappler from being mobile relative to the total environment. This is because the grappler's goal is control: to fix the opponent so he or she can be pounded or further immobilized and strangled. While the grappler is attached to the opponent, working toward the opponent's defeat, the grappler is not free to move rapidly around the environment he or she is fighting in.

In guided chaos, you remain disengaged from the enemy (through trained rapid, convulsive, and yielding movement and sensitivity) and are free to move wherever you want. Further, rapid mobility across the ground (primarily in the mode of rolling) is something that is practiced constantly in guided chaos ground fighting training. This kind of training is notably absent from most conventional grappling programs, simply because it does not fit into the grappling paradigm of constant engagement and the goal of submission. Even when a guided chaos practitioner is forced to fight nose to nose, close range disengagement is a priority.

Sport Versus Combat

The contrasts explored thus far expose the primary difference between conventional ground grappling and guided chaos ground fighting: Most modern grappling methods are designed for a sport paradigm, but guided chaos ground fighting is intended for real combat. Because of the always-present possibility of multiple attackers in real combat, purposefully engaging with a single adversary on the ground, thereby sacrificing mobility, is an extremely risky strategy. Although the story exists of a grounded grappler buying time against multiple attackers by manipulating his engaged opponent as a shield against the kicks and punches of the other attackers, this is hardly a reliable enough strategy to count on. This would require the almost Herculean task of manipulating the opponent's entire body mass against his will while simultaneously defending against his attacks! A far better strategy is the exact same one a guided chaos practitioner would use when standing up: Remain mobile and disengaged in order to prevent the attackers from targeting you for effective strikes and grapples while lashing out with powerful, accurate, full-body attacks against the closest attackers and attempting to create a window to escape the crowd.

This is exactly what the guided chaos multiple attacker strategy consists of: constant, unpredictable movement (rapid, stomping steps to the toes and shins while standing, and rolling when on the ground); rapid, powerful, full-body striking at all angles to the eyes, throat, and other lethal targets (dropping strikes and kicks while standing, and dropping kicks [primarily], body slams, and strikes on the ground); and awareness of opportunities to escape the mass attack (breaking out of the crowd to run away while standing, and creating space to get up and then run when on the ground).

The Strategy Must Match the Goal

The grappling approach of mutually agreed upon full engagement with a single adversary in order to apply pins, joint locks, and chokes is ideally suited to allowing a grappler to convincingly and demonstrably control and dominate a single opponent without seriously injuring him. This is why grappling is such a perfect method for sport competition, where the object is to demonstrate one athlete's superiority over another while preserving both athletes to perform another day. This is performed within the context of weight divisions so that opponents of roughly similar size and weight have a relatively realistic shot at demonstrating superior controlling skills and strength training. Size does matter, and if the goal is submission or knockout, a smaller competitor stands little chance of pinning, locking, or merely "pounding" his opponent for a "win." If we look to the animal kingdom for context, we will see that when smaller creatures are able to take down larger prey it is because the goal is to kill them for food. No controlling tactics are employed; the superior weaponry of a tiger's teeth and claws slash, tear, gouge, and rip at his often far-larger prey's body and points are not awarded for "half-kills." The tiger would go hungry and ultimately die himself. You fight differently when your life is on the line. We repeatedly cite the example of the enraged bobcat in this book; although a bobcat weighs around 30 pounds, you would not want to piss one off and have it dropped on your neck. If you tried to control, hit, or throttle this screaming tornado of teeth and claws, not only would you miss, you'd be torn to shreds for the effort before it escapes. He is not playing the same game as you. The bobcat, by virtue of his evolutionary wiring, simply will not allow you to control and "submit" him because he is not trying to control and submit *you*.

Similarly the guided chaos approach of disengagement, with contact limited primarily to the impacts of powerful, full-body kicks, body slams, strikes, wrenches, rips, and gouges, is not very well suited to pinning an opponent in place or forcing an opponent to admit defeat before serious damage is done within the context of rules. What it is suited for, however, is maintaining freedom of movement and mobility, allowing a guided chaos practitioner to move sufficiently to prevent a lethal piling on or boot party from multiple attackers and to create space to stand up—while dealing out disabling and possibly lethal damage to the attackers.

The Weapon Factor

Another contrast between guided chaos ground fighting and conventional grappling that illustrates their respective foci (combat versus sport) is how the hands are used in each. In conventional grappling, the hands are used almost constantly to hold and control the opponent, and at times to balance on, push off from the ground, or *bluntly* strike the opponent (as opposed to *piercing* him). In guided chaos ground fighting, however, the hands are almost never used against the ground or to hold the enemy, and are used only

Figure 10.1

secondarily for momentary striking, gouging, and ripping. In figure 10.1*a* one combatant attempts a sportive takedown while expecting the other to use grappling or blunt striking tactics to prevent him. Instead, the defender uses piercing and ripping tactics to blind or maim his attacker and a neck wrench, which could do even worse. He might also elbow to the spine or chop to the base of the neck while convulsively delivering a dropping knee strike to the face (see the section on Ground Avoidance coming up soon). Because the defender has attempted up to this point to avoid violence but is now in fear of dying he is not playing the same game. In figure 10.1*b* the two opponents are intent on submitting *each other* and the competitor on the bottom has successfully applied a lock from which the adversary on top has no means of escape. By contrast, in figure 10.1*c* the adversaries are engaged in mortal combat (where either or both could die). However, the combatant on the bottom is *still* employing sportive controlling tactics while the combatant on top is fighting for his life and is ripping his enemy's eyes out. Granted, the bottom combatant could also use life-or-death tactics, but the point is that when you train exclusively to both *deliver and defend* against such tactics you have a far better chance of making yours work and eluding the enemy's. It is not simply a matter of "adding in dirty fighting when necessary," as some MMA purists have stated. We have presented the above scenario as a point of comparison, but it needs to be pointed out that if the defender were employing guided chaos principles from the start he shouldn't even *be* in this arm bar. The groundfighting tactics coming up would keep him disengaged with his boots in the attacker's face instead of his trunk. But you never know.

During guided chaos training, you're admonished to keep your hands as free and unencumbered as possible. This is because guided chaos acknowledges the fact that in real combat, hand-held weapons are often a factor in the outcome. Therefore, guided chaos ground fighting is designed to integrate seamlessly with weapons use. This is inherent in the art's Native American roots, when a practitioner would have been expected to have tomahawks or hunting knives in his or her hands while fighting in close combat, on the ground or otherwise. The modern guided chaos practitioner may instead have a handgun, a carry knife, a cane, or a weapon of opportunity picked up from the ground (e.g., a brick, bottle, rock, or dirt to throw in the enemies' eyes). Ground fighting with weapons, as well as picking up weapons from the ground in the midst of a fight, are frequently practiced aspects of guided chaos training.

Sensitivity and Destruction Versus Control and Submission

The following points sum up what we've covered so far:

- Sportive grappling seeks the ground in order to gain control over a single opponent in order to make the opponent submit to the grappler's will. Once pinned, the opponent can then be pounded to attain a knockout.

- Guided chaos avoids the ground due to the dangers of being on the ground in a real combat situation (as opposed to a sporting match). However, if forced to the ground, the guided chaos practitioner uses disengagement (through sensitivity), mobility, and maximum, immediate destruction of the enemy (including use of weapons if available)—just as he or she would do while upright—in order to minimize the danger while on the ground and stand up as quickly as possible.

- Generally, guided chaos ground fighting uses the same strategy as guided chaos stand-up fighting: Use sensitivity and the disengagement principle to destroy the enemy as quickly as possible while maintaining a firm root no one can find (through balanced mobility), looseness, and body unity.

The major differences that require additional training are the use of different rooting points on the ground—hips, back, shoulders, and so on—as opposed to just the feet while standing up, and the increased availability of tools because both legs may be used simultaneously from the ground and in ways different from when standing up. Because the legs (especially with sturdy boots on them) are by far the most powerful limbs of the body, it makes sense to take advantage of their increased potential on the ground through additional training. Therefore, the main emphasis of solo training for guided chaos ground fighting is the development of balance on and transition between the various rooting points available on the ground; the development of the musculature and coordination necessary to use all the available tools in all possible ways; and of course, the development of the ability to get up off the ground from any position as quickly as possible.

If this ground fighting strategy sounds novel or unproven, note these excerpts from the book *Kill or Get Killed* by Lieutenant Colonel Rex Applegate, one of the greatest works on close combat of the World War II era: "Avoid, if at all possible, going to the ground with your adversary. . . . One injunction you should heed: Once going to the ground, never stop moving. Start rolling and try to get back on your feet as quickly as possible. If you can't get up and can't roll, pivot on your hips and shoulders so you can face your opponent and block with your feet any attempt to close with you. Remember, it is not necessary to go to the ground once YOU have placed your opponent there. You can finish him off with your feet. Your enemy can do likewise if you remain immobile on the ground and stay within range . . . When on the ground, subjected to attack from a standing opponent, the individual can use his feet to prevent the adversary from closing in or administering a coup de grace . . . At the first opportunity he should try to regain his feet"(Applegate 1976 [new revised edition] *Kill Or Get Killed,* Boulder, CO, Paladin Press).

Despite being an expert in sportive methods of ground grappling, Rex Applegate, like John Perkins, understood two facts about real combat conditions, where multiple adversaries may have boots and other weapons fully capable of ending things in an instant if offered a good (stationary) target: Lying on the ground is generally a bad place to be, and when on the ground, the sportive strategy of engagement must be abandoned for one of disengagement and mobility.

Going to the Ground and Ground Avoidance

There are no special anti-grappling grapples or counter-takedown leverage techniques in guided chaos (although some suggestions of tactics to experiment with will be presented shortly). One problem with such techniques is that by the time you realize their necessity in a fight—when you recognize the takedown attempt—it is usually too late to apply them. Instead, the basic concepts of guided chaos, if trained diligently, will usually prevent the circumstances that typically result in fighters going to the ground against their will.

1. Balance. The hyperbalance that is a result of guided chaos training makes it less likely that you will lose your footing and fall to the ground, regardless of the cause.

2. Sensitivity and disengagement. The guided chaos attribute of external tactile sensitivity, along with its application according to the disengagement principle (remain as disengaged as possible while remaining engaged enough to cause damage—to stick but not get stuck), can prevent a grappler from putting you in a strong clinch. Your body always seems to squirt out of attempted grips and holds while striking into vital areas and disrupting the grappler's balance from unexpected angles. This is similar to what one would experience trying to throttle the aforementioned "enraged bobcat." The importance of this combination of looseness and sensitivity cannot be overemphasized. It is the embodiment of all the internal principles trained in guided chaos. You learn to move your body as if the attacker's skin is red hot and scalding, yet you must still feel where the attacker is and where he or she is going. This completely changes the mindset from force and control to touch, evasion, and destruction. The image in guided chaos is one of carrying a hot potato in your hands across a room without dropping it—it's too hot to hold but too tasty to let go. This negates a common grappling takedown strategy: to first tie up the opponent in a standing clinch in order to suppress his strikes and gain control over his balance, and then to take him down from there.

3. Dropping energy and the sphere of influence. Guided chaos practitioners' use of dropping energy to keep strikes within the sphere of influence (to prevent reaching with strikes) means they are unlikely to overcommit to strikes. Taking advantage of a striker's overcommitment is the main means by which an experienced grappler can shoot in for a successful takedown from beyond contact distance. If the grappler cannot force an opponent to overcommit to long-distance striking attacks, it becomes very difficult for a grappler to achieve a clean takedown without first achieving a controlling clinch. Additionally, dropping energy, along with body unity, allows for very powerful strikes from very close range, which can further frustrate a grappler's efforts to safely close distance.

4. Looseness. The guided chaos practitioner's trained looseness makes it very difficult for a grappler to control his or her body even if a grip is achieved. For example, against an untrained person, a grappler can force the other's body off balance simply by manipulating one arm because an untrained person naturally tenses up against the grappler's grip. However, many a grappler has grabbed a guided chaos practitioner's arm only to realize that he's got nothing. Guided chaos principles allow you to move the rest of your body decisively, independent of the controlled arm, to retain balance and attack the grappler.

5. Savagery. Since you fight only to save your life, biting, ripping, tearing, gouging, and crushing body parts is the norm and prevents most grapples; practicing defense against the same through contact flow prevents the grappler from using them on you.

Generally, training in guided chaos principles will allow you to deal with a grappler as with any other fighter. Guided chaos practitioners pay special attention to aspects of contact flow and combat application particularly germane to grappling (e.g., feeling the level change, finding and indexing on the head, body unity and dropping to stop momentum, close-range destruction, destroying the grappler while being taken down, etc.)

Intentionally Going to the Ground: Emergency Off-Lining

Although going to the ground in a real combat situation generally should be avoided, under certain circumstances, going to the ground in particular ways may be the best course of action.

In guided chaos, intentionally going to the ground may be characterized as a form of emergency off-lining. Getting off line from an attacker's charge is a fundamental concept in guided chaos. This is usually accomplished while standing by stepping to the side (and preferably forward) of an attacker with appropriate timing, positioning, and follow-up. However, sometimes you may not have the space or time to move to the side (e.g., in a confined area when there are multiple attackers), or you must immediately get your vital organs further away from the attackers' weapons (e.g., if the attacker is using knives). If you can't accomplish off-lining (as in the CCUE) to either side, and if you cannot levitate, changing the angle can be accomplished in only one direction: downward. You must go to the ground.

The methods by which you would go to the ground are very different from those used by most sport grapplers. Nearly all the methods sport grapplers use to take a fight to the ground (e.g., wrestling takedowns, judo throws) involve bringing their most vital areas (head, neck, chest) very close to the opponent's hands. This creates a major problem in real combat situations that require you to go to the ground—situations in which one goal of the maneuver is to gain distance between your vital areas and the weapons of the enemy. The methods used in guided chaos, based on Native American takedown maneuvers, do not suffer from this problem. They involve dropping, diving, spinning, and rolling to the ground at angles that present your feet toward the enemy as you move your upper body away from the enemy's weapons. The simultaneous takedowns are done with your feet and legs, and these have a good chance of seriously damaging the enemy's lower body, primarily breaking his or her knees. They also set you up to use your legs on the ground (again keeping the vital areas of the upper body away from the enemy's weapons) to quickly end any subsequent ground fight.

Ground Avoidance

But how do you avoid going to the ground in the first place? Extend your sensitivity, so you can treat your opponent the way a matador treats a bull. Avoid the typical response of squaring yourself and stiffening at the prospect of a collision or takedown move. Such tightening would provide a firm handle for your opponent to grapple. Guided chaos is about making yourself unavailable and not confronting force head-on. Don't look at your opponent as the enemy; this makes you angry and tense. Rather, think of your opponent as the carrier of a vile disease and therefore not to be touched (except to the extent of feeling where he is if necessary). This change in attitude will be reflected in the way your whole body moves. Your looseness and pocketing should accelerate until they turn into a kind of spasming we call shedding energy. React to grappling like an angry alley cat. Instead of tensing, squirm and writhe out of your attacker's grasp while you simultaneously rake his flesh.

Let's look at a possible scenario. You're threatened by an attacker from a distance of about 10 feet (3 m). You can back away or run, keeping the attacker in sight as you retreat. If you know you're fast, and the enemy doesn't look it, great. If it's the opposite, then strike preemptively. From this distance, look meek (Jack Benny style), back away slowly, and wait for the attacker to advance. If this happens, explode forward but slightly off line, stomp-step, and kick as if you're making a field goal (these are extremely fast, low, shin-level kicks). Immediately spear-hand to the eyes or throat or palm to the face while stepping in with a knee strike. This is basic close combat and should be practiced in action-reaction drills. You can also do the CCUE.

Suppose, however, that the attacker is a grappler, and he dives for your legs. Fine. The forward drop kick becomes a knee to the face. Dropping causes your diaphragm to contract convulsively (like a cough), speeding your knee to the target while you drop an ax hand or elbow to the neck. If this doesn't cripple the attacker, you'll be in the same situation as if he were closer in and decided to dive for your legs. Drop strongly and jam your fingers from underneath into his eye sockets like a bowling ball. Pocket your vital areas away from his grasp. Use his eye sockets, ears, jaw, and hair as handles to wrench and break his neck. (Remember, you fight to save your life or your loved ones only.)

Because you're striking downward, you can use full dropping energy to power chops, palms, elbows, or hammer fists against the base of his neck (compare with the slambag drills, chapter 6.) As your hands come up between blows, take something with you—his Adam's apple, ears, or hair—or twist his whole head violently (nobody asked him to attack you; he volunteered). If he picks up his head to avoid the initial onslaught, use your fingers to seek out and penetrate his eye sockets. Unless defense against eye attacks is practiced (as in contact flow), it is almost impossible to stop them at close range. Eye gouging can cause convulsions, unconsciousness, and death. We apologize, but real self-defense isn't nice. If you die because you didn't incapacitate your attacker before he regrouped, your grief-stricken family won't be consoled because you showed your assailant compassion.

Tips for Survival

Although there is much more that might be said about the unique and practical characteristics of guided chaos modified Native American ground fighting, what has been said so far should be sufficient to give you an idea of what to keep in mind as you train. Here are some training tips to consider as you begin your path to combative ground fighting expertise:

- Stick with the principles. Because guided chaos ground fighting looks different from guided chaos stand-up training, people sometimes assume that the basic principles of balance, sensitivity, looseness, and body unity do not apply. Nothing could be further from the truth! Balance in any position on the ground is what allows what look like crazy maneuvers to be effective. Both tactile and subcortical visual sensitivity are necessary to guide your movements across the ground and into the enemy, even when your head may be moving and turning rapidly to keep away from danger. Without looseness, your body will quickly be broken against the ground itself, especially during the falling and diving maneuvers. Looseness combined with sensitivity is also what allows you to avoid being dragged into an immobile grappling clinch. You must learn to move your body like a writhing mongoose or a furiously twisting, spitting bobcat. Who would want to grapple with a 160-pound (72.6-kg) bobcat or attempt a headlock, mount, or figure 4? No one; doing so would be insanity. The grappler would never get a grip on the bobcat's body as he or she's being torn to shreds. Finally, body unity is what makes the ground kicking and rolling maneuvers so damaging to the enemy. The attacks come from the whipping and dropping (yes, even on the ground!) of the whole body, not just the legs, allowing them to cleave through the enemies' bodies rather than bouncing off harmlessly. The original Native American fighting methods were characterized by a loose gracefulness and uninhibited use of the entire body as a united weapon to destroy the enemy.

- Become friends with the ground—gradually. Although all the high-speed, ballistic whipping, diving, falling, and spinning maneuvers used in guided chaos ground fighting demonstrations are certainly cool and fun to watch and perform, it's important to start slowly in learning how to do them. The ground can be quite unforgiving if in your eagerness, you don't take enough training time to allow your body to become accustomed to merging fluidly with the ground and moving with it rather than against it. Use soft mats while learning anything new.

Begin learning any falling, rolling, diving, or dropping maneuvers from your knees rather than from your feet—you'll have less distance to fall in case you make a mistake. Practice rolling and moving across the mat in a free, fluid, and creative manner, feeling where you can drop or whip out attacks or contort your body to keep your vital areas safe from attacks from any angle. Only gradually shift your practice off mats and onto hard and especially uneven ground. Remember that no matter how good you get, in the real world, the ground is a hazardous place to be. (Just ask that fire hydrant you didn't see behind you as you began to spin down to the sidewalk.)

- Be cautious about confined spaces. Remember that if one of the possible reasons to go to the ground is to be able to get your vital targets further away from a weapon in confined space, you need to be able to do all the maneuvers in a confined space. Do not practice all of the diving and falling attacks only by diving across the room into wide, ballistic arcs. You should be able to drop to the ground and take out the legs of the person right next to you. This can even be performed in the same movement by shooting the legs out as you fall. Going to the ground like this starts out with a sensation similar to dropping when you're on your feet. Like a marionette that's had its strings cut, your whole body suddenly goes limp and drops—only rather than catching yourself within 1 inch (2.5 cm), you let the drop go all the way to the ground while you spiral or collapse to land at the correct angle to allow you to take out the enemy as you fall. When you do it properly, it should seem to your enemy that you have suddenly disappeared—only to reappear next to his broken legs with your boots against his neck and head.

To practice such tactics, experiment with the following exercises:

Stop the Charge

You must be able to maintain your balance while drop-striking to check the incoming momentum of an aggressive grappler. This drill improves this ability.

1. Have your training partner hold a kicking shield and charge you from various ranges (6 feet [1.8 m] or more away). His goal is to knock you off your feet with the kicking shield.

2. If your partner is holding the kicking shield low, drop-kick to the front to stop him the instant he moves. Don't wait. Kick preemptively. If your reactions become so fast that you can step in and kick his shins before he really gets moving, all the better (the speed of a low dropkick encourages this).

   If you fear you are about to be attacked, just step off line, and drop-kick before the attacker does anything. Emphasize the contraction of your diaphragm with a scream or a cough. Remember to step in and off line slightly. This automatically throws a monkey wrench into the grappler's plans. Your root must be instant and very solid to absorb the energy of the charge and reflect it back at the grappler through the kick. Don't worry about kicking hard. Simply drop well, be accurate with the kick, and keep your body relaxed. Just as the power of upper-body striking comes from dropping, balance, and body alignment rather than from the straining muscles of the striking limb, so it should be with your kicks. If your partner's pads are sufficient, practice full-power dropping and kicking. Note: If your training partner stops his charge abruptly just outside the range of your kick, you should not lose your balance and fall forward. If you are late with your kick or if the charge begins too close for you to kick, replace the kick with a dropping knee strike, again taking care to maintain your balance.

3. If your partner is holding the kicking shield high, stop him with a palm strike delivered in the same manner as the kick and knee described previously. You can also use the CCUE. If your strike is late or he is too close, use an elbow, delivered in a manner similar to the fright reaction.

4. Immediately after landing the first blow, change your root to step off line before your partner can regain momentum. Follow up with anywhere striking, being mindful not to injure your training partner, who won't know where the strikes are going.

Drop-Striking the Grappler

You must be able to effectively drop-strike downward (e.g., on a grappler trying to take out your legs) while maintaining your balance.

1. Lay a heavy bag on its side on the ground.

2. Drop and palm, elbow, and dropknee-strike the bag, being careful to maintain your own balance rather than leaning onto the bag. You should be able to stand right back up after striking, without pushing off the bag.

Close-Range Takedown Preemption Within Contact Flow

Have your training partner suddenly attempt takedowns, throws, and tackles, first at slow speed and then, after you have practiced the following sufficiently, at maximum speed but reduced power. Be careful because this is extremely dangerous.

Perform regular contact flow. One partner suddenly goes for a low takedown. The other partner drops convulsively and delivers one of the following:

1. Multiple machine-gun hammer fists or chops down on the back of the neck, followed by gouges to the eyes using the eye sockets to wrench the head up and sideways.

2. Dropping elbow strike to the back of the neck.

3. Rising knee strike, with convulsive dropping energy, to the falling head. What you will find is that if you have a favorite leg to knee with, you will be able to slam it into your opponent's head regardless of which knee your opponent may go for in the takedown. A safe way to practice this is for the attacker to keep his palms in front of his face as he drops quickly out of sight and dives for the the target knee.

4. Deliver a devastating counterattack that combines the other elements. For example, you can slam in the down elbow at the exact same time as you land the rising knee, forming a pincer to crush the attacker's head, then reach under and rip up into the eye sockets to wrench the head. Use low power but high speed and be extremely careful.

The following can be performed full power if you have a fighting man dummy available to be dropped or thrown at you. (The fighting man dummy is an essential tool we recommend purchasing; see References and Resources.)

Falling in Your Favor

If the tactics just discussed fail for whatever reason, you might still wind up on the ground. Should that happen, there are two options to consider and practice:

1. Think of a cat, perched on your outstretched arm. If the cat loses its balance, it digs its claws in and hangs on as it flops over, ripping your skin with its full body weight. So, if you're going to fall, and you're *already* entangled with the attacker (to the extent that you can't break free as in point two below), fall and take something with you: hair, skin, ears, lips, or the like. Sink your teeth into the attacker's throat, face, hand—anything within reach. Not only may you do some real damage, but by borrowing from the attacker's balance, you might recover yours (of course, there are no guarantees). It's also a distraction that creates other openings. Once on the ground, if you can't get your boots in his face and you're nose to nose, your hands work the same as if you were standing. You yield to the slightest pressure, clear the line, shorten the weapon, and tool-replace, going for the eyes, throat, and groin with chops, spears, rips, tears, eye gouges, palm heels, hammer fists, and elbows. Don't forget to use your teeth.

2. Get to the ground first. If you're losing your balance and you're *not* entangled, drive away with your legs as you fall or dive to shoot your body as far as possible from the attacker and bring your boots into action. This would also allow you to access your pistol if you have one. Use a one-handed, bent-arm "perp shoot" grip, not a two-handed, isosceles grip or you're liable to shoot your own feet as you kick to keep him off you. You can practice this with a toy dart gun or Airsoft gun with eye protection.

Experiment with pulling your knees up to your face when you hit the ground so you can jackknife them back into the attacker. Use your butt, back, and sides as your new root points. Just make sure you fall with your head away from the attacker's feet—and keep it away by rolling and twisting.

Staying Mobile on the Ground

The typical response to a grappling situation is tightness, supreme muscular exertion, and containment. It's when both of you are on the ground that you must really understand and feel the principles of suspend and release, loading the spring, tool replacement, shortening the weapon, and spasming (shedding) energy. This is because your mobility, or disengagement energy, is dramatically altered by being off your feet. Not limited—only altered. This mobility is a very important aspect of guided chaos ground fighting. Rather than the posed side-kick-from-the-ground kicks you typically see in karate, this is much wilder and looks kind of like a mix of log rolling, break-dancing, and the moves of Curly from the Three Stooges.

You must now learn to skitter, spasm, and jump around like a freshly caught catfish in a bucket. To be able to shoot your legs out, flip, roll, and change body position by 180 degrees while you deliver blows, you've got to be loose, yielding, and sensitive. This is so you can avoid pressure and entanglement, then set up attack positions where you can pulse and react off the opponent's energy yet remain unavailable. Do not grab or otherwise wrestle your opponent with the intent of containing or pinning him or her. This is even more important on the ground because there you can be crushed and strangled.

While keeping your head away from the attacker's legs, dive and roll sideways at extremely high speeds by pulling in your arms and legs like a figure skater going into a spin. By rolling we mean both head over heels like a ball and horizontally like a log. Both need to be practiced. You can jackknife your body violently to reverse your head and legs to avoid and deliver kicks. By using your hands to help, you can run in a circle on your side on the floor, a movement that powers many of the kicks described in the coming pages.

Find Your Root
One big difference on the ground is that your root is no longer in your feet. The principle of having a root no one can find is never more important than when ground fighting. Your root can be anywhere your body is in contact with the ground, and it can change like lightning to any other part as you spasm and skitter. An instantaneous drop and spin onto your backside, hip, back, shoulder, knee, or stomach can propel you into a completely different alignment and pivot point to facilitate strikes and redirections. Avoid landing on your elbow because it will shatter against concrete.

Once you're on the ground, kick and knee-strike using your buttocks, hips, and hands to balance you like a crazed break-dancer. For a split second, you can root (be in contact with the ground) and kick or hit off your stomach, chest, shoulder, upper back, lower back, hip, or any other body part you land on while spasming and jerking your body. You'll remain disengaged from the opponent as well as find an attack angle for yourself. Don't just hang out like a flipped turtle! And don't pose like in a karate flick!

Use Bouncing and Contorting Energy
To gain power, kick, stomp, or bounce your feet off the ground or target and kick again. In a flash, contract your whole body into a fetal position (shorten the weapon) and then explode outward. Kick through your opponent's head, bounce your heel off the ground, and kick again. Immediately snap your leg back and hook kick with your heel to the same target. Bounce parts of your opponent's body off the ground like a basketball. Think of bouncing as a form of pulsing because ricocheting off the ground propels you without requiring you to become entangled—something you must avoid at all costs.

Apply bouncing and contorting energy to all your strikes. Don't linger anywhere. When your attacker is on the ground as well, bounce a shot off his head, bounce your knee off his spine, or bounce your forehead into his nose. Twist your body around and mule-kick to the chest, knee, throat, back of the neck, and so forth while bracing with both palms on the ground. If you're lying on your backside, shoot your leg into the air and then drop an ax kick with your heel down onto his neck. Bounce off the neck and drop your heel again onto his thigh or groin. Scissor-kick with one or both legs as you balance, poised on your hip, and chop him down like a tree with roundhouse and heel kicks. When doing round and heel kicks, make sure you are driving the *entire* leg by swiveling from the hip joint to get the most mass into motion. Do not get lazy and just flick the lower leg by bending the knee! After destroying the target, roll with his leg snagged between the toe and heel of both your feet, snapping his knee. If he resists mightily, which is unlikely, release and reverse the energy like a rubber band, and then thrust-kick. Explore all your hitting options in contact leg flow—but do not grapple.

Suspend and Release
The suspend-and-release principle is uniquely effective when you are both on the ground because most attackers are hell-bent on controlling and overpowering you. Think of the bony protrusions on your opponent as tiny foot- and handholds a rock climber might use. Use your toes, heels, knees, elbows, and hands

to climb around your opponent's body. Do not, however, take and maintain a wrestling hold, either with leg scissors or your arms. Instead, actually stretch him out like a rubber band with your feet and hands (suspend and release) and wait (usually a millisecond) for the response. Let his panic propel your whole body into a snap-back reaction (as if you're doing a jackknife off a diving board), either in the form of a strike or a ripping, throttling action. The possibilities are endless. The simple action of digging the heels of your shoes into his ankles or knees and stretching him out for a split second by straightening your legs causes your opponent to have such a bizarre feeling that he may freak out and forcibly pull his body in. Anticipate this energy and use it to propel you like a stretched rubber band into, multihitting strikes like elbows to the neck and knees to the spine and coccyx. Just remember to deliver your crushing or choking assault as instantaneous blows that you immediately abandon as you move on to the next attack. This way, your opponent never gets a fix on you until it's too late for him.

If he grabs and twists your leg (which shouldn't happen in the first place if you're following the principles), don't resist; instead, roll your whole body with it like a log, kicking while rolling. Or, because he's now fixated with both hands on your leg, kick or scrape his hands off with your boot heels or batter the nearest part of his body (now defenseless since he's occupied with his grab). If you find yourself on your back with your opponent on top, sticking comes back into play because your back is rooted to the ground, and your hands are free. If you're on your back and he's sitting on top, you can crush his testicles, even if he weighs 300 pounds (136.1 kg), and there seems to be no room to insert your hand. Convulse your stomach in and slide a spear hand, palm down, under his crotch at the same time as you stab for the eyes with your other hand. Now make a fist under his crotch. The amount of power you can generate closing your hand far surpasses the resistance created by his weight. Now, twist your fist over and crush his testicles. He'll probably get off you first.

Tool Replace To help you avoid entanglement, make sure you use tool replacements with your feet the same as with your hands. In other words, smash and pulse with your boots, but the moment you feel the enemy pushing back or attempting to tie up his legs with yours, suspend and release with one foot, passing the apple to the other foot—or smashing with it. Crack and check, stomp and suspend, tool-replace and destruct—but do not grapple or tie up. Make believe his legs are red hot and keep everything ballistic. Remain unavailable but unavoidable.

Defeating Chokes

One way attackers bring their victims to the ground is with choking. The best defense is to prevent chokes in the first place. If you're aware, sensitive, yielding, and attacking the attacker, the assailant will find it difficult to choke you. The tendency when you're all yang energy is to tense your neck and shoulder muscles against the attack. This gives the enemy a handle and makes you even more susceptible to choking and other mayhem. When you're yielding, retract your head and neck like a garden snail's antenna. If you get choked from the front, it's better to simply step back than to start wrestling with the offending arm. Or, you can stab him in the eye with the other hand. No fancy moves. If it's too late for this, turning sideways and shrugging one shoulder up into the choking arm can break the choke, while leaving both your arms free. The fright reaction accomplishes the same thing.

Defending a Front Choke

If you're following the principles, this should never happen in the first place. However, if an attacker is choking you from the front, you can gouge or chop at his eyes or windpipe, bite his hands, kick his shins, smash the points of your elbows into his arms, and then springboard off his arms into his face, then back to his arms, biting and kicking until you're free. You have lots of options, although the simplest are jabs in the eyes and throat.

Defending a Rear Choke

Despite all your training, a predator can pounce on you undetected and choke you from behind. Unlike in the movies, if this is a serious assassination attempt, and your awareness has not prompted the fright reaction or an answer-the-phone response to prevent the assailant from locking down, you'll probably be unconscious before you can try anything else. So you see, it's vital not to let this happen in the first place. Nevertheless, if you have a split second before passing out, there are some things you can do, but they each depend on the energy he's giving you. Remember, it's a panic from the start, and there's no time for thought. You have to be explosive and flow with the energy wherever it goes. You simply try to augment it.

The instant response is to drop, turn, and chop, gouge, or palm-heel his face. If your arms are already obstructed, and the choke is locking down, you'll feel this as you turn and flow into a chop to his groin or an elbow to his gut. If he's on you fast like a steel vise, however, you'll probably be throttled before you can react. This is why it's important to train your awareness and sensitivity—you have only a split-second-long window to mount an effective response. Turn your head and throat away from the bone of his forearm and into the crook of his arm, shrug your shoulders (to raise his arms) and bite and grab his forearm or his fingers if you can. You can also grab a finger with your whole hand and break it, stomp on his toes, backward head-butt (however, a powerful assailant will pull you back and stifle the movement), or backward finger-poke into his eyes. You need to practice *all* these to see what works for you. In a flash, you may feel that one target is more available than another. His hand may be right near your teeth, or his nose may be near the back of your head. If you haven't been pulled off your feet, you can stomp his toes. Adopt the attitude that you're not going to die without taking him with you.

If you're falling backward, actually help him and launch yourself that way by driving back explosively with your legs. There's a good chance you'll make him hit something hard, and you'll roll over him. Then you're both on the ground, and things are more even. Rolling over your assailant at high speed is often a good tactic because there's sometimes a limb sticking out that can get cracked or dislocated by your full body weight.

If you're falling forward, go with it and turn on your side, keeping your head away from his feet. Snap into a fetal position (loading your own spring) and immediately explode outward, kicking. Like the Anywhere Strikes drills, you need to practice all the various ways of delivering strikes with your feet, knees, and legs while lying on the ground.

Avoiding the Sleeper Hold

The sleeper hold, also known as the mugger's yoke or carotid choke, has been outlawed by most police departments because, although intended only to induce unconsciousness, the carotid arteries of some people will not reopen once the hold is released. We advise extreme caution when practicing this hold and its counters.

The sleeper hold is performed by placing one arm around a person's throat from behind, using the biceps area and the inner forearm of that arm against the carotid arteries on either side of the neck. The hand of that choking arm hooks into the inside elbow of the other arm (figure 10.2a on p. 208), which goes behind the neck, locking it in. The assailant presses the hand of the locking arm forward against the back of the victim's head to cinch it tighter. If you are aware of your surroundings and know the principles in this book, however, you are unlikely to succumb to this deadly hold.

There are a number of escapes to combat this technique before the attacker can fully apply it (not all of them may be available in a particular circumstance):

1. Stick your arm in front of your neck and tuck your chin as someone attempts to apply the lock. Your arm will prevent a solid lockdown as well as elbow strike the attacker (figure 10.2b). This is what the fright reaction is for. You can now use your free hand to reach back and gouge out his eyes, which usually causes a release.

2. Slam the assailant's groin with a chop or hammer fist.

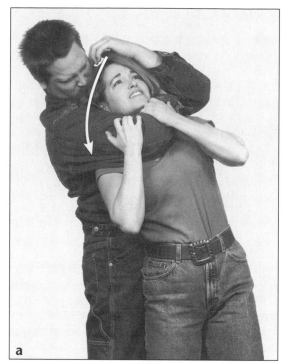

Figure 10.2

While your attacker is still upright, keep your head away from his legs. When you're both on the ground, remember that if he concentrates on throttling or pinning you, you can always snake a finger into his eye or crush his windpipe or testicles.

If you find yourself fully in the grip of this hold because of various factors, such as being attacked by multiple assailants or being stunned by a blow to the head, you could attempt one or more of the following releases. (When practicing them, have your partner hold with full power without pressing on your arteries.) You must perform the releases in under three seconds.

1. Turn your chin into the crook of the choking arm. Simultaneously, raise your shoulders and bear down with your chin to relieve some of the choking pressure. Try to bite the attacker's forearm.

2. While holding the fingers of the attacker's front hand, practice reaching backward and peeling the fingers off the arm that is behind your head. This will make the choke weaker if you are standing or being pulled off your feet.

3. When an attacker feels you releasing his grip, he may try to change tactics. You must seize the opportunity and instantly twist out of the choke.

Remember, you can easily be killed with this choke. It's you or him. Eye-gouge to maximum effect. If necessary, push your fingers into his eye to hit the brain.

Most people will release their grip once their fingers or thumb are pulled or twisted. There are, however, some rare individuals who possess prodigious strength and will not release. Here is where you need a sharp weapon or a handgun. Even a ballpoint pen will do. If the pen is held in the ice-pick grip, gouge it deep into the soft area of the arm above the elbow. If it's in the forehand grip, drive it into his eyes or arm. It could save your life to shop for and always carry a stout metal pen with a large, flat top and a rubber grip. Do not carry it in the V or crook of the neckline of a polo shirt because you may not have access if you're strangled. Keep it clipped in a front pant's pocket, not loose inside or you may never get to it. If you are someone who carries a knife or gun, practice getting these weapons into play in three seconds or less, or they'll be taken from you. An assailant can't squeeze you if you cut through the muscles and tendons of the choking arm. He won't hold on long if shot in the head either.

Getting your weapon into play, whether it be pen, knife, or gun should be practiced diligently. There are rubber and toy guns that shoot rubber darts that can be used; foam or paper sticks are great for hard, high-speed pen and knife training.

Using Anywhere Kicks on the Ground

The kicks you use on the ground are wilder, more varied, and more savage than you might imagine. Experiment relentlessly with all of these.

- Scissoring. By gripping the ground with your feet as you lie on your hip, you can launch into a cleaving action. This should propel you instantly into something else. By positioning yourself sideways on your hip instead of on your butt, you can anchor one foot on the floor to drive the other one through horizontal, round, and hook kicks. The anchored foot then launches and kicks while the other one returns, making for a devastating scissors effect. Make sure you're throwing the kicks from your hip joint, not just your knee joint. A method unique to guided chaos is to anchor your top foot when you're lying on your side and use it to power a round kick with the bottom leg, which bends just enough to clear the anchored top foot (figure 10.3). You are, in effect, running on the floor while balanced on your hip (like Curly from the Three Stooges).

- Hooking and crushing. With your hip on the floor, pull one leg in, taking some part of your opponent with it, and thrust the other out.

- Round kicking. While poised on your hip, drive your foot off the floor in a low, horizontal kick that either arcs through or over the target. At the end of its arc, bounce the foot off the floor and heel kick back into the target.

- Vertical ax-kicking combo. With your butt on the floor, raise your leg straight up and then drop the heel like a guillotine onto a floor target; bounce off and kick up into a higher target, such as the groin or a kneeling attacker's chin (figure 10.4).

- Mule kicking. With your chest facing the ground and your hands in a push-up position, drive the heel of one foot straight back into its target. As with dropping, if necessary, you should be able to switch your kicking and supporting legs instantaneously. Try kicking with both legs at the same time.

- Shredding. As with scissoring, use your feet and legs to scrape and crush against each other and anything in between them. This can be sideways or along their length (figure 10.5 on p. 210). Use it also to load your spring.

You can practice kicking against a swinging heavy bag that is low to the ground. The faster you kick, the better. Remember to practice dog digging simultaneously.

Figure 10.3

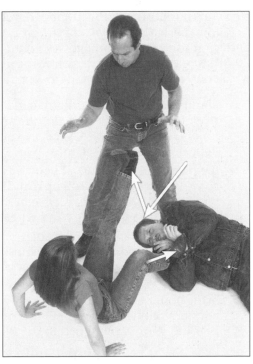

Figure 10.4

Figure 10.5

• Diving and rolling. A significant part of your training should consist of diving, rolling horizontally like a log, tumbling like a boulder, and generally scooting your entire body from any position to any other position in order to do three things:

1. Keep your head away from an attacker's legs.
2. Keep your legs disentangled.
3. Achieve offensive attack positions.

We cannot emphasize these three points enough. You want to be able to replace a root while you shift your balancing from one hip to the other, or from a shoulder root to a butt root. You want to be able to reverse your head position with your feet in one violent spasm (practically levitating off the ground, not sliding) and dive off line to throw out sweeping, round kicks through a standing enemy's legs. This only scratches the surface of what's possible.

Remember, you can shorten the weapon on any kick to increase power or gain a different entry angle. Make sure every kick rebounds into another kick.

All this may tempt you to want to go to the ground, especially if you get good at all the drills. Don't be foolish. No matter how formidable you may get, escaping multiple attackers on the ground is no picnic. Although going to the ground against a knife is sometimes an option (coming up), *looking* to ground fight is sheer stupidity.

Ground Fighting Warm-Ups

Just as we use solo exercises to develop balance, looseness, body unity, internal sensitivity (proprioception), and tendon and stabilizer muscle strength when we're standing, we have exercises that develop the same when we're on the ground. We need different exercises because of the different root points we use on the ground (e.g., butt, back, hip, shoulder, etc.) and the consequently different development needed to balance and move from them.

Before doing these or any of the ground fighting exercises, make sure your core (trunk) and leg muscles are thoroughly stretched and ready to move. We recommend spending 20-30 seconds on each of the following movements. Do each of them slowly and smoothly with constant movement and no stopping.

• Stand with your legs straight, bend forward at the waist as if to touch your toes, and stretch downward as far as you can comfortably go: no pain or strain. Then come up and lean backward as far as you can comfortably go, as if to touch your heels. Repeat for 20 to 30 seconds.

• Lie on your back and roll your legs straight back over your head as far as they can comfortably go. Then roll up to a sitting position with your legs straight out in front of you, reach up for the sky, lean forward as if to touch your toes, reach up for the sky again, then roll back and repeat for 20 to 30 seconds.

• Lie on your back with the soles of your feet flat on the floor and your hands flat against the floor beside your hips; thrust your hips up to the ceiling, then lower them, and repeat for 20 to 30 seconds.

• Do slow Hindu or dive bomber push-ups for 20 to 30 seconds. To do these push-ups, bring your chest and then your pelvis near the floor sequentially, then lift your chest back up followed by your pelvis. An easier way is to perform a regular push-up while keeping your pelvis glued to the floor.

• Lie on your back with your arms outstretched to your sides and your knees pulled up together at a right angle so that your shins are parallel with the floor. Turn from the waist to lower your knees to the floor, or as close as possible, on each side (keep your knees at a right angle, pressed together) while turning your head in the opposite direction and keeping your shoulders flat against the floor. Repeat for 20 to 30 seconds.

Now for the actual ground fighting exercises. During all of these exercises, keep the following points in mind:

- Do not use your hands or arms against the ground for balance. You want to develop the ability to root and move from your hips, butt, back, shoulders, and all areas of your torso so that you can keep your arms free to strike, protect your head, or use a weapon. Whenever you arm is braced against the ground, it becomes vulnerable to damage from any impact or jarring. Keep your hands and arms off the ground throughout the exercises, preferably protecting your head but free to move as needed.

- Keep each foot at a right angle to its shin (i.e., flexed, not pointed) so that the foot is always ready to kick or stomp from any angle. If you let your foot get lazy and dangle at any odd angle, your ankle becomes very susceptible to damage from impact with the ground or enemies.

- Keep your head up, away from the ground. If this overloads your neck muscles, keep at it. You want to develop your neck muscles so that you can reflexively keep your head away from the ground at any angle. If you really can't keep your head up for more than a few seconds, supplemental neck exercises might be warranted.

- Always keep a slight bend in your knees. Similarly, you should never fully extend your elbows when fighting.

- Just as in many of the guided chaos exercises, move slowly most of the time for maximum benefit and impact on your balance and stabilizing muscles.

- Remember that you're doing the exercises primarily to improve your balance, looseness, body unity, and proprioception in any position on the ground. Even though the ground-fighting exercises constitute a great workout for all the core muscles (plus neck and legs), as in all the guided chaos exercises, concentrate on feeling your own body and gaining efficient, effortless movement.

Here's how to complete the exercises:

1. Lie on your back, kick straight up to the ceiling with your left heel, then sweep your nearly straight left leg down until it is only 2 inches (5 cm) above the ground. Then kick straight up with your right heel as your left leg retracts, then sweep down your right leg to 2 inches above the floor. This is like a very precise, mindful bicycle kick motion. Repeat for 30 seconds.

2. Reverse the motion from the previous exercise. Thrust your left heel straight forward, parallel to the ground and 2 inches above it, then sweep the almost straight leg up to a vertical position. Retract the left leg as the right thrusts straight forward and then sweeps up. Repeat for 30 seconds.

3. Lie on your back and ax-kick out to the sides while shifting your hips. Bring the left leg up and around in an outward arc so that it's pointing toward the left, heel toward the ground, and sweep the leg down to 2 inches above the ground. As you do this, lift your hips and bring them down a few inches to the left. Then sweep the right leg up, outward, around, and down while your hips lift and come down a few inches to the right, and the left leg retracts. Repeat for 30 seconds. The hip shift is a critical part of this exercise that helps develop balance and proprioception. Without it, you're just waving your legs around.

4. Lie on your back with your knees pulled up together at a right angle (so that your shins are parallel with the floor); turn from the waist to lower your knees to 2 inches above the floor on each side (keeping the knees at a right angle, pressed together). This is similar to the stretch described above, except that you don't have your hands and arms on the ground for balance, and you do not want to actually touch your legs to

the floor. Instead of being a stretch, this exercise is intended to develop your balance on all parts of your hips and shoulders. Make sure that as you rock back and forth, neither your arms nor legs touch the ground.

5. Lie on your side, balancing on your hip and shoulder (your arms and legs are off the ground); scissor your legs back and forth as widely as possible. The bottom leg (the leg closest to the ground) should not touch the ground at any time. Don't simply wiggle your lower legs from your knees. Scissor your whole legs as widely as possible from the pelvis, feeling the adjustment and balance through the entire body (body unity).

6. After about 30 seconds of doing exercise 5, when your top leg (the leg furthest from the ground) is stretched in front of you, plant the sole of the foot of the top leg flat on the ground. The bottom leg is still off the ground, extended behind you. Push off the ground and whip the top leg up toward the sky in a wide arc. As the top leg passes through the vertical position, the bottom leg whips up to follow it in the same direction. This creates a whipping momentum that switches your root onto your other hip. Stop this momentum by stomping the sole of the foot of the initial bottom leg (now the top leg as you're lying on your other side) flat on the ground in front of you. Your initial top leg is now your bottom leg, extended out behind you, off the ground. During this whipping hip switch, no part of either leg touches the ground except the soles of the feet to initiate and stop the motion. You must train your body to prevent any other part of the leg (especially the outside of the bottom leg's ankle) from hitting the ground, which could result in leg damage. Whip switch back and forth several times, then return and do exercise 5; this time, you'll be on the opposite side from where you began. Visualize cleaving a standing enemy's legs in half with your boots, then smashing his face or any other part of his body into the dust with your stomp as he falls to the ground. Switch.

7. Log-roll sideways and feel the timing as your roll to whip out your legs as in exercise 6. Don't touch the soles of your feet against the ground until you want to stop rolling.

8. While log-rolling sideways, thrust out alternate short, thrusting kicks with your heels. Keep this flurry of short thrusts going throughout the rolling motion, while you roll across your side, front, and back. It takes some practice to get the coordination.

9. Lie on your side, balancing on your shoulder and the soles of your feet; run around in a circle on the floor, with your shoulder serving as the center of the circle. It is optional to make Curly's Three Stooges' whoo-whoo sound (or Homer Simpson's more recent homage to it) while doing this exercise. Whip switch to the other side and repeat.

10. Now that you've mastered a bunch of different movements in isolation, free-form it. Roll around on the floor, going through parts of all the different exercises randomly, concentrating on your balance and proprioception. Imagine threats materializing from every direction and experiment to find how best to bring your legs to bear against these threats quickly and efficiently while keeping your head away. Remember to follow the bulleted list on page 211. Most important, don't start bouncing your head off the ground in an effort to get more creative!

Leg Mania

To do this particularly nasty drill justice, it helps to have some or all of the following equipment as targets for all the kicks and stomps described:

- One or more low hanging heavy bags 5 to 15 feet (1.5 to 4.6 m) apart.
- A heavy bag, fighting man dummy, or kicking shields lying on the ground—alternately, you can use padded trees or poles, but it's not as fun.
- Kicking shields and rubber knives that training partners can use while they run at you.
- Shoes with a composite toe that's as strong as a steel toe but lighter. If you take your self-defense seriously, you can consider adding them to your wardrobe without much

risk to your fashion sense. Using them in this exercise makes you feel like you've got two sledgehammers attached to your legs.

This drill can become totally exhausting, so be sure you're in excellent aerobic condition first. In real life the fight may last only seconds, but you never know. Keep in mind the following two principles of guided chaos:

1. Don't clamp down or maintain pressure on any kick or scissoring move. Don't push. Splash the target and instantly ricochet off it into something else. Grappling with your legs against a larger opponent is suicide.
2. Keep your head away from your assailant's feet at all times, whether he's standing up or lying on the ground.

Practice each of these scenarios on the floor. For simplicity, you can practice any one component against a target before moving on to or combining with others. Don't worry about form. It's not supposed to look pretty.

You can initiate the exercise right out of standing contact flow or practice with your eyes closed while a partner with a shield violently throws you or shoves you to the ground. It can also be initiated out of the gang attack drills (coming later) or against a hanging fighting man dummy so you can claw it before falling, depending on how or if you actually lose your balance.

Thrust your legs and drive your body violently away from the source of the attack to gain distance. Roll on the ground lengthwise while intermittently moving your legs around in big arcs and circles. This looks a little like break-dancing, but it's more focused. When you are wearing strong boots, you have the equivalent of two sledge-hammers at the end of your legs.

1. Practice a wide bicycling motion with your legs. Use it to scissor-kick at a tree, pole, or heavy bag. Now bring your legs in contact with the floor so the bicycling action makes you spin in a circle on your hip or butt (it helps if you've seen the Three Stooges in action).
2. Practice rolling (lengthwise like a log, not curled up like a ball) and straight-kicking simultaneously. Just contract and shoot your legs straight out singly and together.
3. Practice scissoring with both round and hook kicks while on your hip. Use a tree, post, or hanging heavy bag as your target. Practice explosively bouncing your heel off the ground and target to add energy. Brace the other foot on the floor while you do this, then launch that foot out into a kick while the other one hook-kicks back in.
4. Crescent-kick through the target (narrowly missing it) and rebound back to scissor-kick it. The crescent kick from the ground is when you are on your backside and your foot sweeps up and over in an arc; in contrast, an ax kick is straight up and down.
5. Immediately pull your knees to your chest into a fetal position and, with no pause, explode both legs out with heel kicks. This action should be so convulsive that for a split second your whole body comes off the ground. Start slowly. As your legs fly out, twist your body onto your chest (almost a squatting posture), pull them back in, and blast them out again either singly or together, this time as a mule kick, while bracing your palms on the floor.
6. Pull in your legs fast as lightning while simultaneously landing on your left hip. Split them into a wide scissors with the bottom leg forward and the bottom foot anchoring you to the ground. Arc the upper leg forward, upward, and then backward in a sweeping, circular motion clockwise toward twelve o'clock as you simultaneously switch to your rear end. Smash the heel straight down for an ax kick, bounce off the ground, and kick straight up with your toe into a tree, wall, or low, heavy bag. The arcing kick could be to the head of a kneeling assailant; the ax kick to the thigh muscle, knee, neck, or kidney of a recumbent one; and the toe kick to the groin of a standing one.

7. Dive to the side of a low hanging bag while smashing a roundhouse toe kick through it while your body's flying through the air. Land on your hip (with your head away from the bag) and roll at high speed like a log while dishing out short, thrusting kicks at a partner running alongside with a shield. Continue rolling to a kicking shield lying on the floor and end your roll with a crushing stomp kick. While lying on your side, smash the shield by clapping your feet together with the shield in between. Grind the heels and soles of your boots together as if to rip the skin off the shield. Do this by moving your legs in and out, pulling your knees alternately to your chest. We call these shredding kicks. Do a quick sit-up and jam your fingers into imaginary eye sockets on the shield. Roll onto your butt, shoot a leg into the air, and ax-kick down onto the shield, stomping it with your heel. Convulse your body into the air so you're on your hip and drive your knee in, then fall back and thrust kick.

8. Instantly roll like a log to another tree or heavy bag and use the momentum to spin out a round kick into it as part of the rolling motion, then roll back and scissors-kick the first bag while lying on your hip.

9. Snap your legs back into a fetal position, then shoot them straight out into the target, snap in again, and simultaneously round-kick forward with your rear foot and hook-kick back with the heel of your front foot. Dive, but this time into a forward tumbling roll, and land so that both heels come stomping down on a floor target to stop the roll. Dive forward onto the shield with a spearing, downward elbow. Quickly try to tear it in half with your hands, then sink your teeth into it, roll away, and kick. Go wild. You get the idea. The very last point is simple: At the end of each drill, get up and run away. Never stop to admire your handiwork.

Contact Flow on the Ground

Guided chaos ground fighting is not about simply flailing your legs around randomly on the ground. You must gain the sensitivity and targeting skills to make all of your motions as efficient as possible: maximum destruction from minimum effort and movement. You can train this through contact flow on the ground.

Ground Versus Standing

In this variation, you are on the ground; a training partner is standing. Use your legs to feel and disrupt the balance of one of the standing trainees while remaining loose and sensitive. Do not use muscular effort to attempt to shove the standing trainee's legs off balance; instead, feel and make tiny adjustments in angle and position to disrupt the standing trainee's root with absolutely minimal effort. For example, depending on the position of the standing trainee's weighted leg, pushing directly into the kneecap may accomplish nothing, while nudging up under the kneecap at the right angle with the edge of a shoe can make the whole leg collapse with almost no pressure. As in standing contact flow, feel how the pressure of your root points against the ground transfers directly and loosely into the points of contact with your training partner to create effortless power, as in threading the nine pearls.

While you are feeling and experimenting, adjusting your body position, and working with both of the standing trainee's legs, the standing trainee remains loose and sensitive in order to maintain his or her balance and attempt to walk past your legs to stomp on your head. The standing trainee should not try to flex his or her legs strongly to resist your pressures but should yield to any pressure while retaining balance, feeling how to move his or her legs around yours in order to pass them completely. Go slowly and gently with this exercise to prevent knee or ankle damage.

Just as standing contact flow does not simulate a real fight, neither does this exercise. In a real fight, if you find yourself on the ground with an attacker standing over you and trying to stomp your head, you will certainly not be gently prodding and manipulating his legs with yours, playing with his balance. This is why you also do Leg Mania. However, the sensitivity and anatomical knowledge your subconscious gains from this exercise will lend devastating efficiency to the kicks, sweeps, rolls, and slams that you'll use against an enemy. Rather than bouncing harmless leg kicks and strained pushes off the strongest parts of the enemy's legs, your body will automatically position itself to deliver fully-body power from your root through your legs into the enemy at the most vulnerable angles given the fluidly changing situation. This sensitivity, balance, looseness, body unity, and subconscious knowledge are what enables John Perkins, without apparent effort, to sweep standing attackers off their feet from the ground or break their legs at will.

Ground Versus Ground

In this variation, you'll simply do contact flow on the ground. You can start from your knees or back-to-back with your training partner. Get as creative as possible. Use your legs as much as possible—you'll feel how weak your arms are in comparison. Experiment with all the same energy principles you've used in standing contact flow, including yielding, pulsing, and suspending and releasing. On the ground, you also have your full body weight to experiment with.

Place your weight in your legs on top of your training partner's to momentarily pin your partner's legs against the ground, allowing you to roll your legs to his head. If he resists strongly, don't wrestle. Reverse your motion. Roll your whole body onto his while he tries to yield out of the way and let you fall into a trap. Remember to stay uncommitted and yielding, yet recognize when your relative positions and balance give you an advantage. Keep things slow at first, lest someone get a boot whipped into his head. Engage multiple training partners at the same time to create a very strange scene on the training mat. Sometimes add in a goal of getting to your feet while staying at the same constant speed, just as you would be doing in a real fight, without getting stomped or tripped.

Then, experiment with doing regular flow with your arms while you and your training partner are lying side by side or on top of each other. The goal is to get the eyes, throat, and groin. However, be sure to end this part of the drill with an escape to the boots-first position because in reality you want to avoid face-to-face and trunk-to-trunk fighting at all costs. If it happens, it should be brief and nasty. Do not grapple.

That being said, you should also train with one partner grappling or using MMA (preferably if the partner has experience). With the broad popularity of MMA filtering down even to thugs, you may someday be attacked by a criminal with some training. In general, with all forms of contact flow, it is fun and helpful to work with as many practitioners from different styles as possible. What you will find is that the close combat/guided chaos approach precludes MMA effectiveness. We have many MMA students who have begun experimenting with applying guided chaos to their training for purely self-defense applications. This usually requires a drastic change in tactics from a traditional jujitsu approach.

Gang Attack III

Ideally, do this drill with at least three partners. You'll need a low, swinging, heavy bag, a bag suspended between 3 and 4 feet (.9 and 1.2 m) off the floor, and a bag lying on the ground (recumbent bag).

1. Dive onto your hip and roll horizontally like a log, using your momentum to spin out a kick to the recumbent bag. You can try ax and shredding kicks. You can roll over the bag, smashing your elbows backward and chopping into it with your full, loose body weight.

2. One partner swings the hanging heavy bag at you, which you must kick from the ground no matter what positions you get into. Roll or spin off the hanging bag to the recumbent bag, kick it, and roll back into the swinging, hanging bag—its position will already have changed. The wildly different angles are very instructive.

3. Another partner with a kicking shield simultaneously charges you at random intervals.

4. A third partner throws assorted kicking shields at you on the ground while he or she flicks the room lights on and off. It's vital to keep reorienting yourself so your head stays away from the swinging dummy and the attacking shield. Finally, to simulate what would happen when an attacker tries to dive on you, roll under the high bag while it's swinging and try to connect with as many kicks as possible.

One demanding drill we do at our school requires a bit of rigging: Suspend a fighting man dummy parallel to the ground with a system of turnbuckles and pulleys so two assistants can rapidly and violently hoist, lower, and swing the dummy right on top of you. You can just imagine what nastiness is done to the bag.

You can also use this drill to practice getting your gun out when you've been thrown to the ground. In this situation, you must kick first before you can even hope to draw your weapon.

As you will be hitting and kicking with full screaming power against the dummy you will find this drill very disorienting and exhausting, and you need to be in *excellent* physical condition to do it for longer than 10 seconds. You can drill all the ground-fighting principles discussed here, including mobility, scissoring, rolling, jackknifing, shortening the weapon, disengagement, tool replacement, and so on. It may help to break some of them down; for example, experiment using only scissoring or only mule kicking against the various targets. In general though, you should just go wild—but be accurate.

Fighting Multiple Opponents

There are various scenarios in which you may encounter multiple opponents. First, of course, if you see a loitering gang ahead, don't try to show you're a graduate of assertiveness training and walk past them with your head held high. Don't merely cross the street. Go down a different street.

If, however, you're suddenly confronted and immediately feel endangered, don't wait. Attack the attacker, shooting your fingers straight for the eyes of the closest person. Use the CCUE. Keep your body spinning the way you did in the Whirling Dervish Box-Step drill (p. 95) to get behind the first person you hit and keep that person between you and the next attacker. Never fight between two people. Box-step to keep the person you're hitting between you and the next person. Keep up a barrage of chops to the head and neck with palm heels and eye gouges; use a swimming sidestroke motion to get behind your attacker. Don't just back up or you'll be tackled. As you attempt to get out of the circle and run away, hit, change direction, hit, change direction—just like a running back in football. As you spin, lift your knees and stomp, stomp, stomp. This gives you balance, crushes insteps, and makes it more difficult for anyone to grab your legs.

If you grapple for even a second with one of the attackers, you're finished. They'll all pile on. React as if they all have a contagious disease. It will be hard for any of them to get a grip on you with your spinning chops and eye stabs flashing out while your feet are stomping the Mexican hat dance. Spinning may also get you in range of some environmental weapon you can use. Of course, if you've already got a knife or gun, box stepping will give you the precious space you need to pull it. However, simply because you're carrying a weapon doesn't mean you're protected. Many police officers have been shot with their own weapons because they couldn't get to them first.

If you're suddenly confronted with an interview situation as opposed to an immediate ambush, without drawing too much attention, look around for accomplices while you assume the Jack Benny. If a circle is forming, step toward the outside of it. Don't let it close on you. Don't let anyone get behind you. An important point is to keep your eyes, feet, and body moving. Don't settle into a motionless stance. Sway, shuffle, and talk with your hands. These little points keep your attackers from getting a fix on you when they decide to dive in. You deny them the opportunity of prey frozen in panic.

ALL IN A DAY'S WORK

I'm a prison guard, and on Tuesdays and Wednesdays I'm assigned to work in a mentally retarded developmentally disabled unit (MRDD). For the most part, this is a pretty laid-back place to work in relation to the rest of the institution. Most of the inmates are medicated and easy to manage. The state I work for has closed the state hospitals because of budget constraints, and the clients need a place to stay, so off they go to the Department of Corrections.

One night at approximately 7:25 p.m., an inmate approached the officer's station in the unit where I'm assigned to work and asked for a shower. Normally, this is no big deal, but this gentleman was on loss of privileges status and was not allowed out of his cell. There is a zero tolerance policy on this rule infraction. Given where I was and who he was, I explained the rule and told him to go back to his cell. I said I would get him out for a shower after line movement had secured. He walked about two steps from the officer's station and yelled in a loud voice, "This is a bunch of bull----!" He did this in the presence of 60 other inmates, and we couldn't have that for obvious reasons. So I called him to come back to where I was.

I was standing in a modified Jack Benny stance. He spun around and balled his fists. He was not yet within my sphere of influence, so I used a little verbal judo and told him to face the wall. I figured if I could get him restrained, he and I would both be safer. He complied, and I placed him in wrist restraints. Now I don't know what it is, but in my 10 years' experience as a guard, it seems as though any time you restrain a person, that person wants to fight or yell or scream or all three. That was the case with this individual.

I explained to him in a calm voice that he was not necessarily going to go to segregation. I radioed for my sergeant and some escorts, and then I removed the man from the unit. I escorted him outside the unit and had him face the wall. That was where he decided to get combative. This all happened in seconds. First, he turned his head toward me (a big no, no—we don't like to get spit on) and pushed away from the wall. There were four other staff members plus me. As we ordered him to stop and face the wall, another staff member and I attempted to place him back on the wall. The man turned toward me and attempted to kick me. This is where all the guided chaos drills came into play. My connection with his body (I had my left hand on him in a standard escort hold) let me feel all his movements, even the head turn. It is because of contact flow that I felt and perceived his kick subconsciously and was able to react the way I did.

I shot a spear hand right to his throat; once I made contact, I turned the strike into more of a push because I was not justified in using lethal force in this situation (as a side note, this is why we train lethal force but are prepared to bunt at any time). My action totally negated his kick and pushed him back to the wall. I then instinctively skimmed my right hand over his face, grabbed some hair, and placed him on the ground. Where the head goes, the body follows. Others placed him in leg restraints and escorted him to segregation. Later, he actually told my supervisors that I had been kind and professional, and that he had overreacted.

I have studied other martial arts in depth since I was a kid. None of them prepared me for the chaos of a real combat situation. When you study guided chaos and train the drills, it becomes part of you. Although the situation I've described was not life-or-death, I just reacted with no preplanned thought.

If you're brought to the ground, you'll need everything you've practiced in the ground-fighting section to keep them away from your head and stay alive. If you ever want to see your family again, have the attitude that this may be your last fight, so you might as well take as many of your attackers with you as you can. This is why going all out in the gang attack drills is so vital—and why most classically trained fighters' skills go out the window under these conditions.

Fright Reaction IV

1. Find three or more partners for this drill.

2. Stand quietly with your eyes closed and your arms at your sides. Breathe slowly into your stomach saying *in* to yourself with each inhalation and *out* with each exhalation. Relax and quiet your mind. Tune into the sensation of air moving over your skin.

3. Now spin around several times, keeping your eyes closed, and walk.

4. Keep walking. Within a few steps, one partner will shove you forcefully with a padded shield. The shove should come from an indiscriminate angle.

5. Drop and land into a fright reaction. From whatever position you end up in, open your eyes and launch yourself onto the shield with fast, furious, full-power alternating palm strikes, screaming. Meanwhile, the other partners keep circling to new positions.

6. When someone yells "switch!" immediately attack the next nearest partner. Be sure not to take long, awkward steps. Take quick, short, shuffling sideways steps that do not cross each other. Chop with the side of the body that is nearest the new target and step that way sideways. You can chop with that hand repeatedly and then turn toward your attackers with a barrage of palm strikes. When someone yells "switch!" again, move again sideways with quick, short, shuffling steps to the next nearest partner, chopping with your lead hand. Continue switching. In the next step, we'll make it more complicated.

7. As you're hitting one partner, the others circle in continuously, and it becomes up to you when to switch. The idea is to hit and run so you can escape. Don't get bogged down or entangled with anyone. This is pure close combat. Chop, step to the next attacker, chop, step (or box-step) to the next, and so on until you can break out of the circle and run. The most strikes you should deliver to any one person is three or four (two chops and a palm, or one chop and three palms, etc). If your partners are properly protected, you can include low, short, quick kicks with the chops and palms (recall the Hackey-Sack and Puppeteering drills) as well as toe stomps if they've got steel toe boots on.

Keep moving. Do not let anyone get behind you. Keep circling and box stepping so that you keep the person you're hitting between you and the other attackers to the best of your ability. Never fight between two people. Run away as soon as there's an opening.

We have tried to describe guided chaos groundfighting with as much detail as possible. We realize however that the movements are quite different from what you may be used to. The entire groundfighting warm-up and most of the drills can be found on the Combat Conditioning DVD while most of the groundfighting methodology, tactics, and principles are shown in exhaustive detail on the Guided Chaos Groundfighting DVD; both are available from www.attackproof.com.

Preventing Common Mistakes

➤ Don't grapple with a grappler.

➤ Let *your* body react like an enraged alley cat and treat your *attacker's* body like it's covered with some foul-smelling slime.

➤ When you're on the ground, keep your head away from your attacker's feet.

➤ If you're falling, get to the ground first.

➤ Skip the gang attack drills at your own peril.

➤ Whether you understand guided chaos or not, don't neglect the close combat drills in chapter 2.

CHAPTER ELEVEN

STAIR FIGHTING

Fighting on a staircase introduces a variety of opportunities and dangers beyond what you would face on a flat surface. Some of these variables are common to fighting on sloping or uneven surfaces or in confined spaces as well, so stair fighting is a very worthwhile area of study, the benefits of which are applicable to many other situations. Many self-defense instructors pay lip service to the fact that you're unlikely to be attacked on a flat, open dojo floor . . . but then limit the vast majority of training to a flat, open dojo floor or mat. Don't fall into the same complacency.

Because of the isolation and confinement that stairwells in buildings provide, they are favored locations for criminal activity, from drug dealing to rape and murder. Stairwells are commonly crime scene number two in abductions from parking garages. These more secluded, contained areas are where abductors can gain greater control over victims and follow through with their nefarious plans. Simply watch the controversial yet realistic "Rape of Dr. Melfi" scene in *The Sopranos* for an idea of how this happens.

The first variable we'll examine in stair fighting is elevation. Standing on a different level from your enemies can be an advantage or a disadvantage, depending on your balance, prior training for such situations, and knowledge of the possibilities.

Being on a higher step than your enemy gives you easier access to the vital targets on his or her upper body—and decreases access to yours. You may be able to kick the attacker in the torso or head without raising your leg so high as to jeopardize your balance. Leaning against the banister or wall can augment your balance and the power of your kicks (figure 11.1*a* on p. 220). If you are being chased up a flight of stairs and your pursuers are about to catch you, stop suddenly and kick backward like a mule while holding the banister for enhanced balance (figure 11.*b*). This can quickly reverse the momentum of the fight.

Standing on a higher step than your enemy also puts you in a position to use gravity to power your strikes to an even greater degree than usual, as in dropping. Assuming you have undergone the training to develop the necessary balance, agility, and tendon strength in your legs, you can drop down onto lower steps and unleash enormous power while striking and kicking.

When you are above your enemies on a staircase, using all the aforementioned advantages to generate devastating attacks, the impact of your attacks will often have the effect of sending your enemies tumbling down the stairs (figure 11.2 on p. 220). Kind of adds insult (and additional injury) to injury.

Figure 11.1

The major danger in being above your enemies on a staircase is the risk of losing your balance, or generating more downward energy than your body can control. This is what you should learn to exploit if you find yourself downstairs from your attackers. If your attackers are attacking you full blast from above you on a staircase, and you can move to make them miss and augment their downward momentum, it is relatively easy to make them topple down the stairs or at least stumble and struggle to catch their balance, leaving them very vulnerable to your attacks.

Figure 11.2

Being below your enemy on a staircase enhances your ability to damage your enemy's legs by kicking them into the stairs. A kick that might not seriously damage a leg on even ground takes on new meaning if it can lever your enemy's leg against the stairs or smash an ankle against the corner of a step.

We have already mentioned the utility of banisters and walls in stairwells as an aid to balance; using them can magnify your striking power. Banisters and walls are also very useful obstacles to ram your enemies' heads into. Folding an enemy backward over a banister with your strikes makes life far more unpleasant for him than if he had space to step back.

If you lose your footing in a fight on stairs, previous ground-fighting training on stairs would prove itself to have been a wise investment. Stair training should be undertaken slowly and gradually, and only after you have acquired the ability to fall and ground fight dynamically on flat, solid ground (i.e., without mats). The sensitivity and looseness required to save yourself from injury in a fall on stairs are great. From any position and in any type of fall, you must ensure that your head and neck do not impact against the stairs, and that your limbs do not get stuck and broken in the many angles and nooks present on a staircase. If you fall, you don't want to tumble out of control all the way down the stairs. This is what will probably happen if you stiffen as you fall, and you'll break body parts against the steps along the way. Instead, loosen and flop onto the steps to gain traction and balance with any part of your body and stop your descent if that is tactically warranted. Generally, if you feel that you're losing your balance in a stair fight, it may be safer to sit down or fall down under control than to struggle for too long and tumble end over end. Your ground-kicking skills can then be augmented on the stairs just as your standing kicks can be as you use the steps themselves and the differences in elevation to add to your kicks' destructive potential. That being said, just as on flat terrain, you do not want to go to the ground on a fight on stairs.

An incident from John Perkins' police experience illustrates many of these ideas in action (see next page).

Stair-Fighting Exercises

The goal of practicing stair-fighting exercises is to develop the additional balance, tendon strength, and spatial awareness necessary to move combatively with grace and purpose on a staircase. At the same time, you'll enhance your subconscious awareness of the additional uses of gravity and the structures available on a staircase.

Ninja Walk and Vacuum Walk on Stairs

These exercises can be performed on staircases as follows:

1. Start with one foot on the floor and the other on the first step as if you're about to walk up the stairs normally.

2. Slowly transfer all your weight to the foot on the step without moving your feet or taking either foot off the ground. You will feel significant pressure build up in the foot on the step while the other foot becomes light. Be sure you do not lean in any direction, but remain straight and centered over your weighted foot.

3. Keep both feet perfectly flat to the floor without pushing off on the unweighted leg at all. Raise your body by straightening the weighted leg until it is only slightly bent. The other foot comes off the ground without any benefit of a heel or toe push off. This is like a killer one-legged squat.

4. For the Ninja Walk, bend your unweighted leg and slowly tap the toes twice on the floor behind you by bending and unbending the supporting leg, in essence doing partial one-legged squats on the weighted leg. Slowly bring your unweighted leg in front of you and tap the heel twice on the next step, again by doing partial one-legged squats on the supporting leg. Raise and lower your whole body with the supporting leg in order to tap. Do not simply bend and straighten the tapping leg to reach the ground, or you will defeat the entire purpose of the exercise. Do not lean. Keep your hands up and relaxed in front of you.

5. For the Vacuum Walk, use your unweighted leg to vacuum the step you are standing on. Keep the bottom of your foot parallel to the ground at all times by varying the angle of your ankle.

6. Place your unweighted foot flat on the next step up while keeping all your weight on your weighted leg. Do not lean.

7. Repeat steps 2 through 6.

8. Now, try the same exercise coming down the stairs. Do this carefully because it may put more pressure on your knees than going up the stairs. If coming down the stairs is too difficult, stick with going up the stairs for now, and revisit coming down at a later date after building up your legs by going up the stairs.

STAIRWAY TO HELL

John Perkins

One day while climbing the stairs of a housing project in what is called a vertical patrol, I was attacked by two assailants. Because of my training in stair fighting, I was able to overcome the assailants, who were armed and determined to destroy me. They believed I was an enemy gang member, or so they said later.

Although I usually walked when climbing the stairways of the project buildings, which are about 15 stories high, that day I felt like exercising a bit more than usual and began to jog up a few flights at a time.

As I continued up the stairway, I heard a muffled sound up ahead and above me. Using caution, I unsnapped my sidearm in its holster and kept my hand wrapped around the grip. I slowed my ascent and kept a wary eye. I had run into groups of drug addicts or gang members hanging around in stairways before. Usually, I would just rouse them, and they would leave for the time being. This time was different.

As I turned right around a corner of the stairway, I saw a shadow move along the wall above and to my left. I shifted to the left side of the stairs, making a wide loop as I ascended, and turned the corner. Almost simultaneously, the shadow moved in a downward direction and was superseded by two men who were armed and in attack mode. The first attacker did not know that I had abruptly changed my position on the stairs and moved straight downward, hugging the inside wall. I spotted a knife in his hand. As he was taking a downward step, I skipped sideways and side-kicked him in the leg slightly behind his knee, pushing his leg out from under him, which caused him to fall a couple of steps and slam into the wall and floor of the landing below. My ability to keep my balance while delivering a strong kick, move sideways, and check my upward movement resulted from my practicing a stair exercise in which I would run up the stairs while skipping side to side, sometimes kicking against the walls on both sides of the stairway.

As the first man fell downward, his partner had only a split second to realize that I was moving in on him. My hand was on my sidearm, a Smith & Wesson heavy-barreled revolver. As the second assailant attempted to stop his downward movement, I skipped back to the wall, came forward again on the step above him, and slammed him on the back of his head with my handgun. This put him out of the contest immediately. I found it to be quicker and more efficient to slam him in the head at such close quarters instead of shooting him, since shooting a person does not guarantee an instant stop.

Consider the fact that in such tight quarters, a man with a knife has just as great a chance of killing you with his knife as you have of killing him with your gun. Even if you are able to hit him straight through the heart with a torso shot, he often has a number of seconds to get off many stabs or blows before succumbing to the wound. In this particular fast-moving situation, it was easier and faster for me to target the man's head with a backhanded striking motion than to try to shoot him in the head. I had found in the past that a revolver strike to the head could render an attacker unconscious nearly instantly. Two pounds of steel slamming the back of the head with high velocity and dropping power delivers far more energy than a .38 Special bullet could ever approach.

As I disabled the second attacker, I performed my footwork in a seemingly complicated manner. First, I skipped and nearly fell into the wall behind me after kicking the first attacker. This was easy to do because I had often practiced polishing the sphere while on stairs. The next attacker was still coming downward and couldn't check his movement. I ended up above him as I launched forward. I had my left hand ready to check his right arm, which held his knife. Looking back, I realize that keeping my head as well as my balance has served me well in a number of close-quarters situations.

Crazy Walk on Stairs

In this exercise, you'll slowly ascend and descend the stairs while carefully controlling your balance and stepping at unusual angles. This will help you maintain your orientation when moving through the three-dimensional chaos of combat on stairs. Throughout the exercise, do not lean or otherwise compromise your balance. If you need to touch the banister or wall for assistance, do it. It's better to work up slowly to going hands free than to fall down the stairs or blow out your knee.

1. Start with both feet on the floor facing the stairs as if you're about to walk up the stairs normally.
2. Transfer all your weight to your left foot; place your unweighted right foot flat on the first step, toes pointed 90 degrees to the right.
3. Slowly transfer all your weight to the right foot while keeping both feet flat and stationary. Straighten the right supporting leg to bring your left foot off the ground without any kind of left heel/toe push off. Tap or vacuum with the left foot on the next step up.
4. Slowly place the left foot on the next step up, toes pointed down the stairs (i.e., 90 degrees clockwise from where the right foot is pointed).
5. Slowly transfer all your weight to the left foot while keeping both feet flat and stationary.
6. Continue up the stairs in this manner, turning all the way around clockwise, then counterclockwise.
7. Continue up the stairs in this manner, but now stepping at various angles and in all directions randomly.
8. Try varying the speed of your ascent, being careful to control your balance in the same way as when you do the drill slowly. Don't get sloppy with your balance.
9. Make it up, stepping to the most challenging positions imaginable.
10. Now do it all going down the stairs. Be careful because of the additional pressure this can place on your knees. Don't let the downward momentum grow to more than you can control.
11. Add a slow front, side, back, or round kick to each step, dropping slowly on your root leg as you kick.
12. Try doing the guided chaos form (chapter 5), while moving between steps.

Warning: Extra caution must be taken when training on stairs. Failure to do so could easily result in serious injury or death.

Free-Stepping and Kicking on Stairs

Do this drill at your own risk! In this exercise, you're going to pretend you're young again and do what your mother always warned you not to do: run, hop, skip, and jump all over the staircase. Skip from side to side as you go up and down the stairs, sometimes skipping steps. Run up and down sideways, backward, and at any other angle you can come up with. Bounce and jump off the walls and banisters, drop and catch yourself to instantly stop your momentum. Kick the walls as in the Mexican Hat Dance as you go. Doing this while going downward is far more difficult because gravity pulls on you as you skip sideways, which sometimes will cause you to miss a step at high speed. Keeping in mind the method of dropping on one or both feet when breaking a fall comes in handy here. You may find that either one foot will land below where you are stepping or that both feet will land on different steps almost simultaneously. This is where you can develop an advanced dropping ability. One safety precaution in this practice is to hold and release a banister or keep your hands touching the walls as you practice until you master your balance. Eventually, you will find that you can perform this drill with your hands free so that you would be able to grab or hold onto your weapon.

When you can keep your balance with your hands free while box-stepping at various angles up and down the stairs, you'll know you're getting somewhere!

Then, have training partners holding focus mitts and kicking shields stand on the stairs. You have to move around them while striking the targets they present. Kick the shields presented at various heights. Kick or stomp a shield resting right on a step above you, simulating smashing an ankle into a step. Mule kick while holding the wall or railing. Start slowly, making sure you line up your body and drop into each strike and kick. Experiment with the opportunities that differences in elevation and confinement create. When you are able to pick up the speed and hit the various stationary targets fluidly and with balance, have your training partners start to push you with the shields and mitts, forcing you to drop and recover your balance as you move and strike.

Ground Fighting on Stairs

Start out by learning to sit down on a landing (feet facing downstairs), slowly and under control. Hold onto a banister to help control your fall at first. Make sure to protect your head and arms, keeping them up and away from the floor. (If you try doing a traditional judo ukemi or break-fall on stairs, complete with slapping the floor, you'll quickly learn why such methods are inappropriate for real-world use.) Once you are comfortable with sitting down, try it along the stairs themselves (i.e., not on the landing), starting slowly and feeling how your body can best absorb the shocks caused by the corners of the steps. Gradually pick up the pace and vary the angles of your fall. Feel how you can contort and twist your body to change your orientation if you find yourself falling headfirst down the stairs. In most cases, you'll want to change your body so that you're falling feet first, allowing you to slow your descent. *Practice this at your own risk. Uncontrolled falls down stairs account for approximately 2,000 deaths a year in the United States.*

Once you're down on the staircase, try all of the ground-fighting exercises, feeling how your balance and opportunities are affected.

Contact Flow on Stairs

This is where you put everything together. Start slowly, and as usual, make sure all training partners can put their egos aside. Practice both contact flow standing (figure 11.3*a, b*)

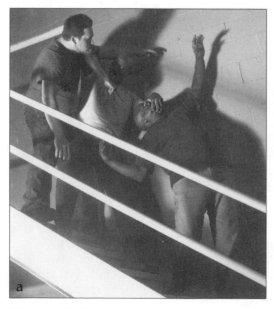

Figure 11.3

Figure 11.3, *continued*

and on the ground (figure 11.3*c*). In figure 11.3*a* the defender attempts to maintain his balance, body unity, looseness, and sensitivity while fighting enemies on different levels. In figure 11.3*b* the defender braces himself with the railing. In figure 11.3*c* the defender uses his low position to topple and blind the enemy pressing from the rear while thrusting kicks (reinforced by his seated position on the step) into the lower enemy's groin.

Preventing Common Mistakes

➤ Raise and lower your whole body with the supporting leg in order to tap or vacuum. Do not simply bend and straighten the tapping leg to reach the ground, or you will defeat the entire purpose of the exercise.

➤ Carefully assess the strain being placed on your knees when you drill on stairs. Stop if you feel pain.

➤ Use utmost care when performing these drills on stairs. Failure to do so could result in serious injury or death. *Practice at your own risk!!*

CHAPTER TWELVE

WEAPONS FIGHTING

If you've made it through the book this far, you've seen how we've exploded many myths about hand-to-hand combat. You shouldn't be surprised to learn this also extends to weapons. Politically correct and romanticized versions of weapons training have proliferated over the years and many have little utility outside of the dojo , movie studio, or local shooting range. Bear in mind that from the ages of 16 to 18, John Perkins trained with U.S. Marshall Thomas Loughnan, the fastest man in the world with a Colt 1911. Loughnan taught Perkins how to shoot under actual combat conditions before he entered the police academy. This experience, combined with his Native American influences and evolving tenets of guided chaos, brought about significant changes in Perkins' applications of knife, stick, and gun fighting.

There are simply so many common misconceptions about using guns, knives, and sticks that it would require an entire book to iron them all out. Nevertheless, we have attempted to summarize some of them here and provide a methodology for training real-life weapon attacks and defenses.

Stick Fighting

The advantages of using sticks or similar objects are that they can physically extend your arms and be thrust through small, defensive openings.

The reality of the stick is very different from what is presented in many traditional arts. Flashy patterns and spiraling, circling movements will get you killed. If your opponent has a stick and you don't, your only defense other than running is getting inside on him or her as fast as possible with an arm raised to prevent a head impact. The best time to get in is immediately. If you attempt to time your attacker's swings and dance outside, you'll be destroyed. If it's a heavy weapon, like a bat, you might be able to get in just as your attacker swings because your delayed reaction will get you there just as the weapon passes you. Think of it this way: If you can't run, absorbing one glancing blow as you dive inside gives you a better chance than trying to survive and fight at a distance, which would only prolong the inevitable. Once you're inside, the opponent's tendency is to fixate his or her attention on freeing the weapon. Take advantage and spear him in the eyes and throat. This principle also applies in reverse: If you both have sticks, and you get inside where you want to be, if you can no longer get clean shots, immediately abandon the stick and go straight for your attacker's eyes and throat with your hands. Your attacker's instinctive reaction will be to hold on to the weapon, rendering him defenseless.

If you have a cane, which is legal to carry, simply raise it into the palm of your other hand, which you should position like a horizontal chop in case your opponent is too close to be speared with the cane (figure 12.1a). If there is still enough room between you and your attacker, grab the cane with the chop hand and jab with a flat, thrusting motion, using both dropping energy and a jackhammer-like delivery. Hit your attacker as if you're a crazed sewing machine (figure 12.1b). Because of the penetrating power, directness, and narrowness of the attack angle, this procedure stops a knife or whirling, twirling stick-wielding attacker cold. Once the attacker is stunned, you can swing the cane, but not in the way you might expect. Hold it like a short ax, with your hands apart, and take short, rapid, hammering swings that limit your opponent's openings (figure 12.1c). Don't change the direction of your attack. Break whatever you're hammering. With this wide grip, you have more leverage, enabling you to hit with either side of the stick by simply twisting your body.

Remember, wide swings are slow, wasteful, and overcommit your balance, creating openings. When you're inside, use short, chopping, hammering, or thrusting strikes with your cane. If your cane gets in your way, abandon it immediately and go hand-to-hand, where you have more options and sensitivity.

Figure 12.1

Stick or Cane Fighting From the Ground

You can really see the Native American influences in Perkins' stick and cane ground fighting. If you haven't seen our DVDs, just substitute a tomahawk for the cane in your mind, and you'll get the picture.

Cane Versus Knife

Let's be perfectly clear: If you see a knife, run. If you're trapped, can't run, or have already fallen, your trusty cane, wielded properly, becomes exceedingly vicious if you've been practicing the ground-fighting drills. It pays to have a sturdy cane that will be up to the task, not one that will blow apart the instant it meets bone. Attackproof.com sells lightweight, chromalloy steel canes that are unbreakable, but there are many other choices capable of serving the dual function of support and self-defense.

Using the same drills described elsewhere in this book for practicing mobility, kicking, and rolling from the ground, carefully add in swinging blows to kicking shields, hanging bags, and properly protected training partner's legs. Use a heavily padded plastic Wiffle ball bat or plastic PVC pipe. People who see our video clips on YouTube may say, "Canes and kicks wouldn't hurt me! I'd just dive on him!" Oh yeah? Try it yourself against a partner wearing boots and weilding a foam stick. After one or two hard shots with either the stick or boots, you'll quickly lose interest in diving. And nobody's diving on anybody after getting slammed with a steel or cocabolo cane. It's virtually impossible to miss because the cane is lightning fast—so nobody's dancing out of its way, either. So don't be too confident even against foam padding—you can still get nasty welts or worse, which you will discover all too quickly.

Your goal is to learn to deliver all the various kicking and rolling movements with cane strikes fluidly and simultaneously. The keys to this are play and experimentation. The freer and more creative you are in your practice, the more adaptive you will be when the spit hits the fan. Try diving to a side roll away from the attacker's legs while taking out his ankles with the cane, followed instantly by ax-kicking to the same or different target. Try double-thrust kicking straight out while slamming the cane over your head behind you into another attacker's feet like a hammer. Slash the cane overhead nonstop like a tomahawk as you roll from one heavy bag to another. Crack your opponents (with kicking shields for protection) in the knees with side, roundhouse, and scissor kicks, then roll and deliver a two-handed baseball bat swing left, right, up, and down. Stab with one end of the cane, then thrust up into a chin (or focus mit) with the handle. You get the picture. Now get up and run.

Knife Defense

Despite what you've read or seen about elegant, wonderful knife defense techniques, don't kid yourself. Put a knife in the hands of a 12-year-old kid, and he or she becomes an automatic twelfth-degree black belt. Tell a 50-year-old, nonathletic woman you're kidnapping her grandchildren, and we don't care if you're Grandmaster Moe: If you put a butcher knife in her hand, you'll be sliced up faster than a Thanksgiving turkey. If you need evidence of this, reread Overqualified? in the introduction to this book.

An important point with both knife and gun defenses is that if you can't run away after the initial strikes, your only recourse is to be merciless and keep on striking until you render the assailant unconscious. Keep hammering with palm heels, chopping strikes, and eye gouges over and over. It's you or the attacker. As described previously, a cane also works well against a knife.

That said, what can you do to survive a knife attack unarmed? First, if it's a simple mugging, be super polite, give the robber your whole wallet (don't stand there counting out bills), and do it quickly. You can't spend your money if you're dead. If he wants more than your money, if he wants to take you somewhere, if it's an ambush, or if you're with your family, you all must either run away if possible, or you must make your stand—right now. Police reports show that if you go with your captor, you'll most likely die or wish you had. So don't think you'll be able to get away later, like on TV. And don't count on being rescued. Instead, train your family to scatter in different directions when in danger and go to previously arranged safe houses. Teach your children to recognize law enforcement officers or safe public places.

A reality check: If someone sneaks up on you successfully and attacks with a knife with the intent to kill, you're dead. That's it. No martial art in the world will save you, nor will a gun. This is an unfortunate fact. Recidivist felons in prison do little else but practice surprise assassinations. Luckily, this is not the intent of most attacks. The goal is to rob, rape, or injure, and then get away. This is why awareness is always the first line of defense.

When you're in a secluded area such as a parking lot at night, always scan the area as you approach your vehicle. One tip is to look into the windows of other parked cars as you pass for the hint of a reflection of an imminent attack. If you see anyone approaching from behind, get a vehicle between you and the stranger as soon as possible. If you see a knife or gun, run. Now, let's address what to do if you are cornered by an assailant who has a knife.

Knife off Your Body

If your attacker is close and facing you, but the knife isn't against your body, you need space so you won't be sliced. Skip backward as if you were a fencer, lunging in reverse to keep from crossing up your feet and tripping. In our tests, nearly 50 percent of people fall down if they don't do this. Keep your hands rapidly rolling in a dog-digging motion as if searching for a buried bone (figure 12.2). This aids in keeping the knife away from your vital areas. If your hands get cut, remember, it's better than getting sliced across the throat.

Figure 12.2

Look around for anything you can throw at your attacker to slow him down or hit him with. Gain distance so you can turn and run. If you have a gun, you'll die groping for it if you can't fight hand to hand or get far enough away to pull it and shoot. If you have a knife, you'll get a chance to whip it out, in which case, the attacker may change his mind. If you have neither, and you're trapped, kick like a Rockette, with your foot tapping against the ground only long enough to bounce back up and kick again. Remember to use only your lead leg to kick. Don't change feet unless your opponent backs up. Aim for the shins and keep kicking until you do some damage.

If you wind up on the ground against a knife-wielding attacker, you're toast—unless you know how to ground fight (in which case, going to the ground *may* be preferable). It is much better to present your boots to an attacker and risk leg slices and cuts than to try and control a slippery, blood-soaked knife hand moving at lightning speed and expose your face, neck, heart, liver, spleen, or kidneys to the attack. In our tests, we find knife wielders very reluctant to go in for the kill when they're getting slammed by boots from the ground as they try to lean or jump in to get a good body slash. Even so, you can't stay there; you're only trying to get enough room and cause enough damage so you can get up and run.

Knife Against Belly or Chest

This is the robbery method most often given as a scenario in martial arts schools. In real life, it is seldom used. Holding the knife to the neck while holding on to another body part or clothing with the free hand is actually the most common technique. Here, however, we'll show you the defense for the former.

If you can, run. If you can't, and the robber asks for an item you can give him, hand it over. If you feel he wants to go further or that he's deranged and is going to cut you anyway, you must act as B does here. B gets her body off line, or out of danger, by twisting her torso out of the way of the knife. Simultaneously, B strikes at and pushes the knife away toward A's body (if the knife arm is pushed outward from the inside, it allows A's elbow to bend the weapon inward and back toward B). While keeping A's knife hand in check,

Figure 12.3

B strikes with the opposite hand into A's eyes with a clawing spear hand strike (or any basic strike described in chapter 2). All three actions occur simultaneously, which is why it's shown in only one picture (figure 12.3). If they were depicted sequentially and practiced that way, they would fail. Don't forget the crucial last step: Run away immediately, screaming.

Knife on Back

The escape here is the same idea as for knife on the belly or chest: a robbery situation gone bad. If you're not boxed in or being restrained, run. Otherwise, if you have complied with A's orders but believe the attacker wants to go further by taking you somewhere else, or if the attacker begins to give orders that might be a prelude to rape or worse, you must quickly do as B demonstrates here. B twists her torso out of the way of the knife, simultaneously pushing it farther off line, left or right (figure 12.4a). Instantly, B palm-heels A's head once or twice, dropping into each strike (figure 12.4b). B runs away immediately. As earlier, getting off line, pushing the knife, and striking are done in one movement. Don't break it down when you practice; you have to keep it simple if you want to live.

Knife on Your Neck From the Front

If the knife is on your neck, it becomes another game. When you're in imminent danger of being abducted, you must act immediately. One tiny advantage you have is that the assailant didn't choose to assassinate you immediately. Thus, he has other intentions. If a knife is pressed against your neck from the front, and you're being held by his other hand from the front also, you must train to do two things simultaneously: Deflect the knife to the outside and perform the drop step–palm heel combo from chapter 2.

For example, A holds the knife with his right hand against the left side of B's neck. After B has offered money and anything else the attacker wants, A decides to move B to

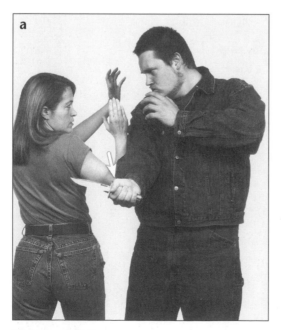

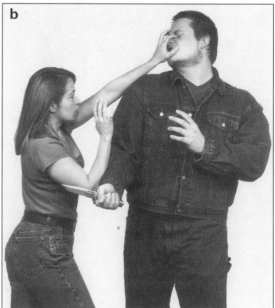

Figure 12.4

another location (where he or she will probably be killed, raped, or tortured). B, not without reason, acts scared and helpless and then, in an instant, simultaneously smacks the knife hand away to the outside from the inside with his left hand and drop-steps forward with a right palm heel or eye gouge. B's right hand should work like a jackhammer, blasting out three or four strikes in one second while his left maintains control of the knife hand. By control we mean anything that keeps the knife away from vitals (stick, parry, smack, or grab, if necessary). B then immediately runs away, screaming. When you practice this defense against a target, use full, howling intensity. Practice using your adrenaline so it propels you to safety, not paralysis. A couple of points:

If you perceive by the way you're being held that one or two strikes will give you the space to get free, than don't try pinning the knife hand. Stun and run. If he's very entangled with a good grip on you, you will have to hit harder and longer and keep the knife hand controlled. There are subtleties involved that are too complex for a book. We greatly recommend the Weapons Series DVDs from www.attackproof.com, which cover every nuance in an extremely comprehensive format, each of which must be practiced diligently. For now, try experimenting grabbing the knife arm with each of the following: a hooking-shaped hand (similar to hapkido), a full arm wrap-up (above the elbow so he won't slip out), a vice-grip between forearm and bicep, a straight double-hand grip that uses head-butting and foot stomping, an inverted double-hand grip that involves stepping under the knife arm and stabbing the attacker in the gut with his own weapon and actual weapon grabbing. You may even find that going to the ground to gain momentary survival space allows you to crack the hell out of his legs with vicious kicks. There are many more, but for now experiment. You will find out many more things that work through improvisation and modification than with rote repetition of standardized defenses.

Knife on Your Neck From the Rear

The usual manner in which attackers use a knife is to reach around from behind the victim and hold the edge of the knife against the throat. This is an extremely difficult position to get out of. The assailant will also use his other hand, either holding the victim's hair or shoulder or covering the mouth. This is scary, to say the least. This is a method taught to specialized members of various armed forces for taking out sentries (and is similar to the method used on Nicole Simpson). In this case, we're assuming the victim is not killed outright, but that the knife-wielding attacker is attempting to control and abduct the victim.

The method used to extricate yourself takes a great deal of practice. The first step to getting free is to get the blade away from your neck by moving several ways simultaneously. Picture the knife being held by a right-handed attacker. His wrist and forearm encircle your neck from behind with the blade pressed against the left side of your throat. At the same time, his left hand is covering your nose and mouth. The attacker is also usually pressed close to your body to control you.

Only you can make the decision of which method to use. One option is to wait until the instant the attacker tries to move you to another place, like a car. Moving tends to loosen the blade and restraining hand for a split second. You can also feign having a heart attack or passing out to change the attacker's grip. Just don't wait too long, because the clock is ticking. When you do act, it must be with total commitment. Dramatically lift your right shoulder toward your right ear while turning your head to the left and tucking your chin. This will exert tremendous pressure against the knife hand, forcing it away from the neck for a split second. Simultaneously, reach up with your right hand, grab the blade hand, (not the blade!) and pull it down with dropping energy. The action should feel like you are doing a high-speed pull-up with your full body weight on his hand. The combined effect of raising the shoulder and dropping into the hand exerts enormous force against the knife arm. Simultaneously, with full extension, drive your left elbow repeatedly into his face, throat, or solar plexus like a jackhammer (figure 12.5 on p. 232). Depending on the attacker's body position, you might alternately strike with left hammer fists or chops to his groin, then turn back to your right with a dropping

Even with a successful escape, you could still be cut, perhaps seriously, but you'll survive. The point is, don't try to be fancy and don't go with your abductor to a second crime scene.

Figure 12.5

left palm heel to the side of his head or stabs through the eye sockets. This should get you free of the blade and allow you to run for your life, screaming. One caveat: Despite its effectiveness, if the attacker is *extremely* large and strong, and you can't get to his eyes, the release will not work. You will be lifted off the ground and eviscerated. Sorry, but we don't want to sugarcoat it for you. This is why we're so big on awareness and the fright reaction—that microsecond of misdirection will keep the assailant from locking down on you and allow the longer-range defenses (eye and throat stabs, dog-digging, multi-kicking, and running) to effect your escape. This is why we say ignore chapters 1 and 2 at your own peril.

Your ability to adapt to changing circumstances is imperative because there are no precise formulas. For example, if the attacker grabs your left arm instead of your mouth, your ability to strike may be impeded. Without struggling against his grip, it would be easier to simply turn your left hand toward his groin and crush. You would follow this immediately with elbows to the face. But suppose he has angled his hip to cut off access to his groin; this would tend to bring his head to the side of yours, which is perfect for smashing a sideways head butt into his face the way you practiced in your Anywhere Strikes drills in chapter 2. You never know how an attack will go down. Sometimes an inexperienced assailant with an extra-long knife will actually keep his wrist instead of the blade against your throat. Because the point of his knife would then be mere inches from his face, your best recourse might be to grab his knife hand and drive it back straight into his eyes.

There are a few key points in practicing knife drills. The first is obvious: Train against both right- and left-handed attacks. The second key point is variability. By being creative, you will develop more subtleties than we can describe here. However, the three things you must usually do with rear-choking knife attacks are

1. drop and pull,
2. lift the shoulder, and
3. hammer repeatedly.

You should know that unless injuries are in vital areas, you could keep on fighting for a period of time even with multiple stabs wounds. Kick, eye gouge, and bite. Unless you are facing an assassin with a death wish, he'll probably lose interest because he never intended to get hurt in the first place. Don't give up. You can survive.

Using a Knife for Self-Defense

If you're using a knife for self-defense, you'd better know how to use it well and be seriously determined to defend yourself. Many men who have spent time in prison see the knife as a symbol of power. If you display a knife to a hardened criminal, and he perceives you're not resolved on cutting him, he may go for you and try to take your blade.

Forget about fancy techniques. Miyamoto Musashi, the great Japanese swordsman, taught himself how to fight and killed hundreds of samurai, many from the greatest schools in Japan, using only a wooden sword. Keep in mind that the knife needs to become a deadly, free extension of your body, moving with all the principles of guided chaos.

Using one of the newly available heavy bags shaped like the human body (see information about the fighting man dummy in References and Resources), learn to thrust into the softer targets—the throat, groin, solar plexus, kidneys, eyes—as well as the chest. You can draw targets of lethal areas on the dummy. Slash at extended targets such as the arms and legs. Learn to cut the main arteries of the upper inner arm, the carotid arteries of the neck, and the femoral arteries near the groin. In general, keep the knife hand out in front with the checking hand in the rear.

If the attacker also has a knife, run. If you can't, all your yielding training must come into play, except that now, instead of imagining that the attacker is holding a knife to make you pocket his punches, you've got the real thing to deal with. Try to cut his knife arm and keep your body away from him. Remember, you can kick also. Don't try any kamikaze moves.

If you're forced to hide in your home or elsewhere, and you're not physically strong, hold the weapon (whether a strong-lock, back-folding knife or a stout chef's knife) in your strong hand in a shake-hands grip with your other hand over it for reinforcement. If you're discovered, stomp-step, scream, and simultaneously drive the knife straight forward into the assailant over and over like a sewing machine needle so you won't be disarmed. Drop your body and thrust your arms rapidly, pulling your arms back faster than you send them out.

A punch-dagger has the advantage of being almost impossible to dislodge or drop in the midst of a hell storm, even when soaked in blood. It takes virtually no skill to use one effectively. Grip it in your hand concealed inside a coat pocket. If you're afraid you're going to die, use it.

There are many more knife-fighting principles in guided chaos that are culled from Native American methodologies, but they are beyond the scope of a self-defense book.

Knife Skip

Use soft, rubber knives, eye goggles, throat protection (a foam collar), and shin guards when performing this drill.

1. Stand with your eyes closed while your partner surprises you with a rubber knife in the stomach. Open your eyes.

2. Dog-dig at the knife while skipping backward as fast as possible using the fencer's step (push off with one leg, then leap without crossing your legs).

3. Once you're at a sufficient distance, turn and run.

4. If you can't get a sufficient distance away for whatever reason, skip backward and unexpectedly stop, drop, and repeatedly kick into the knife-wielding attacker, like a Rockette, with your front leg only.

5. If you can't get away, and there is a wall, run straight at the wall that is trapping you, brace your body for impact with your palms flat on the wall about chest high, and then repeatedly mule-kick backward with your heel at the attacker. Bounce your foot off the floor and then at your attacker like a jackhammer. This has enormous power.

6. If you trip and fall, use your ground-fighting kicking skills. Keep your head away from his feet and the knife and kick mercilessly. If you practice this against a partner who is holding a rubber knife and a kicking shield, and wearing shin guards, you will find that the ground kicks are very effective and your training partner won't enjoy it very much.

Knife Spin

Close your eyes and spin. Your partner should pick a spot on your body to touch with the rubber knife. This can be from the conventional to the insane. As soon as you feel the knife, stop, open your eyes, simultaneously move yourself and the knife off line, and strike. The trick is to pick an off-line direction both for yourself and the knife that minimizes your exposure. You need to experiment because in some cases the deflection should be made by your forearm, upper arm, elbow, or shoulder. In the beginning, in an attempt to get off line, you may find yourself actually moving *into* the attack arc of the blade. As your body awareness increases, this will happen less frequently.

Basic Knife-Fighting Drill

Using very soft rubber knives or a piece of rolled newspaper, eye goggles, and throat protection (a foam collar), have one or two partners rush you from behind or any random direction.

1. Hold the knife firmly in front of you and slash, chop, and stab at your partner from every conceivable angle. Don't patty-cake with this drill. Actually make contact (which is why your knife must be very soft). As with the Anywhere Strikes drills (pp. 37-39), spontaneity is the key: Don't try to emulate some fancy attack you've seen in a movie. Move your whole body and strike with the knife in a blinding flurry like a sewing machine.

2. To avoid being cut yourself, yield and gyrate dynamically as you strike simultaneously.

3. Flow at high speed. Your knife hand should be like a snake weaving in and out. If your wrist is grabbed, twist the blade into the attacker's hand and forearm. Stomp-step and stab like a jackhammer.

4. Use your other hand to strike as well. Note that you can spit in their eyes anytime as well as kick.

5. Practice freely in the manner outlined. Your subconscious will learn more useful information than if you crammed your higher brain with 50 fancy knife techniques.

Chair

Equipped as described for the Basic Knife-Fighting Drill, two people square off with a chair between them. As they try to attack and elude each other, if either one touches or kicks the chair, the one who does so loses a point. This drill is not meant to simulate a real fight except to the extent that you'll see how easy it is to be eviscerated. Kamikaze moves will get you killed, and it is vital to focus on *avoiding* being cut rather than being fancy and flashy. Having to avoid the chair dramatically improves your balance, reaction timing, and looseness. A little tip you can try is to wait for a stab, slash the stabbing hand, then stab to the throat. Keep the blade out in front and the rear hand just behind for parrying.

Gun Defense

The gun is a unidirectional weapon as opposed to a blade, which can slice sideways, too. But a bullet fired from a gun can penetrate you or your loved ones from close-contact distance to at least the length of a football field. Defense against the gun is absolutely dependent on the gun's angle and distance from you.

Always remember when dealing with any life-and-death situation that almost all attacks are dynamic, easily flowing from one position to another without warning. If you're ordered by the gunman to do something that would allow him further control of you, if he hasn't already grabbed you or put the gun on your body, and if you're in a public area, such as a parking lot, run away immediately, even if the gun is already drawn. The chances of his firing at you in public are slim. If he does, the probability of your being fatally wounded are even slimmer.

Everything changes if the gun is right on you, if he's holding you, or if there's no place to run. First, remember that most assaults occur without a weapon, at least initially. Second, know that there's no way to defend against a gun if it's out of reach. Defense is feasible only if the weapon is in close proximity to or in contact with your body. The best you can do is cooperate until the gun comes within close range. Sometimes you can encourage this by feigning paralyzing fear or illness (although this will probably be closer to your true reaction than you'd like). The gunman may need to come closer to move you if you no longer seem to be in control of your muscles (voluntary and involuntary muscles, if you know what we mean; you could also use this as a ploy).

Make no mistake: If you aggressively resist moving, the gunman probably will fire, and you may be hit. At the very least, you'll be deafened by the noise or suffer burns. He may fire even if you don't resist. But your chances of survival are more reasonable if you fight back than if you go with your abductor. The trick is when.

As opposed to hand-to-hand combat, gun and knife defenses are specific techniques you must practice thoroughly; they change with the angle of the weapon, and there's no margin for error. Not surprisingly, bullets are much less forgiving than hand strikes, especially when the barrel is already on you. Because of limited space, we can't go into all the variations of gun defenses. Many of them are more appropriate for video or personal instruction and are simply too advanced to convey practically in a book. The principles, however, are similar. We have included the most elementary ones here. (For more information, consult the References and Resources at the end of this book.)

Gun Extended Toward Face or Front of Body

If the attacker is extending his gun hand away from his body but the barrel is within easy reach, move your body off line while using the same-side hand to hit his arm from the outside in (figure 12.6*a*). The reason you don't do this from the inside out is that the joints of the body are designed to fold inward, so there's a slim chance the gunman's arm may simply bend with the strike and shoot straight at you anyway (figure 12.6*b*). Simultaneously, strike to the eyes or throat with your other hand in a dropping motion and run away, screaming. Remember, it is not enough to move the gun off line; you need to move your body as well to decrease the margin of error.

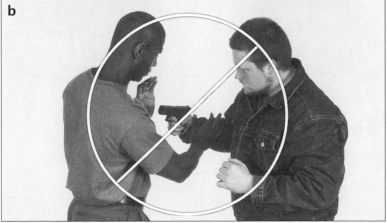

Figure 12.6

Figure 12.7

Gun Against Front of Torso

The gun is against the front of your stomach or chest. You press the gun off line and against the attacker's body with the same-side hand. Immediately palm-strike, eye-gouge, or V-hand-strike the throat three or more times with the other hand like a jackhammer (figure 12.7). Drop on each strike and run when you can. If you're in a confined area, keep hitting until the gunman is disabled.

Gun Against the Back

In this case, you may want to see which hand is holding the gun. Say, "Hey! What's going on?" or "You got me! What do you want?" as you turn and look. Then, turn in the direction of the gun hand so your same-side arm and hand strike the gun arm and hand (figure 12.8a). As you twist around, step into the assailant, pressing the gun arm against his body while pummeling him with chin jabs to the jaw (figure 12.8b). Sometimes it's better to grab and control the gun hand. You need to practice both.

Figure 12.8

Gun Against Back of Head

Put your hands up in the air. Throw your head off line by twisting it back and toward the side you're going to turn toward (figure 12.9a). When you whirl, your lead hand, which is already up, pushes the gun farther off line while your rear hand palm-heels two or three times like a jackhammer against the attacker's face (figure 12.9b), eye stabs, or throat strikes. Run.

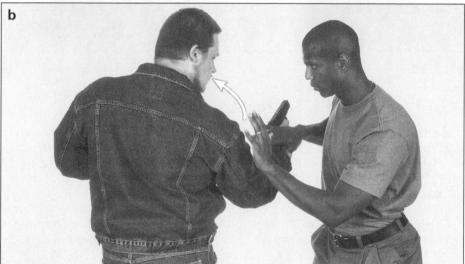

Figure 12.9

Gun-Choke From the Side or Rear

This very dangerous scenario involves an attacker behind you, covering your mouth with his left hand and pointing the gun in his right hand to the rear or right side of your head. With a lot of practice, you can do the following: In one movement, drop your weight while you simultaneously raise your right shoulder and arm dramatically (figure 12.10a on p. 238) and turn in toward the right. Your right elbow clears the gun, smashing it into the attacker's face with blinding force (figure 12.10b). This works very well and is extremely dangerous with training partners, so be careful. Use a foam gun when practicing. Within the same motion, using multihitting principles, drop your right elbow into his face while whirling to the right with your right hand chopping to the side of his neck. Visualize cleaving his head from his body. Instantly check and grab the gun arm with the right hand and palm-smash and claw his eyes with your left (or, alternately, palm-heel his jaw or ear).

Figure 12.10

Gun-Choke From the Front Side

In this case, the gunman is in the same position (figure 12.11*a*), but the gun itself is pointing at you from an angle somewhere between the side and front of your head. Simultaneously drive your head backward out of the line of fire (your head might hit his nose as a bonus), bring your right hand up, and pull the gun hand forward and down (figure 12.11*b*). Drop as you do all these things simultaneously. Instantly, switch your grab on the gun arm from your right to your left hand as you whirl to the right with hammering elbows to the face or ribs. Try head butting (figure 12.11*c*). Remember to move into the attacker as you strike. Keep stomping while striking to maintain your balance.

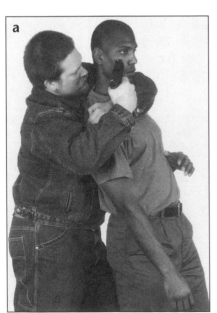

Figure 12.11

IMPROVISED WEAPONS
John Perkins

My radio car partner and I responded to a family dispute at a particular address. When we arrived, I spoke to one female who was apparently injured from a punch to the eye. She stated that her husband was in the kitchen. As my partner and I walked toward the kitchen, we saw there were two open doorways. I entered the closest doorway and saw the husband standing near the second door, holding a large, double-pronged fork in his hand. I heard my partner's footsteps and knew he was just about to enter that doorway. There was no time for me to give him a verbal warning—I knew I would have to act. In front of me was a heavy, old-fashioned metal and wood kitchen table. I stepped forward and dropped into the table. Although it felt like my fingers barely made contact with it, the table flew off the ground and flattened the fork wielder. Although I'd used adrenaline-powered dropping on inanimate objects before, this particular instance seemed like one of those mythical tales of chi.

There are also techniques for taking a gun away from an assailant that require grabbing the weapon and twisting it out of an assailant's hands. These techniques are more difficult to apply under real, adrenaline-rush conditions. If the gun is held with a choke combination behind your back, remember that the gunman still has a free hand and his feet to attack you with. Twisting the gun has some value when the gun is in front of you, but it is dangerous when the gun is held behind you. It's far simpler to push the muzzle away from you and into the attacker while simultaneously jumping off line, striking, and running.

Gun Defense I: Simplified Off-Lining

Practice this drill with a partner and a plastic gun. If you have one that shoots toy darts, you can actually see if you'd get hit. You typically have a half-second delay in the response time of your attacker. This amount is increased by obvious paralyzing fear or feigned submissiveness and decreased by assertiveness or apparent setting up for a counterattack on your part. This drill is used merely to quickly train every possible reaction to random gun placement. Regardless of what drills you practice, always remember: 1. If you have distance and you see a gun, RUN; 2. Do not go to crime scene number two if you want to live.

1. While spinning slowly with your eyes closed, have your partner press the plastic gun against or near *any* part of your body he or she can think of. Variation is vital to your practice.

2. Open your eyes and instantly smash the weapon off-line. Simultaneously move your body in the other direction to maximize your off-lining and avoid getting your head blown off! Take the shortest path to make your body unavailable to the vector the bullet will take on leaving the muzzle. This will require you to experiment, possibly using some unusual arm deflection angles. Add control as necessary (as outlined elsewhere) and simultaneously strike an available vulnerable target (like the eyes or throat) and then run like hell. Just remember not to hurt your training partner! As just mentioned, depending on the placement of the gun, you may need to additionally immobilize the gun and/or gun arm while striking. The possible variations are too great to elaborate on here and so we highly recommend you practice all the scenarios in our Weapons DVD Series, especially Part 4 (Bare-hands to Hand Guns).

3. If you are being restrained in such a way as to make counter-attack impossible (arm tightly around your throat lifting you with gun jammed in your mouth, etc.) you will have to feign a heart attack, fear paralysis, etc. to get him to change his gun and restraint position on you to allow your counter-attack. This may happen, for example, as you're walked to or positioned to be placed in a vehicle.

Gun Defense II

Now practice with both a partner and a heavy bag. You can draw a face on the bag or purchase one of the lifelike dummies commonly available through martial art supply distributors (see References and Resources).

1. Spin with your eyes closed.
2. As you spin, have your partner touch you with a padded stick from behind the bag.
3. Twist off line and drive your partner's stick (the gun arm) against the bag while delivering screaming, full-power dropping strikes.
4. Run away.

Using Handguns for Self-Defense . . . an Introduction

Guided chaos shooting is an entire book in itself. Nevertheless, we present here an introduction to the subject to get your mind thinking and whet your appetite should you want to take this training further.

A well-trained person with a pistol in hand, ready for action, is a rarity. All too often, a person buys a gun and some ammunition and goes to the nearest range or empty lot and fires off a few rounds, thinking he or she is now ready for anything. Conversely, a person can train for years by firing at static targets, get high scores, and still not be ready to defend him- or herself with a handgun. Over 90 percent of gunfights occur within 21 feet (6.4 m). More than half of these occur within 5 feet (1.5 m). Most people, when put to the test, can't even get their guns out in time to defend against a person rushing them from across a large room. You must also know hand-to-hand combat to be successful.

The first step toward carrying a handgun for self-defense is to find a competent trainer through the National Rifle Association (NRA). After you've learned some basic home defense and the principles of safe gun handling, practice simple marksmanship for 10 to 20 hours. Once you can hit a man-sized target with sighted fire (i.e., using the gun sights), you can graduate to the more serious aspects of shooting for self-defense. At close range (0 to 21 feet, or 0 to 6.4 m), it's not necessary to bring your handgun up to eye level. Here is where point shooting, or what's called instinctive shooting, comes into play. This information is not widely available.

Gunfighting is a term that has different meanings for many people. There is the old fashioned idea of the duel at dawn: Two men strap on their six guns and walk down the main street of a frontier town until a particular distance is reached, and then suddenly they draw against each other, and one or both are shot. This is a Hollywood romance at best. In the majority of shootings in the Old West, people were not often given a fair chance to defend themselves against an armed aggressor. Quite often, a lawman would simply come up to someone from behind with a large-bore shotgun, have that person drop the sidearm, or just shoot if the person did not cooperate. In reality, a bad guy would probably not even warn you before shooting you in cold blood. The point of this digression is to show you that gun fighting has *never* been "fair," not even in the good ol' days.

Today, many law enforcement officers, military members, and civilians are not well trained for what happens up close in a gun fight. As stated earlier, well over 90 percent of handgun fights happen within about 10 to 20 feet (3 to 6 m). There is a methodology known as point shooting that is specifically designed for this type of situation. Point shooting is a method of aligning a handgun with a target at close range and firing. The target can be nearly anything. For our purposes, we will assume that we are practicing to shoot at an armed attacker.

1. Draw a handgun from a holster, belt, or pocket and point it at an antagonist as quickly as possible and fire it without looking through the sights.

2. The point shooter looks at the threatening individual with both eyes open while pulling the trigger of the handgun, either with one hand or two on the weapon. The point shooter keeps pulling the trigger until the threat has stopped.

3. If you're confronted with the possibility of an attack by one or more gun-wielding assailants, get to cover instantly if possible. Cover is anything that will stop a bullet from penetrating and will prevent the bullet from hitting you. Do not mistake concealment for cover. Concealment is something like a sheetrock wall, which may prevent the assailant from seeing you but not prevent a bullet from penetrating and striking you.

There are many ways to practice point shooting. Here's a way a point-shooting beginner can have great success:

1. Take four standard sheets of paper from a legal pad and make a rectangle out of them. Number each sheet either from right to left or in mixed order. Place this target at about 18 feet (5.5 m) from your position.

2. While holding your handgun at the side of your body, have a friend call out the numbers in random order.

3. As the numbers are called out, smoothly shoot each sheet without using the sights of your handgun. In some cases, taping over the sights may help you not to cheat. You can practice this smoothly without pushing your speed. Your speed will pick up as you continue to practice. Remember to hold onto your weapon as tightly as comfortable. During an actual gunfight, you will more than likely be crushing your grip while pulling your trigger as fast as possible. Keep in mind that the usual target-shooting principles hardly have a place in close-quarters gunfighting. The adrenaline response will make it nearly impossible to take a sight picture and then obtain a perfect, smooth trigger pull as in bull's-eye shooting.

This exercise will help familiarize you with your particular handgun; it's shown great results with the vast majority of our students.

1. First, empty your handgun. Check it several times to make sure it is empty. Hopefully, you will have a handgun that is ergonomically correct for you. Because this is often not the case, this exercise will help you point your weapon as well and as naturally as possible.

2. Go alone into a room that has a number of items on or against each wall. While holding your empty weapon, look at a particular item. Remember where it is and close your eyes.

3. As smoothly as possible, point the handgun at the item while your eyes are still shut. Hold the weapon steady, open your eyes, and look through the sights to see how close you got to the center of the target item. One-handed practice is usually easier. Your body should move naturally as you turn and aim toward your target.

4. Pick a target that is on the opposite side of the room from where you are facing. Look over your shoulder at a particular item.

5. Close your eyes and repeat this exercise until you can move and aim well enough to get a centered sighting on the item. If you try to get into a particular stance, you will usually fail to get on target, except for those items that are already in front of you. You can practice this using both hands, too.

You will probably find two-handed practice to be far more difficult than one-handed practice. Becoming proficient with one-handed shooting has many advantages at close range. When a sudden attack occurs, you will be more able to get off a fast shot with one hand. If the attacker or attackers are already on you, you may need your free hand to push or strike while drawing your weapon. One thing to seriously consider is the possibility that your weapon will be covered and you will not be able to get your hand on it during an attack. This is where close-quarters fighting will be of paramount importance. Following is a description of the content of the basic Barehands to Handguns course that we teach.

Introduction to Guided Chaos Gunfighting

The operative part of the word gunfight is fight. Many trainers today teach gunfighting as merely an extension of the shooting one might do on a target range. In most cases, unfortunately, reality does not conform to these trainers' assumptions. A recent study of cop killers showed that violent career criminals, with their disregard for the conventional fundamentals of shooting (e.g., sight alignment, stance), their aggressive mindset (i.e., no compunction against killing), their use of surprise attacks, and their more frequent practice with firearms (average once per month versus a police officer's practice twice per year), often achieve a far higher level of real-world effectiveness with firearms than do conventionally trained police officers. This is one reason why guided chaos handgun training differs so greatly from conventional handgun training.

One of the biggest missing links in most armed citizens' and police officers' preparations is the ability to access, present, and use the carry gun while under attack. It seems that many students and even trainers assume they'll see any attack coming from far away, or perhaps that the violent criminal will announce his intentions from a distant, stationary position, allowing time for the victim to execute his practiced stationary draw from concealment into a perfect shooting stance and obtain perfect sight alignment. Reality, unfortunately, usually doesn't happen that way.

First of all, if someone with half a brain wants to assassinate you with a gun, there is little you can do about it once he gets the drop on you. You will probably not even be aware of his presence until he fires.

If the criminal wants to move you somewhere else at gunpoint or tells you to do anything suspicious (e.g., kneel down—a frequent precursor to execution), your best bet is usually to attempt an immediate escape.

Let's summarize what we've learned up 'til now.

1. If you are threatened with a gun and you are not restrained at all, your best bet may be to simply run away. If the attacker has not shot you already, killing you is obviously not the first priority, and criminals often want to avoid the attention a gunshot would bring, at least at the initial location (i.e., before he can move you to a more isolated crime scene). Therefore, the odds of his shooting at you as you flee are low. Even if he does shoot at you, his odds of inflicting a lethal wound decrease significantly with every additional yard of distance you can create. Run straight away from the attacker, preferably to the closest cover. Don't try to zigzag or do anything fancy like that. It is better to get maximum acceleration and create maximum distance as quickly as possible.

2. If the criminal is restraining you, or if you are cornered and cannot immediately run, in order to create the opportunity to escape, you must attack—unarmed. There is simply no way to draw your own gun with any chance of success while a bad guy has the drop on you.

3. The ways criminals usually use handguns to threaten people differ significantly from what is taught in most martial arts schools and training programs. Rarely will a criminal stand directly in front of you and stiffly point a gun at you. More often, the attacker will be very close, controlling you and possibly pulling you off balance with one hand while the other hand holds the gun in various places; sometimes, the weapon moves around. A gunman often will strike a victim in the head with the handgun to make sure the victim knows the gun is present and to achieve maximum intimidation effect. These conditions, among others, make dealing with a handgun-wielding robber or worse much more dif-

ficult. It's impossible to memorize—and then recall under stress—enough preplanned techniques to cover every possibility. Adaptability is key.

4. If you are restrained at gunpoint or have no space to run, and you feel you are about to be killed or moved somewhere else, your best hope in many of these cases is to fight. One thing you could try before you attack is to act extremely compliant or even overcome with fear. This may prompt the gunman to relax a little. You're more likely to be successful if you can attack while the gunman's talking because this lengthens his reaction time. Under no circumstances should you verbally antagonize a gunman who has the drop on you, nor do anything to make him more nervous or alert.

5. Your first move must get your body out of the line of fire and put yourself in a balanced position to attack the attacker and control the direction the weapon is pointing. Using dropping energy is essential because it overcomes inertia (granting you immediate, maximum speed with no warning), gives you instant balance, enables you to strike hard with no wind-up, and lets you break many holds on your body without concerted effort. Just the lowering of your body can help get you out of the line of fire when a gun is pointed at your head.

Beyond that, there are no guarantees. Sometimes you'll be able to wrap up or lock up the weapon-bearing limb while striking the attacker's throat, eyes, and head with hand strikes and head butts, but sometimes you'll only be able to grab or redirect the gun arm as you attack. Seemingly insignificant characteristics of different bodies (e.g., the protuberance of the elbow joint) can make all the difference in how you can control a person. A criminal will move when you suddenly attack, even if it's merely to flinch away from your strikes or fall to the ground. You must rely on your sensitivity, developed through contact flow practice, to guide your attack. Generally, allowing the attacker to move away from you will be lethal because he'll be able to bring the gun back online. You must strike to destroy him where he stands, not to push him away. This requires sensitivity in striking. If he falls while still in control of himself and his gun, you may have to fall with him to prevent him from bringing his gun back online. You may be able to momentarily pin the gun arm on the ground as you access your own gun, knife, or other carry weapon. Sometimes it may be sufficient to knock the attacker's gun off line, strike once, and run. Sometimes, however, you may have to finish the job.

Of course, the probability of multiple armed attackers complicates the situation exponentially. If you carry a gun or other weapon, and you do not walk around with it constantly in your hand, you have to learn how to access and use it under the pressure of a surprise attack or in midfight. The following drill will help.

Combat-Draw Movement

Begin with a semiautomatic gas-powered or fast electric Airsoft replica (or Simunitions if available) of your carry handgun concealed as you would on a daily basis (e.g., same holster, same carry location, fully concealed). As in any such drill, you'll need to wear eye protection.

Have your training partner, wearing head and throat protection impervious to close-range Airsoft shots and holding a padded cane or stick, stand about 20 feet away. Increasing the initial distance makes the drill easier and less realistic; decreasing the distance makes the drill more difficult and more realistic.

Close your eyes and spin in place. After a few seconds, your partner shouts and charges at you with the goal of whacking you in the head with the padded stick.

As soon as you hear the shout, open your eyes and run off line from the attacker's charge to gain enough time before contact to draw your gun and shoot the attacker.

Several points will become evident from repeatedly running this drill:

1. Drawing your gun before beginning your movement off line will result in being whacked before you can fire. Your first movement must be to get off line and keep moving while simultaneously accessing your weapon.

2. Extending your weapon away from your body in any of the classic, one- or two-handed target shooting stances is dangerous. This can put your gun within reach of the attacker, allowing him to knock it off line. Point shooting with one hand (allowing maximum mobility) from below eye level is usually the way to go.

3. Shooting as many pellets as possible, as quickly as possible, into the center of mass of the attacker until the attacker stops is a likely outcome of getting whacked by the padded stick. Your partner should not stop quickly after the first pellet impact but should continue to move just as an actual attacker would, even after being shot.

4. Moving your feet quickly, with balance and coordination (including the split-brain multitasking of performing separate tasks with the upper and lower body), is a more important factor in this drill than any sort of target-shooting skill. Most students, given normal levels of coordination—enhanced by guided chaos training—and firm grips on handguns that fit their hands reasonably well, can make effective hits to the center mass in this drill, even with the movement involved. The difficult part is creating the time necessary to bring the gun into play through effective and efficient movement. Efficiency is key: A smooth, practiced draw that can be executed independently of movement by the rest of your body will be far quicker than a panicked snatch for the gun, destabilized by off-balance movement of your feet.

5. Being able to evade the swing of the stick, hit, and unbalance the attacker with the non-gun hand will prove important as the initial distance decreases.

The next phase of this drill involves going to the ground in order to get off line of the charge. This is appropriate training for situations in which there is no space or time to move sideways, or when you may trip and fall. Just as balance and the ability to move swiftly and nimbly on your feet are the most critical components of a standing drill, guided chaos falling and ground-fighting skills are the most critical factors in this version. Again, the first movement of the drill must be to avoid the charge. Taking the time to go for the gun before beginning to fall will result in getting whacked before the gun is on target. As in unarmed guided chaos ground fighting, you should fall in such a way as to present your legs toward the attacker. This will allow you to stop his charge and briefly keep him at bay, creating time to access your handgun. At worst, getting hit on the lower leg is not as bad for you as getting hit on the head. Once you have your gun, you must have the coordination to fight using your legs while point shooting—*without shooting your own legs*. As described in chapter 10, use a one-handed, bent-arm "perp shoot" grip, not a two-handed isosceles or Weaver grip or you're liable to shoot your own feet as you kick to keep him off you. You can practice this with a toy dart gun or Airsoft gun with eye protection. Keep the gun above or beside your head so it won't be within the attacker's reach. Shoot until the attacker stops.

You can improve your dynamic fighting-while-drawing-or-shooting skills with the following drill (a variation on the unarmed gang attack drills).

Once you are armed with a concealed Airsoft replica gun as in the previous drill, stand in the center of a triangle of hanging dummies or heavy bags. Have your training partners stand behind each dummy; their job is to manipulate the dummies to challenge you by crowding you, hitting you, and knocking you off balance. An additional training partner flicks the room lights on and off, while another may toss kicking shields and other obstacles under your feet. At the starting signal, you must fight unarmed against the attacking dummies, moving and striking to avoid getting crushed, knocked over, or hit from behind. The fright reaction; dropping; simple striking; and fast, spinning, stomping footwork are key—at the same time remaining pliable and sensitive to avoid damage.

On the command of "Draw!" create space and opportunity to draw your replica gun and hit each of the dummies with multiple pellets as quickly as possible while moving and retaining full control of the gun. A designated training partner or instructor might shout, "Ground!" first. At that command, fall and fight off the attacking dummies from the ground, using your legs. You would then execute the draw while ground fighting.

You will find from running these drills that in a close-quarters combat situation, even when you are armed with a handgun, your ability to move and fight effectively when unarmed, whether on your feet or on the ground, will be far more critical to your survival than target-shooting skills. In effect, close-range gunfighting involves dynamically placing a gun and the coordination and skill to use it into the same fight you were fighting without the gun.

These drills should be combined with live-fire point-shooting practice against inanimate targets for full effectiveness. During your live-fire practice, move as dynamically and shoot as quickly as safety constraints allow. Just as in guided chaos unarmed combat, you'll learn to isolate different parts of your body where appropriate; during shooting practice, try to isolate your shooting hand from the chaotic motion of the rest of your body to make good hits no matter what the circumstances.

MACHETE ATTACK

I have been a student of John Perkins since October of 1996. Several weeks prior to a confrontation, I had terminated one of my employees for stealing equipment from me. I had warned him on numerous occasions to stop, but he continued to steal. Finally, I had no other choice but to fire him.

After I fired him, we were in a parking lot. I told him not to steal my customers. We were arguing, but when I realized it was futile, I turned my back to leave the scene. Using blinding speed, he retrieved a machete from his vehicle and came at me. I remembered the principle of attack the attacker. I quickly moved in on the weapon and his body, attacking with both hands and knees. If I had stepped back instead, he would've severed my hands and perhaps my head.

He was holding the machete with two hands at about shoulder height. Using a combination of body unity, balance, and dropping force, I stopped the sideways and slightly upward swing of the deadly 3-foot (.9 m) blade by slamming his lead arm, stopping his forward movement. My strikes got him to release one hand from the weapon. However, he was very skilled with a machete, which he used on a daily basis; he fell back to a second position and raised the machete over his head for a downward stroke.

At this point, I realized this was going to be really bad if I didn't take some drastic measures to end the attack. It was literally do or die, so I went for it. Luckily, I had stuck close to the attacker, taking his space and room to maneuver. I pushed the blade off line and downward while palm-heeling him in the face, and then I cranked on his head, twisting his neck. He immediately dropped the weapon and spun away, falling to the ground. I booted him twice in the torso, causing further damage. I stopped attacking him when a man who identified himself as a city marshal stepped up to me.

I would have never thought that someone I had known for years would try to kill me. A machete is a very serious weapon. A person with little strength can cut small trees in half almost effortlessly. All of this happened in a split second; I had no time to think, just react. I am convinced that what made this a successful outcome for me was being able to put myself ahead of this guy before he knew it. It was a seamless series of reactions and body alignments that prevented him from seriously cutting me and made my counterattack so successful. A witness said that if I had not stopped this guy with such force, he would have cut me up. His intent was obvious, and by the look on his face, he meant business.

Authors' note: Our student's biggest mistake was getting into an argument with the attacker in the first place. By observing the principle discussed in chapter 1 and avoiding all fights, the entire incident (at least for the moment) could have been avoided. Of course, who's to say our student wouldn't have been assaulted at some future date when he couldn't have just walked away. Regardless, the training saved his life.

The machete wielder was arrested and charged with assault with a deadly weapon, battery, and menacing.

Preventing Common Mistakes

➤ If you're the victim of a mugging, be the most cooperative victim your attacker has had all day. If he tries to move you to another location, feign paralyzing fear, then attack mercilessly and run.

➤ Practice the gun and knife drills with an eye toward randomness, versatility, and creativity. Don't just go through the motions or fall into routines.

➤ Skip the gang attack drills at your own peril.

➤ It's better to drop your stick at close range and go hand to hand than to wrestle over a weapon.

➤ Learn to pull your handgun and get off line simultaneously, or you may never get the chance to access your weapon.

Afterword

THE SURVIVAL MANIFESTO

By Lieutenant Colonel Al Ridenhour, U.S. Marine Corps Reserves,
instructor in unarmed combat in Iraq, guided chaos master

One thing we want to stress is this: Unlike in many systems that create techniques based on hypothetical situations, in guided chaos we don't make stuff up. Every drill, training scenario, technique, or principle has its roots in some horrific real-world attack that actually happened.

Everything that we do is based on the more than 100 extremely violent encounters and over 150 homicides that Grand Master Perkins has been personally involved in as a detective and forensic expert for the Yonkers, New York, Police Department. This also includes the experiences of the many instructors and students with law enforcement, corrections, emergency medical technician (EMT), and military combat experiences. The body of knowledge that makes up guided chaos is written in blood, not some made-up nonsense based on what people think real violence is. There is a difference.

If you want to debate the merits of the sportive or classical techniques or the bogus, so-called reality-based scenarios that would work only on a drunk and how they're supposed to save your life in a brutal, homicidal attack, you need to go elsewhere because we're not talking about the same thing.

The Pillars of Guided Chaos

People think that just because something is simple, it can't work. We are conditioned to make fighting, like other things, more complex than it is. Witness the plethora of overly specialized martial arts systems. Some have attempted, with good intentions, to develop a more holistic approach by blending disciplines. The only problem is, once again, if you start off from the wrong mind-set (i.e., trying to blend in sportive techniques), all you have done is created a well-rounded sport. This is fine for mixed martial arts venues but a recipe for disaster against psychotic street killers.

The current systems being taught in the armed forces are based on sportive techniques and a sportive modality of training. Rather than being focused on killing the enemy, they are focused on winning a sportive duel or controlling people. Just as one couldn't expect to win a grappling match without grappling techniques, it's doubtful one could fight for his or her life without training what is required in order to survive blood baths against a determined killer, which is what war is all about. It's no different if you're assaulted on the street and you think you're going to die.

The major principles of guided chaos can be thought of as a pyramid. There are other subprinciples to each one of these, but none of that matters if you don't have a basic knowledge of how they interrelate on a macrolevel.

In our pyramid, balance is the foundation for all the other principles. On top of balance is pliability. Without balance you can't be loose no matter how gifted you are. On top of looseness is sensitivity. Without looseness you can't respond sensitively. Even if you are loose, without balance you can't connect to your root and bring your power to bear. Balance is nothing more than being able to control your equilibrium under dynamic conditions, and it has both a physical and mental aspect.

Looseness, or pliability, is not just muscular relaxation. It involves subtle muscle control, allowing you to strike from one point to another while simultaneously avoiding an attacker's strikes. It is the ability to be hard and soft and everything in between all at the same time. It is the ability to slip through the smallest space possible or elongate your body when you need to. It is the ability to be solid, liquid, or vapor simultaneously by isolating various parts of your body through subtle muscle control.

Sensitivity is nothing more than what you mentally perceive based on touch (kinesthetic awareness) or what you see in the context of the fight (subcortical vision). As with balance and looseness, there is a mental as well as physical aspect to sensitivity that cannot be ignored. Sensitivity tells you where to be and when, and it drives the other principles without thought.

The culmination of these principles working together is body unity, or proprioception. If you want to know what allows some practitioners of guided chaos seemingly to transcend the physical limitations of their bodies and continue to improve, it is the development of body unity through the principles. Through the development of proper body unity, you can do what you want to people and in some cases instantly master various techniques that normally take people years to develop.

Body unity starts with proper foot placement in relation to your root and is the key to proper skeletal alignment. When you strike with body unity, you're hitting with your skeleton, assisted by gravity and with full control of your momentum within your sphere of influence. In other words, you're blasting the enemies with minimal effort, and their bodies just seem to get in the way of your weapons.

Body unity allows you to appear faster and more agile than you really are. You are able to cut off angles of attack and penetrate people with little or no movement. You're never overextended, out of alignment, or restricted in movement. Your balance enables you to instantly change your root point in order to control your equilibrium. As enemies advance, you can easily step off line. As they retreat, you can take their space.

- Through looseness you are able to contort your body to avoid being penetrated. As you move in to strike by yielding, you can align your weapon with your body, lengthen or shorten your weapon, cut off angles, and strike with maximum power from virtually impossible positions simultaneously.

- Through sensitivity you know where the other person is in relation to your weapons. You maintain contact and flow with the battle effortlessly, seemingly always knowing what others are going to do before they do it.

- In guided chaos, balance + looseness + sensitivity = body unity.

- Body unity facilitates blinding speed, economy of movement, endurance, energy awareness and manipulation, internal energy (qi), and striking power (fa jing). Striking power is enhanced by mass, speed, structural alignment, and muscular elasticity, all of which are enhanced by muscle and tendon strength.

- Body unity facilitates the fifth principle of guided chaos, which is total freedom of action.

With guided chaos principles, you are able to develop multiple responses. As long as it is within the laws of physics and human physiology, you are limited only by your imagination.

Awareness Concepts

Without becoming paranoid, learn to direct more of your attention outward into your field of vision, which is as far as you can see and assess potential enemies. Resist the modern tendency to blithely trust your surroundings and withdraw completely into your iPod or personal thoughts. Your field of vision gives you "the big picture." Remember that distance equals time and the sooner you can observe the enemy's actions, the greater the distance they have to cover, allowing you to react or pre-empt.

Within your field of vision is your sphere of influence, which encompasses the reach of your arms and legs and is the area within which you can do actual physical damage to an enemy. Ingrain your sphere of influence into your nervous system. Anyone who enters it is fair game. This is why criminals use the interview technique. It allows them to get close without setting off alarms. But if your mind is focused outward, it's not so easy for a stranger to simply walk up and attack you.

Balance in Relation to Your Sphere of Influence

Your sphere of influence extends to the maximum range of where you can strike with effectiveness. Since your limbs are just long enough to protect your body, regardless of body type, you want to learn to fight within your own sphere. While moving your equilibrium and balance forward and backwards or side to side by shifting your weight from one foot to the other without stepping, you are also moving your sphere of influence. As long as you follow the principles governing controlling your balance, you're able to move your sphere accordingly and maintain control over your weapons.

From time to time, you may find that your attacker is just beyond the distance where you can effectively strike him. Rather than reaching out, becoming overextended and off balance, step to a new root point, and move your sphere of influence while maintaining control over your limbs. Be aware that even a microstep of 1 inch (2.5 cm) can make all the difference in terms of your power and angle of attack!

Moving your center of gravity with you as you step to a new root point enables you to strike with maximum power and cutting force because you are able to penetrate an opponent's center.

No matter which direction you turn or step, your sphere of influence remains the same, as does your center of gravity. No matter which way you line up your weapons, you are able to strike in every direction with power.

Proper Mind-Setting

The foundation of a martial arts program is a proper mind-set; just as sport fighting in its variety of forms has a different dynamic that governs them, so does fighting for your life. If a program is developed from the wrong mind-set, then the underlying theory of the whole system is fatally flawed. This is why sport fighting almost always fails in real fights—unless you're exceptionally gifted—because if a system is not based on killing the attacker from the start, it is incapable of developing a realistic training regimen for street combat. Deadly self-defense training can always be tuned down as necessary, but the reverse is never true: Soft-ball training can never be ramped up in an emergency to save your life. The nervous system simply doesn't work that way.

The guided chaos principles of balance (control of your equilibrium), looseness (muscular and mental pliability), sensitivity (kinesthetic awareness and subcortical vision, eye–hand coordination), body unity (coordination, subtle muscle control, economy of movement, proprioception), and freedom of action (anything goes in a real fight) have always been factors in real life-and-death combat since the dawn of mankind. The principles of guided chaos are rooted in physics and human physiology, so like gravity, they are universal and available for anyone to develop, provided the individual is willing to put the time in.

It's been shown that those who train for survival as opposed to training to win trophies and merit badges are better able to deal with both the psychological and physical aspects of close combat. Even if injured, many people have said that because they were both physically and psychologically prepared to deal with the reality of violence, including being seriously injured, they were able to control their fear; rather than become paralyzed by it, they became empowered.

If you are not mentally prepared to deal with what happens in a real attack on your life, you are finished. Therefore, whether armed or unarmed, you must develop the mind-set to think and strike like an assassin and attack the attacker. An assassin doesn't want a protracted fight—he wants to get in, finish it, and get out.

Accordingly, focus on developing the proper mind-set, body unity, and body mechanics when performing all the striking drills; emphasize realistic body movements rather than the flashy moves common to many martial arts that lack true effectiveness. In your contact flow and all other drills, visualize tearing the enemy limb from limb; engrain it deep into your nervous system so that all your movements, no matter how small, have devastating intent.

Entering to Win

Even with heightened awareness, you may find yourself in a situation where you cannot run due to space, health, or the proximity of loved ones. Also, you cannot maintain your awareness on red alert indefinitely, or you'll suffer nervous-system burnout. If an attack is imminent or a mugger wants to take you to a second location, you must attack the attacker with the mind-set of a cornered sewer rat. You do this by entering to win. The key is to always move in at an angle.

By changing your body position or stepping off line but in (at about a 45-degree angle), you can thwart an initial attack. You then must be able to penetrate your opponent's center with bone-crushing force. To do this, you often must move your sphere into your opponent by long-stepping so that you do not overreach, overcommit, and lose balance. Step in but off line from your enemy's weapons. This renders you unavailable yet unavoidable.

Keep in mind that the attacker's center will change depending on his or her orientation. No matter which way the attacker turns, your strikes are still focused on penetrating his or her center. A typical flaw of the untrained fighter is launching glancing attacks at an enemy. You see this with long, looping hook punches straight out of a John Wayne movie that only chip away at the target. If practiced against a heavy bag, they simply set the bag spinning, waste power, and throw you off balance. Even straight shots suffer from this strategic error, often resulting in broken hands and wrists. The solution is to train to always hit your target dead center, no matter what the angle of the weapon or the position of the enemy. This is why we stress balance, looseness, body unity, and adaptability in guided chaos. This is one interpretation of what we mean by finding the straight line in the circle. Your movement resembles the whirling of a projectile in a slingshot: It circles about your head, gaining speed, until you let it fly, straight and true, to its target. So, too, your looseness and sensitivity may have you circling to find the path of least resistance, but by using the enemy's energy, your final attack is sharp, straight, and immensely powerful.

If you anticipate an attack and move in preemptively, it shouldn't matter which way you step as long as you simultaneously strike and protect your eyes and throat. That is the combat efficiency of entering to win: By stepping off line and attacking at the same time, you make yourself both unavailable and unavoidable.

You never know how you're going to be attacked, but you can always throw a monkey wrench into the attack by stepping off line in either direction. With the CCUE you can deliver a side chop simultaneously; as long as you do not move beyond your sphere of influence, you can recover quickly. If you miss, you're still on balance because you're capable of changing your root point at will. If there are multiple assailants you can box step in the direction that places the closest attacker between you and the next nearest attacker, constantly circling to avoid being trapped. If the attack is so sudden and close that there's no time to step, dropping into a simple, direct, chop or fright reaction effectively takes you off-line because your structure and balance are no longer where the enemy expected them to be (higher up), even though the change is in mere inches (centimeters). Even then, you use the rebound (ricocheting) energy from the impact of your strike to immediately initiate your moving off-line (even subtly) for your next strike, and the next, like a machine gun. You become like a rabid mongoose, impossible to hit yet impossible to avoid.

These entries need to be practiced free form within contact flow so you can experiment with variables.

Once you have struck the enemy, you know where he or she is in relation to your body. If the simple close combat entry hasn't destroyed the enemy, and the enemy moves, blocks, or counters effectively, pure guided chaos principles now come into play (the principles can also be used to imbue straight close combat with more adaptability). It is because of the guided chaos training that you are able to remain loose, balanced, sensitive, and coordinated on the way in as you strike. Any changes in the enemy's body are immediately met with more punishing blows. Also because of guided chaos training, you can strike from anywhere to anywhere regardless of the enemy's body position.

As you enter, you should only be concerned with two things: the opponent's weapons and yours. You do not strike hard or soft—you strike to kill (ramping down force is easier than ramping it up if you train properly and you only fight to save your life). Your opponent either deals with it or is destroyed. Your strike becomes your block, and your block becomes your strike. In guided chaos, we never play, we never do sportive training. This is what we call fighting with ruthless intent.

Ruthless Intent

Miyamoto Musashi states the following in *The Book of Five Rings*:

> *Whenever you cross swords with an enemy you must not think of cutting him either strongly or weakly; just think of cutting and killing him. Be intent solely on killing the enemy. Killing is the same for people who know about fighting and for those who do not . . . cutting down the enemy is the Way of strategy, and there is no need for many refinements of it. (2000)*

Ruthless intention is but an extension of your will; it is more mental than physical and totally achievable by the average person. Guided chaos will not allow you to levitate a 300-pound (136 kg) prison-trained monster, but it will give you a chance to survive an attack by one. You must be able to strike to penetrate people with the emotional and moral will to cut through them. When you feel as if you're going to die, your intention must be to destroy the attacker, and you must set it in your mind beforehand that no matter what, you will take him or her out. With the development of guided chaos principles to the nth degree, the merest thought becomes deadly. Although appearing ordinary to the uninitiated, your movement becomes imbued with incredible intrinsic power that is only apparent to the recipient on impact. What appears like a simple natural movement on the surface has the crushing force of an ocean wave crashing against the rocks, of lightning splitting a tree down the center, of a tornado tossing a house like a toy. In truth, real killing skill looks like nothing at all, which is why people miss it even when it is staring them in the face. All systems that attempt to structure a fight through forms or rigid dogma are actually divorcing themselves from the natural, wild, free-flowing motion your body is capable of. It is in this chaotic motion where the deadliest skills are found. Through guided chaos training, you are able to harness these lethal qualities and focus them with little or no thought.

How ruthless must you be?

If you or a loved one is going to die and the enemy's arm is in the way, you break it. If the enemy's eyes are available, you tear them out. If the groin is available, you must knee or kick so hard that you crack the pelvis. You must chop the throat and neck with every intention of cleaving the head from the body. If your enemy takes you to the ground, you must kick with all that you have with every intention of breaking every bone in the enemy's body. If your enemy falls to the ground but is still capable of causing you lethal harm and you can't escape, you must stomp and kick and utterly crush him or her.

In short, you must be willing to do to enemies everything they intended to do to you and develop the will to do what must be done. Generally speaking, your attacker, no matter how bloodthirsty, doesn't want to be hurt, either. Your attackers are not superhuman or invincible, which is why they use speed and surprise to overcome you, but they are determined. You must be willing to fight on *their* level: Strike without mercy and survive. We cannot overemphasize this point. This is why we say at the beginning of the book to avoid all fights and challenge no one; ignore all verbal assaults no matter how heinous and walk or run away; and ignore all assaults on your pride, manliness, politics, religion, or whatever. All of that is B.S. The only time you fight is if you think you are going to be killed. Laws regarding appropriate use of force in self-defense vary state by state and federally, but in general, if you think you're going to die, you can do what's necessary to live. That's often the best thing to tell the judge, but there are no guarantees. You may turn the other cheek and be killed for it. The female kickboxer we told you about in the beginning of this book knocked her assailant down and was subsequently stabbed in the face with a punch-knife, an injury from which she could easily have died. Bernie Getz, who was mugged in New York City, shot his attackers and probably would've gotten off if he hadn't been heard to say, "You don't look so bad; have another!"

Do yourself and your family a favor by becoming a man of peace and save your life—and your harasser. Remember that any fight, even if you're the good guy, can result in your imprisonment by the justice system. But if the enemy's serious and you're left with no choice, then unleash the dogs of war. All of them. You can always ramp down your counterattack once it begins, but if you don't fight back with everything you've got initially, you may die. If luck is on your side, and you have witnesses and a good lawyer, you'll be all right.

The Five-Second Fight

The five-second fight concepts epitomize guided chaos:

1. All real life-and-death altercations are won or lost within the first five seconds of contact—especially with multiple attackers.

2. Although a number of styles have made statements that 90 percent of fights go to the ground, the truth is that this applies only to the person who is losing.

3. This does not include prefight, juvenile, asinine nonsense, such as tough talk, bouncing, or dancing around like in ring fighting. This is not self-defense, and if you engage in it, you are an idiot and a menace from a societal viewpoint and in the eyes of the law. Walk away, carefully, keeping your eyes on the enemy.

4. All close-quarters police and military altercations are life-and-death situations and must end as quickly as possible.

5. Run at the first sign of danger; don't wait until you've scoped things out. Listen to your gut. If you can't escape, attack the attackers immediately. Crime statistics show that attacking with all you've got immediately is vastly preferable to letting a violent criminal take you to a second location, where you may wish you were dead. You can expect nothing less than being raped, tortured, or mutilated in the most barbaric fashion and then finally killed. No amount of negotiating, begging, or pleading for your life is going to stop a determined psychopath from gutting you. These people cannot be bargained with or reasoned with—if they were reasonable, they wouldn't be attacking you in the first place. The more time you take to react to an attack, the

more time you give the attacker to bring you under control, both physically and mentally.

6. Escape now! Don't hang around to see if your assailant is okay or admire your handiwork (reread The Battered Kickboxer in chapter 1). Don't wait for the police at the scene; your attacker(s) may have accomplices coming to finish you.

7. Never, ever give up! People have escaped and survived after having been riddled with bullets, stabbed repeatedly, fallen from buildings, burned, blinded, and more. No matter what happens, so long as you don't give up, you can survive. John Perkins was seconds from losing his life when attacked by the Williams brothers, but he was saved by a ferocious desire to survive. After being kicked and jumped on by multiple attackers, he almost lost consciousness but fought back and lived. His skills would have been worthless if he had just given up.

The concept of attacking the attacker is only one aspect of the five-second fight. In most cases where a serious criminal attack is involved, the victim does not always have a warning or control of the environment or know the actual mindset or number of attackers. Sudden attacks often involve subterfuge, distracting you from what is about to happen. Even though you are moving and making yourself a difficult target, you must know how to take out multiple attackers in five seconds or less because the more protracted the fight, the less chance you have to survive.

In guided chaos, there are no fancy pressure points to worry about. The eyes, neck, and groin are the primary targets and have the greatest chance of taking out an assassin. All of the attributes that are developed in guided chaos must be developed and coordinated at high speed with extreme focus and power to make the five-second fight work. You must also develop extreme accuracy—a glancing blow to the head won't cut it. As described earlier, you must penetrate the attacker's center deeply, for example with direct, ax-hand strikes to the side of the neck. This way you don't have to rely on extreme strength. Nevertheless, having slambag training for pounding, ripping, tearing, and crushing power can only help your chances.

Close Combat to Guided Chaos

Simple, basic close combat strikes will cut through almost everything. Close combat strikes consist of moving in obliquely while delivering repeated jackhammer chin jabs, eye gouges, chops, hammer fists, head butts, foot stomps, knee strikes to the groin and thighs, and kicks to the shins. They should be delivered in a whirlwind, augmented by the dropping principles you've now trained into every strike.

Against true monsters of this world, the instant your strikes meet with a block or resistance, your guided chaos training automatically kicks in. Remember, a snake can't drill through a rock, but it can twist around it and bite the enemy in the throat.

You become unavailable yet unavoidable as you get closer and strike. This is faster and more efficient, bewildering your opponent. At the highest levels of guided chaos you may dispense with close combat almost entirely and simply ghost in and pierce the enemy unimpeded.

This book, detailed as it is, represents only about 10 percent of guided chaos. If you train diligently and realistically, absorbing only a small part of this material will yield remarkable improvements in your fighting skills, whatever the style. You may surprise a few people with diligent training in the following ways:

- You'll be more aware and better able to avoid dangerous situations.
- If you can't escape, you'll attack the attacker.
- As the attack ensues, you go on autopilot. It will seem as though you have no idea what you're doing or what you're going to do next. To your assailant, you seem invisible (which is why we also call guided chaos ghostfist).

- Though unavailable to the enemy as a target, you are at the same time unavoidable as a weapon, dishing out tremendous mayhem. To your opponent, you feel like a sponge with steel spikes buried in it. A spring-loaded multiple of your entire body weight is behind every blow, no matter what the angle.
- You're without thought, tension, or form. You generate colossal force because you're not fighting your own muscles or balance. Your higher brain is a mute witness to the melee, a mere bystander. Your primitive brain, the one that houses the million-year-old animal, does what evolution created it to do, except now the reactions have been electrified and tuned.

Train and ingrain these reactions into every fiber of your being. Ultimately, unbounded by dogma, myth, or arrogance, you'll move freely and hopefully survive a deadly onslaught. You'll be able to create what you need, when you need it, without thought, until you become pure, unbridled energy, raining down chaos upon the enemy. The winds of hell will swirl around you, the center. All will be quiet, and the terrible forces will be guided, diverted, and destroyed, never blocked, as they are whipped and slingshotted *around* you, the eye of the storm.

Attacking the attacker is close combat in a nutshell, and guided chaos is like being nuked by a stealth bomber. You can see the enemy on your radar screen, but you can't be seen on his. Using stealth energy, if you can ghost through your opponent's attack while dropping, multihitting, yielding, and moving behind a guard, your attack is your defense.

Striking Concepts

We place a premium on blows versus throws. However, we do not spend a lot of time working on strikes but rather on the delivery system that makes them work. Guided chaos can be broken up into the following broad areas:

- Principles: Balance, looseness, sensitivity, body unity, and freedom of action are the principles. These are supported by subprinciples, such as always move behind a guard and always bring a weapon online. There are many others that have been explained in this book.
- Techniques: We don't advocate rote techniques other than the entries and preemptive striking techniques within close combat.
- Tools: These include chops, palms, kicks, knees, elbows, teeth, and so on. In guided chaos, the entire body is the tool.

Many people think that to develop your hands you need to engage in psychotic tool-developing methods, such as doing knuckle push-ups on concrete, kicking palm trees until your shins bleed, practicing Maki-wara board training, and more. These methods cause excessive calluses, calcium deposits, bone spurs, arthritis, blood clots, and permanent nerve damage among others. However, one thing these will not promote is your development into a better fighter.

When striking, you want to feel the ridge (striking surface) of your weapon and the relationship between your body and the strike. As described earlier in the book, try to feel your feet in your hands. Whether you move quickly or slowly, alignment is key. If you're striking with the side of the hand, ensure that the thumb is fully extended, fingers are together, and the strike is delivered with the side of the hand and not the fingers. If you're executing a side kick, aim with the heel and keep the foot as flat as possible. Do not crescent or turn your foot.

Targets

If you are fighting to save your life and use your power to strike an attacker (regardless of size) in the eyes or throat, or at the base of the skull or in the neck, that attacker will either die or experience some form of incapacitation.

READING BETWEEN THE LINES

John Perkins

Police officers are obligated not to use unnecessary force against a perpetrator, even though there is always the potential the officer could be severely injured or killed in apprehending a criminal. This mitigated the kinds of strikes I was allowed to use. As an unarmed civilian defending yourself in a situation where you feel you could die, the laws are different (varying state to state), and you do what you have to do.

On a cold November evening, I was walking my beat in a high-crime area of Yonkers, New York. As I approached a bar, I heard a loud commotion coming from inside. Just as I got to the front entrance, a crowd of men came pouring out and almost knocked me over. The crowd encircled two combatants who, I later learned, were brothers fighting over a girl. I tried to call for backup, but the radio signal wouldn't go through. The two brothers were ferociously throwing punches, and many were causing damage.

I attempted to separate the two men, who were both 6 feet 4 inches (1.9 m) each. Apparently the crowd did not care that I was a uniformed police officer and saw me as an unwanted interloper. The crowd then closed in on me. Just before they did, I felt the change in the mood of the crowd and moved accordingly. As the first attackers closed in, I circled the two fighting brothers and ended up on the other side of them. This gave me a second's respite. Here is where dynamic balance played a great part in keeping me safe. At first I thought I could just escape the crowd, but a few belligerent members prevented my exit. This forced me to go into a deep-rooted fright reaction, which toppled a few of them onto others who were also coming forward. A reverse box step took me to another part of the group that wasn't ready for me. Here, extreme balance along with dropping force enabled me to keep my feet while I turned and slammed one into another, causing confusion. A few times during this fight, I stomped like a flamenco dancer, crushing the feet of whoever came close. This made some of them back up, giving me more room to maneuver. I then went into a frenzy, pushing, tripping, and pummeling a few more of the crowd members.

At one point, one of my legs was grabbed by an attacker on the ground. I dropped into the leg that had been grabbed and quickly drove my fingers with a clawlike motion into his eyes and yanked his head backward, releasing the hold. As I continued to move, I remained loose. I combined this looseness with body unity to slam and maneuver my assailants in all directions, using the ricocheting energy gained from each impact to increase the power of the next. Rather than letting fear freeze my body, I was able to sense where there were openings in the line of attackers and was able to move nearly at will between them, while using their energy against them. This created an ideal environment for multihitting as I unleashed a storm of damaging blows that ping-ponged from target to target and person to person. I was on autopilot and delivered flurries of chops and elbow strikes, spinning like a whirling dervish. These moves used a combination of single-leg balance, whirling dervish box stepping, dropping, looseness, body unity, and sensitivity—and kept me safe until backup arrived.

Almost any portion of this fight could be broken down into individual altercations with one or two attackers engaging me. Most styles, even if they could handle the chaos of this limited scenario, completely break down in a multiple-attacker situation. Other styles might provide robotic, regimented responses that are applicable only to a dry textbook. However, it is the unique, adaptive, and reality-based energy principles of guided chaos that allow you to move easily from one line of attack to another against multiple attackers, borrowing power to launch you into new attack vectors. This is what guided chaos is all about. A person trained in sportive scenarios or typical "you do this—now I do that" self-defense would be inviting nervous-system overload in a split-second fight against even one of these attackers (or pairs of attackers). Against multiple, simultaneous attackers, a non—guided chaos defense would prove difficult if not disastrous. This is not theory but rather my professional experience as a forensic homicide investigator anyalyzing thousands of bloody melees and deaths.

Key Points

- Stay on balance and maintain your body unity. Start off performing contact flow at ultraslow speed, then half speed building to full speed. Begin with light contact and progress to full drop hitting (against a heavy bag, as in the Anywhere Striking series).

- When striking against a bag for practice, focus on penetrating and denting the bag through its center as opposed to pushing it. Splash the tissue when striking a person as opposed to just pushing.

- Ensure that your other hand is up to protect your throat when striking.

For the lower body, focus on the groin, kidneys, and abdomen as well as the spine and tail bone. Kicks (preferably with steel-toed shoes) should always be kept low. Target the shins, with the groin being the highest target and the spot you aim for to stop all incoming kicks. Additionally, you should practice incorporating foot and toe stomps with your heel into contact flow.

Tools

The most well-made tools are worthless in the hands of those who are unskilled in their use.
—*Alexander the Great*

Figures 1*a-c, e, f,* and *h* show the parts of the tools to make contact with. Figures 1*d* and *g* show the direction of the strikes.

a. Spear hand and side of hand (figure 1*a*). Note the exaggeration of the thumb in the figure. This is critical when striking with the side of the hand to augment power and looseness. When using the spear hand, the thumb can be held against the hand.

b. Side of hand as knife hand (figure 1*b*).

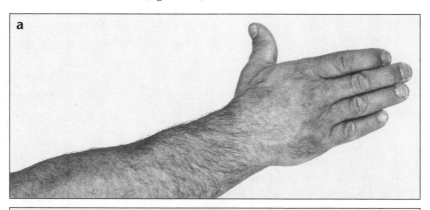

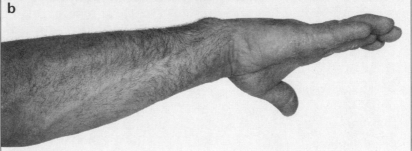

Figure 1

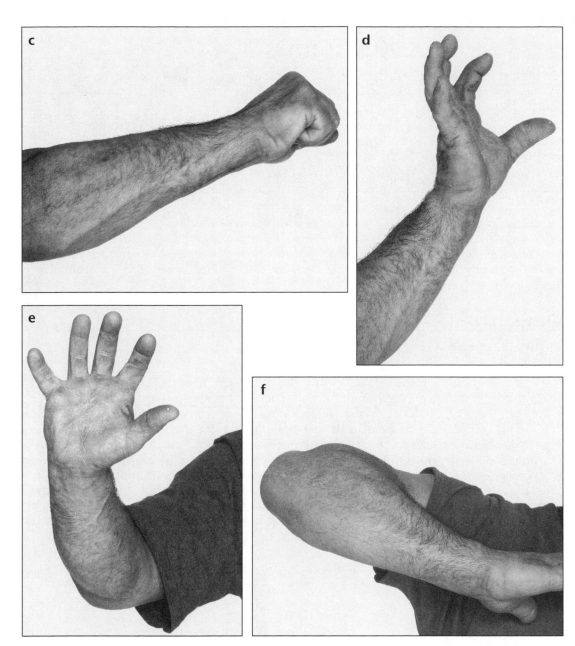

Figure 1, *continued*

   c. Hammer fist (figure 1*c*).

   d. Palm-heel strike (figure 1*d*).

   e. Palm-heel striking surface (figure 1*e*).

   f. Elbow strike (figure 1*f*).

   g. Y strike for the throat (figure 1*g*).

   h. Regular fist strike (figure 1*h*). This strike is generally used on the body and soft parts of the head and neck. Though made popular in sport fighting, it is generally the least effective bare-handed fighting tool for real combat. A punch with a regular fist takes years to develop (as opposed to a hammer fist). This is why boxers wrap their wrists before fights. You don't have time for this.

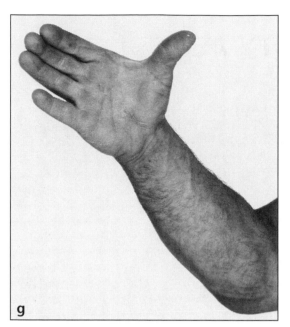

Figure 1, *continued*

Figure *2a* shows a front kick. Use only the toe or the heel to hit with. Hitting with the ball of the foot (as is used in many styles) actually cushions the impact. Crush with the heel. This is not a dojo or the Octagon. You've got shoes on. Use them! Also use the toe for round kicks to spear in the weapon. Do not use the top of the foot or shins. Figure *2b* shows a back or side kick. Use the heel of the foot, not the edge (figure 2, *a-b*). Do not blade your foot as in many styles. Use your shoes for blocking kicks, not your shins, unless you've been bashing banana trees or fire hydrants with your shins for half your life. When you kick, ensure your feet are always in the right position. You want to aim with the toe or with the heel when using either a front kick, side kick, or back kick, maintaining about a 90-degree angle to provide a mechanical advantage and structural integrity to the foot. For the roundhouse kick, use the toe.

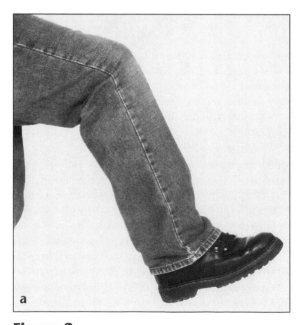

Figure 2

OFF-DUTY ASSAULT

This account comes from one of our military officers.

"When I was stationed in a garden spot somewhere in Asia, the following event took place.

"It was a very hot, humid August night. I was walking home to my apartment near the post where I was stationed. Normally, the walk home was relatively peaceful as long as there were Americans around. I had just passed the last block of vendors in a shopping area before my street when a voice in my head told me to slow down and take a look around. I did just that and noticed a few things out of the ordinary. First, two street lights had been shot out. Second, a bunch of trash cans had been moved in such a way as to channel any person who was not paying attention toward a central spot. Third, a group of college-age males were positioned in what looked like an L-shaped ambush.

"I had calmly started to turn around so I could take another way home when two other males appeared in front of me. Then, the other group of males started to close in on me. Fearing for my safety and not speaking the language, I did the only thing I could think of: I attacked the closest guy to me with two quick palm strikes to the head followed by an elbow to the back of his head. He dropped, and then the next closest guy tried to kick me.

"Before he could raise his leg to chamber his kick, I took his space and multihit by stomping down on his shin and foot. My body unity allowed me to immediately follow the stomps with a very hard strike to his solar plexus. I held on to him long enough to box step and use him as a shield to block the bottle that one of his buddies on the sidewalk threw at me. After the human shield had served his purpose, he became very well acquainted with my foot as it pressed his head into the pavement. The others turned and ran away. I guess they had seen enough. The following week in the same area, six other soldiers were attacked, and their military IDs and wallets were stolen.

"The close combat training and dropping principles I had learned from John Perkins saved my life. Because I was trained to be aware of my surroundings, I was able to see the little details that were out of place, giving me enough time to be proactive instead of reactive to the situation. The key is to always attack the attacker. Make it quick and very violent. Don't waste time because you never know how many other knuckleheads are around. Take the attacker out as quickly as possible; make an example of him, and the others are less likely to attack."

Final Thoughts

Where does the swordsman strike? Nowhere.

—*Takuan So Ho, The Unfettered Mind:*
Writings of the Zen Master to the Master Swordsman

One thing that will help you in your development is to assume nothing. The only things we can count on in a real fight are utter chaos and change. Assume that the enemy is capable of anything. This is why so many fighting systems fail when the poop hits the oscillating device. They assume the wrong things. In guided chaos, we assume everyone understands the same principles we do. This is how we keep ourselves honest.

In all that you do, understand that no one can do anything to you unless on some level you allow it to happen. When someone punches or grabs you, it requires your cooperation. In other words, you have to make your body available to the attacker for him to make his stuff work. This is what happens when your intent is to challenge the attacker instead of survive and escape. Move even slightly, and you completely change the fight. Whether by pocketing, stepping off line, or attacking the attacker, any change in your body's position (if the attacker fails to adjust fast enough) causes his body to get out of alignment. This causes him to fall behind as he tries to adjust. As long as you continue to make your body unavailable, he can never catch up.

Preemption through moving off line or striking first is paramount. Think of it like this: If you let someone strike you in the throat with all their might, there's probably a good chance you're not going to make it. There's no good counter to a crushed windpipe. When someone attacks you, how do you know he or she isn't trying to kill you? The point is you don't—so you can't allow it to happen in the first place. Once that type of hitting starts, you will never get back into the fight—unless the attacker really doesn't want to kill you, and that's a mercy you can't count on.

If someone attempts to grab you, just doing the simple fright reaction changes the dynamic of the attack process. As simple as it sounds, this is the truth: If you change your body, you change the fight.

As shown throughout this book, if we will not yield to the five universally applicable principles (balance, body unity, looseness, sensitivity, and total freedom of action or adaptability), we become our own worst enemies. For the most part, this is purely mental. We say it can't be done before we examine the possibility, or we refuse to take the leap of faith. Some physically gifted people only develop to a certain level because their natural abilities are almost never challenged. They get away with things because they *can*. If they are ever challenged by those of greater physical ability, they will be helpless because in training they relied on talent rather than the principles. The principles are the great equalizer for people with limited physical attributes.

Lack of creativity will hold you back in guided chaos. You get good at thinking outside the box when you use experimentation instead of regimentation as a core principle in your training. As our students have heard me say on numerous occasions, "Owning a hammer doesn't make you a carpenter." From the basic principles, one is able to develop infinite responses. As long as it is within the laws of physics and human physiology, don't ever let anyone tell you what you can't do. From there, you are limited only by your imagination. When we show people a manifestation of a principle, we stress that it is not a technique carved in stone but only an idea of what you could do. Don't fall in love with any specific technique.

Points to Remember

➤ Maintain an outward focus. Be especially receptive to sudden movement.

➤ If you get a bad feeling, listen to your gut and go another way *before* something happens.

➤ Forget about being "assertive" and avoid all potential confrontations.

➤ Control your sphere of influence or personal zone.

➤ Do not allow people to encroach on your space.

➤ Do not allow yourself to be cornered or boxed in.

➤ Never ever allow yourself to be moved from one location to another; it's always better for them and worse for you.

➤ Don't ever assume the enemy will behave in a predictable manner; the enemy will always do what he or she wants.

➤ Assume nothing.

➤ The enemy is capable of anything.

➤ Never let an attacker get the drop on you, and never drop your guard.

➤ Always be prepared to go into action and use deadly force.

➤ Think about what you want to do in the event of an ambush, kidnapping attempt, and so on beforehand. Develop your battle drill and practice, practice, practice. Then imagine every possible scenario you can think of and repeat the previous steps.

➤ Always be prepared to step off line and in.

➤ When striking, keep the majority of your strikes above the shoulders.

➤ Strike to the neck from every angle.

➤ Strike with all of your might and strike to penetrate.

➤ Strike to kill; never strike to wound. Just like bunting in baseball, you can always back off the energy, but you can never raise it if you need it.

➤ Work to develop the ability to preempt a person's attack either by moving off line and in or by striking first.

➤ Do not attempt to grapple or control people. It will only slow you down. If someone grabs or attempts to grab you, strike that person in the eyes or throat. Do *not* grapple back, or you could die.

➤ Do not go to the ground and grapple with an attacker. If you fall to the ground, keep your head away from the enemy's feet, strike and kick with all your might, get to your feet as quickly as possible, and run.

➤ If someone attempts to grab you, following all the previous points changes the game entirely.

➤ Never, ever give up fighting. The will to survive will find a way if you let it.

➤ Be sure that in the totality of your training, every movement is consistent with the natural principles of balance, body unity, looseness, sensitivity, and total freedom of action (adaptability), or you will be wasting your time.

Creating a Training Regimen

To help you create a training regimen, we'll make two assumptions:

1. Your primary interest is in improving your self-defense skills, not impressing your friends with flashy moves.
2. You're not a monk living in the mountains, and your free time is probably limited. To reduce your training time, we advocate training smarter, not harder. It's better to train frequently for short periods than infrequently for long periods. Studies show that reducing downtime, even between short workouts, aids retention. You're reprogramming your nervous system, so consistency and repetition are crucial. It's also more convenient for most of us to squeeze in a few minutes every day than to schedule a large block of time for training.

Most of the drills don't require a Herculean amount of strength; however, some drills (such as the Gang Attack drills on pp. 36, 41, and 215 and Leg Mania on p. 212) can be very exhausting, so it's important to know your physical condition and limits. Any time you start a new training program, consult your doctor first.

All the drills are valuable and build on one another. Some are more specific to training a single attribute, like the dropping drills, while others simultaneously train many or all of the guided chaos principles. The absolutely essential exercise is Contact Flow (p. 135) and its variations (p. 138). This is a drill you should start to do early in your program and repeat often. Although the best thing you can do for yourself is to get a training partner, you will find that even if you get to do contact flow only once a week, if you regularly do the solo exercises, you will derive the maximum benefit from these sessions, retaining and augmenting the attributes you've already developed.

Variety is important in your training to keep your enthusiasm high as well as to focus and build on all the nuances of self-defense preparation. This book provides a wide range of drills to work with. Keep in mind, however, that you should continue to review the close combat drills in part I even as you become more advanced.

Moreover, if you're already highly trained in a martial art, you don't neccessarily need to abandon what you already know. We have many students with high-ranking belts from other styles who, because they're in law enforcement or the military, find guided chaos to be the grease that makes their other skills work better.

If you have only a limited amount of time to train, the Anywhere Striking series (part I), Polishing the Sphere I, II, or III (pp. 131-132), and Washing the Body (p. 132) are drills you should do every day—ideally, for five minutes each. These drills concentrate the principles in a practical way, and you can do them by yourself. Include contact flow as often as you can. If you have a variety of partners and can do contact flow every day, your development will be phenomenal. We highly recommend you register on the Training Groups Page on our Web site, www.attackproof.com. There you will find like-minded people willing to work out with you virtually anywhere in the world. Be aware, however, that *they may never have been to a class,* and you never know whom you're dealing with. *Attackproof Inc. and Mad Squirrel Productions Inc. cannot be held responsible for training injuries, accidents, or your physical condition. In other words, you're on your own, kids, so play nice!*

The best way to arrange your guided chaos program is to perform six or seven drills each day: Polishing the Sphere I, II, or III; Washing the Body; and RHEM, as well as three or four different drills—one from part I, two from part II, and an occasional drill from part III. This approach allows you to hit every neural pathway and keeps things interesting.

Work your way down the drill finder on page xv; after a few weeks, start from the beginning again. Don't get too crazy with this: After a while, you may decide to skip some drills and double up on others but always strive to do them correctly. If you make stuff up or mix in drills from other styles you could potentially set back your development by decades or even go backwards. Check with us on our Web forum; we can point you in the right direction and keep you from wasting your time. If you need video guidance, the Combat Conditioning DVD has most of the drills set to Native American music that you can follow along with. Note that it has no explanations of the drills in order to keep your workout continuous. The Attackproof Companion DVD Part 2 has detailed explanations of most of the energy drills in part II of this book.

Glossary

anywhere principle—In a real fight, a strike can come from or be delivered anywhere.

anywhere strike—Any kind of strike from any angle and any body position.

attack the attacker—A philosophy of striking preemptively without blocking; refusing to be a victim and fighting offensively instead of defensively. The phrase was coined by Professor Bradley J Steiner in the 1970s.

awareness—Being in the moment when out in public as opposed to being lost in thought; achieved through calm visualization and learning to extend your tactile sensitivity outward beyond your skin so that your nervous system actually begins to recognize and flow with the movement of people around you; learning to trust your gut feelings about dangerous situations and people.

balance—The ability to maintain your center of gravity over your root point no matter what your body position or root point—your foot, back, backside, shoulder, or even hip when lying on the ground; also refers to the balance of each bone and its relaxed relationship to every other bone.

blind attack—An assault with no interview or warning of any kind, with the intent to mug, rape, or kidnap; this is defensible, as opposed to an assassination attempt, which is virtually indefensible no matter what your training or weaponry.

body unity—Having your entire body weight behind every movement you make, no matter how small or subtle, by perfectly aligning all the skeletal joints while still keeping them relaxed.

box step—An effective way of moving that keeps you close to your attacker while enabling you to avoid being attacked.

chambering—A method of striking that wastes time by requiring you to withdraw the weapon (object or body part) before moving it forward to strike.

chi (energy)—Internally applied grace and balance; the circulating point of finesse within the body.

close combat—A simplified system of striking culled from methods used to train U.S. soldiers in World War II to deal with Japanese troops proficient in judo and karate.

close combat universal entry (CCUE)—A simplified series of strikes applicable to almost any initial assault that also moves you off line.

contact flow—Free-form sensitivity and fighting drill incorporating all principles of guided chaos.

containing the over-travel—To prevent overcommitment and loss of balance, strikes and kicks are delivered in such a away as to reflect and recycle the energy back to your root where it can circle or snap back out into another blow. This requires dropping and a single-leg root among other things.

counterturning—Turning to strike with the side opposite to that being attacked. For example, driving out a left palm strike when you're struck in your right shoulder.

disengagement principle—Remaining in close physical contact with your attacker while exerting the least pressure.

destruction energy—Full-power pulsing meant to destroy incoming strikes that are then ricocheted off of.

drac—Horizontal triangle defense where your elbow extends out in front of your face.

dropping—A method of delivering energy by a spasmodic lowering of your entire body weight into a current or new root. When you drop, you create a shock wave of energy that travels down your body and rebounds explosively off the ground and back up your legs to be channeled any way you desire.

external energy—A source of energy that relies solely on muscular power and is usually characterized by whole-body tension.

flipper—Raising your hand from the wrist; a sensitive lever for launching elbow strikes, stopping wrist breaks, and guiding inside palm strikes.

fright reaction—Your body's natural, adrenaline-fueled response to sudden shock or fear, wherein your whole body instinctively drops its center of gravity, your back curves out protectively, your head sinks low between your upraised shoulders, and your arms come up around your face and neck.

guided chaos—A system of self defense created by John Perkins in 1978 that accepts that all fights are hell-storms of unpatterned and unchoreographed chaos. By augmenting natural animal and human movement with an awareness of physics, you make chaos work *for* you instead of against you. Also called the way of adaptation.

hello hand position—Vertical hand position for intercepting high outside strikes.

hostile awareness—An everyday visualization technique and mental exercise wherein you calmly imagine counterattacking assaults launched by passersby in the street, carjackings, or virtually any other attack you can conceive of; visualizing hitting to destroy. This conditions the subconscious for real combat.

instant balance—An extremely brief period of balance created by dropping into a new root, which is then instantly abandoned for a new, better root as the balance point necessarily shifts.

internal energy—A source of power that is a byproduct of muscular and mental relaxation, perfectly and economically aligned bones, and an attuned nervous system that conducts fear impulses without tension. This power is contrasted with external energy, which relies on pure muscle power.

interview—The verbal banter a scam artist, rapist, kidnapper, mugger, or harasser will use to distract your attention, gain your trust, draw you closer, and further gauge your ability to defend yourself.

inward pulse—A method of pulling against your attacker to provide a reaction.

isolation energy—Maintaining static contact at a reference point while moving the rest of your body to a more advantageous position without the enemy noticing.

Jack Benny stance—Named after the late, great comedian, a position that protects your face and neck without tipping off a potential assailant that you might be about to strike preemptively.

looseness—The ability to change direction with any part of your body with the smallest possible impetus, with no conscious thought or physical restriction.

Mexican Hat Dance—High-speed kicking and stomping drill.

Moving behind a guard—Keeping some part of your body between an impending strike and its target. The guard should be as fluid as the body position.

multihitting—Striking as many times as possible within the flow of any one movement.

neutral balance—A 50–50 weight distribution over the feet.

passing the apples—Tool replacement from hand to hand.

personal comfort zone—An area surrounding your body that you do not allow suspicious strangers or hostile relations to enter. The area is usually as far as you can reach with your arms and legs; however, in tighter spaces such as subways, your personal comfort zone may necessarily contract. An intrusion into your zone prompts you to attack the attacker.

plyometric—The full elastic rebound potential of the muscles and tendons.

pocketing—Stretching only the target area away from a strike while keeping your body close to your attacker.

pulsing—Pushing, pulling, or otherwise adding energy against your attacker to instigate a reaction. This is an offensive, not defensive, tool.

puppeteering—Lightly applying a two-fingered grab (with thumb and middle or index finger) on each of your opponent's wrists and following his limbs around without adding any energy of your own; a body unity drill building the hand–foot relationship.

recognizing energy—What you do with the information picked up by your sensitivity.

RHEM (relationship of human energy to movement)—Slow, free-form solo movement drill often done by a leader with a group of imitators.

ricocheting—Bouncing a strike off a target to create additional strikes.

riding the lightning—Using a combination of skimming, ricocheting, and destruction energy to deliver multiple strikes against and through the enemy's strike on the way to a soft target.

riding the vortex—Using sliding energy to maintain contact with the general orbit of the enemy's high-speed movement without bearing down on any particular reference point.

rocket step—A one-two dropping step to maximize power and weight transfer.

root—Your loose, balanced, and sensitive connection to the ground. Usually you use your foot, but you can use anything (e.g., your backside when ground fighting).

sensitivity—The ability to detect and create changes in the type, amount, or direction of energy through your skin without conscious thought.

shortening the weapon—Instantaneously pulling back a blocked strike using the limb's joint of origin (e.g., the shoulder for a palm strike) while continuing to step in and strike at a slightly different angle.

skimming energy—Skipping a strike through an intended block or the enemy's strike in a flat trajectory, like a stone across the surface of a pond.

skipping hands—Walking technique for the hand over incoming strikes or pushes.

slambag—Specially constructed training tool for dropping and hitting.

sliding energy—Allowing your attacker's body to slide past your contact point while maintaining your guard position.

sling-shotting—Increasing the speed of a circular strike by shortening its arc.

spike-in-the-sponge—An analogy for simultaneously yielding and striking.

splashing energy—Hitting a target so that your striking tool penetrates only a few inches and then relaxes immediately, allowing you to stick.

stealth energy—Sensitivity so high that you can stick to the heat emanating from your attacker's skin and react to changes in intent before your attacker actually moves.

sphere of influence—The area within which your weapons are effective, usually the range of your arms and legs.

sticking—Remaining in contact with your opponent's body.

sticking energy—Creating suspend-and-release situations with a subtle stretching of the opponent's skin.

stomping drop-step kick—Stomping straight down onto your lead leg as a prelude to kicks. Used to close the gap, adding power to a strike or kick. Prevents you from slipping on ice, blood, beer, oil, sweat, or similar substances.

suspending and releasing energy—Exploding like a mousetrap in response to a deliberate or accidental pulse.

tactile sensitivity—Using your skin to stick to an opponent.

taking something with you—Using the retraction of a strike to hit, rip, gouge, or pulse your attacker.

taking your opponent's space—Expressed by attacking the attacker or moving in on your opponent while remaining unavailable to him by your looseness and pocketing.

tool-replacing or transferring energy—Transferring your opponent's energy by passing his pressure or strike to another contact point that allows you to take more of his space. For example, folding your arm so that your elbow contacts his arm instead of your palm.

triangle defense—The shape created by keeping a forearm horizontally or vertically in front of your head and neck, with your head tucked low behind your shoulder and your elbow always threatening to extend into your opponent's face at close range, like a spear or a spike, forming the point of a triangle or wedge.

vibrating—High-speed dropping and multihitting that results in your striking with the rapidity of a machine gun.

yielding—Moving your body away from pressure being exerted on you; exerting zero resistance to your attacker.

yin and yang—Opposites. In martial arts, may refer to soft and hard, yielding and pushing, and others.

yin-yang generator—Reading and amplifying the attacker's energy.

zoning—Taking space by obliquely moving in and to the side of your attacker.

References
and Resources

Applegate, Rex. 1976. *Kill Or Get Killed*. Boulder, CO. Paladin Press.

de Becker, Gavin. 1999. *The Gift of Fear: And Other Survival Signals That Protect Us From Violence*. New York: Dell.

Kuo, Lien-Ying. 1994. *The T'ai Chi Boxing Chronicle*. Trans. Guttmann. Berkeley, CA: North Atlantic.

Liao, Waysun. 1990. *T'ai Chi Classics*. Boston: Shambhala.

Musashi, Miyamoto. 2000. *The Book of Five Rings*. Trans. T. Cleary. Boston: Shambhala.

Steiner, Bradley J. 2008. *The Tactical Skills of Hand to Hand Combat*. Boulder, CO. Paladin Press.

Strong, Sanford. 1997. *Strong on Defense: Survival Rules to Protect You and Your Family From Crime*. New York: Pocket Books.

Sun Tzu. 1963. *The Art of War*. Trans. S.B. Griffith. London: Oxford University Press.

Yang, Jwing-Ming. 1996. *Tai Chi Theory and Martial Power*. Boston: YMAA.

Since the first edition came out, *Attack Proof* has been adopted by many schools and institutions as their training manual. Nevertheless, though a picture is worth a thousand words, video is worth a billion. All the concepts in *Attack Proof* are demonstrated on DVDs available from www.attackproof.com, where you can also find classes, private lessons, and seminars for civilians, police, security personnel, and the military. You can learn about close combat; guided chaos; modified Native American ground fighting; gun, knife, and cane fighting; and essential training tools like the slambag.

An invaluable training aid is the fighting man dummy, a human-shaped, heavy bag. Fighting man dummies are available from www.iisports.com (800-898-2042) and other sources.

The focus gloves, kicking shields, beanbag fill, muay thai heavy bags, and much of the other equipment described in this book can be purchased at most martial arts supplies stores.

What could be more accessible weaponry than your feet? Steel and composite toe shoes are now available in virtually any style from sneakers to boots to dress shoes (sorry ladies, no pumps!) A great source is www.steeltoeshoes.com.

Index

Note: The italicized *f* following page numbers refers to figures.

A

abdomen, as target 256
abduction, avoiding 8-9, 10
alarms
    home security 5-6
    personal 6
    portable door alarm 4
alcohol and safety 4, 6-7
anger, awareness of 7
answer the phone movement 186-188, 187*f*
arm pressure 56-60, 57*f*-59*f*
Art of War, The (Tzu) 148
assaults, preventing 3-7
attacking the attacker 14, 71, 177-179, 250-253
automated teller machines (ATMs) 3-4
awareness
    concept of 2-3, 44, 249-250
    drill 3
    hostile 7-10
    strategies 3-7

B

back
    gun against 236, 236*f*
    knife on 230, 230*f*
balance
    breathing 87
    components of 82
    drills 87-95, 140
    in economic movement 169-170
    flow 140
    in guided chaos 82-84, 248, 249
    momentum 82-83
    neutral 155-156
    sphere of influence and 249
    stances 83-87, 84*f*, 87*f*
ballpoint pen 7
belly, knife against 229-230, 230*f*
biting 21, 163
blind attacks
    description of 16-18, 17*f*
    drills 25-29
blocking, from Jack Benny stance 16, 17*f*. *See
    also* shield, body as
body unity
    chi and 73-77
    description of 73
    drills 76-81
    enhancing 76
    guided chaos and 49-50, 145-147, 248-249

bouncing energy 205
box step
    defensive response 171, 172*f*
    drills 92-95, 93*f*-95*f*
    zoning and 170-171, 171*f*
breaking strikes 166-167
breathing
    balance and 87
    drills 61, 64, 64*f*

C
cane fighting 227-228
carjackings, tips for surviving 8-9, 10
cell phone 5, 6, 8-9
chambering 23
chaos. *See* guided chaos
checking 178
chest, knife against 229-230, 230*f*
chi
    defining 73, 75
    projection 75-76
chin jab 15, 16, 18-1
chokes, defeating
    front 206
    rear choke to ground 207
    sleeper hold 207-208, 208*f*
chopping 15, 19, 31
clawing 20, 32, 163
close combat
    battlefields 42-47
    drills 25-31, 34, 36-42
    to guided chaos 253-254, 256-258
    schools 42-45
    strikes 18-24
    visualizing attacker 25
close combat universal entry (CCUE) 31-34,
    44, 251
closed-fist strikes 19, 21, 22-23
combat boxing 23
comfort zone. *See* personal comfort zone
confrontations
    avoiding, advantages of 11
    beginning of 13-14
contact flow
    drills 135-138
    drill variations 138-143
    faults with 141-143, 143*f*
    on ground drills 214-216
containing the over-travel principle 24, 38, 94
contorting energy 205
cross-tie lock 185-186, 185*f*
crushing strikes 166-167

D
decision-making process 8
defense
    airliners 45-47
    economic movements 169-173
    gun 234-240
    knife 228-234
deflection 15
destruction energy 114
disengagement principle 105, 196
dog, for home security 5
dog-dig entry 178
double grab, breaking 188-189, 188*f*
downward-spearing elbow strike. *See* elbow
    strikes
drac entry 178-179, 179*f*
drills
    balance 84-95, 140
    body unity 76-81
    close combat 25-31, 34-42
    contact flow 135-138
    contact flow on ground 214-216
    contact flow variations 138-143
    dropping 29, 121-125
    economy of movement 180-181
    energy 128-143
    footwork 96-98
    grip 190-191
    ground fighting 203-204, 211-214, 218
    ground fighting, multiple opponents 216-
    218
    guns 239-240, 243-245
    knives 232-234
    looseness 61-72
    sensitivity 120-121, 147-148
    stair fighting 221, 223-225
    tendons 191-192
dropping
    into chop strike 19
    description of 17-18, 17*f*, 18*f*
    drills 29, 121-125
    as economic movement 170, 173
    energy 109-111, 110*f*
    in ground fighting 201

E
economy of movement
    defensive 169-173
    drills 180-181
    offensive 173-177
    principles of 169

elbow(s)
    getting trapped 171
    overbending 158
    pressure 60, 60f, 61
    strikes 21, 22f, 257, 257f
    as weapons 163-165, 164f
elevator attack 81
energy
    chi 73, 75-76
    creating 107
    drills 128-143
    opponent's 170-171, 171f
    recognizing 120
    sensing 104-107
    types of 107-119
engagement principle 196
Enter the Dragon 74
entries 178, 179f
environment, response in 11
escape(s)
    carjacking 8-9, 10
    plan (home) 6
eye-gouging
    eyelids 20
    in Jack Benny stance 15-16, 16f, 17f
    practicing 26, 34, 36
    strikes 18, 24, 163, 201, 254
    using 26

F

face, gun toward 235, 235f
fakes 179
fear
    drills for using 25-29
    effects on awareness 3
feints 114, 179
fish-hooking 163
fist strikes 257, 258f
five-second fight 252-253
fixed-step flow drill 139-140
flagging 44
footwork, drills 96-98
fright reaction
    description of 16-18, 17f
    drills 26-29, 218

G

Gift of Fear, The (de Becker) 7
grabs
    double grab, breaking 188-189, 189f
    resisting 186-189
    using 182-183

grappling 194, 195-199
grip, strengthening drills 190-191
groin, strikes 24, 256
ground fighting
    avoiding 201, 203
    chokes 206-208, 208f
    contact flow 214
    drills 203-204, 211-216, 218
    emergency off-lining 200-201
    intentional 194-195
    kicks 209-210, 209f, 210f
    mobile, staying 204-206
    multiple opponents, drill 216-218
    takedown attempt 199-200
    vs. conventional grappling 195-199
    warm-ups 210-211
guarding movements
    drill 153-155, 155f
    from formless stance 155-156
    rocker movement 158-159, 159f
guided chaos. *See also specific principles*
    close combat and 253-254, 256-258
    concept of 48-49
    ground fighting *vs.* conventional grappling
        195-199
    handgun training 240-245
    internal-style arts and 74-75
    kicking 99-100, 100f
    natural movement in 50
    perception of 145-149
    principles of 49-50, 247-249
    results of training 179-180
    shooting 240-242
    training 253-254
    vs. martial arts 48-49
guns
    defense 2, 6, 234-238, 240-243
    drills 239-240, 243-245
    running from 10

H

hair-pulling 163
handguns. *See* guns
hands
    in ground fighting 197-198, 198f
    skipping 165-166, 167f
    strikes 15, 16f, 256-257, 256f-257f
head
    gun against 236, 237f
    strikes to 173, 254
head butts 21, 21f, 163
hitting and sensitivity 120

home, defending 5-6
hyperbalance 82, 83

I

intention, guided chaos and 145-147
internal energy 74-75
interview
    defined 13-14
    drill 29-31
intuition 2, 3, 13-14
isolation energy 117-118, 118f

J

Jack Benny stance
    description of 14-16, 14f, 16f, 17f
    drill 29-31
    scenario 35
jackhammer strikes 19, 83
jogging safely 6-7

K

kicks
    areas to target 256
    in close combat 23-24, 25f
    ground fighting 209-210, 209f, 210f
    in guided chaos 99-100, 100f
    strikes 258, 258f
kidnapping, avoiding 8
kidneys, strikes to 173, 256
Kill or Get Killed (Applegate) 199
knee(s)
    bending 86-87
    strikes 23, 33, 33f
knives
    defense 35, 228-233
    drills 233-234
    using 232

L

leaning *vs.* yielding 156
legs
    drills 141, 212-214
    using 19
lethal force training 11
locks
    executing 183
    resisting 184, 186-189
    types of 184-186
    using 183-184, 184f
looking terrified 15
looseness
    in body movements 50

description of 51
drills 61-72
extreme 53
in guided chaos 49-50, 248
obstructions 52
pocketing and 53-56, 55f, 56f
reactive 52-53
relaxed 51-52
rooted 53
yielding and 53-56, 55f, 56f
Lost in Space 76

M

mace 35
martial arts
    internal *vs.* external 74-75
    Native American 174, 194, 195-199
melee flow drill 140
mind-set, proper 249-250
mobility in ground fighting 196, 204-206
momentum 83
muggers
    abduction by 8
    attacking 253
    avoiding 5
multihitting 173-174, 174f
murder, preventing 3-7
muscular strength, body unity and 76

N

Native American martial arts movements 174,
    194, 195-199
neck
    knife on 230-232, 230f, 232f
    strikes to 173, 254
neck-breaking 163
nine pearls 73

O

offense
    body as weapon 163-167
    economic movements 173-177
open-handed strikes 21, 22-23, 165
opponent
    energy of 170-171, 171f
    vortex 170
    weapons of 251

P

palm(s)
    strikes 15, 18, 18f, 31, 32f, 257, 257f
    as weapons 163, 165, 166

pepper spray 6
perception, guided chaos and 145-149
personal comfort zone
　　drill 29-31
　　establishing 7
pickpockets, avoiding 5
pinching 20, 163
pocketing
　　concept of 54
　　as defensive response 170-171, 171*f*, 172*f*
　　example of 55-56, 55*f*, 56*f*
point shooting 241
police
　　phony 4-5
　　reasonable force 10-11
posture, balance and 87, 87*f*
preemptive striking, confrontations and 14
prefight orientation 7-10
pressure responses, examples of 56-61, 57*f*-60*f*
proprioception and guided chaos 145-149
pulsing energy
　　examples of 113-114, 113*f*
　　purpose of 112
　　vs. yin-yang generator principle 112-114,
　　　　113*f*
puppeteering drill 80-81, 80*f*, 183
purse snatchers, avoiding 5

R
rape, strategies for surviving 35
relationship of human energy to movement
　　　　(RHEM) drill 134-135
relaxation
　　drills 61-62
　　for looseness 51-52
ricocheting energy 114, 170, 251
ridgehands, description of 20
ripping 16, 20, 163, 166-167
robberies, preventing 3-7
rooting
　　balance and 84-86
　　common mistakes 85-86
　　description of 19, 84
　　drills 63, 84-86
　　fixed-step rooting 86
　　in ground fighting 205
　　in looseness 53
　　50-50 (neutral balance) 84-85
　　plyometric rooting 85
　　single-leg balance 84-85
ruthless intent 251-252

S
schools, personal safety in
　　bullies, three-step attack process for 42-44
　　criminals, tactical awareness of 44
　　gangs, getting jumped by 44
　　suicidal gunman 45
screaming as defense
　　confrontations and 13
　　environment and 11
　　in Jack Benny stance 16
security. *See also* awareness
　　at ATMs 3-4
　　at home 5-6
　　in hotels and motels 4
　　while jogging 6-7
self-defense. *See* defense
sensitivity
　　description of 103
　　and destruction *vs.* control and submission
　　　　199
　　drills 120-121, 147-148
　　eye-hand coordination 103, 104*f*
　　in guided chaos 49-50, 143-145, 248
　　hitting 120
　　using against opponent, analogies of 106-
　　　　107
set-up attack flow drill 140
shaking the tree 174
shedding energy 201
shield, body as
　　elbow, overbending 158
　　flipper 162-163, 163*f*
　　formless stance 155-156
　　Harley position 158, 158*f*
　　hello hand position 160-161, 160*f*-161*f*
　　hello hand position with triangle defense
　　　　161-162, 162*f*
　　moving behind guard 153-155, 155*f*
　　rocker position 158-159, 159*f*
　　taking opponent's space 156-157, 157*f*, 158*f*
　　triangle defense 159-160, 160*f*
　　yielding 155, 158
shoes, steel-toed 7, 23, 256
shortening the weapon 175-177, 176*f*, 177*f*
skimming energy 116, 116*f*
slambag training
　　partner training 128
　　slambags 125
　　solo training 126-128
　　using 23, 126
　　vs. iron palm training 125-126

sliding energy 114-115, 115*f,* 120
solar plexus, strikes to 173
spear hand strike 19, 20, 20*f,* 256, 256*f*
sphere of influence 7, 249
spike-in-the-sponge 55-56, 56*f*
spine, as target 256
spitting 163
splashing energy 116-117
stair fighting
    drills 221, 223-225
    risks 220
    training 220-221
    variables in 219-220, 220*f*
stalker flow drill 140
stances, formless 155-156
stealth energy 111-112
stick fighting 226-228, 227*f*
sticking (constant contact) 105, 154
sticking energy 116
stomps
    in close combat 23-24, 25*f*
    target areas for 256
    as weapon 163
striking concepts
    in guided chaos 254
    tools 256-258, 256*f*-258*f*
striking intervals drill 141
Strong on Defense (Strong) 7
super-slow flow drill 139
survival manifesto 247-260
suspending and releasing energy 117, 205-206
swarm of bees movement 188
swimming drills
    backstroke 66, 66*f*
    benefits of 64-66, 65*f*
    sidestroke 66, 66*f*

T
tactile sensitivity 105
T'ai Chi Boxing Chronicle (Lien-Ying) 75
tail bone, as target 256
taking something with you 174-175, 175*f*
target areas 254, 256
tearing 20, 166-167
tendons, strengthening drills 191-192
tension, releasing and taking up slack 120
testicles, crushing 163
throat strikes 15, 19, 24, 35, 254
timed flow drill 140
timing your movements 179-180
tool destruction
    resisting grabs with 189, 189*f*

using attacker's energy 177-178
tool replacement 206
tools for strikes 256-258, 256*f*-258*f*
torso, gun against 236, 236*f*
training regimen 262-263
transferring energy 118-119, 118*f,* 119*f*
traveling
    close combat 45-47
    staying safe while 4
turning
    in defensive response 171, 172*f*
    drill 64, 64*f*

U
unmarked police car 4, 5

V
valuables, protecting 4, 5, 6
vibrating 174
vise lock 184-185, 184*f*
visualization 7, 19, 25
vortex, of opponent 170

W
water, in human body 50
weapon(s)
    body as 163-167
    drill 141
    improvised, on airliners 46
    opponent's and yours 251
    use in ground fighting 197-198, 198*f*
weapons fighting. *See specific weapons*
whipping strikes 83
wrenching 20

Y
yielding
    drills 64-66, 65*f,* 66*f*
    examples of 55-56, 55*f,* 56*f*
    guarding and 155
    overbending elbows in 158
    principle of 53-55
    striking and 163-164
yin and yang
    description of 83
    generating energy 107-109

Z
zoning, as economic movement 170-171, 171*f*

About the Authors

John Perkins has been training and teaching martial arts and self-defense for over 50 years. A former Yonkers, N.Y., detective, he has taught hand-to-hand tactics to Marine Corps combat units, Marine Corps scout sniper units, and military counterdrug forces. He also has instructed law enforcement personnel from the FBI, New York City Police Department, New York State Police, and the New York City Transit Police. A former bodyguard to Malcolm Forbes and Israeli Defense Minister Moshe Dayan, Perkins is a forensic crime scene expert and a master handgun instructor and marksman. He has extensive experience in the martial arts of hapkido, taekwondo, kyukushinkai, kempo karate, judo, jujitsu, goju, and tai chi chuan. He has trained in Native American fighting principles since the age of five. Perkins has battled in unlicensed pit fights, a savage forerunner to today's Ultimate Fighting Championship competitions. He is the founder of guided chaos, an adaptive, internal energy art whose principles are detailed in this book. Perkins' system is recognized by the International Combat Martial Arts Federation, through which he holds a fifth-degree black belt in combat martial arts. Perkins lives in Nyack, New York.

Al Ridenhour, a lieutenant colonel in the United States Marine Corps Reserves, has been training in martial arts since 1985. He has studied tai chi, isshinryu karate, and ken jitsu. An all-conference wrestler in high school who later learned boxing in the Marine Corps, Ridenhour is also a sixth-degree master in guided chaos. He is a veteran of Operation Iraqi Freedom and the Gulf War, where he commanded a 50-man infantry unit and served as an instructor in unarmed combat for his Marine Corps unit and for the battalion's scout sniper platoon. He has also worked with various law enforcement agencies, U.S. Customs, U.S. Border Patrol, and the U.S. Drug Enforcement Agency during counterdrug missions. He is a member of the International Combat Martial Arts Federation. Ridenhour lives in Hartsdale, New York.

Matt Kovsky is an editor for CBS Television. His work has earned him two Emmys, one for outstanding editing and another for producing an outstanding entertainment series, as well as many other awards. He also co-produced the debut CD, *finally...,* of songwriter Keri Shore, which won runner-up in the 2002 John Lennon Songwriting Contest. He has trained in isshinryu karate and jeet kune do and has a fifth-degree black belt in guided chaos. Kovsky lives in Westchester, New York.